ZIMBABWE

Challenging the stereotypes

Other books by Robert Mshengu Kavanagh:

The Making of a Servant and Other Poems (Ophir Publications, 1971; reprinted Ravan Press, 1974), translation from Xhosa with Z.S. Qangule

South African People's Plays, G Kente and others (Heineman African Writers Series, 1981), edited with introductory material

Theatre and Cultural Struggle in South Africa (Zed, London, 1985)

Making People's Theatre (Witwatersrand University Press, Johannesburg/University of Zimbabwe Publications, 1998)

Ngoma: approaches to arts education in Southern Africa (Zimbabwe Academy of Arts Education, Harare, 2006)

ZIMBABWE

Challenging the stereotypes

Robert Mshengu Kavanagh

Harare, Johannesburg, Cairo and London

Themba Books is a new family publishing house, established in loving memory of Thembani Ndiya McLaren (nee Nene)

Themba Books
407 Earls Court
2nd Avenue
Johannesburg
South Africa 2193

13 Mountbatten Drive
Marlborough
Harare
Zimbabwe

First published 2014

ISBN: 1500186244
ISBN 13: 9781500186241

British Library Cataloguing in Publication Data
Zimbabwe: Challenging the Stereotypes

DEDICATION

To Solitude and the Half Corona

ACKNOWLEDGEMENTS

Egypt: My daughter, Thando Nomhle Amankwah (Naima bint Robert – author of *Far from Home* and *From My Sisters Lips*), who was one of my readers, gave invaluable feedback and has been part of the process all the way down the line. My son, Henry Kofi Amankwah, who contributed to financing the publication.

England: My son, Ivor Njabulo McLaren, who contributed to funding the publication of the book. Ian Scoones, who found time to read the manuscript and write a preview.

South Africa: My daughter, Mary Gugu Tizita McLaren, who played and is playing a big part in marketing and publicising of the book. My dear friend, Hildur Amato, in whose tranquil and beautiful garden cottage the bulk of the book was written. Cultural activist and celebrated poet and playwright, Maishe Maponya, for reading the manuscript and writing a preview.

USA: My dear comrade, Micere Githae Mugo, for finding the time and strength in trying times to read the manuscript and provide an encouraging comment.

Zimbabwe: Tainie Mandondo of African Publishers Network, my expert, professional copy editor. Richard Knottenbelt (Mukoma Richard), my elder brother/cousin, who gives so much of his time to encouraging my efforts

Finally, the children and youth of Zimbabwe, without whom my life in their country would never have been the same.

Some pre-publication comments on "Zimbabwe: Challenging the Stereotypes"

An intricate lace-work of history, politics, economics, culture and profound political commentary, artistically interlaced with storytelling and biographical sketches, Zimbabwe: *Challenging the Stereotypes is a masterpiece on Zimbabwe. The narrative is refreshingly daring, original, inventive and captivating. It is also highly controversial and likely to stir heated debate. A revolutionary artist/cultural worker, Kavanagh echoes Amilcar Cabral in his advocacy for progressive culture as a critical tool in creating a truly liberated Zimbabwe. Without a doubt, this book is poised to become a foundational reference text for intellectuals, scholars and activists who are truly serious about unpacking the extremely complex and oftentimes elusive, narrative behind Zimbabwe since independence* – Professor Micere Githae Mugo, Kenyan poet, playwright, essayist and literary critic, Meredith Professor for Teaching Excellence, Syracuse University

'No simplistic assumptions can do the story of Zimbabwe justice', argues Robert Kavanagh in Zimbabwe: Challenging the Stereotypes. *This book offers a personal account of Zimbabwe's post-independence story. It has been a tumultuous period, where any simple assessment is impossible. This book confronts the complexity, the controversies and the challenges for the future. Not everyone will agree with the assessments, but the book will confront those who have become used to the standard narrative about Zimbabwe's downfall. Anyone interested in Zimbabwe's recent history should read this book; it is an accessible, fascinating and engrossing read. Thoroughly recommended* – Professor Ian Scoones, Professor, Institute of Development Studies, University of Sussex, UK, co-author of *Zimbabwe's Land Reform: Myths and Realities*

Without doubt, Zimbabwe: Challenging the Stereotypes is an inspired and significant entrée into Zimbabwe's literary canon that will become a point of reference when the future reveals itself. Mshengu is a storyteller whose account represents without claim the voices of millions of Zimbabweans who experience a freedom mired in punishing sanctions because its leader dared to challenge western imperialism. Mshengu's stay in Zimbabwe since its attainment of liberation grants him the voice of a man who has loved his country, to speak the truth to those in power as a way of reminding all why chimurenga was critical and that it cannot remain in the I.C.U. The insights provided in this book are compellingly relevant to the new South Africa…a book all South Africans - and indeed all who wish to learn - must read – Maponya, South African poet, playwright, director and cultural activist, author of The Hungry Earth and Gangsters.

CONTENTS

"*DIEPE GROND*" – THE SECOND DECADE

"*ONDER DRAAI DIE DUIWEL ROND*" – THE THIRD DECADE

MAP OF ZIMBABWE

MAP OF AFRICA

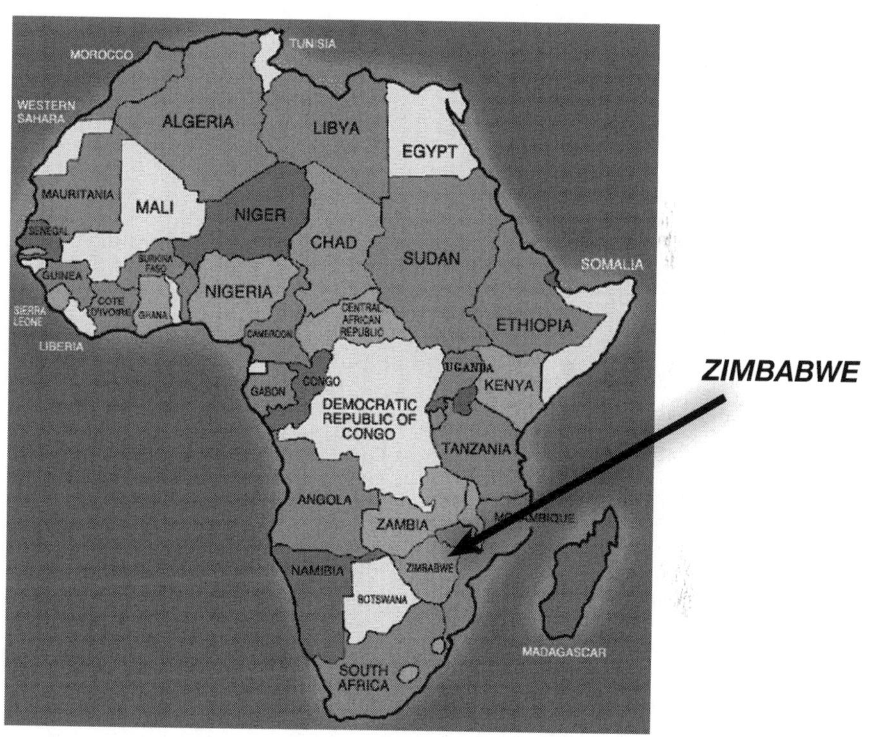

PREFACE

I came to Zimbabwe from Ethiopia in 1984, four years after independence. I have lived here ever since. During these years I experienced and observed some of the most dramatic and significant events in the history of Africa. Wherever I went outside Zimbabwe, people used to ask me what my take on what was happening to Zimbabwe was. I always felt there was no easy answer. I felt the only answer that would do the situation justice, needed thought, time and space - in short, a book. This book is my answer. This book represents *my take* on thirty-three years of Zimbabwean history I was privileged to be a part of.

I do not claim that I have anything resembling a monopoly on understanding what happened to Zimbabwe. I have no idea what will become of Zimbabwe in the short term and even less can I pontificate on what should or rather can be done to put things right – though I think I have a few ideas to share. In this book I have written down my own interpretation of what happened, not suggesting that it is definitive but hoping that some of the insights or perspectives I offer will help in provoking fresh thought.

The writers of a learned article on Zimbabwe described the question they wished to answer in their article as follows: "What happened to Zimbabwe? How did one of Africa's most bountiful and promising countries descend into violence, deprivation and decay?" There have been many writings and pronouncements on Zimbabwe that raise the same or similar questions. My objective is to suggest that many of the underlying assumptions about Zimbabwe are almost certainly fallacious –almost certainly wrong. They are wrong because they are simplistic. I don't think any simplistic assumptions can do the Zimbabwe story justice. That is my first guiding principle in writing this book. I am going to try and communicate to you my own confusion and ambivalence and the mixture of different thoughts and feelings that possessed me when I observed at first-hand an extraordinarily complex piece of history over a considerable period of time. My second guiding principle is that forming judgements on what happened to Zimbabwe without reference to history and the big picture is almost certainly bound to be misleading. In this book I try to place the events and the personalities in the context of history, geopolitics and – my own experience.

We live in a quick fix world and people tend to get their opinions from the monopolistic media reports they have access to. There may have been a time – once - when the media did not dance entirely to the tune of powerful governments and even more powerful corporates. This is hardly the case now. Economic interest, politics and the media work hand in hand. The media is embedded and in bed with financiers, industrialists and politicians and they deliver the goods. They handle what Gramsci called 'hegemony'. They ensure that whatever course of action is in the economic and political interest of their bedmates, is accepted by their viewers as 'legitimate'. The politicians produce the spin, the moral and other justifications which mask and obscure the bottom line, and the media then get their viewers to buy it.

To a large extent, this is how a lot of people get their ideas and form their opinions. Then, without having checked the facts themselves, without having been exposed to any alternative viewpoints, without really knowing anything about the person, government, idea, situation, event or phenomenon involved, they tend confidently to parrot them.

But there are many people, who, like me, are profoundly uncomfortable with the version of world events that is dished up to us on a daily basis by the media. Many in Africa and other parts of what was once the Third World, as well as in Europe and North America, question the images and opinions the so-called 'International Media' churn out – this includes the news, because in this age the news is so loaded with judgement and preconception that it is less news than propaganda. These people feel sure that there is more to it – that there are other stories that need to be told. What are the facts? What is the truth? They ask, they look, they write – seeking these other stories. And they find them very hard to come by.

Rarely have I experienced a situation as polarised as that in Zimbabwe. In Zimbabwe Rudyard Kipling's words, 'East is East and West is West and never the twain shall meet', take on new meaning. Two diametrically opposing viewpoints have developed. Those on the one side can never admit that those on the other might have a point – and vice versa. Politics in its bitter subjectivity thrives on polarisation. The truth doesn't. During my time in Zimbabwe, perhaps because I was both an observer and a participant, I found this polarised vision frustrating - to say the least – myopic, unproductive and tragic.

Polarised thinking is nurtured by and perpetuates 'blame'. I do not find the 'blame game' an interesting or useful approach to history or politics. I prefer 'cause and effect', 'intention and function' and understanding a situation rather than making moral judgements about it. Polarised vision produces stereotypes. I have tried my best to go beyond them.

I am indebted in writing this book by Galil. A. Amin's *Whatever Happened to the Egyptians?*. Galil's book is a mix of knowledge and first-hand experience of a process in the development of an African country. That is exactly what I have set out to achieve in this book. In essence, this is a personal account of the Zimbabwe I saw and came to know - as an outsider but also as a deeply involved participant in some sectors and as a resident for 29 years.

I do not lament the fate of Zimbabwe though its vicissitudes have been lamentable. I believe that what has happened – and is happening as I write – is a robust mixture of the heroic and the traitorous and a tale that every South African, every African, indeed every progressive person, needs to be properly informed about, consider dispassionately and draw his or her own conclusions about.

I am deeply and gratefully aware that my opposition to and indignation at the actions of NATO and governments and institutions in the countries of the West, are shared by many fine and fair-minded people in those countries. I am also acutely aware of their sacrifice and commitment to the peoples of southern Africa in their times of need and in their struggles.

Finally, my reading of what happened in Zimbabwe differs from the Liberal or Right Wing critique of Robert Mugabe, ZANU-PF and the events that took place. I am an African, a supporter of the revolutionary struggles in Africa for independence and sovereignty and a Socialist. I viewed what happened in Zimbabwe from this perspective. The Left critique in Zimbabwe – as in South Africa – where it might exist, has been relatively underexposed. Perhaps this might account for why, in Zimbabwe, ZANU-PF has tolerated criticism and why in South Africa the ANC tolerates it too. Nationalism does not fear the Centre and the Right. But criticism from the Left attacks the very basis of its credentials and recent history is full of examples of how it reacts to it – mostly by suppression, imprisonment and sometimes murder.

INTRODUCTION

The period between the elections in 2005 and the introduction of the dual currency in April 2009 was one of the most extraordinary times in the life of any nation – and in my own life. Things happened which, if but one of them had been all that happened, it would have been memorable enough. But in Zimbabwe lots of extraordinary things happened, sometimes all at the same time, sometimes in different combinations. One never knew what tomorrow was going to bring – something better, something worse? And all the time the headlines in foreign countries proclaimed that Zimbabwe was experiencing a 'meltdown', it was 'on the brink of collapse', 'the country was dry' – meaning there was no fuel - the country 'faced starvation' and so on and so on. Yet here were people getting up every day and going to sleep every evening and life went on. The roads were full of cars. At one stage, there was no food in the shops but it was surprising how many were still eating. There was no cash in the bank but somehow people were making transactions. There was no electricity so people cooked on fires outside. There was no water so people carried water in buckets from the nearest borehole. The traffic lights didn't work but somehow not too many cars collided. The government ceased to govern but somehow the people governed themselves.

Extraordinary things happened. But not to everyone - with money it was possible to lead a relatively normal life. Powerful generators and fuel to power them, gas stoves and fridges and the gas to keep them going, boreholes and large tanks, solar panels, trips to South Africa to stock up, all made life almost normal – for some. But those who were able to achieve this kind of normality, were relatively few. On the other hand, there was the people, the vast majority, who had no advantages and bore the brunt.

With the coming of economic hardships, that new word, 'load-shedding', entered everyone's vocabulary - the closer to the city centre, where all the important things are, the less 'load-shedding' there was. People who lived or had their offices in the outer suburbs, were in trouble. Office workers used to spend the whole day sitting chatting in the sun or getting a fire ready outside to cook their lunches. Generators cost a fortune to buy and another to run – if you could get the fuel, that is - and there was so much that needed power that a normal generator hardly made any difference. Inverters only lasted for an hour or two before going flat.

Many people came home from school or work and finding that there was no power, simply went off to sleep, thinking perhaps that when the power came back they would wake up. Mostly they didn't and just slept right through. Mothers had to get everything ready for the next day, for the husband to go to work, for the children to go to school, and so they cooked the breakfast and did all their other preparations late at night. In the beginning when the power came back there were shouts of glee all over: "*Magetsi adzoka*! The electricity is back!" You would think it was New Year! As the years rolled by and the situation never seemed to get better for long and slowly got worse, no-one shouted any more. By then people were used to it and had taken to doing without. Food was cooked outside on the fire. People went to bed early. Life went on.

Which is worse – going without electricity or going without water? A difficult question. For many electricity is life and so the answer for them would probably be 'going without electricity' – until the next time the bath, the swimming pool and the *zvigubhu* (containers) empty and there is still no water in the pipes.

As time went by a new problem came along. There was a time when one could drink Harare water straight from the tap. Masvingo water was particularly good. Then the quality began to deteriorate and water had to be boiled before it could be drunk. At times, even that was not good enough as a certain greenness or taste of urine turned the stomach. Or when left standing, as in the bath, a deposit of black particles built up on the bottom.

Then there was cash. For instance, most of the time, owing to inflation and the shortage of bank notes in the banks – elsewhere the city was awash with them – the amount one was permitted to withdraw from an account per day was strictly limited. At one stage, it might have been, say, $5 000 000. With two or three activities in the week which needed funding to the tune of, say, 20 or 30 million each, things got complicated. That would mean about $90 million required for the week and 6 days to withdraw it at $5 million per account per day. It became so complicated that it meant doing banking every day. An intricate labyrinth of transfers from one account to the other had to be plotted so as to be able to withdraw the daily limit from every available account – and then arrange to transfer it all back again so as to balance the books.

But it was the fuel shortages that really demonstrated the character of the Zimbabwean people. When a tanker moved through the streets, everyone would follow it until it arrived at the particular service station where it was going to deliver fuel. At the service station they would find that there was a queue already

– people had all sorts of ways of knowing when and where the next delivery would be. In no time the fuel queue was snaking down the road, sometimes starting in one suburb and ending in another. People would park their cars and wait as car by car they inched forward. They would get out of their cars and chat. Many an enjoyable conversation took place between people who had never seen each other in their lives and never would again. Some even brought braai stands and beers along and enjoyed some *gochi gochi* (roasted meat). In other cases, people slept all night in their cars – and then, when they at long last got to the pump, found that each car was only being given 20 litres!

From time to time the government tried in vain to solve the fuel problem – with exciting promises that soon the fuel crisis would be over. They tried to do deals with South Africa, Libya, Iran – based on barter, Zimbabwean products for their oil. After an initial delivery, Zimbabwe would, I suppose, fail to fulfil its side of the bargain and the agreement lapsed. Throughout the entire period of fuel shortages, government was more or less impotent. Corruption scandals at Noczim (the National Oil Company of Zimbabwe), the national oil importer, did not help. Some of the traditional big oil suppliers sold up and left. New indigenous players entered the market. As with many aspects of social and economic operations at that time, where the government abdicated, the people took over. To an extraordinary extent, Zimbabwe during those years was actually run by its people. And the people were ingenious. The new fuel companies that came into existence offered unique services. It became possible for your relatives in the diaspora to buy fuel for you in England or the States. Proof of purchase would be emailed to an office in Harare where you would be given a voucher. With that voucher you were able to fill up your tank at designated service stations. Others who had access to fuel at official, i.e. crazily cheap prices, would sell it on the black market. There was a time when, driving down to Beit Bridge on the way to South Africa, wild-looking men would suddenly jump out of the bush brandishing cans of petrol for sale.

People became absolute experts in knowing what the needles of their car fuel gauges really meant. Being on the red meant nothing. That was like a security zone. It all depended on knowing how far below the red the needle could go without the fuel actually running out. That did not mean that people did not constantly run out of petrol and then have to disappear into the back streets, *chigubhu* (container) in hand, to try and find someone who would sell them a few litres. Of course, this caused all sorts of fuel problems as fuel pumps sucked up the sludge at the bottom of the tank and clogged fuel filters and carburettor jets.

Then, after all the problems relating to power, water, fuel, cash and inflation, came food – and the never-ending tussle between a government, on the one hand, that could not control or improve production but wanted to control prices, and producers and sellers, on the other, who had to make a profit. Every time government gazetted prices, the shops emptied and the black market flourished. Every time they gave up, the shops filled and the prices went up. This cat and mouse game continued for some time until government took drastic action. All retailers were ordered to slash prices overnight. The shopkeepers had no option and teams of cashiers and supermarket workers stayed up all night for a few nights and soon the shops that had been full of goods at high prices were now full of goods at low prices. But before the doors opened to the public, the cashiers and supermarket workers, the managers and accountants, bought up most of the stock for resale later at black market prices and the little that remained was bought up by the public in a few hours. So the shops that had been full of goods at high prices and then became full of goods at low prices, now had no goods at all. They were empty – and they stayed empty for quite some time. No-one was going to supply or sell goods at the stipulated low prices! Those who could do so, crossed the border into South Africa or Mozambique to buy food. The only thing government could do to assist was to lift duty on imported foodstuffs. Once again, only if the people took over, would there be cooking oil, *upfu* (maize-meal), sugar, flour and rice again in Zimbabwe.

An image of the times - a visit to the Wimpy in Masvingo on the way down to Johannesburg. This Wimpy was very conveniently placed, in a highway services facility just outside Masvingo on the Beit Bridge road. It was a useful place to stop and have breakfast after having left Harare in the early hours of the morning. Expecting a good breakfast and a cup of coffee? Take a seat. The waiter comes. Sorry, no coffee. Tea, then? No, tea. Breakfast? Eggs, toast – a sausage? No, none of that. What do you have? Pork chops. Nothing else? No, just pork chops. Literally nothing in the whole Wimpy except pork chops!

There were other things people had to endure – on top of everything else. There was the diaspora and there was AIDS. There was hardly a family in Zimbabwe that did not lose its nearest and dearest to the flight into the diaspora or to AIDS. And then on top of all this, there was communication - telephones, email, the internet. Need to talk to someone, your children or other family members outside the country, to friends, to anyone at all or expecting a call or an email from loved ones outside the country? The phone is down. Email was dial-up then so that meant no email, no internet.

How to survive? Who knows? People did. They always found a way.

***

So, by the end of the third decade of Zimbabwean independence, this was the situation. How did it come about? In my Preface I suggested that the common belief that at Independence Zimbabwe had everything going for it was simplistic. In my opinion a closer look reveaks that such a belief can only be grounded in an ignorance or neglect of the country's history.

When a new country is born, paradoxically it is, for obvious reasons, not 'new'. It is the result of a long history and, in that sense, already old. Those who govern the 'new' country, may or may not try to create the new. Frelimo in Mozambique definitely saw itself as leading '*o povo Moçambicano*' in a post-Independence struggle to build a new society – '*uma sociedade nova*'. Though the same or a similar concept was not touted in Zimbabwe, it is obvious that the new government was going to bring about fundamental changes. Any efforts to bring about change or create the new, must take the old into consideration.

At Independence when the new country, Zimbabwe, was born, its history waited on the doorstep and therefore willy-nilly the old had to be picked up and carried into the new. I am not sure to what extent the Patriotic Front ever attempted an analysis of the old in order to assess the opportunities and dangers that would confront them as the new government at Independence and by so doing consciously evolve policies to exploit the latter and mitigate the former or at least ensure that the new policies took them into account. Subsequent events would seem to imply that they may not have. But there is no doubt that the baggage of the past had a profound impact on whatever happened later.

It would be extremely difficult for anyone wanting to know whatever happened to Zimbabwe to understand why events unfolded as they did, without a fair grasp of what baggage the new nation had inherited at Independence. Only if we consider this, can we avoid the expressions of incredulity as to how a country that had everything going for it, ended up in the situation it did – 'from the breadbasket of Africa to a basket case'. So we have to go into that. We have to inform ourselves, however superficially, as to what the new country had inherited from the past which was going to make a difference to its future. I wish therefore to share with you my reading of Zimbabwe's past and how that past could have been expected actively to impact on the course of events at Independence and thereafter. These are factors that, in my opinion, *defined* the situation in Zimbabwe at Independence. They are factors anyone who wants to understand what happened to Zimbabwe thereafter, has to know. Taken together these factors combined to create a situation at independence that, far from being 'bountiful and promising', was, as I hope to demonstrate, a delicate and fragile mix of opportunities and challenges – golden apples and dragon's teeth - and fraught with very serious dangers.

PART ONE

ZIMBABWE AT INDEPENDENCE

CHAPTER ONE:

THE LEGACY

'*Mviromviro yemhanza mapfeka'* - great events are foreshadowed in little signs

For those who do not know the stories of the golden apples and the dragon's teeth, let me recount them briefly.

Once in ancient Greece a man named Hippomenes loved a woman called Atalanta. The only way she would consent to marry him was if he could beat her in a foot race. However she was an extremely fast runner. So Hippomenes got hold of three golden apples and every now and again he dropped a golden apple and Atalanta would waste time picking it up. It also meant Atalanta had to run holding golden apples, which must have played a major part in slowing her down – though that little fact seemed to have escaped the attention of the story-tellers! So in the end Atalanta got the apples but Hippomenes won the race – and got Atalanta for a wife, which meant he probably got his apples back.

In the second story, again in ancient Greece, someone called Cadmus was told by the oracle to found a city. To get water he had to kill a dragon, which he did. He was then told treacherously by War, whose dragon it was, that he should sow the dragon's teeth in the soil. He did so but a mighty crop of warriors grew up from the soil and, being the sons of War, they were all armed to the teeth and ready to polish Cadmus off. However, he was given a stone by Wisdom and he threw it in amongst the warriors. It hit one of them and the one who was hit by the stone, thought that one of his brother warriors had attacked him. So he started a fight and then all the warriors joined in and started killing each other. In the end only six of them were left. Cadmus persuaded them to join him in founding the city. War decided to make his peace with Cadmus and gave him his daughter, Harmonia or Harmony, in marriage and thus was the great city of Thebes built. Harmonia's mother was - Love.

I have called the opportunities Zimbabwe faced at Independence, the 'golden apples' and the challenges or dangers 'dragon's teeth'. The following are selected phenomena from the past which presented the new country with their store of golden apples and dragon's teeth at Independence.

The Mwenemutapa Empire

The majority of Zimbabweans could pride themselves on having a proud history and heritage as a nation, being the descendants of illustrious forebears - an ancient Iron Age Empire that built cities and citadels, whose ruins are scattered across the country and into South Africa and Mozambique and who traded in iron, gold, ivory and to some extent slaves with all the major maritime nations of the Indian Ocean littoral as well as China. From this comes not only the name of the new nation (taken from *Dzimba dza Mabwe*, meaning 'Houses of Stone', which refers to the ancient capital of the empire now known as the Mwenemutapa Empire) but also its national symbol (the fish eagle the sculptured effigies of which were found there) and its totem (the bird again). It is not certain how much Zimbabweans know about this history and certainly not all Zimbabweans felt included in it – as we shall see.

A relatively homogeneous population

The inhabitants of the Mwenemutapa Empire must have been predominantly speakers of the languages which have come to be collectively called Shona. They include present-day peoples in Zimbabwe as well as in Mozambique (Sena), South Africa (Venda) and possibly Malawi and Zambia. In Zimbabwe they include the Karanga, Kalanga, Zezuru, Manyika and Korekore.

In the period before the Nguni invasions, though there were small minorities such as the Tonga and Nambya people in the north, the Shona-speaking peoples made up the vast majority of the population. This was in contrast with many other nation states that emerged after the colonial period. For instance, Mozambique, from the Rovuma River in the north to the Maputo River in the south, is a country consisting of an immense number of different peoples and languages. In Zambia there are 46, in Kenya 68 and in Tanzania 126!

The Nguni invasions

There were a number of invasions by Nguni peoples from south of the Limpopo, which upset the previously existing relative cultural and linguistic homogeneity. The major invasion was that of the so-called Ndebele[1] under Mzilakazi ka Khumalo. Other Nguni peoples founded kingdoms in Mozambique, Malawi, Zambia and as far afield as Tanzania. In Zimbabwe they contributed to the development of the present-day Shangane and Ndau minorities. Though the Nguni conquerors established their rule over the local Shona-speaking peoples in the areas where they were hegemonic, they constituted only small ruling hierarchies. In the case of the Shangane and Ndau peoples little of Nguni domination remains save for their history, some vocabulary, nomenclatures and cultural features, including songs and dances.

---

1 'So-called' because 'Ndebele' is not their historically authentic name – see p.81

The Nguni of Mzilikazi established a multi-ethnic nation called Mthwakazi, later referred to as amaNdebele. The Mthwakazi nation established hegemony over a large part of Zimbabwe and, even where they did not settle, they commanded tribute and from time to time mounted punitive raids when they would seize cattle and abduct women. This historical legacy is still a powerful factor in the contemporary Zimbabwean psyche. It was exacerbated by the colonial regime's characteristic policy of '*divide et impera*' – divide and rule. In the ideology of the colonial state, flattering stereotypes were fashioned for the Ndebele – strong, warriors, superior breed etc. Derogatory ones were likewise fostered for the Shona. Ndebele-speaking policemen were posted in Shona-populated areas and vice versa. Shona humiliation was further exacerbated by the way white administrators, bosses and madams forced them to communicate in a bastardization of the Nguni language, called '*Chiroro*' or '*Chiraparapa*' in Zimbabwe and '*Fanagalo*' in South Africa.

The Pioneer Column and the First Chimurenga

The coming to Zimbabwe of the Pioneer Column in 1890 marked the beginning of colonial suppression and dispossession. Prior to the arrival of the Column, John Rudd, an associate of Rhodes, tricked Lobengula, the king of Mthwakazi, into a grant of mineral rights, which significantly did not include the right of settlement (known as the Rudd Concession). Once the white settlers were in the country and it became clear that they had come to take over the land and settle, Mthwakazi rose in what came to be called the First Matebele War (1893-4). As this was the first colonial war in which the Maxim gun was deployed, the forces of the British South Africa Company, aided by a sizeable force of Tswana, were victorious. As a result, Rhodes laid claim to what later came to be known as Zimbabwe. In 1895 a proclamation granted the land to his British South Africa Company and subsequently it was named in his honour – Rhodesia. The settlers were then permitted to grab almost limitless tracts of the best land and where this land was already occupied, the original inhabitants were unceremoniously evicted - sometimes, when there was resistance as there often was, by force or by war.

A few years later, 1896-7, war broke out again, this time with both the Ndebele and the Shona rising in desperation against the loss of their land. In later times, as events made the need for a Second *Chimurenga* obvious, this uprising was called the First *Chimurenga* (struggle for freedom). A factor of some importance was the role played by the shrine of Mwari (Shona) or Mwali (Ndebele pronunciation) in the Matobo Hills (*eMatojeni* or *eMtonjeni*), at which both the Shona and the Ndebele worshipped and consulted.

The legacy of the First *Chimurenga* provided much of the mythology and inspiration for the Second *Chimurenga* – the War of Independence - especially through its major actors, the three spirit mediums or *masvikiro*, Mukwati, the medium of Mwari (the Supreme God in the Matobo), Ambuya Nehanda and Sekuru Kaguvi. Both Nehanda and Kaguvi were captured and executed by the settlers. The continuity of this tradition of struggle was maintained when the process of repossessing the land which began in the late 1990s, was called the Third *Chimurenga*.

Settler expropriation of the land

In the beginning the whites who came to Zimbabwe, believed that it would turn out to be some kind of Eldorado, not flowing with milk and honey but full of precious metals[2]. When their efforts to find the metals largely failed - at that time they had no idea of the mineral riches that would later be discovered - they turned to the land. Once the resistance of the local people had been suppressed, the settlers proceeded, during a period of over sixty years systematically to dispossess and remove the local people from any land or any resources they wished to exploit. This included not only agricultural land but also any mineral deposits they subsequently discovered.

Thus the vast majority of the population was banished to the lowest grade soils in regions of poor rainfall while the small settler minority had access to the wealth of the land, turning it into what they called 'the breadbasket of Africa' and 'a gold mine' – a basket and a mine the proceeds of which provided them with a spectacularly comfortable lifestyle while the rest of the population had to work hard – mostly for the settlers – to make ends meet.

Settler population of predominantly British origin

Unlike in South Africa but like in Kenya, the settlers who came to make up the white minority in Southern Rhodesia, were largely of British origin. It is often suggested that Southern Rhodesia did not become the fifth province of South Africa because it disagreed with its racial policies. This is not true. Even a conservative historian such as Eric Walker, in his *History of Southern Africa*, testifies that it was its distrust of the Boers, distrust of Afrikaner Nationalism

2 The settlers must have known of the tradition of mining in the hinterland. Basil Davidson tells us that earlier when the Portuguese attempted to take possession of the minerals at source by seizing the mines, the local inhabitants closed them down. This is probably why the settlers were at first disillusioned as to the mineral wealth in the region. Little did they know that the country they had invaded was indeed a mineral Eldorado!

and its adherence to the Mother Country that put the kibosh on Rhodesia throwing in its lot with the Union.

The special racism of the Rhodesian settlers is attested to by the late Nationalist leader, Maurice Nyagumbo, in his book *With the People*, when after working as a waiter in different parts of *apartheid* South Africa, he got a job in the Orange Free State and remarked that now he was meeting whites just like those he left behind in Rhodesia!

Christian Missionary activity

Zimbabwe must be one of the most 'missionarised' countries in the world. The result is that Christianity is deeply entrenched in Zimbabwe. It also has a very high level of education.

Two factors that make this significant are, firstly, the mission schools were not stopped from providing education (and with it the propagation of their ideas, values and ideology) to blacks – as they were in South Africa - and, secondly, unlike in Mozambique, the Christian missionaries, especially in the countryside, to a significant extent supported the armed struggle of the people of Zimbabwe for Independence.

The accumulated effect of missionary education and Christian proselytisation was to alienate those educated by them from their parents as well as their traditional culture. Christian priests forcefully suppressed not only traditional religious rituals but also the practise of traditional song and dances. They associated the performing arts of the pre-colonial culture with spirit possession and witchcraft. This induced a serious crisis of identity where the people were alienated from their own culture.

It is obvious from a consideration of these two factors, taken in conjunction, that the influence of Christian missionary activity was an important feature of Zimbabwe's national character.

A strong education system

Zimbabwe inherited at Independence a good but dramatically skewed education system. The system was both segregated and discriminatory. The government provided schools for blacks in their own areas, both rural and urban. There were relatively few secondary schools and facilities were far inferior to those available at the white schools. Mission schools contributed substantially to black education. The importance of education was stressed in the black community as being the only possible way to escape or partially escape from poverty and as a result black Zimbabweans took it very seriously. Thus by Independence there existed a relatively large class of educated black Zimbabweans with a good command of the English language. A small minority of these had studied at the University College of Rhodesia, later to become the University of Zimbabwe, and gained university degrees.

In addition, in the period of the political and then armed struggle for liberation, many black Zimbabweans left the country and were able not only to attain a higher education but also a wider understanding and experience of the world, its thought, politics, economies, technologies and communications, history, current affairs and social values and ethics. At school and universities abroad, many opportunities were opened up to them to study a wide range of subjects. Many went on to colleges and universities, some to advanced post-graduate study.

The result was that at Independence there was a relatively high degree of literacy, an ability to read, write and speak English and a significant number of black Zimbabweans with qualifications in a wide range of fields.

Urban migration and urbanisation

The combined effect of colonial education and the deliberate suppression of black agriculture and independent economic enterprise in order to eliminate competition and ensure a ready supply of labour, led to significant migration from the black 'communal lands' to the white towns. However the level of urbanisation remained relatively low and there were few black urban dwellers who came to see their urban homes and suburbs as 'home'. 'Home' *(kumusha)* was the rural home and links to home were actively nourished and kept active by the ties and socio-religious practices of the extended family and a corresponding adherence to the pre-capitalist culture.

This resulted in three extremely important factors in the country's later history - the centre of gravity of black life, relations and consciousness remained rooted in the rural areas, despite their impoverishment and lack of resources and infrastructure; the labour movement was relatively weak; and the war of liberation was to a large extent a peasant-based phenomenon, rooted in the countryside.

The extended family

The continuing dominance of the extended family, despite the introduction of capitalist relations and urbanisation, was, in my opinion, an extremely influential factor in the life of black Zimbabweans, determining everything from motivation to social life. The extended family involved the individual in a complex and all-embracing network of social relations and obligations, which, in the modern context, could prove to be advantageous or detrimental both to the individual and society at large.

Agriculture and mining

Rhodesia was fundamentally an agricultural economy. Agriculture was the backbone. Though maize, wheat, citrus fruit, sugarcane, soya beans, tea and coffee were important, the cash cows were cotton and above all tobacco. On this agricultural base were founded the other sectors of the economy, in particular a vibrant manufacturing industry, banking and tourism.

However, in the Great Dyke, which provides the diagonal east-west backbone to the country, Zimbabwe had a treasure trove of important minerals - many of them of strategic importance - not only to high-tech industry but also for the military.

UDI and sanctions

Zambia (previously Northern Rhodesia) became independent from Britain in 1964. In 1965, what was Southern Rhodesia declared itself independent despite the opposition of the colonial power, Britain. This was called UDI (Unilateral Declaration of Independence). For 16 years up to its Independence as Zimbabwe, Rhodesia was not recognised and was subject to sanctions, which it survived in two ways, first of all through a dependence on the support of apartheid South Africa and, secondly, by the energetic and resourceful development of a self-sufficient economy as well as sanction evasion.

This meant that for a decade both white and black people in Rhodesia were relatively cut off from the world. Television was introduced in 1960 but far from providing a window on the world, it was employed by the Smith regime as a narrow instrument either of old-fashioned entertainment or state propaganda.

Thus, owing to UDI and the resultant sanctions, Rhodesia, which was a small country, became for a decade and a half something of a backwater, out of touch and clinging to illusions of a decadent West and of its own excellence – and propagating various myths to that effect. In actual fact, it was both behind the times and out of touch and this went for its ideological consciousness, its politics, its education theory and practice as well as its arts and literature. The combined effect of the above impacted equally on many blacks as well as whites. When Independence came, it came to a country, very much unprepared, like Rip van Winkle, to cope with its re-entry into the modern world.

A bitter armed struggle

When it was obvious that the Smith regime was obdurate and no other means would serve, both ZAPU and ZANU took up arms in order to bring about democracy and the liberation of the black majority. From bases in Zambia and later Mozambique, the 'comrades', as they were called, infiltrated into the Rhodesian countryside and were able from time to time to mount daring raids on urban installations. The war was a savage one and the Smith regime employed a combination of rigid indoctrination and ruthless and often murderous terror and massacre in order to cling on to power.

As with all liberation struggles, the wounds went deep. Many black Rhodesians either supported and fought for the UDI regime or became allies either through fear or other inducements. To make matters worse, Muzorewa's United African National Council (UANC) and Ndabaningi Sithole's ZANU-Ndonga[3] entered into a separate agreement with Ian Smith's regime and participated in the joint government of a sham substitute for independence called Zimbabwe/Rhodesia. Muzorewa became Prime Minister. Thus Muzorewa and Sithole went into active opposition to ZANU and ZAPU, who had come together to form the Patriotic Front.

This further deepened the wounds as substantial numbers of black Zimbabweans were now actively involved in killing their own people on behalf of the new government. This in its turn increased the scale of killings of 'traitors' and 'sell-outs' by the guerrillas. It also meant that at Independence the black people of Zimbabwe had been by and large split along ethnic lines – the Ndebeles in ZAPU, the Shangane and Ndau in ZANU-Ndonga and the UANC and general support in Shona-speaking areas for ZANU. Despite initial unity, African nationalist resistance had split into four rival factions based to a large extent, but not entirely, on ethnicity.

The armed struggle ushered in revolutionary change in many ways other than political. First of all, both movements espoused socialism as the ideology of the struggle. In the case of ZAPU, led by

3 Ndabaningi Sithole, like Mugabe, had been a senior official in ZAPU under Nkomo. He likewise broke away to form ZANU, of which he was initially the leader. When he renounced the armed struggle, he was deposed in favour of Mugabe. He continued to lead a rump ZANU, which later came to be called ZANU-Ndonga.

Joshua Nkomo, there were strong links with the Soviet Union and the ANC of South Africa. Their ideology was primarily Marxist-Leninist. ZANU had closer links with China and the Pan Africanist Congress of South Africa and thus their ideology, while not being clearly defined, suggested an allegiance to Pan Africanism and Maoism.

Another important development which challenged the stereotypes of history, was the fact that it was ZANU that registered the greatest success in waging the armed struggle. ZANU, though not specifically developed on ethnic lines, was nevertheless made up of people from those parts of the country in which the Shona-speaking peoples were in the vast majority while ZAPU, again by no means exclusively, was made up of people from the west of the country where Ndebele was the most widely spoken language. Historically and in colonial propaganda and policy, the Ndebele had always been 'top dogs' while a consistent effort was made to denigrate the status of the Shona. In the liberation war, these stereotypes were overturned and, when ZANU-PF won the Independence elections, this only further made the turning of the tables more pronounced. This quite naturally affected the attitudes of both Shona and Ndebele-speakers to each other.

Finally, the liberation struggle had other deep social, cultural and artistic effects: the cult of Ambuya Nehanda, as the spirit that guided and inspired the struggle; the revival of the historical and traditional consciousness and culture, which missionary education had gone a long way to extinguish; the *pungwe*, nocturnal meetings, in the countryside led by the 'comrades', in which the peasant masses were 'educated' in the aims and causes of the struggle; the great corpus of revolutionary songs which the struggle inspired and which in turn inspired the struggle; not to mention the influx after Independence of 'progressive' ex-patriates, Zimbabweans returning from abroad, and ZANU and ZAPU ex-combatants and militants from bases in neighbouring countries. All these had profound repercussions when, like alien and aggressive fresh water being pumped into a stagnant pool, they were injected into the narrow, racist, Christian, conservative mix in the isolated, out-of-touch backwater which was Smith's Rhodesia.

A legacy of the liberation war was that many black Zimbabweans did not support or only superficially supported the victorious freedom-fighters when they returned. They had their own grudges, some dating from pre-colonial history or the colonial policy of divide-and-rule, from punishments exacted by the freedom-fighters on 'sell-outs' who happened to be close relatives, or from their support either for the Smith regime or other movements such as the UANC. With some, the antagonism was bitter and verged on hatred – and while *jongwe* (the rooster, election symbol of ZANU-PF) crowed, they remained silent. When the crowing lost its first, fine rapture, these people began to vent their feelings. A lot – of course not all – of the intensely bitter opposition to ZANU-PF which surfaced later within the country, could be traced back to this legacy of the time of armed struggle.

The Lancaster House Agreement

The birth of Zimbabwe and the final demise of Smith's Rhodesia and white minority rule was arranged in London where representatives of the Zimbabwe-Rhodesia government met with those of the Patriotic Front under the chairmanship of Lord Carrington and with the participation of the then Commonwealth Secretary General, Sonny Ramphal. What was agreed there, rather similar to the agreement reached between the ANC and the Afrikaner Nationalist Government in South Africa in 1994, was the result of a conflict which neither side had actually won. It was thus a compromise document, designed to hand over power to the black majority but limit that power in the interests of the white minority while at the same time ensuring that the interests of the colonial power, Britain, and the most powerful capitalist power, the United States, were also taken care of.

Though provision was made for free democratic elections and majority rule, the rights of the white minority were accorded special recognition. Twenty seats were reserved specifically for whites in the first parliament. Commercial farmland was protected from alienation except under the 'willing seller, willing buyer' principle. Rhodesian perpetrators of human rights abuses were also accorded immunity from prosecution or reprisal. What made it especially significant in terms of understanding subsequent events in Zimbabwe was a provision whereby the agreed constitution and all its provisions should be respected and not changed in the first ten years.

The Patriotic Front nearly rejected the agreement over the entrenchment of white property rights with regard to land. As the winning back of the land that had been taken away from the black majority over the previous ninety years, was possibly the major objective of the war of liberation and certainly one of the main reasons why rural Zimbabweans supported and sacrificed for the struggle, this was a bitter pill to swallow. There was another reason not to like it. They believed that they were winning the war and would ultimately take the land by force of arms anyway. Only unwritten guarantees from President Carter that the United States would finance the acquisition of land for re-distribution, finally paved the way to acceptance. Other regional presidents such as Samora Machel also urged the two leaders, Mugabe and Nkomo, to accept the deal, saying that they could always sort out the problem of the land once they had the power.

Revolution divided at Independence

Despite coming together in the last years of the war to create a united front in the struggle for freedom, the two components of the Patriotic Front, ZANU and ZAPU, fought the elections separately. Not only did this serve to accentuate the potential for divisions among those who had fought for freedom but it also exacerbated the already existing tendency of black politics in the new Zimbabwe to be defined by ethnic and regional divisions.

The elections produced a resounding victory for ZANU-PF (57 seats) and Robert Mugabe became Prime Minister. However PF-ZAPU had also won a sizeable number of seats (20). Muzorewa's UANC won three seats. Sithole's ZANU-Ndonga failed to win a seat. What was significant – and regrettable – however was that ZANU-PF had won all over Shona-speaking Zimbabwe and ZAPU had won in Ndebele-speaking Zimbabwe. An ominous precedent had been set and an unfortunate legacy for the newly-born Zimbabwe bequeathed.

Policy of Reconciliation

> *"If yesterday I fought you as an enemy, today you have become a friend and ally with the same national interest, loyalty, rights and duties as myself. If yesterday you hated me, today you cannot avoid the love that binds you to me and me to you. The wrongs of the past must now stand forgiven and forgotten."* – Robert Mugabe, 17 April 1980

These were the words of the new leader of independent Zimbabwe at Independence – and it must be said that the man rose to the occasion in his finest hour for these words have a ring of greatness he was rarely able to attain again.

Mugabe himself was regarded as a terrorist – and depicted as such – not only by the Rhodesian government and the white minority but also by much of the 'international' media. The wheel later came full circle and there is little difference between the demonization Robert Mugabe has suffered over the last thirteen years and what he endured in the years leading up to Independence.

Not only was Mugabe regarded as a terrorist, so were his comrades, his organisation as well as the organisation with which ZANU-PF made up the Patriotic Front, Joshua Nkomo's PF-ZAPU. Further, they were routinely referred to in Rhodesian propaganda as Communist.

Thus at Independence, after Muzorewa's miserable eclipse in the elections, when the Rhodesian propaganda machine had led the whites to believe he would be victorious, a largely racist white minority saw their fate fall into the hands of what they had been taught to believe was a savage and backward horde of black Communist terrorists. It is likely that very few Rhodesians thought it possible that this black Communist terrorist had the capacity to utter the words quoted above – and what's more that he would be extending the olive branch in such loving and humane terms.

This was the first clarion call of Reconciliation, which became the new government's policy and which was never formally revoked though it was overtaken by events. Reconciliation without transformation, re-education and behaviour change, though expedient in the short term, turned out in the long term to be a recipe for disaster.

Summary

The above-mentioned factors combined to create a potentially dangerous mixture. A considerable number of them seemed either to flatter to deceive or were outright recipes for disaster.

For instance, while the majority of Zimbabweans could be proud of and unite around their ancient history, their new name, national symbol, flag and totem, and also benefit from their relative ethnic homogeneity, there were two substantial minorities who might not have been expected to feel the same – namely the Ndebele and the whites. Besides, the homogeneity of the Shona-speaking peoples was more apparent than real. While a clear golden apple on one hand, it concealed its dragon's teeth - as each regional group, principally Zezuru, Karanga and Manyika, had separate identities and pursued different interests and ambitions.

The Nguni invasions and the subsequent raids as well as the ways in which the settler government manipulated Shona/Ndebele relations, had left a legacy of distrust, bitterness, chauvinism and prejudice, which were enhanced by the substantial ethnic divisions between the two liberation movements and their separate contestation of the election at Independence.

While Zimbabwe's agricultural and mineral riches might have appeared to be a great golden apple, the fact that the land and the mines were in the hands of the white minority and foreign companies was a veritable battalion of dragon's teeth. That the land had been taken by deception and force was not only an embittering memory. It also meant that, in the minds of the dispossessed, its taking had no basis in law and that, if taken from them by force and deception, it could be taken back by the same means. And in this regard Zimbabweans could draw on a long tradition of struggle, going back to the Matebele Wars and the First *Chimurenga*.

The next phase of the same struggle was the Second *Chimurenga*, an aftermath of which was that there were many people who nourished bitter grievances against the new Government arising from experiences in the war. Also many Zimbabweans had fought in that struggle and expected to benefit and see change in accordance with the goals they had risked their lives for. Others had fought and massacred to prevent the nation from being born at all – and these were not only whites. Though many of the whites left the country, many stayed. Reconciliation simply left them alone. It did nothing to change their attitudes, their bitterness or their allegiances. Even Ian Smith himself, the great defender of minority rule and racial inequality, was still at large in the country and, until his death in 2007, twenty-seven years after Independence, actively continued to propound his unchanging belief that he was right but had been betrayed by the British

The new people's government had a majority in parliament but it had little power elsewhere. The white minority and foreign interests owned and benefitted from almost all the commercially irrigable land, the entire banking sector, manufacturing industry, tourism and real estate – virtually the entire wealth of the country. And, owing to the combined effects of state propaganda in the Smith era, the knowledge they had of those who had now taken over the government, was either minimal or fatally distorted, their racist attitudes and habits in no way transformed. What is more this minority was of British stock – hence, despite UDI and British sanctions, kith and kin to an influential nation as well as partners to enormous financial and other British interests in Zimbabwe.

Nothing illustrated the golden apples/dragon's teeth dialectic better than the tremendous mineral wealth the new Zimbabwe inherited. It was indeed a two-edged sword. It was a source of wealth, yes, but a source which, if exploited democratically and for the benefit of the people, would, like the land, put the new government on a collision course with the entire capitalist establishment, which has long regarded the world's minerals as theirs by right to exploit - untrammelled and for their profit.

It was the same with the deep penetration of Christian missionary proselytisation and education in the colonial era. True, to a considerable extent, many missionary establishments assisted the popular struggle for democracy. True, they helped lay the foundations for a sound educational infrastructure. Though the education system at Independence, missionary, state and private, discriminated along racial lines and had to be reformed, once reformed it proved to be one of the great success stories of the new nation's first few years. However, the Christian religion, in the form that it was taught, and the education system it produced, created profound crises of identity - to the extent that many would not, could not, embrace their own historical culture, traditions, religious practices and performing arts as a valid and acceptable heritage. When the forces fighting for freedom did so, this led to yet another division – between those who upheld them and those who believed they were anti-Christian.

The effects of UDI and the sanctions that followed were once again both golden apples and dragon's teeth. On the one hand, they stimulated the Rhodesians to develop a resourceful and self-sufficient independent economy, which became available to the new state. On the other hand, they isolated the country and fostered a backward, conservative culture, out of touch with the modern world. This culture gave rise to numerous Rhodesian myths as well as general contempt for organisations such as the United Nations and for Africa as a whole – attitudes which were not only espoused at Independence by whites but by many black people too. The liberation movements and the expatriate 'progressive' individuals and organisations who entered the country after Independence, were operating on a completely different wavelength from those who stayed behind.

The peasant-worker or rural-urban divide at Independence was a particularly sensitive challenge for the new state. Obviously, the imbalance had to be redressed and the peasants and the rural areas had to enjoy their birthright. However at the same time the workers and the towns must not be alienated. ZANU-PF either did not seem to be sufficiently aware of the danger or would not – could not – handle it. It later turned out to be the dragon's tooth that nearly put paid to ZANU-PF's jugular.

Lancaster House made it possible to cut the Gordian Knot and put on the table a treaty which both those fighting for their freedom and those protecting their considerable vested interests would accept. Though it facilitated change, paradoxically it also made change difficult if not impossible. It was the political expression of a struggle not yet won and not yet lost. South Africans cannot fail to hear the echoes here. The policy of Reconciliation was its ideological counterpart. Thus all the challenges that attended the policy of Reconciliation, also attended the agreement made at Lancaster House – the most pressing and dangerous of all being the unresolved question of the land – and this was obviously bound to upset the golden apple cart.

Thus, far from 'bountiful and promising', the situation that faced the people of the new nation as they set out on their hitherto untrodden path together at Independence, was extremely complex, with many positive possibilities but also many extremely dangerous pitfalls. And all this had to be negotiated by those, who had never, with few exceptions, been allowed any experience or offered any training whatsoever in the arts of government or all the other political and economic sciences that are involved in rule. They had to do this on behalf of and in the interests of a people who had been relegated to the lowest functions of Rhodesian society. Both for the governors and for the governed, taking on such a task in such a situation must have seemed a daunting one indeed. The next decades would show how they fared – and, hopefully, those who judge them, will bear in mind both the task and the circumstances in which it was performed.

STILLE WATER – THE FIRST DECADE

There is an Afrikaans saying:

> *Stille water, diepe grond*
>
> *Onder draai die duiwel rond*

which translated literally means 'where the surface of the water is still, there are deeps below and down in them the devil churns things up'. I don't know but for me this little rhyme has a special resonance in the Zimbabwean situation. I see the first decade of Zimbabwe's Independence as *Stille Water* – still, possibly ominously still, water. The second decade I see as *Diepe Grond* – the deeps below. The third decade I see as *Onder draai die duiwel rond* – a time of upheaval and turmoil.

Not only is the way in which I apply the words of this Afrikaans proverb, impressionistic and relative but so are the titles given to the parts. For instance, calling the first decade a honeymoon and a time of 'still water' may well raise a few eyebrows, given some of the events that took place in it. It is only by comparison with other periods in Zimbabwe's history that the decade could be so called.

PART TWO

THE LANCASTER HOUSE HONEYMOON

Independence laid the foundation for a new society. It ushered in a majority government. It saw the end of the sanctions that had been imposed on the Smith regime. Lancaster House and the agreement concluded there had paved the way. Such was the excitement that Independence had at last come to Zimbabwe after all those years and such were the heady opportunities that opened up for those who had previously had few, that on the balance it was possible to call the first decade 'The Lancaster House Honeymoon'.

There was a general sense that anything and everything was now possible. Government set about trying to redress the inequalities of a century as if it could all be done in a decade. There was a dramatic increase in education, in social services and infrastructural improvements, which were at last aimed at benefiting the previously disadvantaged. Job, career and business opportunities opened up. People could buy houses in the former white suburbs and send their children to schools which had been out of bounds to them before. A great feeling of euphoria prevailed, not only in Zimbabwe but all over the world. Zimbabwe was a hot property.

There seemed to be golden apples galore. However, the dragon's teeth were also very much in evidence. Despite the excitement, the situation in the country was precarious and the hopes fragile. Zimbabwe took its first steps in nation-building as a racially and ethnically divided state, clearly reflected in the first parliament. The consequences might have been catastrophic as they were in other newly independent states. Fortunately the slide into chaos was arrested in time. Bitter hostilities did break out between the two erstwhile partners in the Patriotic Front but to Zimbabwe's great credit, total disintegration into civil war was avoided by the conclusion of the Unity Accord between the two main parties, ZANU-PF and PF-ZAPU.

However the new Zimbabwe was full of contradictions. It was riddled with problems of race and ethnicity as well as attitudes related to class and status. Despite all the advantages that Independence had brought with it and ZANU-PF's role in that, there were many people, including the young, who nursed resentments and negative feelings.

The government's determination to redress the inequalities of the past led to an almost obsessive preoccupation with 'keeping up standards'. It was not that easy to balance the interests of the economy and those of redressing past injustices and inequalities. By the end of the decade Zimbabwe was, if not quite bankrupt, sinking deeply into debt and forced to borrow.

Key to the future fate of Zimbabwe was the nature of its leader, Robert Gabriel Mugabe, and the party he led, the Zimbabwe African National Union (Patriotic Front) – ZANU-PF.

Not all honeymoons are sheer bliss and many marriages come down to earth with a bump when they are over. So it was with Zimbabwe.

CHAPTER TWO:

FREEDOM

'Zimbabwe yauya' – our country at last

The very first official words spoken in independent Zimbabwe were: "Ladies and Gentlemen, Bob Marley and the Wailers". The announcement, a few seconds after midnight on 18th April, 1980, precipitated pandemonium among the thousands of people attending the Independence Ceremony at Rufaro Stadium in Mbare. People outside the stadium burst through the gates – and the police fired teargas at the crowd. Order was only restored by a detachment of ZANLA fighters, who, it is reported, marched into the arena with their fists raised. When the clouds of teargas had dispersed, Bob Marley, returned to the stage and shouting "Freedom!" went on to play his song 'Zimbabwe'. The packed crowds sang along with him. When a white organiser told him from the wings that he had two minutes left, it is reported Marley roared: "War!" and went on playing for another 15 minutes. With that Zimbabwe was part of the world again.

It was a fitting and possibly portentous overture to the new Zimbabwe's future history. 'Freedom!', 'War!', teargas, the march of the liberation war veterans, raised fists - euphoria! The very first years in the life of Zimbabwe saw an explosive conflict between the armed forces of the erstwhile partners in the Patriotic Front, who had a few months earlier negotiated together at Lancaster House. It saw the 5th Brigade's brutal repression and reprisals against the population in so-called Matebeleland. It saw the terrorist attacks of Super ZAPU, the so-called 'dissidents', and *apartheid* South Africa's blatant and covert operations in Harare and Bulawayo against the African National Congress. It saw the escalation of Renamo banditry and atrocities in Mozambique, as South Africa took over from Rhodesia in supporting it. It saw the involvement of the Zimbabwe National Army in Mozambique, which fought side by side with Frelimo to suppress it.

Yes, there were lots of things to rock Zimbabwe's honeymoon boat but, as alarming as they may sound and were, they could not overshadow the immense ecstasy of freedom, the heady sense of new growth and the freshness of hope that characterised those early years. The sanctions that had been imposed on Rhodesia were of course lifted. Suddenly Zimbabwe was re-connected to a world that went far beyond the *apartheid* Republic of South Africa, which had been just about the only country which had not officially applied sanctions against Rhodesia. Others, like Israel, circumvented them unofficially.

The newly independent country now occupied a unique position in southern Africa. *Apartheid* South Africa, the region's largest economy, was still out of bounds. It would be another ten years before the situation there began to open up. Zimbabwe's strategic importance both in the region and in the Frontline of free Africa attracted immense international interest. People all over the world had followed the struggle for freedom in Zimbabwe and when it finally came, many were ecstatic. I remember my English Ph.D. supervisor at the University of Leeds telling me how excited he was and what the very name Zimbabwe meant to him. Robert Mugabe was showered with honorary degrees and Harare became an important regional hub.

The British Council returned. The Alliance Française opened up. Embassies mushroomed, including, as was to be expected, all the major countries of the West. But imagine what it must have been like in the once little backwater where Communists were the devil itself when the Soviets, the Chinese and the Cubans came to town. Embassies of all the socialist countries, including the People's Democratic Republic of Korea, were there. Africa too came to Zimbabwe as many African countries also established their embassies. Thus not only had Zimbabwe become part of the world, very importantly it had become part of Africa again.

Most of the major airlines introduced direct flights to Harare. Important international conferences took place in Harare. Many were the Harare Declarations that emerged at that time. The streets and tourist spots of Zimbabwe filled up with tourists. Zimbabwe sports teams could now compete on the international stage, including attending the Olympic Games, where in the year of Independence the women's hockey team stunned the world by winning the gold medal in Moscow. The National Dance Company was formed, which now brought to prominence the neglected traditional dances of Zimbabwe, including the famous *mbende* or *Jerusarema* dance, which finally received international recognition when it was accorded World Intangible Cultural Heritage status by UNESCO in 2005. The *Jerusarema* drums were played to introduce all radio and television news broadcasts. Zimbabwean musicians could now freely perform and tour internationally and soon Zimbabwean artists like Thomas Mapfumo, Oliver Mtukudzi, Stella Chiweshe and Biggie Tembo and the Bhundu Boys became household names for many music-lovers abroad. Zimbabwean sculpture could be accessed and exhibited freely and soon scored spectacular successes and won prestigious awards with exhibitions in the most select international art galleries.

Black and white could mingle without restrictions. The colour bar – or rather the official colour bar – collapsed. Blacks went into previously all-white restaurants, hotels, bars and nightclubs. It is true though that for some time – until quite recently in fact – there were certain white haunts where a black man was not welcome and could enter only at his peril. But generally the transformation was breathtaking.

A feature of Zimbabwean Independence was how quickly Zimbabwe changed from a white country with an excluded black majority to a black country with a reclusive white minority. By 1984 when we arrived in Zimbabwe whole swathes of public life which had once been all white, were now black. The previously all white suburbs began their transformation quite early on as black Zimbabweans bought fine houses that once belonged to those who had 'gapped' it, as the expression went. In other words, they had taken the gap and fled to South Africa, the UK, the United States, Australia and so on. Houses were therefore cheap and those who bought a house at that time, did very well for themselves.

By the time we bought a house, a year or so after arriving in Zimbabwe, the prices had begun to rise again. The suburb in which we did buy, was called Marlborough. Originally a farm, I gather it had been divided up into rather large plots and sold cheap to what in South Africa were called '*die arme blankedom*' – poor whites. These poor whites were living in what the Smith regime had considered to be 'regrettable' circumstances, in other words, circumstances resembling those in which many black Zimbabweans lived. What's more – and this was the real problem – they were beginning to mix and live together with other races.

It seems to be a truism among the British or their descendants, both in Britain and abroad, that the lower they are on the social scale, the more fanatically royalist they are – and this was manifested in the distinctly aristocratic names the new suburb sported. Not only was the suburb itself called Marlborough but there was

Princess Margaret this, Queen Elizabeth that, Marlborough this and – the street we came to live in – Mountbatten that. After some time, as incidences of crime rose, Neighbourhood Watches were formed. I joined ours a little while after we moved in but left in embarrassment when one night someone I knew, who was innocently jogging along the side of the road after dark, was harassed and insulted. Of course, he was black. The Neighbourhood Watch was simply reviving, so I was told, the racial harassment that characterised the suburb in the colonial days. Apparently, Marlborough in the colonial days, like many others, was not a suburb for a black man to be caught strolling in after dark.

Demographic change took longer to act on the town centres than the suburbs so that, for instance, Harare city centre remained for many years the old two-in-one of colonial times. There was the European-looking upmarket precinct of banks, hotels, smart office blocks, government buildings, the art gallery, parks etc., still rather sparsely inhabited and quiet at night and weekends, on the one hand. Then there was a black quarter, full of bus and taxi ranks, Indian shops, motor workshops, fabrics, building materials, tools, low-class nightclubs, and always crowded even at night and weekends, on the other. But that did not last long and by the 1990s the city centre had been totally transformed and become a recognisably African city everywhere.

The euphoria of freedom and opportunity also penetrated, though I believe unequally, the countryside too. There too Independence brought many possibilities. Peace came at last. People who had been displaced or herded into 'protected villages', could now go home. The refugees and liberation war veterans returned from neighbouring countries. People could move around freely without curfews. They could travel to the towns or other parts of Zimbabwe and relatives could travel from town to the countryside without the endless army searches or the fear of landmines. Soon, there were more schools, better roads, in some places electricity, agricultural inputs like seeds and fertilisers, better access to health services as well as food in times of drought. The new growth points promised the possibility of rural development. With regard to electrification, Zimbabwe, like the Soviet Union in its early days, faced a situation in which the vast masses of peasants lived in darkness. Both countries very early on introduced rural electrification programmes. As a footnote, astonishingly the rural electrification programme was sustained even through the dark years of sanctions, hyperinflation and power cuts, though obviously greatly curtailed.

I tried to imagine what experiencing all these momentous changes was like for the black people of Zimbabwe. I could only do that by thinking about my own experience when my family and I made the change from life in Ethiopia to life in Zimbabwe. Although I had visited Zimbabwe briefly in 1982 and 1983, I missed out on Independence itself and its first three years, only arriving to take up an appointment at the University of Zimbabwe in July, 1984.

After a short period living in a staff chalet on the campus, we moved into a staff house. Our impressions of life in Zimbabwe at that time were sharpened by the contrast between where we had come from and where we were now. In a way, by coming from Mengistu Haile Mariam's Ethiopia to the new Zimbabwe, my family and I were experiencing in miniature what the great majority of Zimbabweans were experiencing on a grand scale. Ethiopia, at the time we were there, was a tightly-controlled society, controlled to a large extent by fear. Freedom was not a word that leapt to the lips. One's movements were restricted. There was a curfew at midnight. One could not go beyond a certain radius outside Addis Ababa without a permit. Local neighbourhoods and urban districts were ruled by revolutionary committees usually headed by the military. Consumerism, modcons and free importation of anything that was not essential, did not exist. Television and radio, for us foreigners, had nothing to offer. There were no films worth going to see. Fuel was rationed and so on.

Now in Harare all was changed for us. None of these restrictions existed and many of the conveniences and pleasures that we lacked in Addis Ababa, were freely available. This is not to say that life in Addis Ababa was not enjoyable for us. On the contrary, we loved Ethiopia. Nevertheless, Zimbabwe, by comparison appeared to be, as our children put it, 'magic'. By that they meant they could watch music videos on the Sounds on Saturday programme on television and buy all sorts of nice things to eat and drink in the shops.

Similarly, under Smith, the black people of Zimbabwe had lived lives that were hedged in by bans, restrictions, no-go areas and suppression. Many of them had been herded into what the Smith regime called 'protected villages'. Everywhere, all the time, there had been the menacing presence of the army and the police, sometimes their dogs too. There were so many things they had not been able to do or be, so many places they could hardly go, live, work or study in. Now suddenly, as for us, all was changed. We witnessed, if not the first fine rapture, at least the early years of the people's freedom. Like prisoners, they had emerged after decades in captivity to freedom, from darkness into light. Everything now seemed possible.

It was a time, for instance, of learning, of amassing skills, of moving into spheres of knowledge, expertise and employment that black people had never been permitted to enter before. In an astonishingly short time, black Zimbabweans took over, if not yet all the commanding heights, but at least the major functions of a modern economy. Soon once all-white or 'coloured' banks, hotels, department stores, supermarkets, government offices, police stations, post offices were being staffed by blacks. And the learning never stopped – colleges were teeming, people were taking evening classes in all sorts of subjects from secretarial through accounting, business studies, public relations (PR), and marketing to management and human resources (HR). Government, corporate and non-governmental organization (NGO) training workshops and courses were the order of the day – agriculture, gender, health, co-operatives, even theatre for development. There was a great build up of mass education.

The independent government addressed the problems of the unfair discrimination in the colonial education system with great speed and commitment, setting about immediately to expand both the education system and access to education. Previously all-white government schools were opened up to the excluded majority and transformed. The private schools, formerly either white or only tokenly multiracial, were required to open their doors to black children and admit all on merit. New schools were built – especially in the previously neglected countryside. Crash teacher-training programmes were initiated – at the so-called ZINTEC (Zimbabwe Integrated National Teachers Education Course) colleges, often high schools or other institutions which were converted into teacher training facilities.[4] A Curriculum Development Unit (CDU) was set up to revise and reform the school curriculum. Many teachers and educational experts from all over the world flocked to Zimbabwe from various 'progressive' backgrounds in order to participate in the re-building of Zimbabwe. All government education, including the university, was either free or made

4 Zimbabwe Integrated Teacher Education Course – a crash programme set up to produce enough teachers for the new schools being provided for the previously excluded black majority.

available on a loan and grant basis. Teachers' salaries, even at private schools, were paid or subsidised by government.

At Independence, the University of Zimbabwe, formerly the University College of Rhodesia, was the only university in the country. By 2010 there were at least ten. The University College of Rhodesia had been conceived as an elite institution for the white minority - though by independence black and white students were more or less 50-50. At Independence, the numbers admitted to the university were small and university education was a far off dream for the vast majority of black children. With the enormous expansion in secondary education and despite the high standards - at that time all Zimbabwean secondary schools were writing Cambridge 'A' Levels - many thousands graduated with university-entrance grades. Somehow these school-leavers had to be accommodated. How was this small elite institution going to cope?

The university coped by expanding massively. The new students came from all over Zimbabwe and a great many of them from rural schools. This was unprecedented in the history of the country. Massive new residences were built. New courses and even departments and faculties were introduced. Professor Walter Kamba became the first black Vice-Chancellor as dingdong battles in many departments saw the new black lecturers contesting in many different domains, such as promotions, appointments and syllabi, with the senior, tenured white establishment inherited from the days before Independence. The university cricket ground was sliced in two to produce two football pitches – which was a pity given the interest in cricket which later saw Zimbabwe playing international cricket test matches with teams composed largely of young black players.

An experience which brought home to me dramatically – literally – the collapse of the old order and the coming of the new was when in 1986 our political theatre group, Zambuko/Izibuko, visited Mhangura, a small copper-mining town about 140 kilometres north of Harare. We did two performances. The first was in the open-air arena, obviously built by the mine for the black workers. It was a space well-suited to the performance of traditional dances and music groups. The raked football stadium-like auditorium was built of cement. Of course, there were no cushions. In the evening, we did a show in the little theatre in the staff club. It was a beautiful little theatre, small but well-suited to theatre performance. Obviously this is where the all-white managers, administration and their families would have put on their pantomimes and amateur theatricals in the old days. Now, in the club, the new members, all black by then, filled the bar and the lounges. By way of contrast, the walls were covered with photographs of the whites who had once held sway at the mine. I wondered to myself whether any of this was being documented. It would have been fascinating to pan round the bar and the lounges with a camera back in the days, say in the 1950s or 60s and then dissolve into what it was like now. And this dissolve – from white to black – was happening all over the country in the years immediately after Independence.

As a result of the vast expansion of opportunities in education, Zimbabweans became pretty good at a lot of things. It is difficult to pinpoint what it was about Zimbabwe's education system which produced results of this kind. In my experience, the education system left a lot to be desired. The pedagogy was uniformly top-down and autocratic. There was an absolute emphasis on rote-learning and exam-oriented teaching methods. Yet, *here* is Zimbabwe, a powerhouse of skills and expertise in Africa. This must have owed a great deal to the significant expansion of the education base in the first decade of Independence. Now, as a result of later developments, its products are sprayed all over the world, many of them occupying high and important positions in other countries in almost every sector you care to name.

It is a truism that Zimbabweans are pretty good at English. I discovered this quite shortly after our arrival in Zimbabwe. I have never liked being in an environment where, because of me, people are forced to speak English when they would much rather be speaking their own language. As a South African I had made it my business to speak Zulu, Xhosa and some Sotho. In Ethiopia the English language had very shallow roots and the people loved their Amharic and the culture that went with it. They welcomed a foreigner who showed that he too loved their language or at least was trying hard to learn it. Those foreigners who did, suddenly found that everyone around them was an Amharic language teacher – and so I learned to speak Amharic rather quickly.

When we came to Zimbabwe, I already had a smattering of Shona from the previous times I had visited – both before and after Independence. As I was able to speak other so-called 'Bantu' languages and because I had a fascination for comparative linguistics, I thought I could quickly pick up Shona. Well, it was a lot harder than I had anticipated. I came, rather ruefully, to call Zimbabwe, 'the Land of *Mangwanani*/Good Morning' – in other words, it was a country in which it was very common to greet someone in Shona and be answered in English. Of course, I wondered why. Zimbabwe had a completely different history from Ethiopia – and, with regard to education, different even from its neighbour, South Africa. Unlike Ethiopia, Zimbabwe was colonised – and, unlike South Africa, the colonists were exclusively British. Its school system was English medium. As a result almost all Zimbabweans speak English and many speak it as well as in any English-speaking country outside Britain, North America and the white Commonwealth. In fact, black Zimbabweans visiting Britain are often convinced that their English is a lot more educated than that of the natives – with some justification, I suspect.

The new rapidly replaced the old. "Bliss was it in that dawn to be alive/But to be young was very heaven!" Thus William Wordsworth put it after the French revolution. Zimbabwe was new and young. Everyone, but particularly the young people of Zimbabwe, now seemed to have something to look forward to. Many could go to school for the first time and to university. They could work anywhere, live anywhere, move anywhere. The past, with its pain and uncertainty, appeared over. The future was full of hope. Not many people were thinking of Wordsworth or even knew anything about him in those years after 1980 in Zimbabwe. But there was no doubt that many people were living the spirit of his words. '*Mafaro*' perhaps was the Shona word for it. Was it then, in that first decade after Independence, that Zimbabweans developed their great capacity for enjoying themselves – for *mafaro?* It was a happy time. A honeymoon it certainly was, despite the tragic and distressing episodes that marred it.

But like all honeymoons, it had to come to an end – and, as with many other honeymoons, as the young couple comes home from their short sojourn in some romantic place and a seductive taste of marital bliss, the first intrusion of the real world into their euphoria is likely to be money problems. As they set about redressing historical wrongs and injustices, it must have seemed to those in power that the financial resources of government were unlimited. They just *had* to be as there was a lot that had been neglected for a long time and therefore had to be done and done fast. Now Zimbabwe was independent, what could stop them doing it?

The old saying that one cannot live on love alone, in the case of the new Zimbabwe, might aptly be adapted to: 'Dreams cannot be built on Independence alone.'

Can a revolutionary dream? Yes, as long as his dreams are rooted in hard work and in reality. Thus said Lenin in Nikolai Pogodin's play, *Kremlin Chimes* – a play which was produced at the University of Zimbabwe to coincide with the 70th anniversary of the Russian Revolution in 1987. In the same play, H.G. Wells calls Lenin 'the dreamer in the Kremlin' because Lenin thought electricity could be brought to the rural masses in Russia. Was there anyone who could tell Zimbabwe how to make a revolutionary dream come true?

CHAPTER THREE:

THE NEW SOCIETY

'Keeping up standards'

So here was Independence and all sorts of changes but what would all these changes add up to? Did the new government have some sort of blueprint, some sort of vision in mind?

During my visit to Zimbabwe in 1983, I attended a conference at the University of Zimbabwe that was being convened to establish an all-Africa theatre project. I noticed then that three years after Independence the previous standards as they applied to the small elite institution the university had once been, were still being scrupulously maintained despite the colossal expansion. There were three-course meals in the residence dining rooms and the bedrooms-cum-studies were extremely well furnished. All the services were as one would expect in an *apartheid* South African white or English university. When the residential capacity of the university was dramatically expanded, a Quixotic effort was made to extend to the new residences the same standards that characterised the old.

When I returned to the university in 1984 as a Senior Lecturer, I discovered that the maintenance of the standards that had applied when the university was a small elite establishment, was the practice in facilities and services other than those offered in the student residences. For instance, before we moved into our nice, big house, it was given a fresh coat of paint – standard practice, I was told, for staff accommodation. The facilities and the grounds were scrupulously maintained. There was abundant transport, which was freely available for university business.

There were other things too. Not only were expatriate staff given allowances to buy furniture for their new houses and also visit their home countries every few years – which was standard practice in most African universities at the time – but all staff, including Zimbabweans, could go on fully funded 'contact leave' every two years and take sabbatical leave every four years. In the latter case, the university paid fares and subsistence for the whole family. Years later when our salaries had shrunk and the situation in the country was no longer so 'magical', these privileges were still maintained to the last. After some time, I noticed that staff members, who earned the same as I did or even less, were driving very nice imported Japanese cars. As I could never have afforded such cars on my salary, I wondered how they did it. I asked someone and discovered the secret. Staff would apply for sabbatical or contact leave, save all the money they were given for subsistence by getting a job or living with relatives and then use it to buy a second-hand car from Japan.

Another enormous increase in expenditure was the government loan and grant scheme. Any student gaining admission to the university could apply for it. In this way, students from disadvantaged rural and urban backgrounds were able to pursue a university education. The government would fund their tuition, board and lodging and give them a living allowance. Students were expected to pay the government back in instalments after they had graduated.

Given the fact that staff and student numbers had ballooned, academic staff salaries and perks, new residences, faculty buildings and other facilities, services, transport, staff accommodation, student loans and grants, all taken together, meant an extraordinary and sensational increase in government spending on the university.

The intention was noble. The liberation struggle had not only been fought for the land and political power. It had been fought to extend the advantages and facilities enjoyed by the white minority to the black majority – education was considered a right not a privilege, a slogan I used to see prominently displayed outside the Organisation of African Unity (OAU) headquarters in Addis Ababa. However, the new Zimbabwe government took the slogan further. Education was not only a right. Not only should the many black Zimbabweans now enjoy what the few whites had enjoyed before but they should enjoy them at the same level of luxury. And this is what was meant by 'keeping up standards'. The buzz word was 'standards'. The new government was determined to 'keep up standards'. And by 'standards' was meant the standards that had prevailed in white Rhodesia and were enjoyed by a tiny minority.

There were two reasons for this. The first was the understandable refusal on the part of those who had sacrificed their lives for Zimbabwe, to accept lifestyles, facilities, services, conditions of service, salaries – in short 'standards' - for blacks that were inferior to those the whites had enjoyed and many still did enjoy - despite the fact that these 'standards' had been applied to a small racial elite in a highly unequal and repressive economy.

The second was the determination of the new black government to prove to the whites, to the world and to themselves that they could do things just as well as the whites. And that meant 'keeping up standards'. I say 'the whites'. Yes, there was that but more especially for the black Zimbabwean elite, it meant the British - for they were the model. I remember participating in a very dignified – or pompous, depending on your point of view - Honorary

Degrees Ceremony in the newly-built University Great Hall. The Great Hall was cavernous and it was built to accommodate the massive new influx of students. But so rapid and substantial was the explosion in student numbers that in no time at all it became too small even for graduation, which had then to be held outdoors.

The dignified – or pompous – ceremony was being staged in order to award honorary doctorates to Mwalimu Julius Nyerere, the former President of Tanzania, and Nelson Rolihlahla Mandela, who of course was still on Robben Island. There were orations and choirs and processions in gowns and all the trappings of a British university function. Do they still do all that in Britain? I have no idea how a British university holds its graduation ceremonies. I graduated *in absentia* from both Oxford and Leeds. But I imagine that it was a British graduation ceremony the University of Zimbabwe organisers had in mind. This was borne out afterwards when a Dean who had been in charge of the whole thing, read out to me some extracts from letters of congratulation that came streaming in after the event, from government ministers, other dignitaries and party officials. The general tenor of these messages was 'Congratulations. We showed the British that we can beat them at their own game'.

Whatever the reason, it was obvious that the determination to redress the unjust inequalities in the country but do so while 'keeping up standards', would have serious financial consequences and by the end of the decade it had become a major contributing factor to the financial impasse Zimbabwe found itself in.

It was not only the university that had expanded and must operate according to the same standards it had when it catered for the children of a small and privileged white minority. The Civil Service in general had expanded likewise. In terms of perks, allowances and facilities, black civil servants must have what whites in the tiny civil service of Smith's time used to have when they were in office, including commensurate salaries – of course, it was only right. Conferences, meetings, functions must all be at the best conference centres, hotels or other facilities, with drinks and lavish buffets. But this again contributed to the massive increase in expenditure after independence nation-wide.

But there was another side, a dark side, to the whole 'keeping up standards' phenomenon. Like education, the transport infrastructure inherited from the past, was totally unable to cope with the greater demand after Independence. Just as emergency ZINTEC crash programmes had to be introduced to provide the teachers for the new schools and residences had to be built at the university to house the vast increase in students, so something drastic had to be done about transport. But nothing substantial was. Into this vacuum entered '*maEmejensi*' or 'Emergency Taxis'. The 'Emergency Taxi' was a station wagon or estate car, usually rather rattle-trap. The seating arrangements were two - or three if possible - in the front seat with the driver, four in the back seat and four sitting in the back-back, two on either side, with their legs stretched out in front of them so that they dove-tailed. Gender and age meant nothing. After all, it was an emergency. There just wasn't enough transport for all the people who now needed it and so emergency measures were in order. An emergency taxi operated according to emergency rules. In an emergency all distinctions and cultural considerations fall away – and so women of all ages in skirts were now seen to be climbing publicly up into the back-back of emergency taxis, grateful to have the lift, and then sitting with their legs out in front of them, closely jammed in with men doing the same. It made no difference if the woman was old or pregnant or the man a greybeard or a youth. In an emergency no-one gives way to anyone else. Everyone looks after himself. And so the new phenomenon called 'Pressure' came into being - survival of the strongest and fittest. Seats were limited, taxis few and queues long. King Pressure ruled. People pushed and shoved and the Devil took the hindmost.

But what was 'normal' in an emergency then came to be accepted as 'normal' in everyday life – for some – not just with regard to transport but in all sorts of other sectors where the great influx of emancipated black Zimbabweans was just too much for the existing facilities and services. The 'normality' of '*maEmejensi*' became the normality there too and it soon appeared that when it came to the ordinary people, emergency 'standards' were going have to be good enough. Like rising damp, the rot spread.

So here was a paradox. Here was a government that wanted to 'keep up standards' – and prepared to bankrupt itself in the process. White standards must be maintained – for those who could access them. But for those who could not? Among the ordinary people - the masses - women, children and old people were climbing into the back of taxis in public and sitting thigh to thigh with men. People boarded buses at Mbare Musika by pushing and jostling each other – a godsend to the pickpockets. People were insulted and pushed about and treated like cattle at border posts, at police stations and government offices generally. Thousands and thousands of Zimbabweans had to go for the new metal Identity Document. As they could at last travel freely, thousands applied for passports. At the offices where they had to apply, they had to go through hell to get them. What had happened to '*tsika*'? What had happened to '*hunhu*'?[5] Where were the so-called 'standards'? Everything that made the traditional cultures of the African peoples of Zimbabwe so fine, was chucked out of the windows of the

5 '*Tsika*' – culture, '*hunhu*' – the quality of being human

emergency taxis, the government offices, the police stations and the rural buses.

Take accommodation. In Mbare there are numerous hostels. These were once single men's hostels, housing the migrant labour needed by the Rhodesian city of Salisbury and its light industries just over the road. Most of them are not far from the Musika (a term which strictly-speaking means 'market' but is used for the area around the market as well, including the bus rank). After Independence, with the relaxing of influx controls, people came to live in the hostels, men, women and children, generally two or even three families to a room, in conditions that only the title of Maxim Gorki's play, *Lower Depths*, can properly describe. There were no separate facilities for men and women. Everything that was once there, was stolen and then stolen again if ever the City of Harare replaced it. As a result, there were no taps, no light bulbs, no toilet fittings. Children grew up cheek by jowl with adults. Often these were men who came home drunk, and the children witnessed, on a daily basis, fights, quarrels, swearing and open fornication.

What was the reaction of the authorities? No-one seemed to care. No-one seemed to care that people were waiting for days in queues. No-one seemed to care that they were being treated like animals by officials of all kinds. No-one seemed to notice that the brutalisation and lack of respect for the people knew no gender nor age. No-one revolted against the culture of Pressure. No-one seemed to be outraged by the violations of *tsika* and *hunhu* in the lives of ordinary people.

Thus, the ordinary people did not benefit from the famous 'standards' and then saw their own standards, their own African cultural standards, abused on a daily basis. How do we explain this? Standards for some and none for the rest? Not quite.

When ZANU-PF returned at Independence, they brought back from Mozambique two words that described two very important concepts, both of which came to play a major role in shaping the new Zimbabwe. The first of these words was '*povo*'.

'*Povo*', meaning 'people' in Portuguese, was adopted to refer to the masses. The *povo* had risked their lives supporting the freedom fighters against the Rhodesian soldiers in the bush and in the villages and their children had played an active role as combatants or collaborators. After the war the combatants were demobilised or, if they were lucky, they were absorbed into the army and police force. Otherwise they were simply left to fend for themselves. The ZANU-PF leadership seemed to display as little concern for them – until later, as we shall see - as it did in daily life for the rest of the *povo*.

But here was another paradox. I say 'in daily life' because on the national level and at the level of policy, ZANU-PF worked wonders for the people, the *povo*, in particular the rural masses. Not only were the benefits of education extended to them for free through the construction of schools and their admission to institutions of higher learning but there was support for agriculture, roads previously extremely rudimentary in the colonial 'communal lands' were built or upgraded, the electrification of the countryside á la Lenin was commenced, growth points as foci for rural development were set up, health services were expanded and provided free, rural newspapers opened, basic foodstuffs were subsidised, in times of drought, relief was made available and so on. But this prioritisation of the rural and urban masses in terms of policy and development was directly contradicted by their treatment on the ground.

The point is that ZANU-PF's conception of upholding standards was based on the standards that prevailed in Rhodesia under the whites. The standards they were anxious to uphold were 'white standards' – and in Rhodesia 'white standards' meant dual standards, based on inequality, and the one made the other possible. By maintaining low standards for millions of blacks, it was possible to maintain very high standards for a few thousand whites. In independent Zimbabwe, government was determined to ensure that there would be no diminution in quality in sectors of the society which had previously been white. Here the existing white standards were maintained. But they did little to raise the standards maintained by the white regime in the previously black sectors, the colonial 'standards'. Colonial standards meant insults, humiliation and degradation. The *povo* had always been treated like cattle by the Rhodesians. That is what they were used to. These were their standards – and these were what they had in the main to endure in their own country after Independence and up to this very day. Busy keeping up colonial white standards, ZANU-PF seemed to show little interest in rejecting and replacing the colonial standards that had been inflicted on the black masses, the *povo*.

The concept of 'keeping up standards' was problematical in another way. The struggle for Zimbabwe had been a revolution. Social revolutions, if they are serious, generally involve intense debate as to the kind of society to be built after the revolution. In Mozambique they called it '*uma sociedade nova*'. All over Southern Africa people fought against colonialism and racial discrimination. Surely they did not only fight to end it. Surely they fought because they wanted to replace it – but with what? Did they just fight the system because it excluded blacks from participating in it? Did they not fight it because it was deficient as a system and they hoped to replace it with a better democratic society which was built on their shared values as Africans and the hopes, aspirations and values of the people – the very *povo* we have been talking about?

In South Africa, back in the day, people did not believe that the struggle was for a white South Africa, to which all those the whites had formerly excluded, would finally be admitted. It wasn't just a question of wanting to live with the whites - like the whites lived. To some, this idea seemed racist. It seemed to be rejecting integration and blacks and whites living together. Steve Biko, who was one of the founders of the Black Consciousness Movement in South Africa, did think and write quite a lot about ideology and culture. He answered the critics when he wrote: "If by integration you understand a breakthrough into white society by blacks, an assimilation and acceptance of blacks into an already established set of norms and code of behaviour set up by and maintained by whites, then YES I am against it (integration)." What Biko called 'norms and code of behaviour' was what the Zimbabweans meant by 'standards'. Unlike Steve Biko, ZANU-PF (and the ANC in South Africa) seemed to be happy simply to be assimilated into white society and accept its standards i.e. its norms and code of behaviour. In both countries, there seemed to be little interest in ideology, transformation and notions of cultural revolution. In fact, in both Zimbabwe and South Africa, from what I could see, the predominant perception was that the society the whites had created was just great and all that was needed was simply to maintain it and open up access to it for the people who had been previously excluded from it. The revolution seemed to be about taking over the Rhodesian or white South African social model as was, rather than re-fashioning society according to the needs, values and culture of the majority - one of the reasons, perhaps, why the Mozambicans called what happened in Zimbabwe, the 'Swimming Pool Revolution'. Certainly a hell of a lot of swimming pools changed hands in Zimbabwe!

It was par for the course. ZANU PF as a liberation movement showed little interest in ideology or political education during the struggle and subsequently in Zimbabwe itself after Independence. There was some talk of socialism (*gutsa ruzhinji*), both during the struggle for Independence and also in the first decade after Independence. The very Shona term used to mean 'socialism' seemed to betray its ideological weakness. '*Gutsa ruzhinji*' literally means 'feeding' or 'making full the majority'. The ostensible objectives of the Zimbabwean revolution appeared to relate to material things – food, schools, hospitals and above all the land on which to produce the food. I say 'ostensible' to distinguish the official objectives from the private ones pursued in practice by the majority of the leadership. The espousal of socialism by ZANU-PF was probably little more than rhetorical bait to win the support of the *povo*. In his book, *Zimbabwe: A Revolution that Lost its Way*, Andre Astrow reported that Mugabe said as much to placate his audience of business people in the United States shortly after Independence. If ZANU-PF ever showed any interest in Socialism after Independence, the kind of socialism they had in mind was a form of social democracy more akin to the 'socialism' of the British Labour Party – pre-Blair – or the Social Democrats of Germany.

There was almost no political education and almost no effort to introduce socialism to the people of Zimbabwe after Independence. Having been cocooned for many years in the censorship and propaganda of the sheltered backwater created by the Rhodesian Front, the people of Zimbabwe had very little knowledge of things like socialism. If P.K. van der Bijl, Smith's Minister of Information, and his ilk were to be believed, socialism meant nationalising people's wives and stealing their toothbrushes. See Julie Frederikse's book, *None but Ourselves*, for the tragicomic excesses of Rhodesian propaganda with regard to socialism. The only rather half-hearted doff of the cap to some sort of national education on the topic was a television programme called 'The Road to Socialism', where Shadreck Gutto, a Kenyan exile, a Marxist-Leninist comrade - in those days - lecturing in the Law Faculty at the University of Zimbabwe, used to appear on a weekly basis desperately trying to educate on and defend, virtually single-handedly, the tenets of Marx, Engels and Lenin in the face of national incomprehension and conservative prejudice.

What 'standards', what ideology, what kind of society, what values, what form of government, what culture, what arts, what literature? All this was of relatively little concern either to the party or to the government. If it had been, Zimbabwe might have been able to resolve the contradiction between access to social services and a better lifestyle, on the one hand, and maintaining 'standards', on the other. Different standards, more appropriate, more indigenous and more culturally relevant, might have been more sustainable, cost less money and at the same time helped to create a society more in tune with the spirit and values of the African revolution that had made it all possible. It took twenty years for someone in ZANU-PF to wake his comrades up to the need actually to think about such things (see Chapter 28). His enemies called him Goebbels then. Had someone like Jonathan Moyo done it in the first decade after Independence, they mightn't have.

CHAPTER FOUR:

POLITICAL ATTITUDES

"So you sing songs like *that?*"

As the new ZANU-PF government set about things, trying to open up and transform in the interest of blacks what had been a society dominated by whites while at the same time doing its best to 'keep up standards', what was the attitude of those who benefited? The University of Zimbabwe was a good place from which to observe that. By the time I arrived, black staff and students had largely replaced white. The students came from all over the country. They all owed their jobs or their places at the university to the victory of the armed struggle. What did they make of it all?

After my arrival at the university, it did not take me long to get involved in setting up a political theatre group, which drew its membership not only from the students but also from the academic and administrative staff, workers and the community outside the university. While working on our various productions, I was introduced to the marvellous canon of Zimbabwean revolutionary or *chimurenga* songs, 'The Songs that Won the Liberation War', as the title of Alec Pongweni's book has it. Pongweni was on the staff of the university at the time. Hundreds of revolutionary songs flowered during the struggle, most of them so catchy and inspiring they took possession of one's head. And so I often rode my bicycle around Harare or walked into offices unconsciously singing or humming them.

One day, I walked into the office of the English Department, where a young lady by the name of Dadirai was one of the secretaries.

Already girls with names like Dadirai – which means 'be proud' in Shona – were attending the kind of schools where their Shona names sounded too Shona and it wasn't long before they were Anglicised into something along the lines of 'Daddy-rye'. I was not concentrating at all on Dadirai and busy doing something in the office when suddenly I heard her say, not with any admiration or surprised pleasure but with barely suppressed contempt: "So you sing songs like *that*!" It took me a moment to realise that, without being conscious of the fact, I had been singing a *chimurenga* song and this was the '*that*' she was referring to. When I did, I was taken aback.

Perhaps Dadirai's point was that she didn't expect me, a white person, to sing such a song. But the tone of her voice and the sneer on her face made her attitude to 'songs like *that*' very clear. I had not expected it at all from someone like Dadirai. After all, it was only a few years ago that the liberation struggle had brought to an end the long nightmare of white rule. The two organisations that had fought the struggle, had won a landslide victory in the first democratic elections in the nation's history. The 'songs like *that*' I had been singing had sprung from that struggle. Such songs were still featured sometimes on the radio, at political events and over political holidays such as Independence or Heroes Day. Surely, I thought, there must be overwhelming support for Mugabe, ZANU-PF and the comrades who risked their lives in the bush fighting the Rhodesian army so that Zimbabweans could be free. Surely there can't be many black Zimbabweans who do not support ZANU-PF and who do not approve of the songs of the struggle?

After I had collected myself, I managed to say to Dadirai: "But, Dadirai, don't you realise that if it had not been for 'songs like *that*', you would not be sitting behind that desk and a secretary in this office?" It seemed obvious – not to Dadirai though, and, as I later discovered, not to many, many other Zimbabweans, particularly in the towns, where the liberation fighters had not been able to penetrate as effectively, and among young people in Harare who were too young to know what it had been like during the days of Smith or to remember the triumphant return of 'the boys' – *vakomana* – and the euphoria of Independence. After all, it was already five or six years after it had all happened. Dadirai was young. She was a devoted church-goer. She had probably gone to a school where once children like her were not welcome and where a lot of the teachers were still white and the ethos at the school was generally 'un-African'.

Take a school like Arundel, for instance. Arundel is a very select private school for girls not very far from the university campus. I was invited to go there and talk to the girls about the theatre I was doing at the university. I chose to highlight one of our plays called *Samora Continua.* We had put this play together to commemorate and honour the President of Mozambique, Samora Machel, who had recently died in a mysterious plane crash in South Africa on his way back to Maputo. In the audience that day there was only a smattering of black girls. The attitudes to Mozambique and Samora Machel that I encountered there were exactly those the white Rhodesians and South Africans entertained at that time, namely that Machel was a terrorist communist who had died in a crash caused by a drunken Russian pilot. This was all the black girls were exposed to as well. They were excited to hear that there was a different story and apparently a debate raged in the school for some time after I had left. Perhaps it was that kind of situation which accounted for attitudes like Dadirai's among some of the black youth in Harare.

Zimbabwe's process of Reconciliation differed from South Africa's Truth and Reconciliation and Mozambique's political education, just as both differed dramatically from the post-Second World War Nuremburg Trials. At least in South Africa those who committed crimes were required to admit their guilt before they could expect to benefit from the policy of Reconciliation. Though this led to a measure of national catharsis, it still left the vast majority of racists racist. In Mozambique, Frelimo saw racists, sell-outs, and reactionaries as what Machel referred to as 'professors of the negative'. Mozambicans were enjoined to learn from their negative behaviour and attitudes. Others were subjected to political re-education. In Zimbabwe neither of these approaches was adopted. Instead, unconditional reconciliation seemed in effect to have been offered on the basis of 'let's build Zimbabwe together and let bygones be bygones'.

Yet Mugabe's words, spoken after winning the election in 1980, implied a condition: "*If* you have become a friend and ally in the national interest...*if* you cannot avoid the love etc". The basis of Reconciliation then was to be patriotism and transformation. But no steps were taken to evaluate to what extent the Rhodesian whites had become friends and allies or had accepted the love Mugabe offered. Nothing was done either to ascertain to what extent the minority whites and the black majority had anything like the same idea as to what their national interest was - or to insist on transformation. Thus to a large extent ZANU-PF, inheriting an unequal and racist system and an exclusive economy along with an unreconciled and unredeemed racist white minority, forfeited its advantage and embraced its enemy – without knowing or taking steps to ensure that he was no longer its enemy– as if he was its friend.

In actual fact, the majority of whites remained in fundamentals their enemy. This was evidenced by the fact that in the first elections after Independence (1985) the Conservative Alliance of Zimbabwe, to all intents and purposes the Rhodesian Front, won 55% and 15 out of 20 seats on the separate white voters' roll. In my experience there was little sign after Independence of the white minority 'seeing the light', changing their attitudes or developing a commitment to the building of a non-racial, democratic and just Zimbabwe – and still less to the prospect of giving up any of their privileges or their monopoly on wealth and property – including crucially their 'gold mine', the land. The word 'Rhodie', as used in this book, refers specifically to these unregenerate whites, who never wanted to and never became Zimbabweans in any real sense.

And, in the process, the wounds of the struggle, the massacres in Zambia and in Mozambique, all the years of dispossession, insult, arrogance, mistreatment and exploitation, all that - remained unexpiated, unhealed. Any attempt to educate the children of Zimbabwe about it was condemned as 'raking up the past'. And so the new generation, the so-called 'born-frees', grew up as if it had all never happened and 'anyway', many of them thought, 'what's all that old stuff got to do with us?' Like Dadirai, they had been denied their history.

In my first year of working with students at the university I was working on a production which was going to be performed for Heroes Day, the day that had been dedicated as a time for the new nation to remember those who had sacrificed their lives for its freedom. I was working with a Zimbabwean Staff Development Fellow, who happened also to be a well-known Shona writer. I began the project by getting the students to talk about their concept of a hero. He and I were astonished to discover that, for the majority of them, 'hero' had nothing whatsoever to do with liberation struggle and the comrades who had sacrificed their lives so that they could have a university education. The 'heroes' of Heroes'

Acre[6] and Heroes Day were far from their thoughts. To them, a hero was someone who became a doctor or a lawyer or developed a successful business. I suppose in a way they were confusing 'hero' with 'role model'. But they did not hide their contempt for the heroes who would be commemorated at the upcoming Heroes Day events.

One of the students was particularly passionate about this. His father was a businessman and he had tried to employ the odd ex-combatant from time to time but it had not worked out. The young man explained that the 'comrades' were not educated, they were rough and crude, like people from the bush, they didn't always do as they were told etc. At this point my Staff Development Fellow, who was a staunch member of ZANU-PF, was so disgusted he suggested we drop the play. I disagreed as I believe working on plays is an educational process. It educates the actors sometimes as much, sometimes I think even more, than it does the audience. But he wasn't having any of it and he refused to be associated with it. So I continued with the production alone.

Well, as it happened, theatre proved me right. The passionate young man who couldn't stand ex-combatants, played the part of the ex-combatant in the play and did it with a passion and the whole class learnt to re-adjust a lot of its thinking.

The polarisation that later threatened to destroy the country had already begun to widen. On the one side, were many people, particularly young people and particularly those in the towns, who had little respect for the liberation war veterans, for ZANU-PF or

6 National Heroes Acre is a site on the outskirts of Harare built shortly after Independence to commemorate national heroes. There is a museum, the statue of the Unknown Soldier, murals depicting scenes from the 1st and 2nd Chimurengas and the Eternal Flame. Artists from the Democratic Republic of Korea and Zimbabwe co-operated in its design and art work.

the liberation struggle. On the other, were the masses, particularly those in the rural areas, who had experienced the struggle first-hand and had a far deeper commitment to it and its ideals.

Some of the issues were powerfully illustrated when a detachment of highly politicised women came to attend the 'workshop performance' of another play I was working on with students.

'Workshop performances' were rehearsal runs for an invited audience during the process of playmaking. One held them quite some time before presenting the play to the public. They were designed to get third party comments, which would then be evaluated to see what in the play might need to be changed in the light of them. Many times very good ideas came up that could be incorporated. The particular play in question was called *The Adamant Eve*. It was about Zimbabwean women. One of the strengths of working with a large cast of university students at a national university was that the students came from all over Zimbabwe. They would go home during the vacation and do the research needed to create the plot, content, characters and dialogue of the play. Because they came from all over the country, their research data was fascinating and made for extraordinarily rich texts. With regard to this particular play, they brought back with them the voices of women from all over Zimbabwe. Basically the play ended up being what we called 'an echoing chamber of women's voices'.

As a footnote on gender in Zimbabwe, when the men in the audience heard what the women in the play were saying, words that real women all over Zimbabwe had actually said, they retorted by saying: "These are not Zimbabwean women"! Anyway, at the end of the 'workshop performance', this detachment of strong, politicised women made a number of very powerful but useful comments, including noting the fact that, purely coincidentally, many of the surnames in the play suggested that they were Ndebele rather than Shona – names like Moyo, for instance. I don't think anyone in the cast had given the issue a thought. They were obviously very touchy and quick to suspect a clandestine PF-ZAPU influence. They demanded to know why. "Was the play a ZAPU play?" they challenged. And then they turned to the ending. At the end of the play, the iconic revolutionary leader of Frelimo in Mozambique, Samora Machel, was featured making a motivational speech on gender equality. "Why do you have the leader of another country giving that speech at the end of the play? Do we not have our own Zimbabwean leader, Comrade Mugabe?" one of the women asked.

Well, the answer, in fact, was simple. Mugabe, to my knowledge, had never said anything inspiring about gender equality. But the comrades' questions struck a few notes which were in tune with the tone of the times. First, there was the power of Mugabe as the leader and what kind of man or leader he was. Failing to honour him alone cast doubts on one's loyalty to ZANU-PF. Again there was the suspicion. Was this a ZAPU play? This was a measure of how far apart the two parties had drifted since the days of the Patriotic Front. Then there was the narrow chauvinism of it. They wanted the one who makes the final speech to be their own Zimbabwean leader. Why would they object to another leader, I thought, our neighbour, in a country that was so close to Zimbabwe in spirit and culture and which had supported the struggle in Zimbabwe at great sacrifice? Why not the leader of Mozambique? Why not Machel?

And then there was the menace in the question. Already people were becoming afraid to say what they thought. There was a fear that you could be reported and there was a feeling that ZANU-PF would force you to agree with them or support them if you didn't. Already the dragon's teeth were giving birth to armed warriors.

The divisions, superficially hidden at Independence by the general euphoria, were widening and cohering into the antagonism and conflict of later years. The Dadirais, the students, the urban-dwellers, the Ndebele on one side - the party stalwarts, the liberation war veterans and the rural masses on the other.

The process had not yet gone too far in those early days and, for most of the first decade, there was still strong support both for Mugabe and for ZANU-PF, even among the students at the university – despite the attitude of many of them to 'heroes'. But things were already changing. Young people noticed that Mugabe was travelling widely in the world and no doubt at great expense to the country. Being young and relatively ignorant about global politics and economics, they had no idea why it was necessary for Zimbabwe's president to globetrot. Smith never went anywhere, I suppose – except to Pretoria! Yet, it was also true that some of Mugabe's travels did seem suspiciously like international in-house junkets. Mugabe was at that time enjoying the adulation of many countries in the world for his leadership of an armed struggle that had successfully overthrown a notorious racist regime. Whatever the case, it was at about this time that the students started calling him Vasco da Gama.[7] Then when he was out of the country on one of these frequent travels, a demonstration broke out on the University of Zimbabwe campus. The riot police came in. There was chaos and confusion. Everyone waited for Mugabe to come back. The students hoped he would listen to them and attend to their grievances.

When Mugabe did come back, without meeting the students or giving them a chance to air their grievances, he backed the university authorities and laid down the law. There was profound

7 Vasco da Gama, a Portuguese naval commander, who was the first to sail from Europe to India via the Cape.

disillusionment among the students as a result. This to me was the turning point. Mugabe lost the respect and support of the students and from then on there were annual 'demos', invariably anti-government in tone, and the university was frequently closed down. Only a relatively small group of students, who actually belonged to the party, continued to support him. Student politics from then on was anti-ZANU-PF and anti-Mugabe. That is probably why, when later the Movement for Democratic Change (MDC) set itself up in opposition to the government, quite a number of both its membership and its leaders were former students or student leaders.

If ZANU-PF did nothing to prepare the country for socialism, they did no more to educate Zimbabweans politically. Of course, there had been no political education in the country under the Rhodesians. After Independence the situation did not change. Even within ZANU-PF there was little if any political education. The *pungwes* or all-night meetings with the people during the struggle, which were ideal opportunities for political education, were mostly occasions for generating *morari* (morale) and support and were characterised by slogans, motivational speeches, singing and dancing. Rhodesia had been a highly insulated and insular society in which ideas and knowledge of the world had long atrophied. Though there were Zimbabweans who had received an excellent political education outside the country during the years of the struggle, they were very few in number. With the new government and the ruling party itself doing nothing about it, it would be true to say that, in terms of political economy and ideology, the people of Zimbabwe were uneducated – certainly in marked contrast to the level of their academic and technical education. It was therefore not surprising that when the students at the University of Zimbabwe staged demonstrations, they were either related to issues which had nothing to do with politics – like the new curtains in the residences not matching the old bedspreads, an issue which once provoked a 'demo' – or, if purporting to be political, they were totally confused mix-ups of what one might call 'progressive' and 'reactionary', serious and petty, demands.

In Part One I tried to describe the factors that I felt characterised the situation in Zimbabwe at Independence. I suggested that whatever happened subsequently would be influenced by them - the golden apples and the dragon's teeth. There is another consideration too. History, I suppose, is a constant dialectic[8] between the circumstances on the ground and the individuals who are called upon or who take it upon themselves to negotiate them. The circumstances shape the individual and the individual shapes the circumstances. The founding of Thebes was in the hands of Cadmus. The founding of Zimbabwe was in the hands of Robert Gabriel Mugabe.

In the early days of independence, a lot of people rapidly came to consider the ZANU-PF leadership that returned from exile a bit of a poor lot but for a long time there was still immense respect for Mugabe. My Zimbabwean uncle obviously thought Mugabe was a cut above the rest. My uncle was a man who, give or take a few, had taught all the leaders of the new ZANU-PF government. He himself had got into trouble with the Smith regime from time to time with his forthright and sometimes idiosyncratic protests.

8 The dialectic is a concept first developed by the philosopher, Georg Hegel, and adapted by Marx and Engels as the cornerstone of what Marxists called Dialectical Materialism. It is the key for understanding change and motion and embraces concepts such as the Law of Quantity into Quality, the Unity of Opposites and the Negation of the Negation. Put simply – and this is the way it has proved useful for me – development and change is characterised by the fact that everything is always moving and changing and leaps forward are generated by contradictions between apparent opposites, which conflict and in the process give rise to an alternative, deriving its qualities from both.

However, after Independence, he rapidly became disillusioned, just as teachers will do who expect so much from their pupils, only to see them not practising what they were taught. My uncle used to say: "To the best of my knowledge, there are only five socialists in Zimbabwe – Robert Mugabe, myself and...well, er..I haven't yet met the other three!"

So, what was it with this Mugabe, Gushungo, the man they write and talk so much about, the man who has been in the driving seat in Zimbabwe from Independence to the present, the so-called 'devil', the 'murderer', the 'bloodthirsty tyrant', Hitler, Attila the Hun – what has he not been called? He might not answer to any of those soubriquets but to Gushungo he must. Just as 'Madiba' is Nelson Mandela's *isiduko* or clan name, Gushungo is Mugabe's.[9]

---

9 Clan names – in many southern African cultures, lineage is indicated in the clan names that are part of the naming of an individual. In Nguni cultures, the *isibongo*, what has come to be adapted as the modern surname, is accompanied by a short version of the *isithakazelo*, which would appear to be a part of the praises of the individual's clan, in which the linkages between the individual's clan and other related clans are spelt out. In other cultures – Sotho, Tswana, Shona – the totem fulfils a similar function but does not preclude the use of clan names and praises. It is customary in many situations to refer to someone by one of their clan names – hence Mugabe is Gushungo, Mandela Madiba, Zuma Sholozi etc.

CHAPTER FIVE:

ROBERT GABRIEL MUGABE (I)

The portrait of a 'dictator'

Mugabe was a key factor in the shaping of Zimbabwe. To understand him is to understand a great deal about whatever happened in Zimbabwe between 1980 and 2014. What follows is an attempt to share with you my personal take on Robert Mugabe, as I observed his performance over the entire period, 1980-2013.

Robert Gabriel Mugabe was born in 1924 in the Zvimba District northwest of Salisbury in the then Southern Rhodesia. He was educated at mission schools, notably Kutama, and went to the University at Fort Hare in South Africa. He subsequently became a teacher and taught in Kwame Nkrumah's Ghana for a number of years. He returned to Rhodesia in 1960 and entered politics by joining the National Democratic Party (NDP), which was led by the veteran Nationalist, Joshua Nkomo. From there he went on to hold leadership positions in Nkomo's Zimbabwe African People's Union (ZAPU), which he left in 1963 to found the Zimbabwe African National Union (ZANU). In 1964, he was arrested and detained. He put his ten years in prison to good advantage by studying, managing to acquire two university degrees by correspondence. On his release he left the country for newly independent Mozambique to spearhead the armed struggle against the Smith regime.

I myself never met my namesake, Robert Mugabe, though he did once greet me as he left an outdoor function at the Murehwa Culture

House, thinking possibly that though he did not know me, being white – which was a rarity at such functions - I might be someone important. But I did observe him over a long period of time, watched him on television, read his speeches, read about him in the press and listened to the gossip. I shall try to write about him without fear, favour or prejudice. I shall try to speak of him as he was, 'nothing extenuate nor set down aught in malice'. I was never convinced by the sweeping and mostly ignorant, hasty, unthinking or biased 'judgements' and stock stereotypes of him as a leader, a statesman and a man whom the western world has demonised day in, day out for the last fifteen years. As in all men, the elements are mixed in Mugabe too.

Mugabe has in the last fifteen years received about as bad a press as it is possible to get. So successful have the media been that one could pull up at a service station in South Africa and the black petrol attendant would take one look at the Zimbabwean number plate and say: "Mugabe! Mugabe's bad. Mugabe must go." When you ask him what is bad about him or why he should go, the best he will do perhaps is to say that he has stuck around too long. But beyond that, he doesn't have a clue. Funny, very few people say that about Museveni, to take but one example, who has been President of Uganda since 1986, came to power unconstitutionally and for a long time never held an election at all.

The reason an ordinary person, like a petrol attendant, even an African petrol attendant, will say Mugabe must go, is mainly because the 'international', the South African and the local 'independent' Zimbabwean media go beyond the bounds of all reason, even sanity at times, to denigrate and demonise him. To them he is the devil incarnate – just as he is to the Rhodies.

The prevailing assessment of Mugabe in the 'international' media is obviously over the top. It is not accurate – and it does no-one any good, except as a safety valve through which those who have reason to hate him, can vent their feelings. Mugabe's enemies in the West and in South Africa might have done well to heed the sentiments of Sun Tsu, the Chinese military strategist, who went one step further than Socrates when he said: "Know your enemy and know yourself and you can win a hundred battles." They would have been a lot wiser to try to know Mugabe better rather than create or believe their own phantasmagorical fiction – just as they would have done a lot better to try and get to grips with what was really happening in Zimbabwe rather than believe what they wanted to hear and parrot what they wanted people to believe. Much more seriously, the same goes for those who essentially are not his enemies but whom the media barrage has convinced that they are.

In Chapter 28 I talk about the tendency on the part of the media to 'tag' someone. I can think of no better way to start an assessment of Robert Mugabe than by examining his prime 'tag' – 'dictator'. Only today, as I was writing, I came across a reference in the *Christian Post* to Mugabe. The writer referred to him as 'the infamous dictator President of Zimbabwe'! I bet that if you were to ask the *Christian Post* and all those people, including journalists and reporters, who automatically apply the tag 'dictator' to Mugabe, what a dictator actually is and in what way Mugabe is a dictator, most of them would be flummoxed.

What is a dictator and to what extent can Robert Gabriel Mugabe be said to be one. The way I see it, a dictator is someone who wields total power and tells everyone what to do. A dictator does not like anyone to disagree with him – so far almost all dictators have been men, hence the 'him' bit. A dictator wants people to do as they are told and anyone who opposes him is in for a very bad time. That just about sums up what I think a dictator is.

Now many people might think this is actually a pretty good way of describing their father, their wife or their mother-in-law – or perhaps their boss or the company director. I cannot say for sure but I have good reason to believe that Mugabe's Politburo and Cabinet would probably think it as good a way as any to describe him in that context. I have it from the usual 'impeccable sources' – in this case a former Permanent Secretary to whom it happened personally – that if someone rocks the boat at Cabinet meetings, the Chairman, if the cabinet session is being chaired by Mugabe, is quite capable of shouting 'Shut up!' at him if he does not like what that someone is saying. But then this seems to have been par for the course with the generation of British-trained headmasters and schoolteachers that ran Zimbabwe in the early years.

Professor Walter Kamba, for instance, before Independence a member of the Law Faculty at the University of Dundee in Scotland, was the first black Vice-Chancellor of the University of Zimbabwe. Professor Kamba was well-known for the way he yelled at professors and senior lecturers both in Senate meetings and elsewhere. When I proposed to him that the University had unfairly altered the terms of my contract and that I would therefore work to rule, he exclaimed: "Gosh!" a number of times in a very loud voice and thumped his fist so resoundingly on his desk that the whole Administration block heard it. Everyone thought I had been sacked on the spot. This was the style, especially in the early years of Independence, not only in universities and schools but also in the corporate sector. Dictatorship was the order of the day and dictatorship the dominant management style.

I think therefore that there is little doubt that within the party and in his work environment, Mugabe, like so many other Zimbabwean headmasters and bosses at that time and even now, could safely be referred to as a dictator. But the media, when reporting that someone's mother-in-law or boss was involved in a case of drunken driving or financial chicanery, no matter how dictatorial they may be at home or in the office, do not forever after call her or him 'a dictator'. They call Heads of State that. It is Mugabe as Head of State who is categorically and at all times referred to as a dictator. Was he – is he?

In the context of the state, a dictator, who runs a dictatorship, like his counterpart in the family or the boardroom, similarly takes all the major decisions. His word goes. He brooks no opposition. Those who oppose him had better beware. And he has no objection when his sycophantic underlings create a personality cult. In fact, he often obliges, not only by posing for photographs but also by penning little books for everyone to read – if they want to be anyone and get anywhere.

Now, let's look at Mugabe *qua* statesman and his pedigree as a 'dictator' in that context. First of all, in Mugabe's Zimbabwe, between 1980 and 2013, there have been regular parliamentary and presidential elections, two democratic constitutional consultancy processes and two referenda. In the first few elections ZANU-PF, as they did in the very first election in 1980, won with ease – to the point that there was talk of a One-Party State. Mugabe did not go for that option. Small opposition parties won some seats and PF-ZAPU continued to win in its Matebeleland constituencies until the Unity Agreement in 1987 when the two major parties merged. Later, with the growth of the Movement for Democratic Change (MDC), ZANU-PF began to lose more and more seats in the parliamentary elections, the President lost more and more votes in the Presidential elections and the 2000 referendum on the Draft Constitution, widely assumed to have been a ZANU-PF document, was actually lost (see Chapter 16). This trend continued until in 2008, when ZANU-PF lost ground dramatically even in its rural heartland, lost its majority in Parliament to the two MDC factions, and lost the first round of the presidential election.

Now in terms of elections alone it has to be admitted that this is not the characteristic behaviour of a dictator. A dictator rarely brooks an opposition party at all, certainly not one that is going to win seats! Then, in the unlikely eventuality that he holds elections, he does not allow himself to lose. It has often been alleged that ZANU-PF rigged elections. It is possible it did but extraordinarily, unlike in your average dictatorship, despite rigging, it still lost! If Mugabe was a dictator then he must have been a very unusual one. When a pukka dictator rigs elections, he makes sure the result is a landslide. Perhaps the reason ZANU-PF found it hard to make a really good job of rigging elections was that Zimbabwean elections were monitored and observed, not recently by European observers it is true, but by Zimbabwe's African peers, the African Union, SADC and individual African governments – again very unusual behaviour for a 'dictator'. Contrary to the general impression conveyed by the international media, elections in Zimbabwe have been, with the exception of the second round run-off in the 2008 presidential election, generally remarkably well-organised, openly observed and surprisingly peaceful.

I really can't see an 'infamous dictator president' subjecting himself to all this bother – let alone giving the opposition the opportunity to say all those nasty things about him that they will obviously say when campaigning to win an election! So I think, despite existing anomalies in the election process – eg. access to media and use of coercion - when it comes to elections one can hardly accuse Mugabe of living up to his reputation as a 'dictator'.

Then there is the press and the other media. With the short exception of Joy Television, television has been a state monopoly ever since Independence – as it was before Independence. We'll come to that (Chapter 25). So, that means ZANU-PF has had its way on television. But for the last ten years or more a large section of the population has abandoned Zimbabwe Television in favour of DSTV, with which they are able to access SABC and Botswana news broadcasts and many even BBC, CNN, Sky and Al Jazeera, all of which are traditionally Mugabe's harshest critics. However when it comes to the print media, I have no hesitation in saying that Zimbabwe has had a remarkably free press – contrary to what many people believe and commentators go on denying. Interestingly, even the 'unfree press' freely went on claiming that there was no press freedom. They never seemed to see the irony of their claim. I really know of no dictator who ever tolerated the kind of intensely oppositional journalism churned out on a daily and weekly basis by the so-called 'independent' press in Zimbabwe. A feature of it was the often quite insulting and obsessively negative reporting on the President himself. I really doubt how many other African countries and countries elsewhere in the world, whose presidents have never been accused of being 'dictators', would tolerate the volume and ferocity, often quite simply the mendacity, of the so-called 'Independent Press' in Zimbabwe. The sheer scope of opposition newspapers that have been freely available on the street indicates the freedom the press enjoyed – *News Day*, *The Daily News*, *The Financial Gazette*, *The Daily Gazette*, *The Standard*, *The Independent*, *The Zimbabwean* (funded by the British Government and printed outside Zimbabwe) and even a special edition of the rabidly anti-Mugabe South African weekly, *The Sunday Times*. If you doubt this assessment of the press in Zimbabwe, many of these newspapers are freely available on the internet to this day. Go to them and check out for yourself what they write about Mugabe and his party.

So I think we can safely say that when it comes to the press and the freedom of the press, Mugabe was no dictator.

Now what about the much heralded 'rule of law'. No dictator tolerates for one instant the 'rule of law' or the rule of any law except his own. Yet Mugabe, his party and his government have been regularly taken to court and on many occasions have lost their cases. When results in individual constituencies, for instance, went to court, judgements were handed down for and against both the MDC and ZANU-PF without favour. The Treason case against Tsvangirai, the leader of the opposition MDC, and two other high officials was likewise thrown out. So again on this charge, Mugabe cannot be said to have demonstrated the typical behaviour of a dictator. (For more discussion of the Rule of Law, see Chapter 24.)

Next let us look at the opposition. An open opposition that speaks its mind, holds rallies, publishes publications and regularly insults the president or threatens to remove him by force or incites its supporters to undertake 'final pushes' by marching on State House, is also not a common characteristic of a dictatorship. Those who oppose dictators, not only in Africa, often disappear or end up being fed to the crocodiles, kidnapped, murdered and dumped in the forest or at the very least thrown into jail where they either languish or die in mysterious circumstances. Such occurrences were not that unusual in white Rhodesia but in Zimbabwe, despite the efforts of the opposition to give the impression that they were, they were not. It is interesting how many people in Zimbabwe loudly proclaimed that there are no civil liberties in Zimbabwe and that it is a police state, somehow blissfully unaware that if it was, they would either be meat for the crocodiles or rotting in prison.

Finally, the personality cult – on this one, surely there are very few who would accuse Mugabe of fostering a personality cult, not at least on the level of those fostered by thoroughgoing. There is no Robert Mugabe Airport though there is a Joshua Nkomo Airport. Mugabe is not the Father of the Nation. Joshua Nkomo is. There are streets named after Mugabe but no towns, buildings or squares. There are no large statues. There are no large billboards displaying his picture in all the squares and streets of the towns and cities. There is no little red book or Green Book, collecting his thoughts and sayings. It is true there is a 21st February Movement of children who interact with Mugabe on the occasion of his birthday, but it hardly constitutes a personality cult.

So given all the above, I am not and never was convinced that - outside his own party, that is - Mugabe was a 'dictator', despite the fact that every time the 'international' media mentioned his name, they called him one. He may have been many other things but not a 'dictator' in any conventional or accepted sense.

Mugabe has been no stranger to negative images of himself. These days he is a dictator. During the liberation struggle he was a 'terrorist'. He was portrayed then in ways very similar, but no less vociferous, to those in which he is portrayed today – and for many of the same reasons. Whether a dictator or not, it is a fact that 'this infamous dictator President of Zimbabwe' has been hated, vilified and reviled by many people. The reasons for this are clear but at the same time ambivalent - reasons that some people hate him for are reasons that others love him for. For Mugabe has been as loved as he has been hated and as popular as he has been infamous. What to some were faults, to others were virtues - for as I have said, Mugabe is a man, a human being like the rest of us, and he was neither all one thing nor all the other and he was not the same to all people. Like Brutus, the elements are mixed in him. He is, in my opinion, both unjustly hated and justly deplored.

CHAPTER SIX:

ROBERT GABRIEL MUGABE (II)

'Speak of things as they are'

Robert Mugabe has been a Nationalist, a Pan Africanist, an Africanist, a staunch supporter of the ideals of the Non-Aligned Movement (NAM), an anti-colonialist, an anti-Imperialist and, unlike many other African leaders, he never hesitated or feared, no matter what the forum, in no matter who's presence and no matter what the cost, to speak his mind. He has held these positions genuinely. They have been the lodestones of his life, his life of struggle and sacrifice to liberate his country. Mugabe would speak up against anyone he perceived to be an enemy or a threat to his Zimbabwe, the Zimbabwe he gave so much of his life to recover. That is why he told Blair to keep his England and let him, Mugabe, keep his Zimbabwe.

He has believed in and stood up for African unity and united action in Africa's interests – a dangerous tendency in a continent with so many resources and where the need for pliant and obsequious leaders is vital for their exploitation – a need that unfortunately, it would appear, is so easy to supply. He did not take kindly to anything that implied a slur on his race, the race of the majority of the people of Zimbabwe and the continent. He not only refused to tolerate slurs but he refused to tolerate those non-Africans who would impose, order around or lecture Africans. On that he has been obdurate. In the context of world politics and economics, he has opposed bullies and has never recognized the right of any one power to dictate or interfere in the affairs of another. This has made him an implacable enemy of many developed countries who believe the contrary. In other words, Mugabe believed in democracy at the international level. One of his favourite slogans was: "Zimbabwe will never be a colony again" and he has fought untiringly against all forms of colonialism and imperialism.

All this accounts for many powerful and influential enemies, enemies who control the world, its resources, the world bodies, both political and financial, and the media - so that their revenge is effectively applied and their hatred of him broadcast into almost every home all over the world.

It also accounts for the fact that where he may be vilified in some quarters, he has received rapturous standing ovations in others, in international fora all over the world - such as the Earth Summit on the Environment in Johannesburg in 2002 - despite walkouts by the West and the prolonged anti-Mugabe media campaign. It accounts for the fact that he was placed in the top ten by African readers voting for their greatest Africans in a poll conducted by the New African Magazine a few years back. Even in South Africa, where his press has been as negative as it could be, he has regularly received ecstatic receptions, like his tumultuous entry at the Freedom celebrations in Pretoria in 1994, at the Inauguration of Jacob Zuma as President in 2009 and at the memorial for Mandela in 2014. He repeatedly received ovations at the United Nations, notably in 2009 when he called President Bush 'god' and Tony Blair 'his prophet'. A little while back, he received yet another on a state visit to Uganda.

The Janus-like nature of Mugabe's impact has been nowhere better exemplified than in his attitude to and pronouncements on homosexuality. There is no doubt that this has been one of the major factors that account for his having been so unpopular, especially in Europe, and the fact that the worst examples of his homophobia were uttered in Holland did not help. Yet, when he said the things he did, he was speaking for literally millions of people, not only in Zimbabwe but all over Africa and possibly people in other parts of the world too. Tolerance of homosexuality was not the problem for him or for Africa. The problem was the pressure to force Africa to accredit and promote it. It would appear that those from the North who castigated Mugabe and other African leaders for their refusal to do this, have as usual spent little or no time trying to understand the roots of the Africans' attitudes in history, culture and religion. Yes, everyone in Africa knows that there are those whose sexuality is not the same as others. Culturally this has always been accepted as a fact but it has never been accepted as a viable alternative to heterosexual relations. Africa tends to be fairly fundamentalist in its religious perceptions too and both Christianity and Islam do not accept homosexuality.

But perhaps even more powerful is the historical experience of homosexuality in colonial relations. Very few Zimbabweans – and possibly few others in Africa – conceptualise homosexuality as a consensual love relationship between adults. Colonialism has entrenched a quite different image – the coercive relationship between a white adult and a black child or even between white and black adults. Many of Africa's leaders, including Mugabe himself, went to schools where white male teachers may have sodomised their black pupils, something which those who have attended such schools sometimes attest to privately.

Simply branding the African position on homosexuality as backward without attempting to appreciate its genesis, smacks of the West trying yet again to impose what it thinks is right on Africans who do not agree – and as mentioned above, this is something that

Mugabe and many other Africanists are very allergic to. What I am trying to explain here is not by any means intended to be a defence of homophobia. It is simply an attempt to explain that Mugabe's attitudes are general on the continent and that they are rooted in its particular history, culture and religion. What is required on the issue is the dialogue of equal partners not arrogant hectoring and threats.

As we shall see, Zimbabwe is rich in minerals. Thus another reason for some to resent Robert Mugabe was that, as a nationalist and anti-colonialist, Mugabe consistently opposed the alienation of Zimbabwe's wealth, whether to foreigners or to the white minority in the country. One of the characteristics of his political economy has been black empowerment and indigenisation. At the time of the land seizures and the negative impact of sanctions, many workers were losing their jobs and beginning to bewail the situation in post-independent Zimbabwe. They compared it unfavourably with the old colonial days when there seemed to be more jobs, jobs seemed secure and the prices of food and other necessities were low. Mugabe tried to explain to them – not well or consistently enough, unfortunately – that the time had come for black Zimbabweans to get rid of the 'working for the *baas*' mentality and face the challenges of real independence by thinking in terms of owning the economy, creating their own companies and generating their own jobs. This was his vision. Mugabe wanted not just political independence for the black people of Zimbabwe but economic independence as well and he consistently pushed for that.

All the above, as powerful as it might have been in shaping people's opinions or inciting feelings about him, was superficial in comparison with the fact that Mugabe was seen as the man who took away the land from the white farmers. I argue later (Chapters 15-19) that his role in the reclamation of the land was not necessarily central but it was inevitable, given his own personality, his beliefs and convictions, the exigencies of history and the prevailing situation in Zimbabwe in the period leading up to it.

In fact, Mugabe occupied a position rather similar to that of the Cuban leader, Fidel Castro. He too was never afraid to speak out and he too presided in similar circumstances over a process of nationalisation and redistribution of the assets of the minority – and, just as the blockade against Cuba will never be lifted until those assets are restored, so the United States has often made it clear that its sanctions against Zimbabwe will never be lifted until the ownership of land in Zimbabwe is restored to its pre-2000 status.

Mugabe's 'clinging onto power' is almost universally adduced as an argument for why he should go. He has been at the helm in Zimbabwe for thirty four years now. He is an old man. Somehow people feel that if he would just go, the whole situation would change and all would be well.

It has become fashionable these days to condemn a statesman simply on the basis that he or she has remained in power for a long time. I say 'these days' because I believe it is a relatively new idea – and when I ask the young people who are convinced that it is a well-established tenet of democratic politics that a statesman should not remain in power for long, 'why?', they can give no reason. All they can do is to re-iterate their assertion that to remain in power for too long is wrong and not good for the country. They invariably use the phrase 'clinging onto power'.

Obviously in terms of the laws of logic this attitude is not sound. I have always thought that in a democracy, who rules is determined by the people, who express their will through their democratic right to vote for whomsoever they wish. If the electorate considers that the ruler is doing a good job, if they do not see the reason to make a change and they go on electing the same ruler year after year, is it not undemocratic to complain that the ruler has been in power too long and must go? The democratic way would be to campaign for the people's votes and if one's arguments win their support and they vote for change, well and good.

Another reason why a leader may stay in power longer than he might have in other circumstances can best be explained by a fable of Aesop. It is the famous story of a traveller with a cloak. The sun and the wind have a dispute as to who is the most powerful. They see the traveller and agree that the one who can get the traveller to let go of his cloak, is the winner. The wind howls and buffets but the more he does, the more tightly the traveller clutches the cloak around him. Then the sun comes out and, as soon as he feels its warmth, the traveller takes off his cloak and the sun has won.

When a people or a party perceive themselves to be in danger, the victims of aggression, the objects of compulsion – in short, when they feel they are being subjected to the howling and buffeting of aggressive winds aimed at forcing them to give up something they value, they cling to the cloak. Mugabe is the cloak. Mugabe has consistently shown himself over time to be the one man who can be trusted not to give in to those who might wish to take away from the people or the party what they do not want to give up.

But my intention is not only not 'to set down aught in malice' but also 'to speak of things as they are'. With Mugabe's strengths go his weaknesses, with his credit goes his debit – and the first of these is the corruption and greed that very soon came to characterise the behaviour of his party and its leadership.

The West's objection to corruption as a reason for condemning a weaker state, is applied highly relatively and selectively. In other words, the West has a long tradition of continuing to do business with chronically corrupt states - Mobutu's Zaire is the classic case in Africa - while castigating those that do not toe the line, for being corrupt. Their objection to corruption is often simply a banner to mask the naked steel of their economic interest. But for those, including those in the West, who genuinely wished to see a thriving, sovereign Zimbabwe, it was one of the most fundamental reasons for deploring Mugabe's rule and ZANU-PF's betrayal of the sacrifices and ideas of the liberation struggle. In Zimbabwe, corruption has sometimes been quite justifiably called 'internal sanctions' for it is corruption – and the looting of the economy that has accompanied it – that has complemented the effects of sanctions in almost bringing Zimbabwe to its knees and intensifying the suffering that its people have had to endure (see Chapter 22). Corruption has also radically undermined what measures the state has taken to develop an economy which might have made Zimbabwe impervious to Western disapproval. Corruption has eventually attacked the entire fabric of society – and it is difficult to see how in the future Zimbabwe will be able to restore a culture of integrity and commitment to the national good. Corruption is what transformed ZANU-PF from the organisation that people like me supported, into an oppressive travesty, a party that still propagated the rhetoric of the liberation struggle but cynically betrayed it with their deeds.

Mugabe, as the leader of ZANU-PF and as the Head of State, must take responsibility for this. The extent to which he himself in his own life has been corrupt, is a matter of conjecture and debate. I myself have no way of knowing the truth but it would appear that the extent to which he and his close family relatives might have been corrupt is the only conceivable reason for why Mugabe was not able to rein in those in the leadership of the party and the armed forces who have been the main culprits in the orgy of high-level corruption and looting that has taken place and which has had such deleterious effects for the country. Given his life and his continued dedication at the level of policy to the goals of the liberation struggle, it is difficult to understand how he allowed himself and his close associates to betray them in the way they have.

Along with the corruption and looting is the violence and coercion, at times torture, that elements in his party have resorted to in order to browbeat and cow the people into continuing to support them. Mugabe himself often spoke out on the need for peace and the importance of eschewing violence. He has on a number of occasions pointed out that the use of violence is actually counter-productive and simply alienates the people. But the fact remains that the party structures and the youth have consistently brutalised the people. Together with the corruption, the violence was one of the major reasons for the alienation of support for the ruling party and for the President himself.

As a President, Mugabe also failed in uniting the nation. Zimbabwe as we have seen came into Independence threatened by division and a divisive history. Mandela did a great job. When it came to uniting the nation, Joshua Nkomo, Father Zimbabwe, as he is called, would have done a much better job than Mugabe. Divisiveness has been a hallmark of Mugabe's rule. He was forged in the crucible of oppositional struggle, first in the nationalist phase against a ruthless, racist opponent, and then in the armed struggle, where anyone who seemed to be against one was an enemy, a potential betrayer, spy or even killer. Such people were regarded as '*mhandu*', the enemy, and usually dealt with ruthlessly. In the period we are looking at, Mugabe never made the transition from that kind of mentality to a sense of being the president of a whole nation, of all the people in it, even when they disagreed with him. (See Chapter 28 for Mugabe's recent but alas temporary metamorphosis.)

He was always quintessentially the leader of ZANU-PF and he mistook ZANU-PF for the nation. Others citizens of the country he led as president, who had divergent views or were not fully-fledged supporters of the party, he often ridiculed. If not that, he saw them as the source of threat.

When Mbare, the oldest high-density suburb in Harare, the old Harare location, stopped voting for ZANU-PF, he belittled them by referring to the people of Mbare as '*vanhu vasinamutupo*' (people without a totem). This might have provoked some jeers in the rural areas but it did not go down well in Mbare. Thus instead of finding out where ZANU-PF had gone wrong and how the people of Mbare could be wooed back, he alienated them forever. And this was just one example of his jibes and sneers directed towards those who did not or no longer supported him.

He used to inveigh regularly against opposition politicians for not attending national events such as Independence or Heroes Day. But when they did come, he entertained the crowd with anti-opposition jibes and insults. Even at funerals, he would invariably make political speeches, to the discomfort of those who had come to pay their last respects to the deceased but did not necessarily support ZANU-PF politics. Relatively recently he attacked the policies of an unfriendly country, prompting its Ambassador, who had come to pay his respects to the dead, to have to leave the funeral.

Coupled with this was Mugabe's rather fatal lack of statesmanship. Perhaps another way of putting it is his lack of strategic diplomacy. There is a lot to be said for the strategic diplomacy King Moshoeshoe of the Basotho displayed when, having repulsed an enemy attack, he sent after them cattle and beer so that they would not return to the attack out of sheer hunger, thirst and the humiliation that they had been defeated. Another example is the hawk in a Xhosa satirical poem, who states a cutting truth but then immediately blows on the wound to make it feel better. When Mugabe went to world events and made one of his truthful but reckless speeches, I couldn't help likening him to a rooster (*jongwe* – the political symbol of ZANU-PF), which, accustomed to standing on a dung-heap in his own yard where he rules the roost, suicidally does the same outside the homestead where the hyena and the jackal rule. Yes, Mugabe told them to their faces – and most of what he said was spot on. But all he had done in effect was make the people's already parlous situation at home more desperate by intensifying the determination of his enemies to make Zimbabwe suffer.

Mugabe's quest for national sovereignty, majority ownership and control of the economy was always going to provoke the ire of powerful foreign interests – but not all. It would have helped a lot if, side by side with the implementation of his programme, he had also taken the time to explain to, to persuade and win the support of those others who might have had a lesser degree of hostility to what he was proposing instead of unleashing his customary defiant, provocative and alienating diatribes indiscriminately against them all.

And this in a way is related to another consideration, what I am going to call 'ruth'. Mugabe rarely gave the impression, through the worst times in Zimbabwe, when his people were really suffering, of having any 'ruth', of feeling any sympathy or pity. When one of his comrades or a member of their families died, he never failed to be there to offer his commiserations. But when people fled the country to seek jobs elsewhere, when the people were afflicted by AIDS or cholera, when children had no schooling, houses no water and electricity, garages no fuel, shops no food, when his police and army units had chased them out of their homes and demolished them in front of their eyes, as happened during the disastrous *Murambatsvina* debacle, he was conspicuous by his absence. He was there for the party but never seemed to be there for Zimbabweans. Perhaps if he had had more 'ruth', he would have been more of a statesman and more of a uniting and humanising force as president.

Again, he, like his party, had either no or very poor PR. Not just in the sense of image or brand but also at times where it was crucial for the people to understand what he and his government were doing. He and his party rarely deigned to explain. Mugabe rarely talked to the people – as opposed to making speeches. He rarely explained to them why certain things were happening and as a result was not able to carry them along with him, even when his policy was good and his intentions noble. Instead he left his and his government's actions unexplained and open to interpretation by his enemies. Was it because he shared ZANU-PF's general arrogance and the belief that to explain is to admit weakness, that to explain is to undermine ZANU-PF's struggle-given right to take decisions for the people and to govern them without check or challenge? By not explaining, Mugabe left the door wide open for the opposition and the hostile world media to fill in the gap. Thus the people ended up believing what Mugabe's opponents told them when if he had explained, they might instead have believed him. The classic example was Zimbabwe's involvement along with Angola and Namibia in the Democratic Republic of the Congo (see Chapter 14).

Perhaps another of his failings was his lack of vision or ability to instil in his people or inspire in them a vision of something better to live and work for. In asserting and re-asserting the fundamental demands of the liberation struggle with regard to land, black ownership of national resources, black empowerment, national sovereignty and economic independence, he was unrelenting. However visionaries like Kwame Nkrumah of Ghana, Amilcar Cabral of Guinea-Bissau, Augustino Neto of Angola, Samora Machel of Mozambique, even Julius Nyerere of Tanzania, could open up their people's minds to new possibilities, new visions of the future. Machel did this on a wide range of issues, such as gender equality, the need for all the different peoples of Mozambique to become one, 'from the Rovuma to the Maputo', or a concept like 'the professors of the negative', where he taught the people to see that they could extract something positive even from the traitorous example of sell-outs. Robert Mugabe's strengths were elsewhere. He was no visionary. Instead, he never tried to take the people somewhere where they weren't. He appealed to what they already thought – even sometimes if their thoughts were not progressive or did not constitute a potential for change for the better. Apart from that one great speech at Independence, I do not remember another memorable speech. Some were interesting, some powerful, but they seldom included anything new or inspiring. To a large extent they were dogged re-iterations of his and ZANU-PF's time-worn ideals, most of which in the later years had been to everyone's knowledge betrayed. He said what *his* people wanted to hear. He was, to put it crudely, more a demagogue than a visionary leader. On the election trail, he was in his element, drumming up the people's support by saying what he calculated would win their support. This meant the range of his ideas was limited, his themes, though valid, were unoriginal and predictable.

Finally, along with the corruption went what in my opinion was a serious lapse in morality. Mugabe began a relationship with a very much younger married secretary, Grace Marufu, and had two children by her, while his first wife, Sally, was still alive. Her husband was an air force pilot and Mugabe had him sent out of the country. Up to that point, Mugabe had had an exemplary record in terms of personal moral integrity. Sally Mugabe was a very respected personality in her own right. Marital betrayal, adultery and breaking up other people's marriages is not what many people expect from a Head of State or a revolutionary hero. In a country where 'small houses' are a common phenomenon and a serious problem for wives and their families, such behaviour was not worthy of him.

Most of Mugabe's shortcomings, as they so often are with human beings, were related to his strengths. His stubborn defence of the gains of the liberation struggle and the depth of his ideological convictions, discussed above, probably made it inevitable that he would say his piece on the international stage with no care for strategy or diplomacy. His dogged refusal to be beaten by Smith and his resilience both inside and outside the country, accounts for his attitudes to anyone who seemed to oppose him.

I hope it can be seen from the above, that Mugabe's years of sacrifice and dedication to the struggle for liberation in his country and in Africa, his strongly held views and principles, his commitment to the empowerment of his people and the sovereignty of his country as well as his refusal to kowtow to the interests of the West, were over the years compromised by his many failings as a leader and a president as well as rampant corruption, including his own moral corruption, and the resort to violence and torture.

However, that Robert Mugabe was a great man, history must attest. Great men, with the exception of saints and prophets, are seldom perfect. Sometimes it is their very greatness that creates men in whom just as their virtues, so were their faults - great. I believe Rober Gabriel Mugabe is such a man.

CHAPTER SEVEN:

RACE, ETHNICITY, CLASS AND STATUS

'Bones much heavier than ours'

So much for the leader – what about the people? Though relatively few, the people were extraordinarily divided. Their divisions followed a number of social fault lines. A major and the most conspicuous of them was colour or race. The split was between a small but powerful white minority and a large black majority with two other very small minorities in the middle – the so-called 'Coloureds' and Asians, the last of which being people largely of Indian descent. Though the white minority was relatively homogeneous, the Asian minority and the black majority were not at all. The former was rigidly divided along religious lines – Hindu and Muslim. Ethnic divisions went deep in the black majority. As if this wasn't enough, status and class complicated matters still further – asserting themselves more and more in the first decade of Independence in ways hardly known before.

My wife and I, being South African, one white and the other black, had experienced the racism of both the apartheid system and that of the black reaction in the form of Black Consciousness - along with everything in between. You would have thought that anyone born and brought up in apartheid South Africa, like us, would rank among the world's experts in the field of racism. As veterans of the South African racial battlefield, we could have been forgiven for being a little patronising to the little nation we had ended up in when it came to race. We knew they'd had a few problems but nobody ever spoke much about Rhodesian *apartheid*.

True on a previous visit, in the early 1970s, my wife-to-be, myself and my cousin and his wife – who was of Indian descent - had had to sit up in the gallery in order to watch a film at a cinema in Gweru - then called Gwelo - while the homogeneously white sat down below. But, compared with the laws that criminalised racial mixing in South Africa – the Immorality Act, the Mixed Marriages Act, the Group Areas Act and so on - sitting nicely up in the gallery while the others sat down below in the same cinema, watching the same film, was heaven. No-one came up to the gallery to call us all sorts of scandalous names, break our noses and chuck us out or slap handcuffs on us and drag us to the police station. Compared with South Africa, Rhodesia was a doddle – or so we thought.

So when we came to Zimbabwe after Independence, when the formal racism they had had in the old Rhodesia, had been dismantled, we thought that whatever problems we might face, it wasn't likely to be race again. We were obviously being naive and it wasn't long before we began to realise that. To our surprise, we soon discovered that Zimbabwe was a seriously racist country – in some ways just as racist as South Africa itself. As in South Africa, there was white racism towards the other races, Indian and so-called Coloured racism towards blacks and black racism to everyone else. These racisms were compounded by numerous chauvinisms. Among blacks themselves, there was ethnic chauvinism between Ndebele and Shona and then among the various Shona groupings, not to mention attitudes to the minorities such as the Tonga. Then there was a national chauvinism, which extended beyond Zimbabwe's borders. Just as South Africans, black and white, had a very low opinion of *amakwerekwere*, peoples who lived to the north of them in Africa, so Zimbabweans, proud of their education, what they saw as their 'infrastructure', the way they spoke English – whatever – also had a very low opinion of the peoples to the north of *them*!

Of course, chauvinisms seem to be the human disease and it is not only South Africans and Zimbabweans that suffer from them. Before discussing how they operated in Zimbabwe, I suggest we remember that race or even ethnicity in Zimbabwe, important as they were, were not, essentially, as fundamental a determining factor in people's lives as family (extended family) and by extension *mutupo* or totem groups (clans). The hierarchy of what made the average black Zimbabwean tick was, in my opinion, family then clan, then home locality, then ethnicity, then race and finally nationality. A man from Mahusekwa in Chihota, for instance, was likely to be most influenced by considerations relating first to his extended family then to those with the same totem or of the same clan, then those from the Chihota district, then being Zezuru, then being Shona, then being black – and finally being Zimbabwean.

At the University of Zimbabwe there was a student canteen. It was here I first observed exactly how ethnic chauvinism operated in Zimbabwe. At that time, the beautiful Zimbabwean women of today did not seem to have been born. An ANC student, studying at the university, used to refer to the Shona girls on campus as 'sculptures'. People who remember the joke about a certain cabinet minister and the African mask, will know that the comparison was not intended to be complimentary – more about that in a moment. Yet, a few months later, I found him sitting at a table in the Students Union seemingly very much in love with a girl – who was Shona. Whether he had developed a taste for 'sculpture' or he had simply got acclimatised, I don't know but he seemed to be more than satisfied with his Shona 'sculpture'!

Very briefly, the story about the minister and the mask hinged on the fact that generally this particular minister was not considered to be the most handsome member of the cabinet. One day there was a function that featured dancers who wore masks. At such functions, it was common for dignitaries to take to the stage, as Kenneth Kaunda of Zambia and the late vice-president, Simon Muzenda, always did, and join in a traditional dance or two. On this occasion three ministers took to the stage. The first two were given masks to wear but our particular cabinet minister was not. When he enquired as to why he was not being given a mask, he was told that he didn't need one!

In those early days, working in banks, government offices, department stores and all that was a rather new experience for a lot of black Zimbabwean women and so it took them some time to develop the appropriate dress sense. One day, there appeared in *The Herald* newspaper a cartoon, which depicted a very overdressed lady pitching up for work in the morning and the caption went: "Good morning, Madam. What a lovely evening dress!" If, at that stage, dress sense was at a premium, this did not remain the situation for long and no-one would understand the South African student's chauvinist jibe or the cartoonist's joke now.

However, back to the issue of chauvinism. In the said Students Union, students used to sit at table according not only to their race but also their ethnic group. Over there would be the Karangas from Masvingo and here at this table the Zezurus, by the wall the Manyika and somewhere else the Korekore, the Kalanga or the Ndebele. Government posts followed the same pattern – where there was an attempt to deal with the problem of ethnicity, posts were evenly distributed amongst the Shona ethnic groups. This unofficial but complicated quota system became even more complicated when after the Unity Accord the Ndebeles came into the equation. In those cases where no attempt was made to strike an ethnic balance, whole ministries, departments and, in the private sector, companies could be staffed by a combination of family members, 'home boys' - those coming from one's home district - or people of the same ethnic group – a phenomenon which people referred to as 'nepotism'.

One of the first plays we staged at the University was based on this and related issues – ethnic chauvinism, nepotism and corruption. It was called *Seri kwesasa/Okusemsamo* – translated into English, 'beyond the threshold'. The main plot of the play involved an Ndebele man falling in love with a Shona woman and the two wanting to get married – a prospect that was equally horrifying to both families. In symmetrical scenes, the families go through the litany of ethnic insults Shona and Ndebele commonly used to disparage each other. The Shona father asks what kind of people these Ndebele are that do not know how to respect. When they refer to someone who should be respected, they just use the second person singular '*iwe*' instead of the plural '*imi*'! Shona and a number of other 'Bantu' languages express respect by using the plural – as in French. "Imagine that," the father says, "*Iwe kwandiri Baba*!" – saying 'you' (singular) to me, the Father of the family! What an outrage!

On their part, the Ndebeles talk about what kind of people are these (the Shona) who, when you go and seize their women and their cattle, the men are nowhere to be found! The men disappear! '*Ukushona*' means to disappear in Ndebele – and this is also one of the theories chauvinistically concocted to account for how the Shonas came to be called Shona! They always disappeared when they saw the enemy coming! In another classic scene from the same play, the Employer, who is Shona, is interviewing a job applicant and he wants to know if the man is Ndebele or Shona – obviously if he is not Shona and or a home boy, he's not going to get the job. So, slyly, he asks him what football team he supports. Two of the most famous football teams in Zimbabwe are Dynamos from Mbare in

Harare and Highlanders from Bulawayo. Generally, Shonas support the former and Ndebeles the latter. Being an Ndebele, the applicant begins to say: "Of course, Highlanders" but in the nick of time he sees the trap. He quickly tries to cover up his mistake by saying: "Of course, High...I mean, any team that's high on the log". The job eventually goes to a totally unqualified Shona, a relative of the Employer.

If ethic chauvinisms were rampant among black Zimbabweans, racial chauvinisms were similarly rampant among whites. Before my coming to the university, the lighting equipment that had once existed in what was a thriving university theatre before Independence, had disappeared. Some of it was 'borrowed' and went to white private schools and institutions. One of these was the Reps Theatre, an all-white amateur repertory theatre club. In the process of looking for the lighting, I visited them. Being white I was invited into the bar for a few beers. Everyone in the bar was white. Though not official, this is virtually still the case even now. That evening, as we downed our beers, I was treated to lots of interesting white chauvinisms. An elderly lady, whose family must have been pretty working class when it left England for the colonies, was parading her acquired upper class airs - and bizarre theories relating to 'breeding' to go along with them. The lady in question came from Bulawayo in so-called 'Matebeleland'.

In this book I always say 'so-called' when I get to this word 'Matebeleland' because, as I will explain in a later chapter, the Ndebeles are not even Ndebeles and in any case 'Matebele' is a transcription of the Sotho/Tswana pronunciation of 'amaNdebele'. In the old days the Sotho and Tswana-speaking peoples had every reason to dislike the 'Matebele' so the way they used the word – and still do - was pretty derogatory. Most white Rhodesians seemed to make a point of not pronouncing African words properly and their rendition of 'Matebele' became something like this: 'mat' (as in 'the cat sat on the mat') 'a-beelee' (as in 'mielie' or 'steely') and thus 'Matabeelee'. When this abomination became the name of a province, well, 'so-called' was the least one could call it. Incidentally, the 'tribal' names of the Rhodesian era are still to this day the names of most of the provinces in Zimbabwe – Bulawayo, Masvingo, Midlands and Harare being the exceptions.

Now, this lady from 'Matabeleeland' was of the opinion that the 'Matabeelees' were a far better lot than your Shonas (pronounced 'show-na'), for whom she and many others in white Rhodesia had the greatest contempt. She felt that, as a result of the alleged superiority of the 'Matabeelee', the whites who lived with the 'Matabeelee' in Bulawayo were by a sort of geographical osmosis superior to those from Harare, who had to breathe the same air as the 'Show-nas'. The lady from Bulawayo was particularly concerned about her grand-daughter, Viola, who was living in Harari (Hararee). There was a young German man 'of good stock', she said, who was interested in her but she dreaded that Viola would not go for him but instead go for a 'Show-na'! The thought of what kind of great-grandchildren Viola might produce in that case was enough to give her sleepless nights, she said. "These coffee-coloured children that result from such liaisons," she opined, "are just too ghastly for words". By that time, she and her son, who was a professor at the University, were giving me a lift home. As I said, I was married to a black South African woman and we had three beautiful 'coffee-coloured' children ourselves – whom I expected to come running out at any minute to welcome their daddy home!

Then there was the white senior teacher at the local primary school near the university which my children went to. In the Rhodesian era, the school was a segregated all-white school. By the late 1980s, of course, it was integrated and the majority of the children were black while the majority of the teachers were still white. The Senior Teacher was talking about the problems that she had to deal with as a result of all the new 'African' children that were now attending the school. Whites, when they were being polite, referred to blacks as 'the African' or 'Africans'. They referred to themselves as 'Europeans'. A particular problem, she confided to me, was that school swimming sessions, practices and galas had become a nightmare ever since the 'African' children had come. She rightly pointed out that not a lot of black children had ever been taught to swim. Before Independence they didn't have access to all the swimming pools the whites had – the 'Swimming Pool Revolution' was still to come. "What makes it worse," she went on, "is that 'they' sink so fast. You see their bones are much heavier than ours."

I could go on and on with such stories – not just whites about blacks but also blacks about whites and about 'Coloureds' and 'Indians' - and all of them with their derogatory names for each other and nursing their wild ideas and theories and stories about each other. It was a nightmare – far worse even than school swimming galas!

The racism was deep, entrenched and sometimes very bitter but, unlike South Africa, it was seldom overt. In South Africa, black people used to say that they preferred the Afrikaners to the English. An Afrikaner would tell someone bluntly that no 'kaffir' is going drink from his cup. An 'English'[10] would watch with a strained smile as an 'African' drank from his cup but then throw the cup away after the 'African' had left – or put it aside for the servants, so that it became the 'boy' or the 'girl's' cup, like the 'boy's meat' he bought from the butcher. In other words, you knew where you stood with

10 *The reference here is to the English-speaking whites in South Africa – not the English of England*

the Afrikaner. His racism was bad but open. The 'English' was just as racist but he pretended not to be so.

The white settlers in Rhodesia had been in the main of British descent. The British middle class tends to mask its feelings with a veneer of politeness. This culture seems to have become legitimated in Rhodesia and was carried over into Zimbabwe. The whites in Zimbabwe were seldom openly insulting and derogatory to the other races. They reserved this for when they were alone together or for their workers on the farms. It became the culture and the other races were assimilated into it. When they were alone together and talking in their own languages, their hatred or contempt or scorn for other races was openly expressed. But, in their social interactions, superficial politeness tended to be the order of the day.

This was definitely the case at departmental board meetings at the University. There were these academic meetings going on in the language of agendas, minutes, matters arising, resolutions etc and a fly on the wall would have been forgiven for imagining that the ladies and gentlemen of different races sitting round the boardroom table were really discussing syllabi or examinations or student performance. In actual fact, under the surface, only thinly veiled, there was a racial war going on. The hidden hatreds, contempts and prejudices only came to the surface after the meeting when each racial group was alone with its 'own kind'. I remember overhearing black colleagues walking down the corridor after one such meeting on their way to tea at the Staff Lounge, celebrating a boardroom victory on some point or other as if it had been a skirmish during the struggle for liberation – and in the same language: "*Tawina*!" they said, exultantly. "We triumphed."

When it came to race, ethnicity, nepotism or chauvinism in Zimbabwe, as far as I could see, little changed over the three decades - among the older generations, at least. The hope for something different, at least in the area of race, lay perhaps with the so-called 'Born Frees', many of whom had gone to racially integrated schools - this and the fact that with the indigenisation of the society the white factor became less and less significant.

There were also many other social divisions, relating more to class, status and culture than to race or ethnicity. Among the black youth, for instance, society was divided into those who lived in the old townships, those who lived in the ex-white suburbs and those who lived in the rural areas. The term 'high-density suburbs' or '*mahigh-density*', was a post-independence euphemism for the old black locations or townships. '*Masabhabha*' or low-density suburbs referred to the low-density, ex-white middle class suburbs, equivalent of *emakhishini* or *dikichining* (the kitchens) in South Africa. '*Marurals*' or '*kumamisha*' were the rural areas. Children and young urban blacks of the middle class, living to a large extent in *masabhabha*, developed a contempt for the traditional culture and the countryside where the traditional culture remained to some extent intact. Their parents, who would still tend to have close ties with their rural homes, would meet with increasing resistance from their children as they grew older, either to accompanying their parents on visits 'home' or even more to their spending school holidays there. In Shona the rural home is '*kumusha*' and so the children of *masabhabha* would refer to those from *marurals* as '*kumushas*' or SRBs, standing for 'Strong Rural Background'. But those living in '*maHigh-Density* - or even in the rural areas - would express their contempt for the children or youth of *masabhabha* by mocking the way they spoke English – and even sometimes Shona – with a snobbish nasal tone, calling them '*maNose*'. Another soubriquet was *maSalad* – according to one theory, a term originally derived from food ate by black models in order to become skinny.

Thus, we discovered that Zimbabwe, though small, was a labyrinth of social divisions and prejudices. Yet, all these race, ethnic, class or status chauvinisms paled into relative insignificance in the face of the great Shona/Ndebele divide.

CHAPTER EIGHT:

OPERATION GUKURAHUNDI

The 'Third Matebele War'

Wemba ngomkhonto, wemba ngenduku,	*(He fought with the spear and the battle stick,*
Inkosi yabeNtungwa labeThwakazi!	*King of the people of Ntungwa and Thwakazi!)*

- from the praises of Mzilikazi ka Mashobane

Ndebele is the name given to the people who held sway over most of Zimbabwe at the time of the coming of the whites and who effectively replaced the Rozvi Empire that had ruled before them. As with Shona, Ndebele is not a name they used themselves. They referred to themselves as 'Mthwakazi' or 'Mahlabezulu' and to the Shona as the Lozwi, their adaptation of Rozvi. The so-called amaNdebele of Zimbabwe are not related in any way to the Ndebele people who now inhabit the Mpumalanga Province in South Africa, except for the fact that both are originally Nguni from what is now known as KwaZulu/Natal.

Mthwakazi was a nation of many peoples. There were the Khumalos, Mzilikazi's own clan, and members of other Nguni clans who were in Shaka's regiment that came up from KwaZulu with Mzilikazi. There were baSotho and baTswana whom they met on the way north. Lastly, there were the Rozvi or Lozwi, the local Kalanga people they found already there. The Lozwi were in the majority. The Sothos or *Abenhla* – people from further north – were next and the Ngunis or *Abezansi* – people from the south - a tiny minority. Thus, the people referred to as Ndebele are not a homogeneous ethnic group but rather the descendants of the multi-ethnic nation of Mthwakazi, resulting from

Mzilikazi's wise policy of uniting the people in language but not discriminating against non-Ngunis in other ways.

So-called Matebeleland consisted of three provinces - Matebeleland South, Bulawayo and Matebeleland North. My first visit to Bulawayo after Independence took place in 1985. I was working closely at the time with two colleagues at the University of Zimbabwe, Thompson Tsodzo and Dr Vimbai Chivaura. They were both Shona-speaking and, like most Shonas, they could not speak much Ndebele. Now, I said to myself, now I shall be the one at an advantage. Here in Harare they are at home with their Shona while I struggle. When we get to Bulawayo, as a Zulu-speaker, I will be the one to feel at home and it will be their turn to struggle. I looked forward to it.

Not a bit of it. My hopes were dashed in the very first moment of arriving in Bulawayo. One of my two Shona-speaking companions asked someone by the side of the road for directions and he did so in Shona. The man he asked, answered effortlessly in Shona. From then on that was the order of the day. Though Bulawayo is the very heartland of isiNdebele[11], Shona is spoken by virtually everyone. Ndebele-speakers speak it but there are also many native Shona-speakers and many Kalanga, whose language is simply a Shona dialect. It is a general rule in Zimbabwe that almost everywhere people can speak Shona. Probably everywhere, I suppose, minorities tend to speak not only their own language but that of the majority. Ndebeles, in the main, speak Shona whereas most Shonas, quite arrogantly at times, do not speak Ndebele.

11 In the so-called 'Bantu' languages language or culture is indicated by a prefix before the noun eg, isi(Ndebele), isi(Zulu), se(Sotho), chi(Shona), ki(Swahili)

In the early days of nationalism before Independence, the organisations followed the pattern of other African Nationalist movements – they were not ethnically divided. Shona and Ndebele organised and struggled together. But with the formation of ZANU and ZAPU the Zimbabwean nationalist movement found itself divided into two ethnically based liberation movements, one predominantly Shona, the other predominantly Ndebele. During the armed struggle, with the unhappy exception of an ill-fated attempt to unite, the armed wings of the two organisations, ZIPRA and ZANLA, fought separately. A Nationalist movement based largely on ethnicity was relatively rare in Africa. It was philosophically heretical. Only dubious characters like Gatsha Buthelezi could claim that such an ethnic party was in the tradition of African Nationalism. The danger of his false claim was demonstrated to great cost in the misery and bloodshed that resulted when his Zulu-based Inkatha yeSizwe (later Inkatha Freedom Party), in complicity with the *apartheid* regime, became involved in bitter rivalry with the African National Congress in Natal and in the hostels on the Reef in the last years before the demise of *apartheid.* Buthelezi's antics were well exposed in Mzala's book entitled *Gatsha Buthelezi, Chief with an Agenda.*

ZAPU, and its army, ZIPRA, indeed fought for Zimbabwe, valiantly - in many ways they were the pioneers of the armed struggle - but there was no getting away from the fact that it was ZANLA, the army of ZANU, that was the main liberator of the country. Then, as victory was in sight, ZAPU and ZANU came together to form the Patriotic Front and they negotiated together at Lancaster House. But, when it came to the election, ZANU-PF decided to go it alone and fight the election as ZANU-PF - and they won. So we had the divided government and divided nation I wrote about in the introduction – a virtually Shona majority, a virtually Ndebele minority and a small block of whites voted in by whites on a separate roll.

Now imagine, the year is 1980. The first democratic election in the history of the country has been held. ZANU-PF are the victors. ZANU-PF is overwhelmingly a party of what Mzilikazi referred to as the Lozwi, now Shona. The children of Mthwakazi, of Lobengula and Mzilikazi, wake up to find that, having been the lords of Zimbabwe before the coming of the whites and consistently treated as superior to the Shona by the whites during the colonial era, they are now to be ruled by the descendants of those they once ruled and whom both they and their colonial masters traditionally regarded with contempt. I suppose most peoples, who have been conquered and struggle to be free, hope that when they have got rid of their conquerors, their land will revert to what it had been before the conquest – the Palestinians, for instance, after the First World War. In the case of Zimbabwe that would have meant a Zimbabwe ruled by the nation of Mthwakazi with the Lozwi as their vassals again. It was not to be and many Ndebeles did not – and to this day do not - like it.

The situation was obviously highly unstable. There was little trust. Whites still owned the economy and effectively controlled the armed forces. There were rumours at one point of a white coup. Though some have recently denied it, ZIPRA, the armed wing of ZAPU, had cached weapons all over the place and so almost certainly had ZANLA. It made good sense. When the Lancaster House Agreement came into force the liberation forces were required to hand over their weapons and enter camps, supervised by the British. Perfidious Albion? What if it was all a trick? Of course they had to cache arms in the eventuality that, if it was a trick and they had to go back to the bush, they would not be defenceless.

So here it was – the newest country in Africa, Zimbabwe, with two ethnic liberation movements, this inauspicious ethnic Parliament and arms caches all over the country! Talk about dragon's teeth. It was a highly inflammable situation.

There have been many instances of independence coming to a divided society where the divisions exploited and exacerbated during the colonial period, were bequeathed by the colonial power to the newly independent state. There have also been many instances of countries in which revolutionary governments have come to power after long struggles, in the teeth of Western opposition. In both cases, what followed were often bloody civil wars, sometimes leading to dismemberment. In India, the country fell apart into three nations, India, Pakistan and Bangladesh. Countless people lost their lives and everything they possessed in the ensuing mayhem. In Nigeria, British colonial policy set up the divisions which resulted in the tragic Biafra War. In Ireland, where the colonizer pitted Catholic against Protestant, a large chunk of historic Ireland, Ulster, one of the four great kingdoms of Ireland, was excluded from Irish Independence when it came. For decades after, the bombings and assassinations never ceased.

In Mozambique, Frelimo's struggle for a new society and its liberatory ideas inspired a revolution in Portugal and they were seen as a threat not only by white Rhodesia and South Africa but also by right-wing elements in the United States and in other countries too. These forces reacted by funding a proxy force, the MNR or Renamo (*Resistência Nacional Moçambicana*), with which to oppose the Frelimo government and destabilise the country as well as to disrupt the ability of ZANLA to use Mozambique as a base for incursions into Rhodesia. The war of banditry, destruction and mutilation it waged devastated the country and 'killed the dream'[12] of *Uma Sociedade Nova*. In Nicaragua, the Sandinistas, whose idea of

12 *Killing a Dream*, video by Anders Nillsson & Gunilla Akesson, detailing and depicting the depredations of Renamo in Mozambique.

a new society was also seen as a threat to powerful capitalist interests, had to face a similar proxy war in which the so-called Contras wreaked havoc and slaughter wherever they went. In Angola and San Salvador a similar situation developed.

Now, as Shona and Ndebele squared up in Zimbabwe, there were many who were ready to stir the pot. What made the situation in Zimbabwe worse was the fact that, at the time, there was lots of talk that ZANU-PF was going to 'go communist' or at least introduce socialist policies. The Rhodesians had made great play of that in their 'anti-terrorist', 'anti-commie' propaganda. The Cold War was still on and there was concern that Zimbabwe would align itself with the 'Reds'.

So, the situation in Zimbabwe, independent but ethnically divided – and talking socialism - was perilous. Zimbabwe was in great danger of becoming another India, Nigeria, Ireland, Mozambique, Nicaragua or San Salvador. It didn't. But it was a close call.

As this is an 'As-I-See-It' book, let me be frank. When I arrived in Zimbabwe, I could speak Zulu but no Shona. We lived in Harare and I didn't actually go to Bulawayo very often but, whenever I did, I loved it because being a Zulu-speaker, I felt much freer there than in Shona-speaking Harare. Initially, it was much easier for me to relate to Ndebele-speakers than to Shona-speakers and, initially, I was biased in their favour. But living in Harare helped me to see both Shona and Ndebele with a degree of objectivity. I think I was able to see what to me appeared to be the contrasting qualities that characterised both of them. Of course, neither Shonas nor Ndebeles are all the same. As with any group of people of the same language and culture there exists a wide variety of personalities and behaviours. However, this having been said, it is usually possible to discern certain characteristics which, though not shared by all, are common and sometimes even typical of that people.

I have to say that, in my opinion, both groups contributed to the difficult situation that prevailed between them in the years after Independence. Of course, they could blame history, like the South African writer, Bloke Modisane, who called his autobiography *Blame Me on History*. But, at the time of Independence, both Shonas and Ndebeles needed to make a re-assessment of that history and turn over a new leaf. A concerted campaign of national education was needed. But independent Zimbabwe did not much go in either for re-assessments of history or for educating its people – outside of the formal academic curriculum, that is. The political emblem of ZANU-PF was *jongwe*, the cockerel. They had won the war and won the election so I suppose it was inevitable that they would be cocky – pun intended. After all those years of being the underdog, they were now top rooster and they made no bones about it. But personally, while I noted the new-found arrogance of the Shona, I became rather disillusioned with many Ndebeles. I felt they, most of all, needed to shake off the baggage of their history.

Though the Shonas were the vast majority in the country, historically, as we have seen, for nearly a century both before and during the colonial era, the Ndebeles seemed to have seen themselves – with the collusion of the colonial whites – as the natural overlords of the country. Now that it was *jongwe* that crowed triumphant, many of them found it hard to adjust to the new situation. They seemed to do little else but complain, lament and look for Shonas under the bed. I soon lost patience with them. Zimbabwe was here to stay. Their being a minority in Zimbabwe was here to stay - and as long as there were democratic elections in which the ethnic factor played a significant part, it was likely that their being the underdog was here to stay. The only way, in my opinion, was to shed their Ndebele isolationism, accept the situation and make the most of it. The greatest of them, Joshua Nkomo, showed them the way when he led PF-ZAPU into the Unity Accord with ZANU-PF. Yet, instead of understanding and accepting that the way he had shown them was indeed the only and the best way for the future of the country and for themselves, the vast majority repudiated him. This is not to say that there were not many Ndebeles who rolled up their sleeves and got on with it, as Zimbabweans among Zimbabweans.

But the 1980s were early days. And in those early days, the Ndebeles had not yet had enough time to digest and come to terms with a situation the writing of which had been on the wall ever since the idea of an independent Zimbabwe seized the imagination of the early African Nationalists. What was obvious and inevitable all along but which Ndebeles somehow seemed not to be able to credit, had happened. Shonas ruled the roost. And to be honest, they were enjoying it. For too long – over 150 years – they had been the underdog. Now they were *jongwe* – the rooster, crowing on top of the great anthill that was Zimbabwe. Everywhere people were doing passable imitations of a cock flapping its wings – and crowing. Suddenly Ndebeles, the former overlords and aristocrats, found themselves being crowed at. Many were cowed. Others just couldn't take it.

Even before Independence, the two partners in the Patriotic Front, though united at the top, were still divided down below. Already even before the elections there had been a number of clashes. The divided election did not make things any easier and the young men and women from ZIPRA and ZANLA must have felt themselves strange bedfellows in the national army where many of them found themselves after ZANU-PF's go-it-alone victory at the polls. In the very year of Independence there was a major outbreak of fighting at the Entumbane Barracks not far from Bulawayo. This was followed by another outbreak at the Connemara Barracks near Gweru. ZIPRA cadres began to reject the position they found themselves in. They deserted and were able to locate their buried caches of weapons. They dug them up and began to stage attacks in different parts of the country. This acted as a signal and ZIPRA defections from the National Army increased.

Recently a former ZIPRA cadre claimed that the arms caches were in fact ANC caches and that all these years this had not been revealed because it would have compromised the ANC. It is difficult to understand how the revelation that Umkhonto weSizwe had cached arms in Zimbabwe would have embarrassed the ANC once democracy had come to that country. It is much more likely that they were ZIPRA arms caches. As suggested above, for the two liberation movements after the Lancaster House ceasefire, it would have been sound policy to cache arms after the Lancaster House Agreement. Be that as it may, ZIPRA knew about the caches and used the arms to launch sabotage and attacks against the government. Essentially they had embarked on a foolhardy and perilous adventure, which offered no chance of success and, in its place, only suffering and bloody defeat. What is more they were stirring up a hornet's nest of years and years of Shona bitterness at Ndebele hegemony. An extremely inflammatory – and tragic - situation was the result. Gukurahundi!

Things began to deteriorate rapidly as the new ZANU-PF government discovered more arms caches in various places. ZANU-PF accused PF-ZAPU of plotting an uprising to overthrow the duly elected government and PF-ZAPU leaders were arrested and tried for treason. Their leader, Joshua Nkomo, fled the country. The situation for ZIPRA cadres in the National Army must by this time have become a bit scary and there were now mass desertions. Many simply fled for their lives. Others left taking their arms with them, determined to fight. Former ZIPRA fighters began to converge from all over Zimbabwe to join in a fight which it would appear they were convinced they could win and even as a result secede from or take over Zimbabwe.

There followed an attack on the Prime Minister's official residence, other attacks on army and police posts, abductions of tourists and various acts of sabotage. It was then that the government decided that it was necessary to restore order and in an operation which was code-named Gukurahundi, the Fifth Brigade was sent into so-called Matebeleland to do just that. Like ZANU-PF's much later campaign, Murambatsvina, Gukurahundi got out of control and took a grisly and still not forgotten toll.

The 5th Brigade was the army unit responsible for implementing Gukurahundi. Talking about media tags, the Fifth Brigade is almost always referred to by the hostile media as the 'Korean-trained' Fifth Brigade. The effect was obviously calculated to make them sound sinister -- the 'Stalinist' People's Republic of Korea - another media tag, with its connotations too of the Korean War and then no doubt slanted eyes and Kung Fu. I remember the squeals emanating from the descendants of the British in Zimbabwe when, after Independence, the new Zimbabwe government asked for assistance from the Koreans in the design and construction of the Heroes Monument at Heroes Acre on the outskirts of Harare – a resentment that Heroes Acre to this day still attracts, as in a 2009 article by the Guardian Africa Correspondent, David Smith, in which he describes it as 'a somewhat totalitarian mausoleum'. Later the squeals were reserved for the Chinese. Somehow the involvement of Koreans, Chinese, Russians or Indians always seemed to provoke a squeal of horror. When it was the British, the Yanks, the

French or the Germans - well, that's how it should be, isn't it? - and no-one complained.

'*Gukurahundi*' is a Shona word for the first rains. It is the first rains that come in October - or used to - and restore the parched veld, soften the soil and usher in the hopes for a good agricultural season and a plentiful harvest. Sometimes these rains are also called *Bumbarutsva*. Unfortunately, Operation Gukurahundi was not nearly as poetic and life-affirming in the doing as it was in the naming. By the time the Fifth Brigade went in, there was a lot of bad blood on both sides – and no doubt provocation. Tempers were high and, as pointed out above, a malignant history too was playing its part – shades of the Hutu, perhaps, at last able to sort out their oppressor of centuries, the Tutsi?

I see no reason to believe that, if the situation had been reversed, it would have been any different. If, say, PF-ZAPU had won the election and ZANLA had started digging up weapons and waging a guerrilla war, there is no reason to believe that PF-ZAPU's retaliation on the civilian population in the Shona-speaking parts of the country would have been any different from what the Fifth Brigade perpetrated in Matebeleland.

Apartheid South Africa was not slow to exploit the increasingly unstable situation in its newly independent 'Communist' neighbour. Only a year after Independence they blew up the arsenal at the Inkomo Barracks near Harare. They tried to assassinate President Mugabe and then they struck another base, the air force base near Gweru. All of these actions they tried to make appear the work of ZIPRA. Many white and black Rhodesian ex-police and army personnel had been integrated into the South African defence forces. South Africa provided arms to a group calling themselves Super ZAPU that employed the terror tactics of Renamo, UNITA and the Contras. They murdered civilians and committed acts of sabotage, typically striking at the tourism industry.

The situation was degenerating into the type of catastrophic situation that followed Independence or the revolutionary transfer of power in the countries mentioned earlier and Zimbabwe showed all the signs of following in their footsteps. Zimbabwe was on the brink of a disaster from which it might never have recovered. Fortunately, it did not follow in their path and the efforts of its enemies to try and make it do so, were frustrated – by the intervention of Kenneth Kaunda of Zambia and Joshua Nkomo's far-sighted and patriotic agreement to engage ZANU-PF in unity talks, resulting in the Unity Accord of 1987.

In recent years, especially after the Catholic Commission for Justice and Peace in Zimbabwe issued a report, many organisations, both in Zimbabwe and abroad, have spotlighted the Gukurahundi campaign, citing the torture, the massacres and, in their view, the 'genocide' perpetrated by the Fifth Brigade. They have called for independent enquiries, reparations, justice and the erection of monuments. There have been calls from Bulawayo to seize power so that the atrocities of Gukurahundi could be reported to the International Court of Justice in the Hague! Given that august court's exclusive predilection for trying African crimes, it would no doubt have been happy to oblige.

There is no doubt that Operation Gukurahundi was a terrible and totally regrettable episode in the history of Zimbabwe. Its effects are still being felt today and it is likely that unless an open admission and some kind of process of healing is undergone, the west of Zimbabwe will remain for many generations alienated from the rest of the country. Though no-one asked me - nor are they likely to - my humble suggestion is that it might be a good idea if all the politicians and the armed forces could get together and hold a *bira*, a traditional ceremony, on the site of one of the Fifth Brigade's atrocities, ask the spirits of the dead to forgive and to bless their Zimbabwe and give it peace and teach the people of Zimbabwe to live with each other in respect and togetherness.

However, there is also no doubt in my mind that not all the indignation and outrage emanating in recent years from various quarters is either sincerely felt or expressed in good faith. The curious thing is that little was heard of it after the Unity Accord and until the Land Reform. In other words, I believe the rather belated outcry over Gukurahundi may well be not as much an entirely genuine indignation at the awful tragedy as a stick with which to beat Mugabe and ZANU-PF as a result of the reclamation of the land.

Let us put the whole thing in context. Since the arrival of the Pioneer Column in Zimbabwe in 1890, there have been countless massacres. The settler regime not only conquered the people through violence and military force, they also removed them from their land over many decades and killed or imprisoned anyone who resisted. During the Liberation Struggle there were more atrocities, Nyadzonia and Chimoio in Mozambique, Mkushi in Zambia – some mass graves and mine-shafts stuffed with corpses are only now being discovered in Zimbabwe. There were the massacres of Gukurahundi. And there were those who died in the years of ZANU-PF/MDC conflict.

These horrific atrocities are scars upon the psyche of the young Zimbabwean nation and they need healing. They ALL need healing. The birth of Zimbabwe has been a long labour of much pain and suffering. ALL of these tragic happenings need to be remembered, mourned, expiated and healed. Those whose tender consciences are not touched by all the other terrible things that took place in this long history of tragic and unfortunate events but suddenly find themselves moved to raise a hue and cry about Gukurahundi, cannot escape suspicion that it is not their consciences that were touched but their interests. Zimbabweans need to get together as a nation, remember and mourn all those that lost their lives in the bitter struggles of their history - whether ZANU, ZAPU or MDC, whether in the prisons or in the camps, in the bush or the homesteads? The ghosts have to be laid. This is as important for Zimbabweans as appeasing the victims of Gukurahundi. Zimbabwe must move on. But before it can, I believe it needs to yield to the inspiration of the Unity Accord and achieve real all-inclusive national unity (see Chapter 30).

After Independence, Robert Mugabe and the liberation movements did not take their revenge on Ian Smith, on his cronies in government, on those in the Rhodesian armed forces that planned and executed the massacres of women and children and on the civilian white population itself who in many cases had colluded and benefitted from the many crimes of the colonial period. Instead there was Reconciliation. That reconciliation was never asked for by the perpetrators. They never apologised. In many cases, they never were reconciled. In fact, they are among ZANU-PF's most vociferous critics today – many of them now piously clamouring for the justice, democracy, human rights and rule of law they denied the vast majority of Zimbabweans for all those years, some even for retribution for Gukurahundi!

Joshua Nkomo saw that what had erupted in the country was dangerous and disastrous and it must be put an end to. He did that through an act of reconciliation. He did not base reconciliation with ZANU on Nuremburg trials, on official reports or on recriminations. He knew that for the good of Zimbabwe, this page had better be turned. He and others had fought for Zimbabwe, given their whole lives to that cause. To them it was the preservation and progress of Zimbabwe that mattered - and, for this, sacrifices had to be made. He made yet another sacrifice and the result of that sacrifice is that Zimbabwe never became a Rwanda, an India, an Ireland, a Nigeria, a Mozambique or an Angola. While Zimbabweans may mourn all the loss and the suffering, let them also celebrate that and give credit where it is due. Turning back the page that Nkomo and Mugabe turned in 2008 does no good for anyone, especially Zimbabwe.

And as for the nation of Mthwakazi – Mahlabezulu - secession is not an option. Being again the rulers of Zimbabwe is not an option. It is time to move on. In the past, the nation of Mthwakazi was an enlightened meritocracy, a political fusion of different peoples. Surely the only Mthwakazi that is possible now, is the fusion of the existing peoples of Zimbabwe. Zimbabweans can learn the lessons of history in order to bring about a better future. Ndebeles must become part of the nation again. Zimbabwe would be all the stronger for it. They have so much to contribute. The only path to tread is the one that great son of Mthwakazi, Joshua Nkomo, opened up. And if they tread it, it is up to the other Zimbabweans to welcome them as compatriots and equals, the sons and daughters of a united Zimbabwe. The onus is on Zimbabweans.

CHAPTER NINE:

THE ZIMBABWE AFRICAN NATIONAL UNION (PATRIOTIC FRONT)

'*Tora gidi uzvitonge*' (Take up arms and rule yourself)

Ambuya Nehanda kufa vachitaura shuwa	(Ambuya Nehanda died telling the truth
Kuti tinotora sei nyika iyo	how do we get back our country?
Shoko rimwe ravakatiudza	The one message she left for us (was)
Tora gidi uzvitonge.	Take up arms and rule yourself.)

One night, the Zimbabwean writer, the late Dambudzo Marechera, and I happened to be going home together in the same vehicle after a function. He confided to me that people thought I was a supporter of ZANU-PF. It was obvious from this that 'people' did not expect me to be one and did not approve that I was one. Lots of people in Zimbabwe never supported ZANU-PF, even during the struggle for liberation and in the immediate post-Independence euphoria. They did not support them then and they weren't about to support them later. It is probably true to say that a lot of artists, writers and others in the NGOs, in sectors where they depended on the patronage of foreign and local white liberals, did not support them. Dambudzo Marechera did a lot better out of being a rebel, anarchic and iconoclastic, than he would have had he done something as 'inartistic' as support ZANU-PF. For is there not a prevailing view in the liberal establishment, both foreign and local, that maintains that – particularly in Africa – true artists and writers should always oppose ruling parties and governments? If you are a struggling artist and an African who wants publishers and patronage, it's better to play that game. In the thirty years of Zimbabwe's Independence there have been many such artists who have sold their country for 'a mess of potage'.

Nevertheless, I think I am as much of an artist as the rest of them - and I have no problem supporting either a ruling party or a government - if it pursues the liberating, just and democratic policies I espouse. In those days I used to illustrate my position by citing the story of the Soviet writer, Mikhael Sholokov, who, when asked how he could simultaneously support the party and write with his heart, replied that he did write with his heart and his heart belonged to the party. Though a lot of people in academic and literary circles in Zimbabwe and elsewhere would have found - and did find - Sholokov's words shocking, I saw absolutely nothing wrong with them.

So, I was not phased by Marechera's little bit of gossip. I told him that I am not going to be anti-ZANU-PF for the sake of it – or to win other people's support or favours and rewards from those who have a vested interest in maligning African governments as a matter of course. Where I believe a party or a government has a good policy or is doing a good thing, I will support it – openly. Where it doesn't, I won't - openly. *Chakanaka chakanaka* – what is good, is good. It's as simple as that. I told him I think that artists or writers, especially African ones, are much more useful to society if they do that than if they oppose everything all the time out of principle.

And that just about summed up my position in those early days with regard to ZANU-PF. I supported the African liberation struggle wherever it may be and whoever was fighting it, as long as those doing the fighting were genuine. I was a supporter of the ANC and I saw no problem in supporting ZANU-PF where I felt that they too were trying to do something good for the people and society. But mine was a critical support – and there was already in ZANU-PF's political behaviour reasons enough to be critical. Others revealed themselves or developed with time. When the reasons for criticism outweighed those for support, I no longer supported them. When they didn't, I supported them again.

And so, as we asked about Mugabe, let us ask about the ruling party – what's it with this ZANU-PF?

There is a common assumption that one can put down everything that happened in Zimbabwe to one man – to Mugabe. It is extraordinary how virtually every little thing that happens in Zimbabwe is described as having been done by Mugabe. If police in Matebeleland North take Tsvangirai to the police station in connection with a road accident, the media headlines will scream: "Mugabe arrests leader of the opposition". Though Mugabe plays the star role, he is not the cast. ZANU-PF exists and needs to be examined independent of its leader. The assessment of the party reveals inevitably that it is coloured by the thoughts, character and actions of its leader. But it is also true to say that the thoughts, character and actions of the leader are partly shaped by the party. For this reason, we need to take a look at the party, the party that developed from the movement that played the major part in winning the War of Liberation and which the country has to thank for its freedom, the party that has ruled the country for three decades and more, the party that took back the land but presided over the maintenance of white standards for the middle class and tolerated colonial standards for the people and the party that came to talk one thing but do another.

I have only voted in two elections in my life. One was in an all-white election in South Africa during the 1970s - for a Socialist Party candidate in Johannesburg. I had never heard of a Socialist

Party in South Africa before and I have no idea what kind of 'socialism' it had in mind but confronted with the Afrikaner Nationalist Party, the United Party and the Progressive Party, a Socialist candidate of any ilk seemed to be a better alternative to just not voting at all. And then the second time I voted was for ZANU-PF – in an election sometime in the early nineties I think. I never voted for them again because, dreading that as a white I would vote for the Movement for Democratic Change (MDC), they took my Zimbabwean citizenship away.

My family and I had arrived in Zimbabwe on United Nations refugee documents but I managed to get Zimbabwean citizenship owing to my father having been accidentally born in Bulawayo. When much later all the whites started voting for the MDC, ZANU-PF passed legislation to ban dual citizenship and made everyone renounce foreign citizenship, something which I had already done when I took Zimbabwean citizenship in the first place. However I was out of the country at the time and, when I later appealed, I suppose they were only too happy to uphold their decision and strike one more white MDC supporter off the voters' roll. Little did they know that despite being white and despite ZANU-PF's betrayal, I would never have voted for the MDC.

What ZANU-PF was to become in later years – just as what Zimbabwe was to become in later years – was prefigured in the years soon after taking power, in the period of the honeymoon. Thus I have found it impossible to confine the discussion of ZANU-PF to the early years. The following assessment – as I saw it - goes way beyond the First Decade of Independence and tries to place the party in the wider spectrum of Zimbabwe's history.

My first lesson on the nature of ZANU-PF was in 1982 when I came down from Ethiopia for the African Theatre for

Development Workshop in Murehwa. The atmosphere was strange. There was a sort of tense excitement, a realisation that the whole dynamics of the country had changed and new people were calling the shots. But calling the shots they were and, as if to the manner born, their approach was arrogant and authoritarian with a sense of hidden threat. They evinced the pride at having done it – brought about Independence - and the determination to brook no nonsense from anyone. At the workshop, I myself was in danger of being deported at one point because I mistook jocularity for license. The Bulawayo contingent at the workshop was quite cowed. I remember a ministry official, who happened to be Ndebele but spoke many Zimbabwean languages, and who generally chaired plenary sessions, chaired them in Shona almost all the time. Once when he actually did add a snatch of Ndebele, he said in parenthesis: "Lest we forget the language" or something to that effect. At the farewell concert, a group of us did a little sketch which featured a lovely Zulu farewell song, '*Indlela mhlophe*' – Zulu being a language closely related to Ndebele. The Shona participants drowned it out with their intentional inattention.

The new authorities did not appear to be at all happy about the democratic nature of theatre for development methodology, with its interacting with the country folk and encouraging them to speak freely. Almost all such interactions were monitored by local representatives of the party. A functionary from government noted in a speech at the official opening that theatre for development could be compared with fire. You can cook with it but it can also burn the house down. On the way back to Ethiopia, we discussed the tension, the veiled threat, the nervousness about people other than the party interacting with the *povo* and the fear of democratic dialogue and discussion of issues that related to the people's daily lives. It was rather similar to the way things were being done in Ethiopia under the Derg[13]. 'What kind of liberation was this going to be?' we asked ourselves. We were overheard by a Zimbabwean discussing these issues on the plane and reported to the Zimbabwean Embassy in Addis Ababa.

In a way, this short dip into the waters of post-1980 Zimbabwe was a litmus test for me. It prefigured many of the problems that were to follow - for ZANU-PF came back to Zimbabwe cock-a-hoop. They had won. "*Taitora nehondo*', they – and we - used to sing. 'We took it (Zimbabwe) through war!' This was partly true but it also tended to eclipse the significance of the fact that the actual transfer was the result of the negotiations at Lancaster House and these negotiations ensured that the transfer of power would be incomplete and limited. But the sense that they had won characterised ZANU-PF's style - and that of its government – and it characterised its treatment of the rest of society and the people. Having won, they could dictate. They expected obedience and compliance. They did not tolerate argument and dissent - and they were prepared to use force if they encountered it. It was almost as if they had entered Zimbabwe as a conquering army rather than an army of liberation. They hadn't but there was the sense that they had.

Perhaps this accounted for what would later appear to be a lack of foresight and strategic planning - or was it rather inappropriate planning? Perhaps they were never able to adjust the tactical thinking of the war they had just successfully fought to the new terrain of parliamentary politics and government. I got the impression that the way they read it was that they had a right to govern. They had taken Zimbabwe and anyone calling into question their legitimacy or their decisions was *mhandu* – the enemy – and would be dealt with as such. Perhaps that is also why they seldom

13 *After the revolution in Ethiopia in 1974 a military co-ordinating committee was established, chaired by Mengisti Haile Mariam, which came to be called the Derg.*

bothered to explain to the people why they were doing things. It was their right to govern so why explain? And in any case, is explaining not a sign of weakness? Perhaps too that is also why they felt they had no need for PR. What did it matter what happened to their image? They were the rightful heirs. In fact, ZANU-PF's style was rather similar to that of a hereditary monarch whose every action is sanctioned by divine right. Whatever they did, they seemed to imply, they ruled by right of their having fought the struggle and the people must accept – accept and go on supporting - and, if they didn't, they were sell-outs and must be punished and made to do so.

Their trump card was that it was they who had got rid of the whites, and in every election campaign, this was the carrot. The stick was that the whites might come back if the people did not support ZANU-PF. As the years went by, it was a card they went on and on playing until at one point it seemed to become their only card. There were no other cards left to play - yet.

When that time came, I remember having attended a meeting of farm workers in the commercial farms. A government minister was speaking. Now it so happened that he had a large farm in the same area and by his own admission was buddies with the local commercial farmers, including the remaining whites. He, like them, was an employer of people like those who were in the audience. He knew his own corruption and so did his audience. Attending the function with me was a white woman from a Scandinavian Embassy. The minister was speaking in Shona and he proceeded to play the card, using the two of us as a convenient focus of his tirade. The only way in which this corrupt black commercial farmer cum ZANU-PF/government 'fat cat' could strike a note of brotherhood with the black labourers he and his fellow commercial farmers exploited but whose support he still needed, was to resort to the racist abuse of whites – all and any of them.

As it happens, he didn't know that before he arrived I had performed, to some acclaim, a Malawian traditional song and dance. Many of the workers on commercial farms originated from Malawi. After the minister finished his speech, the workers, much to his surprise, asked if the white man could sing and dance again. I did so – he then changed his tune. No longer '*bhunu*' – the pejorative term for a white - I was now Bongo Man! He was historically and constitutionally unable to accord a white person respectful human status in front of such an audience - it would have been completely against his interests!

Much of the problem was rooted in the pre-Independence years. Obviously an organisation that is locked in an armed struggle adopts military ways – not only for prosecution of the military struggle but in all other aspects of its structures and operations. Military ways include discipline, obedience to orders, no dissent, no debate and discussion, no consultation - and deference to your superiors. If you remember, I spoke of two words which came with ZANU-PF from Mozambique. One was '*povo*'. The other was - '*chef*'.

Chef literally means 'chief', 'boss' or 'big man'. An expression, derived from the military, it was then applied to the civilian bosses both in ZANU-PF and society in general, especially the government. A *chef* is not someone you argue with. You obey. You flatter. Every time you use the word, you highlight the *chef*'s bigness and your littleness. For me this word, *chef*, summed up the relations not only within ZANU-PF and in government but also between ZANU-PF and government, on the one hand, and the people, on the other. It seemed to sum up the culture of rule and of government in Zimbabwe, from the earliest years onwards. Perhaps it was not a difficult thing for people in Zimbabwe to fall in with the '*chef* syndrome'. After all, under the whites there wasn't much room for argument or equality either, a relationship expressed in the obligatory use of 'master', 'madam' or even 'baas' when addressing a European. As I have already observed, autocratic rule, which brooked no dissent and eschewed consultation, was the management style. It characterised the old British school system as well as that of the civil service.

So, instead of ZANU-PF returning from the struggle and bringing with it alternative values and practices that embodied the ideals of the revolution in whose name they fought, it just seemed to confirm the existing order – with one basic distinction, the *chef*, the boss, was no longer white. He was black. ZANU-PF, though it fought for liberty and freedom, did not bring democratic discussion and debate; tolerance of dissent, equality and comradeship; respect for all people no matter what their position in life; a rejection of force and violence as opposed to persuasion; consensus and unity as opposed to 'the party line' and division. They made a political revolution – and they surely brought the *possibility* of freedom. But they were structurally and institutionally not able to realise that freedom. They could not and did not set both Zimbabwe and the people free.

Another legacy of the struggle was the attitude that ZANU-PF consistently evinced, which was that, as they had brought Zimbabwe, they *were* Zimbabwe. This equation between the party and the nation was something bitterly resented by many. As a result, ZANU-PF did little to build the nation – yet the nation had never been a nation before. It was a colony and nation-building was precisely what was needed. Unlike Samora Machel and Frelimo, with their constant education and encouragement of Mozambicans to see themselves as one – as in their slogan '*Viva o povo Moçambicano da Rovuma ao Maputo*' –the nation Zimbabweans were offered was ZANU-PF or nothing. Those Zimbabweans who did not support ZANU-PF as a party or had different ideas about things, had in the eyes of ZANU-PF forfeited their claim to be Zimbabweans. They were *mhandu nevatengesi* – enemies and sell-outs. ZANU-PF could never understand or accept that those who did not support them or saw things differently, were also Zimbabweans, part of the nation of the new Zimbabwe, which had to be built from nothing, and they needed to be included.

I got the feeling that at Independence ZANU-PF's vision of a free Zimbabwe was a Rhodesia which they ruled and in which blacks took their place alongside or in place of the whites. Apart from its racism, its oppression of blacks and its monopolisation of all the good things of life, I don't think that ZANU-PF had a problem with Rhodesia as a society as such. I don't think they had an alternative concept of what society they ought to build. There was never any talk of a *sociedade nova* or 'New Society'. In the same way, they demonstrated a lack of ability or perhaps interest in conceptualising the implications of their basic revolutionary principles in any other areas beyond material development, indigenous empowerment and enrichment for the party hierarchy and its fellow-roaders. Though the leadership employed a rhetoric which seemed to offer promise to the *povo* who supported their struggle, even to the point of propagating 'socialism', it soon became apparent that the rhetoric had been and was still being employed to ensure the support of the masses for the advancement of its own class interests. Thus, the actual behaviour of the echelons that had access to power began almost immediately to diverge from the party rhetoric and the spirit of its policies – a process which was already apparent in the years of the armed struggle as exemplified by the abuse of privilege and in particular the abuse of the female cadres in the camps on the part of the leadership. On the one hand, ZANU-PF continued to project itself as a party of popular revolution in which the interests of the people were being served while, on the other, those in power very quickly began to pursue at the level of personal action quite different and more selfish goals – to the extent of undermining and actually sabotaging the official party line and its own people-oriented policies and programmes (see Chapter 22 on corruption).

The positions of power included those in the armed forces, which the party now dominated. This and the military culture, expressed in the cult of the *chef*, also set the tone for civil relations and the actions of those in power. Though their excesses, abuse of power and illegal self-enrichment were widely known to the rank and file and to the population at large, they could not be challenged. The political and military leadership attained positions of almost complete unaccountability and immunity from check, censure or the consequences of their actions.

Though the party's allegiance to its basic principles of anti-imperialism, Pan-Africanism, national sovereignty and indigenous empowerment, was consistent, it never extended into the domain of ideology. I don't think ZANU-PF ever demonstrated much interest in the political education either of its own members or that of the nation. Even in its own ranks the leadership itself did not inculcate a political consciousness, which might have taken an ideological form and possibly inhibited its personal excesses. In fact, true to its roots in colonial British philistinism, ZANU-PF seemed, as a party, to be suspicious of political consciousness and ideological thought. Its major emphasis seemed to be on the creation and preservation, even through violence, fear and coercion, of a compliant and obedient support base.

Nowhere was this more evident than in the role of the party youth. Direction came from the top and, far from being the vanguard in the generation of political strategy or ideas or even young watch dogs of the revolution, as say in the case of the ANC Youth League in the 1950s or even in a perverted sense that of the post-Mbeki period, the ZANU-PF youth came to be an instrument of support and coercion in the interests of the party leadership. Here again it seems that the military culture of the party inhibited any other possibilities. Perhaps the achievements of the Youth League in South Africa had only been possible in a civilian movement like the ANC in the 1950s or outside party structures as in the time of the mass democratic movement in the 1980s. The insubordination of a Malema within the structures of Umkhonto we Sizwe, for instance, would have been an easy matter to deal with. He would simply have been regarded as a mutineer and subjected to military disciplinary procedures.

The situation of women in ZANU-PF is revealing. The ZANU-PF government framed and implemented some of the most progressive policies and legislation relating to gender equality and the protection of women from abuse in Africa. Many women began to come to the fore and occupy positions of authority and power. Yet, dating back to the days of the struggle, despite the relative equality they achieved in the field as combatants, their actual status in the camps and in the movement was depressingly different.

Female ex-combatants in our political theatre group, Zambuko/Izibuko, who had been in Mozambique, told of how women comrades were regularly treated as sexual perks for the male leadership. This was corroborated by Fay Chung, who was once a ZANU-PF cabinet minister, in her book on the struggle, *Re-living the Second Chimurenga*. She recalls how on one occasion Josiah Tongogara[14]

14 *Josiah Tongogara, commander of ZANLA, who was killed in a road accident in Mozambique a few days after the signing of the Lancaster House Agreement.*

himself arrived at a camp in Mozambique with other male *chefs* and demanded to be provided with 'warm blankets'. Women comrades were regularly parcelled out to *chefs* for their sexual convenience. This tradition continued in Zimbabwe itself after Independence where party and government officials when visiting schools or even spending some time in the locality, sometimes demanded that headmasters provide them with schoolgirls. I have this information from a long-serving headmaster who resigned from the service on account of this abuse.

In other words, both before and after Independence many of those with the power used their positions to pursue totally selfish agendas which were quite in opposition to the declarations, policies and ideals of the party. It was a painful fact that the very people who had ostensibly fought for the liberation of their country and a better life for all, betrayed the cause, seemingly with no conscience or sense of guilt. Women in power were no exception.

Because of the general lack of theoretical political thought, ZANU-PF had no concept whatsoever of the role of the arts, literature, culture and intellectual production in the development of a sovereign democratic state. In fact, so ignorant were government minsters and the party itself of this that in the main the very concept 'culture' was habitually equated with *chivanhu*, the traditional (and often ossified) notions of Shona *tsika* or Ndebele *amasiko* i.e. pre-colonial customs and practices. Development was always and exclusively equated with material progress or services. Politics was equated with party or international politics. Everyone knew that the *chimurenga* songs had played a vital part on the road to liberation and after the attainment of Independence the songs continued to be trotted out at political events and during campaigns. However, as we shall see later, ZANU-PF was not able to extrapolate on this so as to forge a theoretical understanding of the role of culture in struggle and generally in social development. Whereas, for instance, they kept a tight rein on political content in the electronic and print media they controlled, arts and culture, seen as entertainment, were totally disregarded and as long as plays or songs did not attack the party – and even when they did - as far as they were concerned, anything could go. To them, it appeared, art was frivolous, of no account and something they knew very little about. This attitude, already established in the first decade of Independence, became disastrous in the third (see Chapter 26).

As for the concept of 'cultural revolution', ZANU-PF behaved as if the concept did not exist or if it did it was a lot of hooey. Very little effort was made – and that soon abandoned – to develop a new and liberatory climate of arts, culture and literature. The National Arts Council of Zimbabwe in the thirty four years since 1980 has been a national disgrace. Government consistently did little more than pay the salaries of its staff – if that.

During the liberation war ZANU-PF had operated in the countryside with a strategy of encircling the towns. After Independence, this was its base and it was easy for it to establish an effective structure of party branches in the rural areas. As it had never operated in the same way in the urban areas during the war, it was much more difficult to build a power base there. Initially the urban population gave ZANU-PF its spontaneous – as opposed to organised – support, as did the trade unions. However, though most urban dwellers still had relatively strong ties with the countryside, essentially they had different interests from those of their families in the rural areas and the working class had its own organisational base and a set of basic concerns, which ZANU-PF never seemed to have sufficient time for. Already in the first decade ZANU-PF began to have problems in the urban areas, particularly with the Zimbabwe Council of Trade Unions. (See Chapter 20)

Here again it was a strategic and a theoretical failing that seemed to have inhibited ZANU-PF's performance. ZANU-PF seemed to be quite clear as to how they were going to run the countryside. But it was as if they had never thought about how they were going to handle the urban areas and the trade unions. It was as if they regarded the urban population as simply an extension of the countryside or as people from the rural areas that live in town – and they treated it as such. The party's development programme was very clear when it came to catering for the needs of the rural population and in return it was expected to give the party its unconditional support. Their programme was not so clear when it came to catering for the needs of the urban population - and in particular the workers - yet they expected that they too should give the party their unconditional support. If they did not behave the way rural people did and did not give their unconditional support to the party, they were seen as deracinated, rural people who had become corrupted by city ways – or as in the President's infamous remark, already quoted - '*vanhu vasinamutupo*', people with no totem.

Now after this litany of weaknesses and failures, one may well ask why I supported them – even critically. The answer is that I am a Romantic and an Optimist yet my Romanticism and my Optimism are what is called Revolutionary Romanticism or Optimism. That means I believe that human beings have the capacity to make changes for the better but the process of change is a process of struggle and is rooted in hard work, perseverance and time. As a historical materialist, I do not easily give way to disillusion. I try to understand what is going on in terms of historical imperatives and the constraints and limitations of the here and now. As a result, I never expected ZANU-PF to work many more miracles than it did.

But work miracles it had most certainly done. By the end of the first decade, ZANU-PF had liberated Zimbabwe from colonialism and from the clutches of that most anal of all racist fuddy-duddies, Ian Smith, and his devoted band of white supremacists, the Rhodies. That was a miracle – particularly when you remember that Smithy had said they never would - 'not in a thousand years'. They transformed the lives of millions of Zimbabweans by opening up the country to them so that they could go, live, study, shop, have fun wherever they liked, they could get jobs they could never get before, they could go to school, they could get treatment for their ailments, enjoy their music, drive their cars where they wished – excluding of course the road that went past the President's official residence in Harare after 6pm! The ZANU-PF government subsidised the people's food, it provided free education for their children, it ensured that the sick could get treatment no matter how poor, it took care of them in times of drought – but, above all, it made it possible for the people to feel free and equal in the land of their birth. All that was a miracle. And for those miracles ZANU-PF deserved my support.

But they also did some other very big things for which few now give them much credit. At Independence, they did not take their revenge on Smith, his cronies, the population, both black and white, which had opposed them, and murderous military units like the Selous and Grey Scouts. They exacted no revenge for massacres like Chimoio, Nyadzonia, Tembue and Mkushi or for atrocities like mineshafts stuffed with corpses that had been dissolved in acid. They let bygones be bygones – in contrast to Ian Smith who, unrepentant and recalcitrant as ever, spent the rest of his life on his farm in Shurugwi, lost in his delusionary fantasies, writing books which extolled his white Rhodesia and complained that he had been betrayed.

ZANU-PF assisted Frelimo with their army and air force in the defence of revolutionary Mozambique against the ravages of one of the most savage proxy armies ever unleashed on a non-compliant government – Renamo. ZANU-PF and PF-ZAPU frustrated the efforts of apartheid South Africa and others to instigate a similar catastrophe in Zimbabwe and avoided a bloody civil war by joining forces in the Unity Accord, an achievement the significance of which is not often justly acknowledged.

In the international domain, Zimbabwe pursued an exemplary path, fearlessly denouncing injustice and supporting progressive causes. It supported the struggles for liberation in Namibia and South Africa and gave its solidarity to the people of Palestine in their tragic plight. It forged close ties with Cuba and played an active and influential role in the Non-Aligned Movement (NAM), hosting the 8th summit of the organisation in Harare in 1986. Along with Namibia and Angola it played a historic role in thwarting the Balkanisation of the Congo.

ZANU-PF was an instrument of history. As such it brought about a fundamental and inevitable change for the better. Then paradoxically it set up the contradictions within itself and in Zimbabwe which call for a resolution, a resolution that ZANU-PF in its present form cannot possibly oversee. If this is not an example of the dialectic at work, I don't know what is!

Zimbabwe was founded but the teeth were sown. Zimbabwe is now faced with the agonising realisation that progress is paved with paradox. ZANU-PF, which always looked for enemies and sell-outs on the outside – and found as many as it could possibly expect – became in later years its own worst enemy. There is a Pedi expression which translated says: 'When you point a finger, remember that four are pointing at you.' When, in the third decade of Independence, the enemies from without pressed hard, it was the enemy within, the sell-out within, the *chiconhoca*[15] in ZANU-PF itself, that opened the door either for ZANU-PF's neo-colonial enemies or a quite new democratic force with the people's agenda at heart, to enter.

Since then, ZANU-PF has fought and triumphantly won a reprieve through its decisive victory over the MDC in the election of 2013. But the Third Chimurenga has not yet quite come to a successful or definitive conclusion and only the first Battle for Zimbabwe has been fought. The outcome is pending and what it will be - only time can tell.

15 *Chiconhoca* – a term used by Frelimo in Mozambique for 'the enemy within'

DIEPE GROND – THE SECOND DECADE

PART THREE

ESAP (ECONOMIC STRUCTURAL ADJUSTMENT PROGRAMME)

Ee! Satane Asvika Pano (Yes, Satan is here.)

From 'stille water' to 'diepe grond' - more and more the muck below, more and more the unfinished business, the detritus of colonial deformation, the traps and betrayals, the divisions and unhealed bitternesses, came to the surface and squelched the fresh hopes and dreams of Independence and Freedom. In their place, there was ESAP.

Zimbabwe had been independent for a decade. Though a lot had been achieved, the country had overspent and was in debt. It turned to the International Monetary Fund, the IMF. The IMF imposed a Structural Adjustment Programme (SAP). In Zimbabwe, they added an 'e', standing for 'Economic' at the beginning and so it became ESAP. It wasn't long before the inevitable consequences began to manifest themselves as they had more or less wherever a SAP had been applied. The consequences in Zimbabwe were both economic and social. The situation became so disturbing that government began by modifying and then scrapping ESAP – not however before the damage was done. The issue of the land, which in the first decade had not made much progress, began to hot up towards the end of the second. Zimbabwe's armed intervention in the Democratic Republic of the Congo and the listing of farms for compulsory acquisition with compensation drove the last nail into the coffin of IMF co-operation. In fact, everything looked very much like a shaping up for war – the war that, in fact, when it did come, was called the Third Chimurenga. *The events of these years also led to the Zimbabwe Council of Trade Unions (ZCTU) founding a political party, the Movement for Democratic Change (MDC). Villagers and liberation war veterans began to move onto farms and the Constitution Consultation process resulted in a referendum, which was followed by general elections, which shook the ruling party.*

CHAPTER TEN:

END OF THE HONEYMOON

'The muck below'

Zimbabweans had in many ways been economically empowered. Some of their horizons had expanded but others not. A lot of whites had left after independence but those that remained, sometimes in collaboration with largely British and South African corporates, still owned and controlled the bulk of the economy. In the early years there was some of the usual 'fronting' – bringing in black figureheads. However it was the whites who commanded the heights in sectors such as banking, finance and insurance, light and heavy industry, manufacturing, tourism and real estate. Above all, they had the land and the agricultural sector, the mainstay of the Zimbabwean economy, was in their hands. The mines too were largely owned by foreign interests. That left only government, parastatals, non-productive businesses, like rural bus companies and bottle stores, and cottage industries in the hands of the black majority. Outside of these, owners, employers and top management were white.

Meanwhile the people in the countryside, despite the benefits Independence had brought, were disappointed that it had not brought them the land. Thousands of them, including the chiefs and whole clans, had been forcefully removed from fertile and well-watered areas to dry and arid ones in order to make way for the white farmers. In the process they had not only lost the means of their subsistence but also their ancestral homes and were alienated from their shrines and the graves of their ancestors. During the war they had been promised that the land would come back to them. This was one of the main themes of the all-night *pungwes* in the countryside and a central plank in the propaganda pumped out by the liberation forces.

Shortly after Independence some jumped the gun and took matters into their own hands by occupying white farms or moving back onto the land they had held before their removal. They were surprised to find that the party - now the ruling party - which had promised them the land and which they had supported for that reason either persuaded or forced them to leave and return to the places where they had been dumped by the whites during the colonial era. Under the Lancaster House agreement, the land could only be acquired according to the 'willing seller/willing buyer' principle. The British did make some money available for this and farms were acquired. But then the British stopped the funding, claiming that the land acquired was going to party heavyweights and cronies.

But in 1990, the end of the first decade of Independence, the ten years were over. There was no longer any legal reason why ZANU-PF shouldn't move forward on a number of issues that Lancaster House had put the brakes on. This was the opportunity for dramatic changes. The land question could now be settled. A new constitution could be crafted. The indigenous majority could move to take a greater stake in the economy.

It didn't happen. Tragically, one reason for the lack of action was surely the fact that during the first decade of independence the petit-bourgeois leadership and government officials had been able to help themselves. Independence had brought many of them most of the gains that had been fought for – nice houses, cars, children at posh private schools and jobs with lots of potential for unofficial income-generation. In fact, the phenomenon noted and described in many other African countries, had already taken root in Zimbabwe – namely, the petit- bourgeois leadership of the nationalist movement had got its hands on political power and government and was busy accumulating wealth and privilege, in other words, becoming a bureaucratic bourgeoisie and in some cases even a bourgeoisie proper. *Gutsaruzhinji* (satisfaction of the majority), while still the official slogan, had been replaced by *gutsamaChef* (satisfaction of the party heavyweights). Very few of them seemed to have much stomach for exerting themselves or rocking the gravy boat in order to bring commensurate benefits either to the ex-combatants, many of whom had been simply dumped after demobilisation, or to the peasant masses, who had sacrificed so much for the struggle.

However, before this critique degenerates into a stereotype, it is important to record that although the enrichment of the few was probably a factor that inhibited dramatic popular changes on the expiry of the Lancaster House Agreement, it was not the whole story. It is a fact that it was Government's efforts to redress the inequalities and imbalances of the inherited colonial dispensation in favour of the *povo* that was partly responsible for plunging the country into debt and into the arms of the International Monetary Fund. In other words, there was another facet to the paradox referred to earlier. While at the level of official policy and programmes government really did try to bring the benefits of independence to the masses, the rural masses in particular, individuals in government undermined and betrayed the ideals and objectives of the liberation struggle through abuse of power, corruption and their own pursuit of private wealth and privilege.

In any case, the whole question of taking advantage of the expiry of the Lancaster House Agreement to bring about revolutionary transformation was really taken out of Government's hands by the state the economy was in by the end of the first decade – and it was partly government's efforts to bring the benefits of independence to the people that were responsible for this.

Years later, the white-owned South African press maligned Thabo Mbeki for his 'quiet diplomacy'. In his rather highfalutin and abstruse way - therefore little heeded – he explained that the main reason the Zimbabwean economy had got into the mess it did, was the over-spending on education and services in the first decade, which was not matched by a commensurate increase in national productivity. Mbeki with his usual perspicacity had put his finger on the problem. The problem was that Zimbabwe had tried to replicate on a mass scale after independence what had been possible on an elite scale before - despite the fact that the economy had not expanded sufficiently after independence to pay for it.

The government had presided over a dramatic expansion of the Civil Service. This included teachers and, owing to the rapid growth of the school system, their numbers had increased greatly. Government was swollen too as a result of having to accommodate party members and supporters as well as manage and staff the developing public and social services. Then there were the programmes in education, health, electricity and road infrastructure. True to their reputation but also because government subsidised and determined prices, the parastatals that provided utilities and services, lost money. On top of all this, there were crippling droughts in 1982-4 and 1987 and government had to utilise precious resources in providing drought relief.

The defence bill too rocketed as a result of destabilisation by *apartheid* South Africa, including Zimbabwe's military involvement in Mozambique. Independent Zimbabwe, to a great extent independent because of Frelimo and Mozambique's support, went to Frelimo's aid, provided air fire power and fought side by side with them in a number of campaigns aimed at rooting out Renamo bases, in particular the taking of Renamo's main base in the Gorongoza National Park.

One might have expected that after sanctions imposed on Rhodesia had fallen away, there would have been a dramatic expansion in the economy, fuelled by increased production, trade and investment. That this did not happen to the extent it might have, was, as far as I could see, due to a number of factors, including the volatile political situation in the country, the talk of socialism, ZANU-PF's nationalist regulations relating to investment, bureaucratic inefficiency and the government's forthright anti-imperialist pronouncements and alignments in the international terrain.

However, a major factor was the fact that that the economy was still in white hands. My general impression was that many of the whites were never reconciled to the loss of 'their' Rhodesia or to acceptance of a black-ruled Zimbabwe and this attitude would seem to have conditioned the behaviour of many white commercial farmers and businessmen. There was a time, before 1994 when democratic change came to South Africa, when the markets of Africa opened up opportunities for Zimbabwean expertise, business and manufacturing. South Africa, Zimbabwe's main competitor, was still restricted by its *apartheid* status and not acceptable in the rest of Africa. Zimbabwe with its relatively well-developed agricultural and manufacturing infrastructure had what seems to me to have been a historic opportunity to become the springboard for much profitable economic expansion into Africa, similar to what the South Africans achieved after 1994. Although the South African economy is still very much in the hands of the whites, as it was in Zimbabwe, there seems to have been one basic difference. In South Africa, the white entrepreneur was committed to take advantage of the opportunities the new South African dispensation offered and fully prepared to explore and exploit them. I would have thought that white Zimbabweans, who still controlled the vast bulk of commercial production, in agriculture, manufacturing and industry, would have seized the opportunity to profit from markets in Mozambique, Zambia, Malawi and, especially after Zimbabwe's intervention, the Democratic Republic of the Congo and elsewhere. But my impression was that most whites were disgruntled and bitter. The predominant attitude seemed to have been a yearning for the Rhodesia that was. The overall impression I gained was that in the face of black majority rule, most of them seemed more ready to shake their heads and tut over the shortcomings of the country under its black government, hoping it would fail, than energetically work to take advantage of its success and commit themselves to contributing to the general prosperity of the new nation. They seemed to share the spirit in which their erstwhile, idolised leader, Ian Smith, continued to moan and lament the passing of Rhodesia and foster the illusion that things were better for everyone before 'the great betrayal' – the title of a book he wrote.[16]

16 Apropos Ian Smith and his book, I once had a rather bizarre experience in a Johannesburg television studio. I had visited the studio on business in the company of a well-known Zimbabwean film-maker. While we were there, we heard that they were expecting Ian Smith to pitch up at any time for an interview on his new book – the one I referred to above. We were invited to witness the interview. As we entered the sound booth from which we were to watch the interview, a black television technician approached me and began wiring me up with microphones. Neither of us could understand what was going in until suddenly the penny dropped. The technician had heard that there was some old white man called Ian Smith coming from Zimbabwe for an interview. He saw me and immediately jumped to the conclusion that I must be he! Something I will also never forget was the look on the faces of two rather handsome white women, who sat with us in the control room during the interview. Clearly for them they were listening to a hero and nostalgia and hero worship shone from their faces as on the other side of the glass partition Ian Smith spoke of what a great job the Rhodies had done and how Britain messed it all up.

Thus, by the end of the decade, expenditure had increased dramatically and this expenditure was not matched by a corresponding rise in production and investment. In fact, the economy at the end of the decade was not essentially a great deal larger than the economy that had previously supported the 'standards' of a small white minority. Real growth for the period averaged between 3 and 4 percent per annum. Though this did constitute slow but solid growth, it meant that the national economy was not yet in a position to finance the democratisation of the country. The contradiction between the determination to expand access to education, health, housing, electricity, roads, transport etc. and at the same time 'keep up standards', though well-intentioned, was not only an impossible dream but also a mistaken and dangerous policy.

In summary, then, the dramatic increase in expenditure that took place in the first decade of Independence was not matched by a correspondingly dramatic increase in income and the tax base. In order to cope, Zimbabwe had to rely on foreign aid and donations - and borrowing. By the end of the decade, to sustain development and balance the books, Zimbabwe needed to borrow. The government decided, as many before them, to throw themselves into the arms of the International Monetary Fund (IMF) and the World Bank – and soon found themselves wrapped in the coils of that notorious anaconda, the Economic Structural Adjustment Programme (or ESAP), which at that time these institutions inevitably imposed on so-called 'developing economies'.

ESAP was introduced in 1990. Once in those coils, there was no longer any question of taking advantage of the opportunities to transform Zimbabwe which the expiry of the Lancaster House Agreement made theoretically possible. In fact, the opposite was true. ESAP introduced a transformation of its own, a transformation that was not only the virtual negation of what the expiry of the Lancaster House Agreement made possible but one that was possibly as, if not more, revolutionary than that brought about by independence itself!

The second decade of Zimbabwe's independence saw the optimism and euphoria that masked the underlying contradictions, rapidly and traumatically evaporate as the society moved ever more precipitately towards bitterness, violence and polarisation. Zimbabwe began to reap more and more the historical harvest of the dragon's teeth and less and less the golden apples. It had been a mixed harvest from the beginning. Yes, there had been Gukurahundi but there had also been the Peace Accord. Yes, the students at the University had become disaffected and their annual rituals of protest had commenced. Yes, the frustrations were being felt, the rural people wondered why they were not getting the land, the debt was mounting, corruption beginning its process of rot.[17] But the overwhelming feeling of the first decade of independence was still that an extraordinary revolution had taken place. There had been an exhilarating tide of black freedom, empowerment, education, enrichment and opportunity. There had been sweeping social changes. There was still hope in the country – it 'springs eternal in the human breast', the poet, Alexander Pope, rightly warned – and there had been, relatively, '*stille water*'. Now for the '*diepe grond*'.

17 For instance, the Willowgate scandal in 1988-9 in which government ministers abused a motor vehicle purchase facility in order to make a profit. Enos Nkala and Maurice Nyagumbo were among those implicated. The latter committed suicide as a result. The journalists who broke the story lost their jobs.

CHAPTER ELEVEN:

ESAP AND THE NEW WORLD ORDER

The 'Satan' Agenda

> *In the 1980s, Zimbabwe had been a star performer in Africa in the provision of social services and in the reconstruction and development of its public infrastructure. Average life expectancy was on the rise; childhood mortality was down, and other measuring sticks such as the literacy rate and the technical skills capacity were encouraging.*
>
> \- Richard Saunders

The International Monetary Fund's Structural Adjustment Programmes (SAPs) were packages of economic reforms aimed at 'liberalising' and 'deregulating' closed and controlled economies. It was a key instrument in the establishment of the New World Order, a euphemism for the post-Cold War world in which every obstacle in the way of free and untrammelled exploitation of the world's resources and the amassment of wealth by international capital were to be removed.

Generally, as far as I could see, states that closed and controlled their economies mostly did so in order to protect their markets and resources from exploitation by bigger and more powerful foreign economies. Such states hoped to grow their own economies, increase their own productivity and direct their trade and the utilisation of their resources towards their own benefit – either that of a corrupt local oligarchy or the people or sometimes both.

They knew that their national economies were still weak and could not compete with the economic big guns. They feared that if they opened up their economies to unrestricted entry and freedom of foreign operations, they would be overwhelmed, their own economic development would be pushed aside and their markets and resources exploited not for the good or in the interests of themselves and their own countries but rather for the profit of the foreigners in question.

However, looked at from the other side, the big economies saw the controls and restrictions on their ability to trade, invest and make profit as being an 'unfair' denial of their rights, which are enshrined in the doctrine of 'Free Trade'. In order to have protectionist controls and restrictions lifted, there were a number of options open to them. These included diplomacy and advocacy, media campaigns, sanctions, regime change, military force – and debt. This was where the IMF stepped in. But in cases where the troublesome state was not prepared to enter the fateful arms of the IMF, there was an array of other more drastic measures that could be fallen back on, often leading to regime change.

One of the components of the regime change strategy was to finance aid and development organisations, the so-called NGOs (Non-Governmental Organisations), many of which were not non-governmental at all but in fact agencies of their national governments. In response to the availability of funding and donations, local NGOs sprang up, ready to do the work on the ground. Their development programmes, which ranged from genuine development and humanitarian projects to others which had more to do with regime change, were tied to their sponsors' agenda. In the process they nursed a bed of nationals who became willing accomplices and who had a vested interest in hostility to the local government - as they knew which side of their bread was buttered. This meant that when regime change became expedient, there would exist within the country a willing stratum of compliant cadres.

From time to time governments cropped up which were troublesome enough to require direct steps aimed at regime change. In such cases, two options were available. One was force, involving direct invasion, as in the case of Iraq and Libya, or by proxies, as in the case of the Democratic Republic of the Congo (see Chapter 14). The other option was somehow to get the people themselves to bring the change about. This could be achieved by creating surrogate bandit armies such as the Contras in Nicaragua, MNR or Renamo in Mozambique and UNITA in Angola, or through sanctions. This form of persuasion was most effective when banditry and sanctions worked hand in hand – along with an unrelenting media campaign and a barrage of demands for freedom of expression, human rights, the rule of law – and 'free and fair' elections. Thus the fly was caught in a pincer grip. Life was made so hard for the local population that the people ended up blaming all their hardships on the government and in their yearning for peace and release from their suffering, obligingly overthrew the government themselves in the 'free and fair' elections the fly would ultimately lose.

Of course, the concept of 'free and fair' elections is quite subjective. As the decision as to which elections will be 'free and fair' and which not, rests with the spider, basically no election which the fly wins can ever hope to be 'free and fair'. It could win as many elections as it liked. Such elections would, by definition, not be free or fair. The only way to qualify for the 'free and fair' stamp of approval was for the fly to lose. This fact and the fact that no election can be said to be 'free and fair' when counter-revolutionary violence, sanctions and overwhelming media propaganda all favour one side, was conveniently ignored by the regime-changers (see Chapters 21 and 26). The ultimate defeat of the Sandinistas is a classic illustration of this technique.

The above scenarios are extreme ones. They were applied to a fly which was a particular nuisance and which would have no truck with either the capitalist debt web or the IMF's financial pills. In less extreme scenarios, the IMF's SAPS were perfectly adequate instruments of regime change and many observers have noted that among the inevitable consequences of the implementation of a SAP was the fall of the government.[18] It is not difficult to understand why.

When a Third World fly found itself caught in the debt web and turned for a bail-out to the IMF, the IMF would characteristically agree on the condition that the fly swallow its bait and 'reform' its economy. This 'reform' took the form of a Structural Adjustment Programme. A Structural Adjustment Programme was accompanied by a number of standard policy conditions. A key condition was that the role of the state be minimised. Now in many weaker economies such as those in Africa, which did not possess a strong and entrenched indigenous industrial, manufacturing and mining class, there existed no coherent or powerful structure that could protect the national political and economic interest - with the exception of the state itself. In other words, to be more specific, only the government could stand up to the powerful capitalist interests wanting to penetrate the economy.

In the case of a government having come to power on the back of a popular and nationalist struggle, the conditions dictated by the IMF caused serious problems as the IMF package required the abandonment of the very goals for which the struggle had been

18 *See Mlambo, Alois,* The Economic Structural Adjustment Programme: The Zimbabwean Case, *1990-1995 (UZ Publications)*

fought. Thus, obviously, for those wishing to penetrate the economies of such states, their governments were seen as target number one.

It is surely not for nothing that the propaganda agents of these big economies, such as their television stations and newspapers, have laboured untiringly for decades to discredit governments in Africa. It was part of the softening up process, rather similar to the role the missionaries played in preparing the ground for colonialism. It set up an ideological justification for intervention in African countries and weakened the only structures in these countries that could even begin to resist. Populations in the West have been fed, year in year out, with negative stories about Africa and in particular about how bad African governments are. The fact that in many cases their propaganda has had an element of truth simply made their task easier as African elites played into their hands. The readership, viewership and audiences of African media are in the main confined to their own nation states. Despite efforts to establish it, there never has been an effective Pan-African print or electronic media agency comparable to the BBC, CNN or Al-Jazeera. Therefore Africans have always been largely dependent on the media instruments of the big economies and many Africans have swallowed what they were dished up with.

Zimbabwe at the end of the first decade of Independence had not yet become the very troublesome fly it later became but it did seem to have a nationalist agenda and it was indulging in anti-Imperialist international rhetoric and unfriendly international orientations. Efforts by apartheid South Africa – and who knows who else? - to create a Nicaragua-type situation had failed with the signing of the Unity Accord between ZANU-PF and PF-ZAPU and the eradication of Super-ZAPU. However, as we have seen, the Zimbabwean fly had fallen into the debt web and it turned to the IMF to get it out. At this I hear echoes of an old jingle my dad used to trot out when the occasion moved him: "Will you walk into my parlour/ Said the spider to the fly."[19]

So along comes the IMF with its ESAP pill. I am not an economist and the pill of the IMF needs an economics laboratory technician to analyse. This is the way one such technician described it as it applied to Zimbabwe:

> *Trade and currency de-regulation, devaluation of the Zimbabwe dollar, movement towards high real interest rates, the lifting of price controls, chopping of "social spending" and removal of consumer subsidies.. .increasing emphasis on reduction of the government deficit, civil service reform and shedding of public enterprises...finally, a string of large loans and credit facilities from the Bank, the IMF and international donors, aimed at supporting the country's balance of payments and government's plans for substantial private sector infrastructural development...estimated (at) roughly US$3 billion over five years ...from overseas donors to make the reforms work. Zimbabwe would spend its way into a new free market on borrowed money(!)*
>
> Richard Saunders (1996)

Swallowing the ESAP pill was intended to induce, even compel, governments to abdicate their former and expected paternal role and cease actively to intervene - or 'meddle', as the IMF would put it - in the economy and social welfare. Policies government had previously pursued in the interests of the well-being of the people had to be abandoned. Instead some of the basic measures that ESAP demanded were that government cut expenditure and

19 I was a child then and only found out recently that it comes from "The Spider and the Fly", a poem by Mary Howitt (1821). I would have said it was from an old music hall ditty myself, especially as my dad was a singer.

downsize the civil service, increase taxes, sell off state assets, remove food subsidies, place the burden of health and education on the backs of the people, permit companies to retrench their workers, devalue the Zimbabwe dollar - by a massive 40%, as it happened - and give foreign big business a free reign to own, invest and trade with minimum restriction in the local economy.

In the face of its need to get out of the debt web, the fly did more or less what it was told – and in the process found itself even more firmly enmeshed. Government believed that the introduction of ESAP would transform the rather sluggish economy, which was characterised by a stagnant local market, production bottlenecks and rising unemployment, by modernising it and making it more competitive. This they hoped to achieve through boosting exports as a result of a more dynamic involvement of the private sector and increased foreign investment. As Richard Saunders put it, Zimbabwe hoped to solve its debt problem by borrowing and, naturally, by borrowing it just made its debt problem worse.

Government began to implement the ESAP agenda. Prices immediately shot up, basic foodstuffs became too expensive to pay for, people lost their jobs, real incomes declined dramatically, health and education became no longer a right but increasingly a privilege and this impacted on health, resulting in a rise in the percentages of stunted growth and malnutrition. The formal economy began to collapse and the informal mushroomed - and so on. Soon it was a case of survival of the fittest and every man for himself. On top of this there were the droughts and the dreaded new pandemic of HIV/AIDS at a time when nutrition levels were deteriorating. The people became confused. What had happened? Where was 'the people's government', the government they had overwhelmingly voted for?

As usual the ZANU-PF government had implemented ESAP without ever really explaining to the people why they had introduced it and what it was all about. As a result, the people blamed government for what had happened. The people were suffering. It was the government's fault. When after some time the people began to see what this ESAP was all about, they came up with their own explanation as to what the acronym, ESAP, stood for. They said ESAP stands for '*Ee, Satane Asvika Pano*', which means 'O, yes, Satan has reached this place' or more loosely 'Satan has come to Zimbabwe'. They called ESAP Satan and they blamed government for unleashing it on them - and that was the fertile ground in which a new opposition party, initially based in the trades union, was to grow. The ground was particularly fertile in the towns, where the depredations of ESAP were most acutely felt and where support for ZANU-PF was most fickle. Opposition to ZANU-PF was greatly aided and abetted by the NGOs and the bed of nationals they had nursed, who, as I have already pointed out, became willing accomplices in the regime change agenda. They too were based in towns, Harare in most cases.

By the end of the first five years of ESAP, Zimbabwe had implemented much of what the IMF's reform package required of it. There were still significant aspects where progress had been either slow or non-existent, privatisation, significantly, being one of them. Some of this could be put down to bureaucratic delays and inefficiency but others seemed to reflect a genuine reluctance within the ruling party to comply. I personally cannot believe that the ruling party had been unanimous in the first place about swallowing the IMF pill. I have a hunch that some people must have had to do a lot of talking to get the wily old revolutionary, Gushungo, and some of his more cagey comrades to allow his Zimbabwe to swallow the IMF's bait. But, as I mention later, round about this time Mugabe seemed to be sliding into a state of somnolence and senility from which he only seemed to snap out when people started taking over the farms.

It looked very much like some in ZANU-PF had only implemented ESAP with reluctance and that there was by no means general consensus within the ruling party as to its being the right way to go. There were still those who could recognise Imperialism when they saw it. It had not escaped their notice, for instance, that while ESAP was leading to a general deterioration in the lives and fortunes of the majority, it was suiting the white minority very nicely. The six thousand white farmers, who dominated commercial agriculture, were getting far better prices for their crops. They had much freer access to foreign currency and there were greater opportunities to spirit their earnings out of the country into foreign banks.

Experience of the relations between government and the people and, in particular, the nature of the people's perceptions of government, in Ethiopia, Zimbabwe and recently South Africa, has taught me two lessons. Firstly, governments are not monolithic. Yes, the ruling party may control government but government is not only made up of party members. Often only the ministers at the top could be said to be genuine party members. For many others, 'support' of government may be either simply time-serving or in actual fact a cloak for opposition. As a result when 'government' does not do what it ought to, one has to remember that in dealing with government or trying to understand its actions, one is not in actual fact dealing with 'government' but with the people in it.

The second lesson is that in countries like the ones mentioned above, the people tend to see things in purely national terms. Their perception rarely wanders beyond their borders. And because they see government as responsible for their country and the situation in it, they blame it for everything that goes wrong - which is obviously a great plus for those in the country who are in cahoots with outside forces, or for those from outside who oppose the government. As a result, the outside forces can get away with any amount of skulduggery and the people will blame it all on the government.

The lapse of the Lancaster House Agreement had been an opportunity for the implementation of the agenda of the liberation struggle. The IMF had little interest in that agenda – except to replace it. There must have been many, both in government and especially in the party, who would have preferred to junk ESAP and go instead for an economic policy based on the empowerment of the majority, what came to be indigenisation, black ownership of the means of production and, above all, reclamation of the stolen land. By opening the economy up to the vast majority that had historically been excluded, the grounds could have been laid for a far larger and more prosperous economy than that inherited from the Rhodesians – and one that would be sovereign, independent and in the interests of the people. So when Zimbabwe's implementation of ESAP was characterised from time to time by prevarication, I think it is likely that some of it at least could be put down to these internal contradictions.

After the shocks of the first few years of implementing ESAP, the government came up with another plan, an incongruous compromise called ZIMPREST. Government still considered it crucial to retain IMF support and therefore Zimbabwe was constrained to continue with ESAP. However it was becoming difficult to resist other considerations. ZIMPREST was announced in 1998 but was billed as the next phase of ESAP, 1996-2000. The fact that it was late might have been an indication of the degree of disagreement there had been on the way forward. While ZIMPREST professed to be furthering the process of economic reform in the spirit of

ESAP, it also included two other considerations, more closely linked to the realities on the ground – the first being indigenization and the second government action on the HIV/AIDS pandemic.

As a result, Zimbabwe's relationship with the IMF was becoming somewhat strained. For instance, there was a contradiction between, on the one hand, selling off government assets and denationalising the parastatals and, on the other hand, implementing a policy of black empowerment and indigenisation. Selling off in a deregulated economic environment would hand even more of the economy either into the hands of local whites or their foreign cousins. As opposed to this, the indigenisation agenda demanded that, if assets and parastatals were to be up for grabs, those doing the grabbing had to be black Zimbabweans.

Nevertheless Zimbabwe was still doing enough to retain the support of the IMF but the contradictions between what had to be done to placate the IMF and what had to be done to honour pre-ESAP commitments were sharpening. The first manifestation of this was the increasing militancy and dissatisfaction of the abandoned liberation war veterans, who were now threatening to go back to the bush and fight the struggle all over again, this time against the leadership that had previously led it. The second was Zimbabwe's intervention, along with Namibia and Angola in the Democratic Republic of Congo. The way government handled these two situations led to the end of IMF and the international capitalist community's support for Zimbabwe's economy as well as to the end of ESAP. The government incurred considerable expense by sending its troops and air force into the Congo and subsequently endangered the economy still further by agreeing to a completely unbudgeted payout to the liberation war veterans. And so the IMF was able to cite, as the justification for its withdrawal of support, Zimbabwe's breach of the rules of dependency housekeeping – when as we shall see its withdrawal of support was motivated by quite other interests.

Earlier I had mentioned the revolutionary transformation in Zimbabwean society that ESAP was responsible for. Nowhere was this more apparent than in the mushrooming of the informal economy and with it what I have called the 'magabaisation' of society itself.

CHAPTER TWELVE:

THE INFORMAL ECONOMY

The irresistable rise of Magaba

There is one place in Harare that, if you are a Zimbabwean and have never been to or never been a customer of, you have led a rarified existence and Harare knows not you. That place is Magaba. '*Magaba*' means 'receptacles' – and especially in this day and age, 'tins' – and the place, Magaba, is definitely characterised by tin, tin of all sorts. Actual tins, tins made into something else, objects made from tin, corrugated iron and all sorts of other tinny objects, like motor car rims and hubcaps. But *magaba* are not the only things that characterise the place. In Magaba, wood is to be found in abundance, mostly used – just as much as a lot of the tin of Magaba is also used, often very used. Plastic is another thing – and cardboard. In fact, these are the items that Magaba is constructed from. Magaba is a sprawling maze of alleys and workshops largely constructed of tin, plastic, planks, cardboard and black plastic sheeting. However, in Magaba can also be found PVC. There is copper, there is cement. Another name for Magaba was Siya So, which roughly translated means 'leave things as they are'. And I believe the two names complement each other perfectly.

There is another place similar in some ways to Magaba but dealing in quite different commodities and rackets. This is '*Mupedzanhamo*', which means 'a place to end your troubles'. It is a kind of *musika* (market) where second-hand items of all kinds can be bought as well as various crafts – second hand clothing becoming its main speciality, much to the detriment of Zimbabwe's formal textile and clothing industry. I have bought numerous traditional drums and assorted items needed for traditional dance at *Mupedzanhamo*. Both Magaba and *Mupedzanhamo* are between Harare city centre and Mbare, the oldest township in Harare, and they both suffered grievously during the destructive orgy called *Murambatsvina* (No more rubbish), a debacle that took place in the third decade of Zimbabwe's history. In fact, Magaba was razed to the ground, only to spring up again once the fury had spent itself, as good if not better than new - for in fact it is a place that seems never to have been new.

If ever your hubcaps were stolen or otherwise went missing, or your spare tyre, wheel spanner, jack or any other similar item, Magaba was - and still is - the best place to find a replacement. It is quite possible that you will, unwittingly, simply be buying back what used to be yours in the first place. But that is better than going without, isn't it? The only other place I can compare Magaba with is the Mercato in Addis Ababa, which is the largest – or was when I was there – covered market in Africa. The Mercato combined Magaba and *Mupedzanhamo* and included a lot more. It is said that during the revolution in the 1970s, whole tanks would go into the Mercato and disappear without any trace at all.

When you arrived at Magaba, especially if you are a tall white man, you were surrounded by up to thirty eager, quite aggressive and obviously desperate young men. 'Pressure' was king here as each clamoured, pushed and bullied for your custom. I evolved a way of dealing with this. I would select, through my car window, arbitrarily from the crowd, two people whose faces I liked or did not – that was not the point. The point was to select the faces and then shout to everyone else, preferably in Shona, that you are these young men's customer – as if you already had an arrangement or relationship with them. One needed two young men. One would accompany you into Magaba and lead you to the best places to buy whatever it was you were looking for. The other would guard your car while you were away – which might well have been a case of 'setting a thief to catch a thief'. Sometimes what I said about being someone's customer was genuine. I may have on a previous occasion been conducted round, through or into Magaba by the very same young man or had my car looked after by the very same man whom I had managed to spot in the crowd. On the other hand, they may have been more surprised than anyone that I was their customer. But that didn't matter. They quickly snapped out of their surprise and began loudly confirming to all and sundry that I was indeed their customer. They then firmly dismissed all the others and cleared a path for me to go with the one to do the shopping and to leave the car with the other. The others gave way to them, some because they did not see through the ruse and really thought that I was their customer, others with a smile as they saw right through it but appreciated its ingenuity.

In order to illustrate what Magaba was like, I only have to recall what happened to an equally impecunious artist as myself – the knowledgeable and experienced film maker, Steve Chigorimbo - with a car that he, like me for most of my life, was trying desperately to keep on the road in difficult circumstances. He went to Magaba to buy a tyre. It looked fine, it was fitted for him and off he drove. He didn't get further than *Mupedzanhamo* before it fell apart – and *Mupedzanhamo* is not more that 1 000 metres from Magaba. That it fell apart was not really the salt in the wound. The salt in the wound was the fact that, as he did not know much about prices and assumed that everything in Magaba was cheaper than anywhere else, he had paid more for the tyre than he would have for a brand new one!

Magaba and *Mupedzanhamo* were the spirit and the essence of the informal - and the new decade in Zimbabwe was to see the irresistible rise of the informal, in other words the phenomenon I refer to as 'magabaisation'. Along with it, 'magabaisation' brought, among many other things, the new or greatly expanded phenomena of street kids, vendors, flea markets, *'maCross Border'* (cross-border traders) and *'maCommuter'*(minibus taxis) - in short, the informal sector. The informal sector became an ever increasing feature of Zimbabwean life and culture – and the economy. The informal sector turned the ringing revolutionary slogan 'No taxation without representation' upside down, converting it into something like 'Representation without taxation' – for, as more and more of the economic activity of the country was conducted informally, two things happened. Firstly, it became almost impossible to assess statistically what was going on and therefore plan economic development. This was because informal sector activity is not recorded and therefore is not fed into national statistics. The second was that, though a lot of economic activity may have been taking place, the fiscus did not benefit for the simple reason that the informal sector did not pay taxes. This characteristic of the informal sector was one of the reasons why, when all the experts and pundits in South Africa and elsewhere were confidently and, let's face it, rather gleefully, predicting the collapse, melt-down, implosion – or whatever melodramatic word they liked to come up with – of the Zimbabwean economy, the Zimbabwean economy kept banging along.

In the beginning, there were no street kids as far as I can remember. People parked quite satisfactorily in Harare city centre and put money in the parking meters in the 'usual' orderly way. There were even 'meter maids'. There was almost no double parking. People parked in the parkades the City of Harare provided for the purpose. But then the street kids appeared.[20] To be accurate the phenomenon of children leaving depressed and poverty-stricken

20 See above: Unicef Report (*2001 ZIM: A Study on Street Children in Zimbabwe*)

existences in search of an alternative was not new. Formerly, in the colonial times, the children would get jobs, for example, as garden boys - or cooks in mining settlements, often offering sexual services to the miners, who lived in bachelor settlements or compounds. What was new was that with the removal of the white regime's strict zonal policing, it was now possible for such children to eke out a life in the city streets. With the rise of poverty in the rural areas – most street kids were from there – and more and more breadwinners losing their jobs, families breaking up, prices rising, AIDS wiping out whole generations, child-headed families emerging, lots of children abandoned their homes and went out onto the city streets to scrounge for survival – and in the process made for themselves a dangerous but freer Peter Pan existence than they experienced in the ruins of family life. The advent of ESAP gave this phenomenon a vicious turn of the screw.

It wasn't long before the street kids were joined by what could only be referred to as, in the amusing phrase of the late Zimbabwean performance poet, Elliot Magunje[21], 'street fathers'. In other words, they were not kids. They were adults. It did not take long for them to displace the real street kids, who really were kids - children who lived in the city centre, sleeping there by night and roaming its streets by day searching for food and trying to get what they could out of motorists and passersby. The real street kids were pretty pestiferous in their time and would vent their displeasure in various rather unsociable ways if they did not get what they wanted. But when the 'street fathers' took over, naturally their displeasure could be vented far more effectively. It wasn't long before these 'street fathers' had staked out their claims to the streets of the entire city centre and its peripheries. As the situation in the country

21 Trade-unionist, a member of the political theatre group, Zambuko/Izibuko, Elliot Magunje contracted AIDS and became an AIDS activist, eventually succumbing to it.

got worse and worse what started off as a service or a kind of begging, became intimidation, bag-snatching, stealing cell phones and other 'felonious little crimes'.

Meanwhile, what happened to the real street kids? They were busy ransacking dustbins, especially outside fast food outlets, indulging in petty theft and sometimes begging, when the street fathers gave them a chance. But worst of all was their involvement in child prostitution. The girls could be raped even by their fellow street kids and either paid or just abused by men. The boys were the target of homosexuals, often white men from the suburbs, who would take them home, give them a bath, abuse them, pay them and let them loose again on the streets at night. Despite their hard life, many of them preferred the freedom and adventure of the streets to going to rehabilitation camps or homes and they definitely preferred it to returning to their dysfunctional and/or poverty-stricken homes, from which they had fled in the first place. Efforts to remove them were invariably frustrated by their determination to return.

The vendors were, to a large extent, women, who bought their vegetables relatively cheap at Mbare Musika, the great market in the old high density suburb of Mbare, and then took up their places at various sites throughout the city - on the side of the road, on the pavement or in the parking areas outside shops and supermarkets or near bus ranks. They endured years of running battles with the Municipal Police, who would time and time again chase them away and confiscate their vegetables. The City of Harare would also from time to time build them stalls, which the vendors were supposed to rent. However their profit margins, when they existed, were so small that paying a rent drove them out of business and so they continued to sell in their informal sites, sometimes not very far from the official ones provided by the City, which stood empty and derelict while the unofficial ones thrived. Many a household and the education of many a child in Zimbabwe was supported by these women.

The propinquity of South Africa and Botswana, with their plentiful supply of goods at lower prices in the context of shortages and rising prices in Zimbabwe, as well as the new ability of ordinary black Zimbabweans to get passports and cross borders freely, proved to be a temptation that could not be resisted and the phenomenon of cross-border traders of all races and all classes came into being. Depending on the amount of capital and foreign exchange they could muster, the cross-border traders, travelling by *Kombi*, 'chicken bus' or aeroplane, crossed Zimbabwe's borders with *forex* (foreign exchange, usually either US dollars or South African Rand), some with purses and briefcases full of it, others with a few dirty notes they had somehow cobbled together, or with local products such as crocheted doilies, baskets, crafts and carvings. They came back with office equipment or household appliances, including television sets and fax machines, with motor, industrial or computer spare parts and accessories or with clothing, cosmetics, shoes, wigs, hair pieces, weaves and hair relaxers for sale either in the shops that retailed such or in the flea markets that were beginning to mushroom. Cross-border trade was not only a case of going over the border to buy. Many traders were involved in *bona fide* trade. Once across the border they set up with their commodities, sold them then purchased goods to take home. Soon there was hardly a place in South Africa where one did not see lines of Zimbabwean women selling their goods.

In the first decade of Independence, Zimbabwe had had an efficient urban bus service. In the Rhodesian days, it was segregated and there were buses which journeyed to and from the white suburbs and buses which serviced the black townships. Now black Zimbabweans had moved into the old white suburbs – '*maSabhabha*' – in large numbers. Places with resplendent British names like Balmoral this and Churchill that, Queen Elizabeth this or Princess Margaret that, which had once been exclusively white and in the streets of which no black Zimbabwean dared walk after dark for fear of arrest at the hands of the over-zealous all-white Neighbourhood Watch, were now almost totally inhabited by the descendants of those same black Zimbabweans. In the less affluent former white suburbs, leafy streets, once silent and empty, soon became thoroughfares for people walking this way and that, shady bits of grass for others to rest on and chat, playgrounds for little kids or corners for young people to hang out at. Inside the properties, there was sometimes a commensurate acculturation as backyards were given over to urban agriculture and chicken-rearing and swimming pools either became ideal ponds for fish-farming or were filled in with soil and used to grow maize.

The buses that served these suburbs transported the middle-class residents as well as their children on their way to work and school and back. They also transported their servants, in cases where the servants did not live in, and those who worked in the shops, garages and municipal services or public utilities, like clinics, municipal offices, libraries, telecommunications and electricity, that were to be found in each urban district.

By the second decade, my own children were attending three different schools, Mount Pleasant High and later Girls High for my eldest daughter, Prince Edward for my son and Groombridge Primary for my youngest daughter. The two eldest travelled by bus, which they caught at the bottom of the road every morning at the same time and which they then returned on in the afternoon when school was over. As the youngest was still a little girl and also as travelling by public transport to her school would have meant taking a bus into town and then another to her school, my wife or

I would take her to school and pick her up after school by car. And this was a very satisfactory arrangement.

However there was now an aggressive and profit-driven new kid on the block. As a result of ESAP, the public transport sector had been liberalised and de-regulated. The new kid on the block was the privately-owned Commuter Omnibus - '*Commuter*' or '*Kombi*'. These minibuses of all different conditions and descriptions did not run according to schedule. They stopped whenever and wherever they felt like. They had touts or '*mahwindi*' leaning out of the open passenger door, sometimes hailing potential passengers, sometimes shouting out the destination, and at others insulting, in the fruitiest terms, other drivers, women or anyone who took their fancy. The drivers were usually young boys of dubious accreditation, who also did exactly whatever they liked. Their main goal was very far from trying to ensure their passengers were treated well, were comfortable and arrived at their destinations in one piece. Their main goal was to squeeze as many passengers into the Commuter and do as many trips to and from town as possible in one day. As described earlier, 'culture', '*hunhu*'(the quality of being human), '*tsika*' (traditional ethics), '*kuremekedza*' (respect) or any other relic of social behaviour inherited from a former age, had in the epoch of *maEmergency*, already been eroded by 'Pressure'. In the era of *maCommuter*, everyone forgot that they ever existed. Travelling in a *Commuter* made travelling in the old Emergency seem not so bad after all.

If the rules of decent human relations meant nothing to the *Kombi* drivers and their *hwindis*, it stood to reason that neither did the rules of the road - such as those relating to no stopping zones, lanes, overtaking, traffic lights, bicycle paths, pavements, speed limits or roadworthiness. It is not surprising that *maCommuter* of the 1990's rapidly overtook the army vehicles of the 1980's as the single most frequent cause of urban car accidents and concomitant deaths and injuries. A similar contagion affected intercity and international travel where '*Kombi*' accidents - or accidents involving them – competed with speeding and unroadworthy country buses to become the most frequent and horrific cause of death on the roads.

With the introduction of the Commuters, it was not long before the large buses that had always come on time and carried our children safely to school, were supplemented and then slowly replaced by what were called '*maZupco*'. '*Zupco*' referred to a smaller bus, probably about a 25-seater, which no longer followed a schedule and did not only stop at official bus stops. Obviously, the old bus corporation, also called ZUPCO (Zimbabwe United Passenger Company), had to adapt to the times and compete with the competition. As all the buses that belonged to ZUPCO had 'ZUPCO' written on their sides, they were all technically speaking '*maZupco*'. How and why the people then came to call only the smaller buses '*maZupco*' was one of those mysteries which everywhere seem to characterise the way people do things. However, as the new *maZupco* had been introduced by a properly constituted transport company with an infrastructure, many years experience, maintenance mechanics etc., *maZupco* and *maCommuter* were completely different kettles of fish. *MaZupco* were driven by properly trained bus-drivers and they only stopped at places at which vehicles were permitted to stop by law. The bus drivers – a few of them by now women – were mature adults and by and large polite. The buses too were not usually overcrowded. In short, they were generally safe and decent.

But soon, in the face of competition from the Wild West business practices of *maCommuter*, *maZupco* started to disappear until eventually people were left with nothing but the dreaded Commuter Omnibuses. So instead of my children going down to the end of the road, like little children in Noddy books, to catch nice clean buses, with polite drivers, who always came on time, they were now cast into the maw of the *hwindi*, the lawless young drivers and King Pressure – in short, the world of often filthy and rattletrap *maCommuter*. There were also times when I myself did not have a car and needed to get somewhere. I then also entered the same maw and travelled by Commuter. My children put a stop to that. Knowing full well what travel on *maComuter* actually entailed, as by now they were forced to travel on them, they did not want their dad to have to undergo the same dehumanising experience which they and the masses of Hararians underwent almost every day of their lives.

But that was not all. *MaCommuter* were boarded in the less salubrious parts of the city centre and for young girls to walk from school and through the city streets to Market Square, they had to run a gauntlet of theft, sexual harassment, verbal innuendo, racial taunts and abuse at the hands of street kids, street fathers and other disreputable sections of the population. None of us liked the situation but it seemed there was no alternative until one day I happened to be driving my youngest daughter – by now at Girls' High School - to school and something happened that made me realise that finding an alternative was possibly going to be a matter of life and death.

I was coming down Harare Road, hoping to turn left into Park Lane, go past Queen Elizabeth High School and then turn left again into Leopold Takawira (or Moffat, as some people still called it) and so arrive at the main Girls High School gates. There is a traffic light in Harare Road that stops the traffic so that the Girls High School boarders, coming from their hostels, can cross the road safely on the way to school. In Rhodesia, most major roads were designed with a cycle path – presumably the road being for the cars of the whites and the cycle path for the bicycles of the blacks. These cycle paths ran parallel with the road but were separated from it, often by a drainage ditch – which I suppose you could describe as a rather original form of colour bar. I mean, one can get tired of railway tracks. So the girls crossing at the lights in Harare Road would cross the road, walk over a little bridge that spanned the ditch, cross the cycle path and then go in through the pedestrian gate into school.

It was morning rush hour and the lines of cars were long. The pedestrian crossing light was red. The cars, including my own, stopped at the traffic light and a number of girls started to cross the road. Some had reached the little bridge over the ditch and others were crossing the cycle path, when careering up from behind us on the cycle path came a Commuter Omnibus, travelling at high speed. Without reducing speed for a second, it zoomed through the crowd of girls, many of whom had to throw themselves to the ground or into the ditch to save their lives. Off it sped as if nothing had happened until it found a place to swerve back onto the road and proceed with its murderous rampage into town. I was so shocked, disgusted and frightened for the girls' safety by what I had seen that from that day on I would not allow my daughter to travel to school on *maCommuter* and took her every day and fetched her every day after school. Jokingly, I said to her once or twice (fathers can be tiresome): "No-one who ever fetched and carried his daughter to school every day became famous!" It does slightly interfere with one's productivity.

Alas, what I read in a newspaper about fifteen years later, after Zimbabwe had gone through the agonies of its third decade, made me think that death under the wheels of a careering Commuter

Omnibus was cleaner and less desperate for a young girl than what was to come. The newspaper in question reported that a *hwindi* had been caught having sex with a girl in the back of his minibus in broad daylight. On investigating further, the reporter had discovered that the drivers and *hwindis* of *maCommuter* were bragging that they could have a different girlfriend every day of their lives as there were young girls who were prepared to sell their bodies to them for a free lift into town. However, their male paradise had its downside. They complained that many of their number were now dying of AIDS – and they blamed the girls!

As the initial promise of ESAP failed, there was a shortage of foreign currency in the banks and the next great characteristic of life in Zimbabwe in the time of ESAP was born – the Black Market. The goods that had flooded the market with the deregulation of the economy that ESAP introduced, were no longer being imported through the official channels and so the shops either began to become empty again or stock items that were many times more expensive than they were in neighbouring countries. Black marketeers seized the opportunity and foreign currency was now bought and sold on the streets. Now it was *maCross-border* who not only resorted to the black market but also those who supplied the goods either to the shops or direct to the customer. Thus the shortage of goods and the high prices of whatever was available, the overpricing of the Zimbabwe dollar and the unavailability of foreign currency in the banks encouraged the growth of the black market.

It is mistaken to think that shortages were something that began in Zimbabwe during the economic upheavals of the third decade or even in the years after the failure of ESAP. I remember, when visiting Zimbabwe from Ethiopia in 1982, my uncle would come rushing into the house, shouting excitedly that there was milk at so-and-so shop or bread at another – and off he would go on his little Velo to get some before it ran out. And it wasn't long after our own arrival in Zimbabwe from Ethiopia in 1984 that I had to plan a shopping trip to Francistown in Botswana to get tyres and other parts for my car. Over the years, especially after 1990 when it became possible for me to visit South Africa, I earned the nickname 'Spare Parts' because that was what I spent most of my time running around trying to get when I was out of the country.

In actual fact, the only time in the three decades when almost all the goods we wanted were available was in the early years of the period I am describing, namely the early 1990s shortly after the introduction of ESAP – but then few could afford them and it didn't last long! For a short while there was no need for my uncle to get on his Velo and dash off to Avondale to buy bread or milk before it ran out, no need for me to drive off to Francistown to get tyres. The shops were full of goods, the supermarkets bulging. ESAP happened to coincide with the unbanning in 1990 of the African National Congress and the South African Communist Party. Nelson Mandela was out of prison. South Africa, whose profile in the new Zimbabwe had been low, owing to *apartheid* and Zimbabwean economic nationalism, suddenly began to loom large. South African goods appeared on the shelves to compete with local products. South African stores started opening up – the Central News Agency (CNA), Clicks, the pharmaceutical giant, Midas, the car spares and accessories giant, Mica, the DIY and hardware chain. Access to foreign exchange was liberalised and exchange controls relaxed. Soon Harare could boast of shopping malls, Eastgate (1996) in the city centre and Westgate (1995) on the outskirts of the city on the road to Zambia. If the ordinary people quipped bitterly that ESAP stood for '*Ee, Satane Asvika Pano*', for many of the urban middle classes it was as if, far from Satan, the Saviour himself had come to Zimbabwe.

There was a link between the establishment of a mall such as Westgate on the road out of Harare to the north west, a suburban shopping precinct like Sam Levy's Village in Borrowdale or Arundel Shopping Centre in the affluent suburb of Mount Pleasant, on the one hand, and what had been happening to the Central Business District, on the other. As the city centre slowly changed in character, coming to reflect Harare's demographic make-up and with street fathers and other hazards multiplying, fewer and fewer whites went into town to do shopping or business or go to the office. The whites, who, despite their diminishing numbers, were still an influential and affluent market, along with diplomats, expatriates, the staff of foreign NGOs and the new and growing black middle class, lived in the posh suburbs. White business followed its market and fled from the city centre. There were also the wealthy white commercial farmers to think about. Westgate Mall was particularly well positioned for them. It was situated on the outskirts of Harare on the road to Zambia and the rich tobacco and cotton farmlands around Chinhoyi, Raffingora and Karoi. The farmers could now 'come to town' for their purchases, without having to go into town at all. Incidentally, Westgate is architecturally speaking a very attractive little mall. It provides the advantages of mall shopping without its most dreary features. With Old Mutual looking for projects in which to stash its millions and recognising the advantage of real estate, new office parks were opened up between Mount Pleasant and Marlborough.

The ESAP boom didn't last long. There was drought. Water was rationed. Instead of booming, ESAP soon began to bite. As unemployment and costs rose, people found themselves locked increasingly in the bitter struggle to survive.

Whereas in the past there may have been shortages but what goods there were could be bought at an affordable price, now in the new

ESAP era, it was the opposite. For a while the goods were there but fewer and fewer people could buy them. Historically, this seems to have been a perennial problem, not confined to Zimbabwe. Either affordable prices but no goods or plenty of goods but too expensive. How to strike a happy balance? I remember reading how the young Soviet Union was faced with a similar dilemma called, I think, the 'scissors' effect. When prices favoured the working class in towns, the farmers in the countryside did not produce and there was famine in the towns. When prices favoured the farmers and food became available, the workers could not buy it. This became essentially the story of Zimbabwe starting in the early years of the second decade and coming to a sensational head in the last years of the third decade when shelves were literally bare. As fewer and fewer people could buy the goods, shops began to go out of business, businesses began to close down. Soon not only were things too expensive to buy but there were less and less goods in the shops to buy. The currency was devalued. The Black Market stepped in.

Zimbabwe was being 'magabaised'. In many ways the informalisation of society had transformed the lives of ordinary people and posed new dangers. However these were things that people rapidly adjusted to. Indeed they became part of the country's daily culture, even affectionately recognised by those that remained in Zimbabwe as well as those who fondly remembered it in the Disaspora, as being quintessentially Zimbabwean – as a re-read of the famous email that circulated among Zimbabweans at one stage, headed: "You are a Zimbabwean if...", would reveal. The email enumerated all the silly but dear little quirks that characterise life for a modern Zimbabwean. You will find that the informal sector understandably features strongly in this litany of what makes a Zimbabwean Zimbabwean.

Other things also changed and the changes were such that it would not be so easy to survive them or ever remember them with a smile. These were the things that more and more plunged Zimbabweans into the life and death struggle for survival – or escape into the diaspora.

CHAPTER THIRTEEN:

THE SOCIAL EFFECTS OF ESAP

"Something for something, nothing for nothing"

An ESAP pill does not only bring about changes in the economy. It can quite revolutionise human behaviour, attitudes and values. It would not be true to say that the social transformation described in subsequent chapters could be put down to the IMF and ESAP alone. Though ESAP was the key factor, the groundwork had already been laid by the materialism, greed, selfishness and complete lack of conscience displayed by many in the new ruling elite and the contradiction between its socialist or populist policies and utterances and its avaricious personal behaviour. This ambivalence had already begun to affect policy - and government policy in the period after 1985 began to downplay the commitments to social equity that characterised the first five years and develop a tendency to flirt with neo-liberal economic and financial prescriptions. Hence the government's readiness to treat with the IMF.

In the wake of the imposition of ESAP, lots of things changed – as we have seen in the previous chapter. There were changes in economic activity, changes in the supply and cost of goods, services and foreign currency, changes in transport, changes in the Central Business District. But for me of all the changes it was the change in people, the change in the way people behaved and related to each other, that was the most alarming.

The first decade had been a time of *'kushandira pamwe'* - working together. It was a time when there was hope for a society built on democratic equality and co-operation. Co-operatives were the in-thing. Agriculture and all sorts of income-generating projects were being organised on the co-operative principle – crafts, textiles, ceramics, carpets, clothing, furniture factories, catering, even dance and drama groups.[22] In the community itself, people came together readily to work for various causes – social betterment, political solidarity, cultural expression. They gave freely of their time and they were prepared to give it free.

In the 1980s, I had been very active in unpaid co-operative endeavours, mostly for political causes. For instance, I was instrumental in forming something called the Film of the Month on the campus of the University of Zimbabwe. We began by showing alternative films - films from Africa, from the socialist countries or alternative films from the West. Our role soon expanded into solidarity events such as cultural galas, festivals and commemorations. We never failed to mark the day of the Soweto Uprising (16th June), Sharpeville Day (21st March), Workers' Day (1st May), Africa Day (25th May) and Heroes and Independence Days (10th August and 18th April) with some kind of commemorative event. We organised African Film Festivals and a week-long festival to mark the 70th anniversary of the Russian Revolution. We had solidarity cultural galas for the struggles in Nicaragua, Angola, Cuba, Palestine and South Africa. When Chris Hani was assassinated, we mourned his death with an evening of protest poetry, drama and song. We hosted Amandla, the Cultural Ensemble of the African National Congress, in a performance to an enormous audience at the University Great Hall. We were the only ones in Zimbabwe to hold an event celebrating Namibian independence. All this was organised by myself and a small group of lecturers, students and comrades from the community – in our spare time and for free. I also produced amateur drama productions, involving not only

22 See above: Shah, Anup, *Structural Adjustment—a Major Cause of Poverty*

lecturers and students but also workers at the University and artists from the community theatre movement – again in our spare time and for free. All the time and effort we put into the political theatre work of Zambuko/Izibuko, too, was likewise purely voluntary and unpaid.

But, as the second decade kicked in, almost overnight this changed. In no time at all no-one had any time to donate, no-one could afford to work with others unless it was a business venture or there was a realistic prospect of payment. The Zimbabwean singer, Thomas Mapfumo, renowned since before Independence for his social commentary, captured the mood and the phenomenon very early on - in 1989, in fact - with his popular song, 'Corruption', which contains the words: "Something for something, nothing for nothing". Although Mapfumo was referring to the phenomenon of corruption, the words exactly described the change in human relations that ESAP brought about. It is exactly what happened. No-one was prepared – or perhaps could afford - to do anything for anyone else without payment. If you gave something, you expected to get something back in return.

The reason for this was that the struggle for survival suddenly became acute. Unless you devoted all your time and energy to earning money, you and your family would go down. Everyone became busy. Before, they had been busy but often together and for a cause or for the good of others or all people. Now people were busy by and for themselves.

It was a rapid acceleration of a process of social and cultural change that had been going on for decades. It had started the moment the settlers began involving indigenous Zimbabweans in their colonial, capitalist relations. The work of the missionaries and the growth of urbanisation and proletarian labour had given it another twist. As economic and other problems began to multiply towards the end of the first decade of independence, the pace quickened. With the introduction of ESAP at the beginning of the second decade, the process became a rout. By the time ESAP was abandoned almost a decade later, a whole society had been drastically transformed.

Prior to ESAP, social and, to some extent, economic relations in Zimbabwe were still by and large shaped by a combination of three cultures - the traditional culture of the pre-capitalist, pre-colonial period; Christianity; and to some extent Socialism, first introduced during the liberation struggle. Mwalimu Nyerere, first President of Tanzania, and many others recognised in pre-colonial African 'communal' society an early form of socialism. Christianity, especially that based on the actual life and teachings of Jesus, has much in common with socialism – something that socialists, notably Fidel Castro, and supporters of 'Liberation Theology' in Latin America recognised. '*Gutsaruzhinji*', the philosophy touted before and in the early years after Independence, was a form of socialism.

In communal society, in democratic Christianity and in '*Gutsaruzhinji*' there *was* something you did not have to pay another something for. There *were* things that could be done, got or offered for nothing. There were many provisions for collective or co-operative labour. In Shona culture there was the customary good neighbourliness and communal support of the *nhimbe* tradition, where the people would gather at a neighbour's homestead and work together on some task or other, such as house-building, land-clearing or harvesting. The beneficiary would brew beer and provide those who came with food and drink. The extended family network was another very supportive and co-operative institution and family members would help those who needed assistance, with their education, for instance. Christianity, in the manifestations that characterised both the colonial and post-independent years, preached and in many cases practised charity and fellowship, love for one's neighbour and support for the poor.

The cultural base was the rural areas – *kumamisha* – where the vast majority of the people still lived. The umbilical cord that maintained the cultural nourishment of the traditional society among urban Zimbabweans was regular visits between town and country. The sudden and dramatic assault on the common person's pocket caused by the hike in the prices of goods and services combined with retrenchment, while not completely cutting it, pinched the umbilical tightly. Shortage of transport, the high cost of travel and the serious cut in spending power meant that the relatively easy to-ing and fro-ing between town and the rural home was drastically reduced. At the same time, the kind of life ESAP had trapped the town-dwellers in brought pressure to bear on traditional cultural relations and practices, hastening the process of distortion, reduction and even abandonment that had set in many years ago with the coming of the whites.

Probably the most fundamental example of the profound impact of the change on society that ESAP brought about was its effect on the extended family and its practices and values. The extended family was – probably still is – the central and single most important warp in the weave of Zimbabwean life. As I have already suggested, I believe that for black Zimbabweans the extended family commands an allegiance and a commitment far more profound than their motherland itself. In contrast with the nation state, first the extended family and then the clan and people of the same totem, are realities and constructs the roots of which reach deep into the past and are watered by blood (see Prologue to the Future at the end of the book for a discussion of the nation state). The duty and deeply felt belonging and commitment that a man and a woman have to his or her extended family are probably the driving force of human behaviour in Zimbabwe today. Women leave their families ostensibly when they are *lobola'ed* but though their new loyalties in the family of the husband are real and obligatory, they carry with them the bonds and ties of their own families. In the traditional context, this could lead to the two families entering into close and cooperative relations. In the modern context, it can lead to the opposite where the two extended families compete for the benefits that accrue to the labour and achievements of the man and his wife.

In the extended family, the nuclear family is still a relatively weak though obviously strengthening reality. Even now no man or woman can say openly that his or her children belong to him or her alone without general opprobrium. For a start, the children belong to the man's family but also each child has many mothers and fathers and many brothers and sisters outside the nuclear family. Such relationships are not sentimental or symbolic ties, they are totally real. When a child relates to the mother's sister as to a mother and she to the child as her child, or the man or woman refers to his or her cousins as brothers or sisters, this is not just a way of getting off work to attend funerals – obviously a gimmick that has been used over the years with frustrating (for the bosses) success. It is absolute fact.

And this stretches far beyond human relationships – to money, to property, to the home, to education, to health, to clothing and to food. Traditionally, a man or woman cannot claim the exclusive and selfish possession of his or her wealth, home, property, clothing and food. If there are others in the family who have neither, it is the duty of those who have, to give to those who do not. The elder child finishes school and starts working. Not only is that child expected to support a parent where the parent is a dependant but also to care for younger siblings so that all over the country there are older children supporting younger children with their education, with accommodation, with food, with clothing. And as the younger children in their turn start to earn, they then in their turn do the same for those coming after them.

A man or a woman cannot marry or even die alone. He or she needs the other family members. Thus the importance of the extended family is the overriding consideration in the majority of Zimbabweans' lives. It is also the lynchpin of their social lives. Many is the disgruntled foreigner – myself included, I must be honest - who has complained at the lack of hospitality of black Zimbabweans. You may invite them to your home and hope to become friends, even family friends, but it is a rare Zimbabwean who will invite you back to his or hers. The fact is that apart from men who go drinking and women who go to church, social life revolves almost exclusively around family occasions of all sorts. Funerals and marriages themselves are enough to keep the average Zimbabwean busy for life. Take a family funeral for instance – first, rushing to '*rufu*' at the home of the deceased, then the wake, then the funeral, then '*kugova nhumbi*' (dividing up the possessions), then some time later '*kurangarira*' (the memorial) and finally '*kurova guva*' (the bringing back of the spirit to the homestead) and '*kugara nhaka*' (guardianship of the deceased's wife, family and property). Or the similar round of marriage-related family activities – *lobola* (Shona '*roora*', the processes of negotiating and paying bride wealth), engagement, various wedding ceremonies, traditional, Christian and modern – to mention only the two most demanding of the family commitments. When one thinks of the social commitments that these two serial activities demand and how many family members are marrying and dying, especially in the time of AIDS, it becomes easier to understand why one is not invited back and why it is so hard for someone outside the family to become a 'family friend'.

This is not to say that family friends do not exist. They do and they are called '*madzisahwira*' – but in most cases these are people who are neighbours, whether from the same rural area or in town, or very close school friends or workmates.

However, all these commitments fly in the face of the world ESAP came to impose. The world of ESAP - its philosophy, its values and its practices - was diametrically opposed to those of the extended family. To survive in the time of ESAP a man or a woman needed to cling to the money he or she has made. For the home to function, the household fed and the children educated, a completely different approach to the individual's resources was required.

Stephen Chifunyise is an extraordinary figure in African education and culture. He is also Zimbabwe's most influential and prolific playwright. One of his very numerous plays is, in my view, a Zimbabwean literary classic, along with Charles Mungoshi's *Waiting for the Rain* and E.C. Kumbirayi's Shona poetry. The play is called *Vicious* and it deals with middle class poverty in Zimbabwe.[23] At first sight, the concept of middle class poverty seems to be a contradiction in terms. But this contradiction is precisely what became a reality in Zimbabwe at the interstice of ESAP and the extended family in the early 1990s.

The play depicts the family life of a relatively high-ranking civil servant. It soon becomes apparent that far from being comfortable and financially secure on his comparatively generous salary, he and the family are on their knees. His grown-up daughter begs her father for a few cents to buy sanitary pads. He does not have the money. All he has in his pocket are the few cents required for catching a 'Commuter' to work and back. Note he cannot run a car. There is virtually no food to cook and his wife, who also works,

23 In *Intimate Affairs and Other Plays* (Cybercard Trading PL)

escapes her domestic problems by going off to church meetings in the evenings. The son is forced to share a bed with a consumptive uncle. There are up to fourteen children in the house, the children of various impecunious relatives. There are people sleeping in every room including the kitchen. When, finally, the man's elder brother and his wife (*mukoma* and *maiguru*) arrive from the rural areas to live with them, the situation comes to a head. The man and his wife have to move out of their matrimonial bedroom and make way for *mukoma* and *maiguru*. Noteworthy is the fact that the elder brother does not ask permission. He takes it as his right to come and live with his brother. He is incensed when his younger brother suggests that they practise birth control and they threaten to leave. Despite the fact that it would greatly alleviate the crisis in the house, this is met with horror by his brother. The elder brother being forced to leave his younger brother's home in such circumstances would totally disgrace him in the eyes of his extended family.

Chifunyise's civil servant cannot break away from the exigencies of the extended family and its culture and as a result ESAP has him in its grip. Others were not so conscientious and situations like this were driving more and more families to pursue a far more selfish road, leading to violations and breakdowns in the culture. One other stark and chilling note is struck in *Vicious*. When asked how things are in the rural home, the elder brother and the wife laugh and say: "They are dying." They compare it to a graveyard and remark that people only go home these days to die. It was not only the catastrophe of ESAP that barrelled into Zimbabwean society in the second decade like a tornado. It was also AIDS.

The extended family was not the only warp in the social fabric that was at risk. ESAP began to corrode almost every aspect of pre-ESAP culture. Before the coming of ESAP, *lobola*[24], though it had been already corrupted by capitalist relations, was still a respected and respectable institution – in the sense that it was not blatantly commercialised. With the coming of the hardships as well as the need and greed for money, *lobola* became in many cases simply an opportunity for individuals in the bride's family to make money, source food and acquire goods and luxuries. In effect, the bride came to be sold – for the highest possible price that could be extracted.

'*Kugara nhaka*' is a Shona custom whereby on the death of the husband someone in the husband's family can be appointed as guardian to the family of the deceased, responsible for the children and, in particular, for ensuring that the property of his brother would be looked after and utilised for the good of the wife and children.[25] With the corruption of social life and the economic exigencies tightening their grip, this custom came to be seen as an opportunity for the relatives of the deceased to grab all his property and for his brother to jump into the bed of his widow. Not only did this turn of events prove financially disastrous for the lives of the widow and her children, it also exposed them to the equally disastrous danger of infection by HIV/AIDS. At the end of the second decade, the Zimbabwean government introduced new Wills and Inheritance legislation to curb these abuses but, as everyone knows, a law is not enough and any woman who sought its protection would have to face the dire consequences of the wrath and revenge of her deceased husband's relatives.

---

24 Originally, compensation paid by the family of the young man to the family of the young woman to compensate for the loss of the woman's labour and reproductive capacity.

25 See the film *Neria* (1993), written by Tsitsi Dangarembga, directed Goodwin Mawuru, screenplay Louise Riber.

Another basic social and cultural concept that was at risk in the time of ESAP was the nature of government. In many parts of Africa the residual pre-capitalist ideology concerning government and its responsibility for the welfare of its people, is still strong and deeply rooted. The capitalist concept that the citizen's welfare is his own business, that it is up to the individual to make good and, if he doesn't, tough cheese, has not even now quite replaced it. In earlier days, it was not uncommon for African populations simply to migrate when a ruler did not discharge that obligation. Stephen Bantu Biko, one of the founders of the Black Consciousness movement in South Africa, wrote that individual poverty was a foreign concept and that if there was ever poverty in an African community, it was poverty suffered by the whole community as a result of a common problem such as drought or plague.

To this day in Zimbabwe, there lingers on the concept of *Zunde ra Mambo*, whereby the king or chief maintains a granary from which those in need are fed. For the populations of many states in Africa, modern governments are still largely seen to have inherited this role. And indeed whenever there was drought and the danger of famine in Zimbabwe during the first decade, the State was expected to and did provide substantial quantities of drought relief – one of the factors that added to its fatal debt.

So, in Zimbabwe, perhaps owing to the residual consciousness of this traditional political and economic ideology and to the general sense both in Christianity and in revolutionary socialism, that the government, especially a self-professed 'People's Government', has a responsibility for the well-being of the people, the people consistently expected the government to provide and this was implicitly accepted by government. It was a sort of social contract. In Zimbabwe the people saw government very much as a father of the family, who, as the father, must see to it that there is food on the table, that the family is clothed, the children educated, the sick cared for and so on - an attitude to government that ESAP was diametrically opposed to and indeed set out to eradicate. When the exigencies of ESAP led government to cut subsidies on basic foodstuffs, hike prices and the costs of health and education as well as permit bosses to retrench their workers, it was a shock, something the people had never expected – and did not accept. It infringed the social contract and snapped the bonds that were expected to bind the people and their government. Perhaps the large scale emigration of those who have left Zimbabwe and gone off to other countries, was simply a latter day instance of the common practice of traditional communities in Africa abandoning rulers who did not or were not able to look after their interests.

This attitude to government accounts also for the way in which Zimbabweans tended to analyse their woes when problems multiplied and the situation deteriorated after the taking back of the land in the next decade. Despite the obvious effect of sanctions imposed by external forces, government was held responsible for the welfare of the people and the people blamed the government for everything that went wrong.

Thus, to sum up, in the space of the few years in which it was implemented, ESAP, from what I witnessed, entrenched a new ethos and new social and economic relations, which quite revolutionised Zimbabwean society and culture, possibly even more profoundly than the nationalist revolution that had brought independence itself. The people recognised the change and they knew it was a change for the worse. That is why they proclaimed: "Satan is here!"

Satan did not stay long though his legacy endured. A combination of the disastrous effects on society and the economy that transformed the positive achievements of the first decade into something approaching horror in the second, led to the modification of ESAP in the form of ZIMPREST. Before it could be totally abandoned, it was the IMF itself that withdrew from its relationship with Zimbabwe. As already mentioned, this was mainly due to the unbudgeted payout to the liberation war veterans and to Zimbabwe's military commitment in the Democratic Republic of the Congo. The latter, Zimbabwe's involvement along with Namibia and Angola in the Congo, dubbed by some as Africa's first world war, owing to the number of countries it sucked in, is a much misrepresented and misunderstood event, even in Zimbabwe. It is my belief that its importance for Africa and Zimbabwe's role in it have not been sufficiently understood.

CHAPTER FOURTEEN:

WAR IN THE CONGO

'Good news' from the Front

While Zimbabwean troops were fighting in the Democratic Republic of the Congo (DRC), a cartoon appeared in the government-owned newspaper, *The Herald*, which, if my memory holds good, depicted Zimbabwean journalists in the newsroom of a so-called 'independent' newspaper. One of the journalists was announcing to the others that he had received some good news. More Zimbabwean soldiers had been killed in the Congo!

Before saying anything more about the cartoon, I would like to tell you a story quickly about something that happened to us in Finland. You may well ask what Finland can possibly have to do with this cartoon. I'm not sure but I suspect there is a connection.

We were in that country with a group of Zimbabwean primary school children, performing a play that featured five Zimbabwean dances and explained their context. At one of the railway stations in Helsinki our senior trainer, *Tete* (or Auntie) Elizabeth Takawira was racially abused by a member of the public. When I intervened, I was accused of being a Serbo-Croat and told to go back to my country. On another occasion when I was crossing the road with Sis Julie, a black Zimbabwean married to a Finn, I was shoulder-butted by another member of the public. In the town of Tampere a woman set her dog on our children and only called it back when it was already standing astride a terrified little girl with its jaws slavering a few inches above her face.

One of the scenes in the play the children were performing in Finland, featured the *jiti* dance, which was a favourite dance at the nocturnal meetings (*pungwe*) between the comrades and the people in the Zimbabwean countryside during the liberation war. We were due to perform the play for the Ministry of Education but they asked us to drop the '*jiti*' scene. When we asked them why, they said that it 'encouraged child soldiers'. They must have seen and read about the child soldiers in Sierra Leone and Liberia. Although we explained that our play was nothing but patriotic African children *acting out* the comrades who liberated their country, not child soldiers, they persisted and in the end the scene had to be left out.

I thought a lot about this. We in Zimbabwe knew something about child soldiers. Zimbabwe's neighbour to the east is Mozambique and for many years, largely on account of its support for the liberation struggle in Zimbabwe, the people of Mozambique had to endure some of the worst suffering and traumatisation a people ever experienced. The perpetrators of this nightmare were the *matsangaise*, which is what the people called the Renamo bandits.[26] When Renamo bandits attacked a defenceless village, they did so with three aims in mind: first of all, simply to sow terror; secondly to destabilise and create as much havoc and destruction as possible – after all, they were 'killing a dream', in other words, the dream of '*uma sociedade nova*'; thirdly to recruit. In particular, they liked recruiting boys, who, after they had been given the treatment, made very good killers. So, they took the boys as fighters, the girls they took for their pots and their blankets, the adults they left for the treatment. The treatment involved giving the boys AK 47s and making them shoot their fathers and mothers and all their male relatives. After that they gave them *dagga* (cannabis) and a gun - and in that way the boys became pitiless killers.

26 Named after Andre Matsangaise, the first leader of Renamo.

I wondered whether patriotic children in Finland ever performed plays about Finland's eventful history. What about her heroic resistance when the Soviet army invaded in 1939? Did they never act that out? If they did, would they be accused of 'encouraging child soldiers'.

What is the connection? I think the connection has something to do with children (maybe young people too), Africa and patriotism. I remembered in the early days of our arts education organisation, we decided to arrange a concert to commemorate Heroes Day. Heroes Day was a national holiday, a day on which all Zimbabweans were encouraged to remember and honour the sacrifices of those who gave their lives for Zimbabwe. I heard via the grapevine that parents, who knew of my political alignment, when appraised of our intention to hold such a concert, began saying to each other: "You see, we knew he was going to start indoctrinating our children with Communist propaganda."

On another occasion people at the university objected to a dramatisation of Wilson Katiyo's novel, *Son of the Soil*, which showed how the system before Independence almost inevitably drove a young black Zimbabwean into the armed struggle, despite the fact that all he really wanted was an education and a chance in life. They said it was 'raking up the past'.

And then I thought, why do people always seem to see being patriotic as an African and depicting or celebrating the heroic episodes of resistance and triumph in African history, as somehow uncalled for. It reminds me of theatre in the Victorian era when the theatre of the upper classes was actually called 'legitimate theatre' and that of the lower, 'illegitimate theatre'. It is as if arts that depict Africa's brutalities, its injustices, its ignominy or its defeats are 'legitimate'. Patriotism is 'illegitimate'. It becomes worse when anyone tries to pass on the legacy of African patriotism and heroism to children or young people. Then it becomes indoctrination, propaganda, 'encouraging child soldiers'. But there is no need for propaganda or indoctrination. All we need is INFORMATION. We need to teach our history to our children and our youth.

History and 'the big picture' go together. It is much easier to see the big picture if you know the history. We therefore need to provide our peoples, especially our children and our young people, with information about our history, including and especially, the history of slavery, invasion, colonialism, the struggles for freedom and the struggles to deepen and broaden that freedom. History helps in understanding the big picture. But they need more than history. They need information about what is going on *now* – in Africa and in their world. Then they would be able to see things like the SADC intervention in the DRC in the context of history and the big picture. But if they have no information on the Belgians in the Congo, on the Congo's mineral treasure trove, on what happened to Patrice Lumumba, the role of the USA, Belgium and the United Nations in Lumumba's overthrow and murder, Zaire under Mobutu, the end of Mobutu and the reasons for it, the invasion of the DRC by Uganda, Rwanda and Burundi and who aided and abetted them and why – if they do not know anything about this, how can they understand why Zimbabwe, Namibia and Angola did what they did? If they have no idea of Angola's long struggle, first against the Portuguese and then against their surrogates, UNITA, and who aided whom and why – if they have no idea of how the Germans massacred the Herero in Namibia, almost to extinction, how Namibia came to be a mandate of *apartheid* South Africa, how SWAPO fought and how they assisted the Angolans (MPLA), the South Africans (ANC- Umkhonto weSizwe) and Cuba to turn back the *apartheid* South African army and air force at the Battle of Cuito Canavale – if they do not know anything about all this, how can they understand why these countries did what they did in the DRC? And if they don't know and cannot understand, they will believe whatever they are told.

There seems to have been a general failure in Africa to understand the political and social importance of history and current affairs. Almost everywhere generations of Africans have been permitted to grow up not knowing their country and their continent's history – and not knowing what the hell is going on in the rest of the world. It has happened in South Africa too and the African National Congress, like Zimbabwe and ZANU-PF, will reap the harvest of the dragon's teeth they have sown. The South African Broadcasting Corporation (SABC), for instance, includes very little if any African or world news in its national news broadcasts.

Back to the cartoon - the cartoonist was satirising the way in which this 'independent' newspaper and its journalists, who stridently opposed ZANU-PF and everything it did, including Zimbabwe's involvement in the Congo, seemed to be hoping that their own country would be defeated and exulting at every reverse, including the deaths of her soldiers, Zimbabweans like themselves. The cartoon was highlighting the extremes to which the polarisation in the country had gone. It really seemed that the incipient polarisation, which was Zimbabwe's legacy at independence, had split the country. It was as if *nyika yeZimbabwe* (the Zimbabwean nation) was no longer one but rather two nations. One seemed to look inwards to itself, Zimbabwe, to the region, to Africa – and a few years later, to the East. Another was simply mirroring the views, echoing the opinions and feeling the feelings of Europe and North America. Europe and North America opposed SADC's involvement in the DRC – for reasons we shall soon see - and so this other Zimbabwean nation opposed it, behaving at times as if they were not Zimbabweans but citizens of the countries whose governments they seemed to owe their allegiance to and whose media they parroted and echoed in their own.

There were many who had never ever supported Mugabe and ZANU-PF. There were others whom ZANU-PF's betrayal had disillusioned. In any case, according to the way they saw it, if Mugabe and ZANU-PF sent troops to the DRC, they were against it. Kabila was not worth supporting because he was Mugabe's friend. The MPLA in Angola and Swapo in Namibia were just the same as ZANU-PF. And so on and so on. But this was not all.

Zimbabwe's involvement in the DRC has generally been considered by its detractors to have been a historic blunder. For them, it was a blunder because, as they asserted, the DRC's problems had nothing to do with Zimbabwe, it was a waste of money and lives and lost Zimbabwe the support of the West and crucially the money of the IMF. I saw it differently. The intervention was not in my opinion a blunder – far from it. What was a blunder however was that no incident in my experience demonstrated more clearly the President and ZANU-PF's disastrous weakness in the areas of dialoguing with the people and explaining why they did what they did.

For me, the intervention of SADC in the DRC was a historic African initiative and one that provided a model for how Africa could at last pull herself together and take united action to protect her interests against external meddling and exploitation, especially in the light of the more recent NATO violation of African interests in Libya and the United States' military penetration in Uganda and many other African countries. Yet no effort whatsoever was made to explain the reasons for Zimbabwe's involvement and, in this way, to unite the Zimbabwean people behind the move. Because hardly any effort was made to publicise the *facts*,

ZANU-PF handed the opposition and the West a massive propaganda victory. The Western media and the opposition press had a field day.

For the vast majority of Zimbabweans who did not have access to alternative sources of information, there was only one version of what was happening. Virtually the whole of Zimbabwe saw the involvement of their own country in a war from the perspective of the West and their local mouthpieces. The government perspective was simply unexplained and unknown. The talk in all the taxis, the buses, the homes and workplaces of Zimbabwe was almost unanimous in its condemnation of Zimbabwe's involvement in the Congo as a wasteful and uncalled-for adventure which the country could not afford. "Why die for the Congolese?" people said. "We are suffering yet we are spending money to save Kabila." The opposition newspapers waded in with vastly exaggerated and at time fictional reports of hundreds of soldiers dying and their bodies coming home in secret flights at night. Bodies, they claimed, were being buried without heads – and so on and so on. While the government-owned press and television did try to counteract the more lurid rumours, ZANU-PF and the government did not lift a finger to explain to Zimbabweans what had made the intervention necessary, even if it involved the sacrifice of Zimbabwean lives and the expenditure of scarce financial resources.

So, opposition to Zimbabwe's intervention in the DRC could be put down to the polarised state of the nation and the failure of the President and ZANU-PF to give information and explain to the people of Zimbabwe why Zimbabwe had intervened.

What information and how to explain? What really happened in the Congo and why did the SADC Organ on Politics, Defence and Security[27] feel it had to get involved? And why do I say that I believe their involvement was a model for Africa?

Like most explanations of the present, this one starts in the past. For over 30 years, the United States supported, uncritically, the unconstitutional rule of Mobutu Sese Seko, grounded as it was in the overthrow of the Congo's duly elected first head of state, Patrice Lumumba, which the West had likewise orchestrated. Incidentally, I once acted the role of the white mercenary who actually shot Lumumba - in a production of Aime Cesaire's *Un Saison au Congo* in Addis Ababa.

For, all the time the US was being pally with him, it was common knowledge that Mobutu was sacking the country big time. Instead of the censure he deserved, Mobutu was feted by a succession of US presidents. The reason was simple. The Congo is one of the richest sources of minerals in the world and Mobutu was permitting the US and its Western allies free rein to exploit them. When finally Mobutu's human rights record became too embarrassing for even those who had supported murderous dictators like Batista and Pinochet to accept, the US decided to dump him. For this they used – as they invariably do in Africa and elsewhere where they are available – proxies. Their African 'friends', in this case, Rwanda and Uganda, did the job for them by assisting Laurent-Désiré Kabila and his Alliance of Democratic Forces for the Liberation of Congo-Zaire to overthrow Mobutu in 1997. Burundi also did its bit. As a result, for a short period, Kabila became, like Mobutu had been before him, the fêted protégé of the US. This was because the US was convinced that, having put him

27 See www.sadc.int/about-sadc/sadc-institutions/org/. The organ is a troika consisting of three members of SADC itself. It originated in an earlier organ developed by the former Frontline States i.e. the states that were in the frontline against apartheid.

into power, Kabila would extend to them the same favours his predecessor had. However, when to their alarm he gradually began to wean himself off the rather oppressive and unpopular 'support' of his erstwhile allies, Kabila changed from hero to zero.

After the Rwanda genocide in 1994 and the coming to power of Kagame and his Tutsi-led Rwanda Patriotic Army, thousands of Hutu refugees had flooded into Eastern Congo. Among them were many Hutu militants, who had been responsible for the slaughter of Tutsi during the genocide. They then seized control of the Hutu refugee settlements. As Kabila was no longer playing ball, Kagame, together with Museveni, planned to invade the Congo, overthrow Kabila and deal with the Hutu. This they did in 1998. In the process they indiscriminately slaughtered thousands of Hutu civilian men, women and children and plundered Congolese resources. There was no protest or sanctions from the United Nations Security Council, for the simple reason that the invaders were heavily supported by the US, Britain and other Western nations. The US played an active role in the invasion by providing training, arms and advisers. The motives for the US intervention had little to do with Hutus. They were purely political and economic. As ever it was the Congo's vast hoard of mineral wealth they were after. They had been able to plunder it for all those years under Mobutu and they were not going to let some little upstart like Kabila get in the way.

Everything seemed to be hunky-dory for the West until to their utter astonishment, the disciplined armed forces of three SADC countries came to the Congo's assistance and put a spanner in the works. They had every reason to be astonished as for centuries the West had been used to doing whatever it liked on the continent of Africa. This was the first time that an African regional body had intervened in defence of one of its members – the Democratic

Republic of the Congo had recently joined SADC – and stymied the efforts of the West to impose its interests. These three countries were Angola, Namibia and Zimbabwe.

There have subsequently been a number of efforts to distort SADC's intervention, including that of a United Nations report. The United Nations' record in the Congo is abysmal, going right back to its role in conniving with the US and Belgium in the overthrow of Lumumba. The charge the West tried and - because of the West's control of the world's media – managed to make stick, was that the three countries had invaded because they too, like the West from the Belgians to the present, were simply out to plunder the country's resources. It is true that after the SADC forces had saved and stabilised Kabila's rule, the level of gratitude was such that Zimbabwe was invited to partner with the government of the Democratic Republic in re-habilitating and developing the country after years and years of neglect, instability and chaos. After all, Zimbabwe had the infrastructure and the human resources to do so. That it did not or was not able do so became a constant source of frustration for a series of Zimbabwean ambassadors to the DRC. I remember Zimbabwe's Ambassador to Kinshasa making an impassioned appeal on television to the people of Zimbabwe to take advantage of the business and investment opportunities in that country. Zimbabwe's response remained weak and it was South Africa, which had not participated in the defence of the Congo, that reaped the harvest Zimbabwe, Angola and Namibia had sown.

On the part of the IMF, it was no wonder that it and the World Bank disengaged from Zimbabwe after Zimbabwe's frustrating and even humiliating interference in the Congo. Both institutions are totally dominated by the US and its European allies. What Zimbabwe had done to their interests in the Congo was not only a serious setback but also extremely embarrassing. The three countries had set a dangerous precedent. What made it worse was that the American Kaiser could not openly punish Zimbabwe for putting the kibosh on him as he had never openly admitted or revealed his hand in the war and would obviously not like it known that he had used Rwanda and Uganda as his proxies in a war through which he hoped to dismember the Congo and pillage its resources. The IMF of course, for similar reasons, did not come clean on its real reason for withdrawing. Instead it was diplomatic and offered purely economic and financial pretexts.

This was not difficult. As the SAPs routinely demanded that governments cut expenditure and withdraw from interventions in civil society, leaving that up to the 'private sector', so they certainly did not approve of the massive expenditure incurred in intervening in the affairs of foreign countries, let alone waging war in them!

But back again to the guys in the newsroom, announcing the 'good news' that Zimbabwean troops had been killed in the Congo. Sitting there and observing what was going on while Zimbabwean forces were in the DRC was for me an emotional experience – one of those experiences which culminated in my deciding to write a book like this. The thought of Zimbabweans, those journalists depicted in the cartoon, rejoicing at the deaths of their own soldiers! And ordinary Zimbabweans in the commuter taxis saying: "Why die for the Congolese?" and "we are suffering yet we are spending money to save Kabila" haunted me. What would have happened, I asked myself and would have loved to ask them, what would have happened if, during the time of the Smith regime, the Zambians, the Tanzanians and the Mozambicans and all those in the rest of Africa and the world had said: "Why sacrifice, why risk death for the Zimbabweans. We are suffering yet we are spending money on Mugabe and Nkomo"? What would have happened if everyone had had that attitude about the South Africans or the Namibians in their struggle against the apartheid regime?

I also wondered with something akin to horror if Zimbabwe's intervention in Mozambique, a country that had done so much for the freedom of Zimbabwe, had happened later, would Zimbabweans have said the same thing? Zimbabweans wept with the Mozambicans when they read in the newspapers on that fatal day, 20th October, 1986, that Samora Machel had been killed in an air crash. Now here were Zimbabweans who saw no point in making any sacrifices for the Congolese.

Work tirelessly for regime change, if you wish, hate Mugabe, detest ZANU-PF but give due where it is due. *Chakanaka chakanaka* - what is good is good. And above all, just because many in ZANU-PF have betrayed Africa, it is no reason that we should. Africa only became free because Africans took their destiny into their own hands and because Africans supported each other. It was the support that Zambia, Tanzania and Mozambique gave unstintingly to the struggle that made Zimbabwean independence possible just as it was the support of the Frontline and in particular Angola, with the assistance of Cuba, that hastened the coming of freedom to Namibia and South Africa. The Mozambicans had to endure the Renamo holocaust because of their support for Zimbabwe. This is an African legacy that must never be forgotten and one we should be faithful to, no matter what happens.

That Zimbabweans should have fought for the protection and integrity of the Congo was just and noble and something that Zimbabweans should have been proud to have done. It is a pity that so many of them were not. And that is why I suggest that Zimbabwe's intervention in the Congo, side by side with Namibia and Angola, is something that all Africans and those that treasure freedom and justice, should give it credit for.

Two other issues emerged for me from the DRC experience – one was the issue of a base in Africa for US Africa Command (Africom), the other the immense importance of SADC.

It must have been frustrating and humiliating for NATO to watch their proxies being defeated by local foes without their being able to turn the tide with arms shipments. Unlike the Yom Kippur War of 1973, when the United States was able to furnish Israel massive support from its aircraft carriers and other bases in the region when the Arabs seemed to be getting the upper hand, Congo was a bridge too far. Africom was based in Stuttgart, Germany, then because no African power had as yet acceded to US requests to establish a base in their country. For some time, there had been talk of Botswana obliging. It would appear that at long last the US's recent ally, Museveni's Uganda, has proved to be the Judas they were looking for. Need one waste ink pointing out first of all the danger of US armed intervention or assistance to proxies this poses to Africa, given the example of Libya, the hotting up of the scramble for Africa's resources and the US's determination to curb the growing power of China? Or in pointing out yet another in the seemingly endless examples of Western hypocrisy? A base in Museveni's Uganda, did you say? A virtual one-party state, homophobic legislation, a very long-ruling head of state – everything, in fact, in the book they habitually throw at Mugabe's Zimbabwe!

If the US had had its base in Uganda at the time of the SADC intervention, it would have had the capacity to re-arm and reinforce its African proxies when the SADC forces got the upper hand. It might even have been able to get the United Nations to agree to a 'no-fly zone'! It *might* have done so – however, on the other hand, it might not, owing to the involvement of SADC. Zimbabwe's action was undertaken in the name of a powerful and influential regional African grouping, the SADC. It was SADC's refusal to go along with the idea that stymied Tony Blair's plan to do what he so dearly wanted to do – namely launch an armed assault on Zimbabwe.[28] SADC may have similarly been able to restrain the US's involvement in the DRC. SADC's solidarity is rooted in its knowledge that it could be any one of them that is confronted in future by the danger of outside intervention. It is also rooted in the fact that all the most influential members of the regional grouping come from a long tradition of struggle, in most cases, armed struggle.

SADC's intervention in the DRC was not to be dismissed and scoffed at. It was not an irresponsible or self-interested adventure. It was not a blunder. It was an exemplary and strategic operation, which posed many questions for the defence of sovereignty in Africa. There was the effectiveness of solidarity among African states. There was a regional grouping taking decisive steps to protect a member. There was the need for African states to take special steps to ensure that their populations and, in particular, their children and young people have information about Africa's past and the world's present. There was the role of the arts in all this. There was the need to uphold the legacy of African struggle and support for each other despite domestic polarisations, rivalries, disaffection and party politics. There was the need not to condemn a good thing even if it is done by your enemy. In short, there was a lot more to Zimbabwe's 'adventure' in the DRC than it has been given credit for.

28 See above: Tony Blair, *The Journey*

CHAPTER FIFTEEN:

THE LEAD UP TO THE LAND

The *churu* start

> *In 1997, led by their Chief, the Svosve people came down from their barren and rocky land onto the white commercial farm of Daskop and claimed it as their ancestral land. In Shona* 'svosve' *means 'ant'.* 'Churu' *means anthill. A 'churu start' is starting a car with a flat battery by rolling it down a slope, like an anthill.*

I have never ever been to the races. When we were little, my sister and I invented a very exciting card game modelled on the Durban July Handicap – and that was the closest I got to a horse race.

But I did watch a little ceremony on television after one of the big horse races at Borrowdale Race Track in Harare. The OK Grand Challenge maybe – or the Castle Tankard, I don't remember. But what happened at that little ceremony I shall never forget for the rest of my life. The Land Reform had been going on for some time. One of the Ministers was giving a speech. I suppose it was one of the usual glowing glosses that Ministers regularly give to make everything sound rosy and their own performance exceptional – when suddenly, out of the blue, a relatively old white lady, stood up and shouted: "Rubbish!" She was shaking with rage and her voice was shrill and furious. Like a Harpy she then began a strident denunciation of the Minister and the government and of how it had destroyed the country. One or two other whites tried to restrain her but she was not to be thwarted. The part that will stand out forever as one of the great giveaways of history was her punchline. "This country used to be a goldmine!" she shrieked.

A black man in front of her provided the obvious riposte: "Yes - maybe for you, madam."

'This country used to be a gold mine' – and for many of the whites who had farmed or mined or milked it, Zimbabwe was a veritable gold mine. In fact, I tend to think that what they really meant when they said 'Zimbabwe was the breadbasket of Africa', related much more to the bread on their own tables than on the tables of Africa. You can be sure that when the lady said the country used to be a gold mine, she wasn't primarily referring to mining. It was the land she was referring to.

During the First and most of the Second Decade, the 'elephant in the room', the Land Question', had largely been kept in the corner. There were flurries of interest only for interest to subside again – until 1997, that is. Starting in that year a series of events began to unfold which, by the end of the Second Decade, had set the stage for some of the most dramatic developments in the history of any country in Africa.

Going right back to the liberation struggle, it was always clear that the revolutionaries' main objective was to reverse the losses sustained in the years after the First Chimurenga and recover the country that had been taken away from them.

Nyika ya baba	(the land of my father
Yakapambiwa	is in bondage
Handei tiitore	let us go and take it
Tizvitonge.	and rule ourselves.)

The rhetoric and the songs of the struggle are dominated by phrases such as '*tinoda Zimbabwe*' (not only that we love Zimbabwe but also that we want it), '*kutora nyika*' (to take the land or country) and '*Zimbabwe yauya!*' (Zimbabwe has come back) – very much along the lines of the South African slogan '*Mayibuye iAfrika!*' (may Africa return). At the all-night *pungwes* and elsewhere, the comrades harped without stint on the promise that at last the people would get their land back. By their land was meant not only *nyika*, Zimbabwe, the country, but *ivhu*, the soil.

As we have seen, Zimbabwean Independence did not come in the wake of total victory. This was pre-empted by the Lancaster House negotiations. When the question of the return of the land had not been included in the agreement, the Patriotic Front refused to sign. They only agreed when they were given an informal assurance that Britain and the United States would provide the money to make this happen.

When ZANU-PF and PF-ZAPU swept the board at the elections in 1980 and the crowing of the *jongwe* was heard all over the land, the people naturally thought that, in every real sense, including their reclamation of the lost land, *Zimbabwe yauya!* – Zimbabwe has come back. Many went on to the land there and then. What did they know about Lancaster House? And what was their surprise when they found the very people who had been fighting all these years to take the land, the comrades, the people's government, who had told them in the *Chimurenga* nights that they were going to take the land, came to persuade them and at times even force them to vacate!

According to the Lancaster House Agreement, the land was only going to be available on the basis of 'willing seller, willing buyer'. Like the old lady at the Borrowdale race track, the white farmers in Zimbabwe, as those now in Namibia and South Africa, knew they were sitting on 'a gold mine' – and they were not going to give it up that easily. However, a fair amount of land did become available for purchase, much of it marginal. Some of it was bought with British funds and many families were settled on '*mhinda mirefu*' (long fields), which is what the people called the resettlement areas. Despite the 'myths', research has shown that after a difficult period in difficult conditions, the majority of these resettlement farmers did surprisingly well for themselves.[29] More significantly perhaps, black business men and politicians bought into commercial agriculture – significant because, once there, why should they bother about others less fortunate, the *povo*, in whose name the struggle had been fought? Then British support, which had been anything but enthusiastic, ceased altogether, policy began to favour supporting existing farmers in the communal areas and the whole idea of 'taking back the land' went onto the back burner.

By the end of the first decade, with the Lancaster House Agreement about to lapse, little had been done and the two main players - government and the British - began to move sharply apart. The British, never enthusiastic, showed signs of hoping to continue operating in the spirit of the Lancaster House Agreement after it had lapsed while the unified Zanu-PF, with Mugabe and Nkomo to the fore, decided to abandon the 'willing seller, willing buyer' policy in favour of compulsory acquisition with compensation and incentives to sell. However, the drought in the early years of the second decade, the restrictions of ESAP and the need to keep in the good books of the IMF and World Bank led once more to the back burner – despite a series of policy statements and plans that envisaged land reform, including a Land Acquisition Act in 1992.

And this is where the issue stayed until in 1997 when the Svosve clan sent out their clear message to the nation that the people were sick and tired of waiting to get back their land. The heat on the back burner was turned up. A number of factors led to

29 See above: Ian Scoones et al, *Myth and Reality*

this. These included the disastrous effects of ESAP; the increasing discontent and opposition in the towns, led by the Zimbabwe Congress of Trade Unions (ZCTU); and the increasing dissatisfaction of the Liberation War Veterans. At that time, efforts by the liberation war vets and the people to go onto the land were being thwarted by government ministers and even the armed forces. Government was by no means anxious to upset the agricultural apple cart at that time. But then in November, 1997, Clare Short, New Labour's Secretary for International Development in Tony Blair's cabinet, informed the Zimbabwean government that the election of a Labour government 'without links to former colonial interests' meant Britain no longer had 'special responsibility to meet the cost of land purchase'. Poor Clare Short! She has been demonised for saying this. She was only saying what New Labour had generally decided would be its policy. Tony Lloyd, a junior minister in the Foreign and Commonwealth Office, proclaimed the same when he said in 1998: "Colonization is not something that people of my generation in Britain benefitted from." Yet, for someone heading a ministry which was directly responsible for relations with former colonies of the British Empire, Clare Short's knowledge of history was apparently scanty – or perhaps was she saying that when a Labour Government comes into office, history ceases to exist? What about that Privy Council ruling in the last century that whoever owned the land, it was not the indigenous inhabitants, and their alienation of all the land to the Crown, thus giving the white settlers *carte blanche* to grab whatever they wanted? (see Chapter 16)

The result of Clare Short's letter was that in the same month, using the legal framework of the previously unutilised Land Acquisition Act, the government started listing farms for compulsory acquisition, something which the liberation war veterans had earlier demanded.

Even at the time, I remember saying to myself that ZANU-PF had now thrown down the gauntlet. I felt that many would see this as a declaration of war. It was – and it came to be called the Third *Chimurenga*. I wondered at the time whether ZANU-PF had sized up the balance of forces and was ready for the battles that would ensue. As mentioned in an earlier chapter, I always felt that one of ZANU-PF's weaknesses was strategic planning. Many people, both in Zimbabwe and elsewhere, especially in South Africa, had never been taken in by the 'Communist terrorist', Mugabe's, apparent rehabilitation and had just been waiting for something like this to happen. Finally, according to them, the leopard had shown his spots.

Slowly the confrontation built up. A new Land Reform programme was introduced and this led to a key donor conference on the land. There were some rather feeble, I thought at the time, expressions of interest. The World Bank offered money for training when what was obviously really needed was substantial financial support for acquisition of land, compensation, capital, equipment and inputs for the new farmers! Generally, it was a let-down. In fact, it was a clear signal to ZANU-PF that – what they had always suspected – big money and its governments in the West have never been overly enthusiastic about anything that smacks of 'land reform' and it was not going to bank roll even an orderly process of compulsory land acquisition with compensation. Just as people's long-held suspicions about Mugabe and ZANU-PF now seemed justified so were Mugabe and ZANU-PF's, namely that, just as at Lancaster House, when the chips were down, no-one was going to help them get back the land. They would have to take it for themselves. It really appeared to me then that this was a turning point.

Meanwhile, the other side in the looming war was not idle. The ZCTU not only teamed up with the by now rather worried white farmers but also with white capital and industry. The continuing unrest in the cities was characterised by stay-at-homes directed largely against the effects of ESAP – shortages, high prices and retrenchments – and they were now producing an extraordinary situation as bosses and unions, in apparent harmony of purpose, egged on workers to join the stay-aways and not come to work! The interventions of the white bosses in efforts to create social unrest seemed to be particularly conspicuous in the period leading up to elections! By that time, many of the whites were desperately wanting to get rid of Mugabe.

With labour, the urban masses, Matebeleland, the unions, the white bosses and the white farmers all aligned against it, on what social forces could ZANU-PF rely on in the coming war? Obviously there was the possibility that the uniformed forces, including the police, the liberation war veterans, the traditional chiefs and the rural *povo* would support them. But there was only one way in which ZANU-PF could sustain this alliance. In addition to paying out generous benefits to the liberation war veterans and collaborators as well as being nice to the armed forces, they had to give in to the chiefs, the rural masses and the war vets and start taking and handing out the land, at the same time opening up vast opportunities for its officials, black business and the armed forces – largely war veterans themselves – to help themselves to the commercial farms. In fact, when the liberation war veterans had met the President to demand the payouts, they had also demanded a return to the revolutionary agenda, in particular the taking of the land, and threatened to go back to the bush if their demands were not met.

Outside forces had profound interests in Zimbabwe and it was not long before they began to participate in the looming struggle inside the country. It is from this period that the increasingly negative and ultimately obsessive if not hysterical, campaign by the South African and world media began its devastating offensive. This too was the beginning of the withdrawal of investment and donor support and vehement denunciation in international political and business fora. It was still early days – worse was yet to come. The gloves were only just beginning to come off. Some weighed in in an effort to prevent what might happen, others because they thought it was inevitable that it would happen and therefore, they reckoned, the fighting might as well start now.

As with most storms and many wars, for a short time there was a lull. In this case, it took the form of a new plan, what appeared to be a sort of consensus on how to deal with the land issue based on purchase at market prices. It was doomed from the start. Many on one side no longer accepted that there was any justification for finding money to buy back land that had been stolen in the first place and almost everyone on the other side was very reluctant to put up money to fund the acquisition of white land even with fair compensation. The belief that no-one was likely to pay for the reforms had already been quite glaringly demonstrated by Clare Short's fateful letter.

The pace of events quickened. At the end of 1998 a tranche of white agricultural properties were gazetted for acquisition – albeit with compensation. There was an outcry. The IMF threatened to withhold the next tranche of funding. And then the land occupations – what came to be called '*Jambanja*'- began, some involving local people, others led by the liberation war veterans, others involving the participation of the military and yet others being reversed by party and government officials who still did not approve. In 1999, the ZCTU spearheaded the founding of a new political entity, the Movement for Democratic Change (MDC).

This was the situation that prevailed as the Second Decade came to an end and as the Zimbabwean government rolled out its Constitutional Consultation process. Then in the first year of the next decade, two momentous events took place – the referendum on the new draft constitution and elections.

PART FOUR
THE THIRD CHIMURENGA

The second decade, the 'Diepe Grond', had seen the brewing of the storm that was long but sure in coming. As Zimbabwe slid into its third decade of Independence everything seemed to be gathering pace alarmingly. The terrible harvest of the dragon's teeth's was about to be reaped. All the hidden and emerging contradictions that had been in that suitcase when the victorious liberation movements moved into the governmental mansion and had been clamouring to get out in the two decades thereafter were released on Zimbabwe, like the spirits in Pandora's box or Bhetsholude, the tokoloshe *in the sack.*[30] *They came together to produce a decade as significant, as dramatic, as memorable and as traumatic as any in African history. This, the third decade in the history of the African nation of Zimbabwe, was the decade of 'Onder draai die duiwel rond' (down in the depths the devil churns things up). I was there for its entirety and it shaped my life - as it did that of thousands of others who lived through those terrible but strangely exciting times. Somehow, those of us who could look beyond the*

30 Bhetsholude is the name of a *tikoloshe* or *tokoloshe* (familiar spirit) who was made famous in a popular Zimbabwean song.

petrol queues, the empty shelves, the media onslaught, the horrific upward tailspin of the Zimbabwe dollar into the billions, trillions and quadrillions, knew that, despite its horror and despite the frightening experiences we were all going through, something very extraordinary was happening. Zimbabwe was involved in something of momentous historical and political significance - for Africa and the world.

The Third Decade of Zimbabwe's Independence was dominated by a phenomenon referred to by ZANU-PF as the Third Chimurenga. *Just to remind you,* 'Chimurenga' *means 'struggle'. The First* Chimurenga *was the struggle at the end of the Nineteenth Century against the invasion of Zimbabwe by white settlers and the British South Africa Company. The Second was the armed struggle for Independence against both the illegal Smith regime as well as the colonial power, Britain. The Third* Chimurenga *is the struggle to take back the land that was lost in the First* Chimurenga.

After a constitutional referendum and an extraordinarily close general election, the process of taking the land went into overdrive - in what some called a 'land grab' and 'farm invasions'. The MDC retaliated with a political campaign to unseat the ZANU-PF government and restore the status quo. This was supported by Britain, the European Union, the United States and the White Commonwealth[31] *through financial support and the imposition of sanctions. Further undermining the efforts of those committed to the Third* Chimurenga *was the corruption of the ruling party, the government and other elements of society in what the people dubbed 'internal sanctions'.*

---

31 The term 'White Commonwealth' was used to refer to Australia, Canada and New Zealand

As a result of the Land Reform, thousands of Zimbabweans now found themselves on land of their own. The conditions for starting up as a farmer could not have been less conducive. The whole population too experienced an extraordinary series of very difficult circumstances with spiralling inflation, shortages in just about everything and finally no food in the shops at all.

CHAPTER SIXTEEN:

THE FATEFUL YEAR

The alarm bells toll

As we have seen in the previous chapter, by the year 2000, taking back the land was being seen by more and more Zimbabweans as a priority. The government had begun to move more determinedly on the issue. Already farms had been listed for compulsory acquisition. The liberation war veterans had demanded it. The villagers were becoming more and more difficult to hold back. Chiefs were agitating for it. Already in 1999 efforts were being made to replace the old Lancaster House Constitution and the new decade began with the finalisation of the Constitutional Consultation process and the submission of the draft constitution to the people in the form of a referendum. It was a constitution which ZANU-PF was determined would enshrine the right to take back the land.

The constitutional consultation process was an extraordinary display of democratic participation. The Constitutional Commission reported that 4,321 public meetings were held, attended by 556,276 individuals. It received 4,000 written submissions. There were thirty-one television programmes and 143 radio programmes, including programmes in the nation's minority languages. Zimbabweans in the Diaspora were also consulted. It was a humbling experience. I was particularly struck by the intelligence and know-how displayed by a range of 'experts' and ordinary people on matters constitutional all over the land.

However, it resulted in a draft constitution which the MDC and many others, in Zimbabwe and all over the world, believed to be a bad ZANU-PF document and therefore needed to be opposed. How many people jumped on the MDC bandwagon and echoed this assertion without really knowing what was actually in the draft constitution? I found from personal experience that none of those who held this opinion and voted against it, when I asked them, could claim to have read it!

It is difficult to say exactly what the belief that the draft constitution was a bad ZANU-PF document was based on except for the fact that a ZANU-PF government organised it. Some have complained that they had hoped to see a genuinely 'people-driven' process. This was obviously a 'civil society' complaint and it is very difficult to know what precisely was meant by it. I personally know of few examples, outside the conditions of a popular revolution, where 'the people' drew up a constitution. The so-called 'Constitution of 1793' drawn up during the French Revolution is what 'people-driven' brings to my mind. But it was not the result of a constitutional consultation process. It is difficult to see how a consultation of this kind could possibly have happened without the structures and resources required for such a massive national process being provided and organised by the government. It is also surely unlikely that an elected government would hand over such a key democratic process to as amorphous and indefinable a construct as 'the people'. I believe that what the critics did mean is that they would have liked ZANU-PF, the President and the elected government, to have kept out of it and handed the process over to 'civil society'. However, 'civil society' in Zimbabwe has always had little empirical existence outside of the NGOs, which as everyone knows are very seriously susceptible to the influence of the foreign donors and governments that support them.

Critics of the process complain that the commission was selected by the President. Again it is difficult to know how else it could be selected and where such government commissions would not be selected by government. Another grouse was that the submission of the draft was followed by a Government Gazette entitled 'Draft Constitution for Zimbabwe: Corrections and Clarifications'. The revised draft that was submitted to the referendum included some of these 'corrections and clarifications', including the introduction of compulsory military service and the prohibition of same-sex marriages. But crucially it stated that the land would be taken compulsorily and no compensation would be paid except for improvement – and this would have to be paid by the British as they were the colonial power that presided over the theft of the land in the first place.

The draft constitution was rejected in the referendum and this was widely construed to be a defeat for ZANU-PF – as the MDC had led the 'No' campaign and ZANU-PF had *appeared* to support it. Reasons actually advanced for the rejection of the draft seemed to centre on the powers of the president, which included the power to appoint and dismiss public figures, dissolve parliament and declare states of emergency. This is strange as such presidential powers are common, even in the most illustrious of the 'Western democracies'. It is unlikely that 'the people', in the sense of the 'broad masses' would have taken great objection to this. 'The people' in the sense of 'civil society' most surely did.

No, I believe that for all their professions to the contrary, it was the clause on the land that prompted the MDC and their supporters to oppose the constitution and at the same time to label it a ZANU-PF document. It must certainly have been this clause that motivated the whites to come out in numbers to participate in the referendum, when they had previously been conspicuous by their absence at most other elections and national events. Ironically, those who opposed ZANU-PF might have done well to support the draft constitution, which was obviously a great improvement on the Lancaster House constitution, for if they had read it, they would have realised that, very interestingly, the constitution included a clause limiting the President's time in office to two five year terms! Had the draft been accepted, Robert Gabriel Mugabe would have ceased to be President of Zimbabwe some time back.

Then on the question as to whether the 'no' vote was really the equivalent of a defeat for ZANU-PF on the basis of the general supposition that the draft constitution was a ZANU-PF document, I once had a very interesting discussion with a High Court judge, who was himself a liberation war veteran. He posed the question: "Who said the draft constitution was a ZANU-PF document and supported by them in the referendum?" He went on to say that there were many in the party who did not approve of the draft and that was why ZANU-PF's campaign to win support for the document was not whole-hearted. This seems to be borne out by the fact that only 26% of the electorate voted and the 'no' vote was only carried by 54.31% of that 26%. This meant that only 14% of the electorate voted against the constitutional draft! This would suggest that ZANU-PF did not deploy its massive party structures in the rural areas to get its voters to come out in support of the document.

However, many did see the rejection of the draft constitution as a defeat for ZANU-PF. For them, the unthinkable seemed to have happened. After 20 years in power, most of it so dominant that one could be forgiven for mistaking Zimbabwe for a one-party state, ZANU-PF seemed to have lost a national vote.

The 'No' vote was regarded by the liberation war veterans as tantamount to a vote against the reclamation of the land and consequently an alarm bell that tolled the collapse of everything they had fought for. Government moved very smartly to sort this out by using its vast majority in parliament to amend the 1992 Land Acquisition Act along the lines of the rejected draft constitution. However, what they saw as their triumph in the referendum was a tremendous fillip to all those who opposed ZANU-PF – in particular to the MDC and the whites in general. With the parliamentary elections coming up and an MDC victory a distinct possibility, all this nastiness over the land would come to an end, they hoped, and things would go back to business as usual – lucrative as has been noted.

Whatever has been said about the elections that followed, to what extent they were rigged and to what extent they represented the will of the people, the fact is that they reflected the balance of power in the country at that time. The whites voted overwhelmingly for the MDC as did their class mates, the black middle class in the ex-white suburbs. MDC had majority support among the working class and lumpen proletariat in the large towns and cities and majorities in almost all Matebeleland. ZANU-PF retained much of its hold on the countryside in the Shona speaking provinces. But it was a damn close thing. In the previous parliament, ZANU-PF had held all the seats except three! In the election of 2000, ZANU-PF polled 1,212,302 votes, which amounted to 48.6% of the electorate and produced 62 seats, the MDC 1,171,051 votes, 47% and 57 seats – a majority of only five!

Kgosi walla! The alarm had sounded – for Robert Mugabe, for ZANU-PF, for the corrupt fat cats and looters in the party and government, for the military, for the war vets, for the chiefs and those in the countryside who still cherished hopes of getting their land back – and for all those others who believed that the organisation that had fought the liberation struggle, for all its corruption and all its betrayal, was still the best guarantee that Zimbabwe would not be lost again – for all these, the writing was on the wall. Another five years of sanctions and economic hardship and the MDC would sweep into power and then goodbye to it all. Yes, people say that Mugabe and ZANU-PF only decided to take the land when they saw that there was no other way to stay in power. This is true only in the sense that the referendum and the subsequent narrow squeak in the elections brought everyone, everyone who saw the danger – for all their varied motives and hopes – together and created the determined consensus to seize the time – and seize the land, while they still had the power.

In this desperate hour, it was not only the land that was there to be seized. The song says '*Tinoda Zimbabwe ne upfumi hwayo hwose*'. The war of liberation was not fought for the land only. It was fought for the land and all its wealth – the seizure of the land had to be accompanied by 'indigenisation', majority shareholding in mines, black control and ownership of the banking sector, challenging the white monopoly of tobacco sales and export and so on.

Time was now of the essence. The Land Reforms had to be 'fast-tracked'. In the first ten years after Independence policy on the land provided for the principle of 'willing seller, willing buyer'. This had developed into compulsory acquisition with compensation at market prices. Now, accepting the assertion that the land had been acquired from its original owners for nothing, the Fast Track programme offered only compensation for improvements. At first, land that was designated was confined to unutilised land on large farms, multiple farm ownership and absentee owners. But as the international opposition to the process grew more and more intense, as negative publicity and sanctions bit in, restraint was thrown to the winds and whole farms were designated and single farm owners lost their land. The opponents of the Land Reform described what happened as 'farm invasions' and a 'land grab'.

The previous chapter and this short summary of what happened in 2000 is intended to shed some light on why and how it was all of 18 years before ZANU-PF moved to take the land. Hopefully it goes some way towards exposing the oversimplification that the Land Reform was engineered from above as a cynical ploy by ZANU-PF to retain their support base in the face of defeat in the Constitutional referendum and losses to the MDC at the General Election. There was most certainly an element of that. ZANU-PF knew that, unless they returned to the revolutionary agenda, they would have no hope of retaining the support of the armed forces, the liberation war veterans, the chiefs and the rural masses. However, it was not engineered from above. What the party did was to throw its weight behind those who were already trying to move onto the land or were agitating for it. They did not do it only to retain their support but also to seize the land while they still had the power.

Hopefully, too, it might also make it a little clearer why the Land Reform did not go ahead in the nice, planned way some people said it should. Land Reform in Zimbabwe was revolutionary change. Revolution is a more or less fundamental transformation of power and property in a society. It is a structural re-organisation and pits the interests of those who possess power, wealth and property against those who don't. It is often accompanied by violence – and this is to be expected seeing that very few people, social groups or communities possessing power, wealth and property will consent to relinquish them peacefully or in a 'nice, planned way'. One would have thought this was obvious with relation to Land Reform and the Zimbabwean situation. It remains to be seen whether those who hold the power, wealth and property in South Africa will find a 'nice, planned' way to share it with or re-distribute it among those who don't. I hope so – but unfortunately, history holds few examples of it.

In terms of the so-called 'Zimbabwe crisis', there is no doubt in my mind that the fundamental point at issue is the Land. Everything stems from it. When some Zimbabweans decided the time had come to take back what their ancestors had lost a century before them, other Zimbabweans, black and white, opposed it. They aligned themselves with powerful forces in the world, more specifically in South Africa, Britain, the European Union, the White Commonwealth and the United States. In their efforts to oppose it, they crafted a multi-faceted offensive against the ZANU-PF government. In the process they popularised, through their control of the 'international' media apparatus, an effective propaganda portfolio. As the land was the key issue, the interpretation and assessment of the Land Reform is of vital importance for anyone sincerely trying to make head or tail out of events. In the next chapter (Chapter 17) we examine the assertion that the Land Reform was an illegal and unacceptable 'land grab' accomplished by widespread 'farm invasions'. In the two chapters that follow (Chapters 18 and 19) we look at the widely publicised allegations and statements which have come to be accepted as definitive judgements on the issue of the Land Reform and try and show that they have little basis in fact – that indeed they are largely 'myths'.

CHAPTER SEVENTEEN:

LAND GRAB

The power to take

One day about 120 years ago – the well-known political journalist and publisher, the late David Martin[32], tells us - a white man, one of the early pioneers, set out to look for his missing oxen. He saw some very interesting and inviting hills in the distance and decided to explore them. He records in his diaries that he passed a number of inhabited villages as he roamed. He was 'enchanted' by the lush green topography, the rich forests, the delightful 'burns' and the agreeable views. There and then he decided to set up his beacon and proclaim the entire area as his 'pioneer farm' of 3 000 acres. He called it 'Cloudlands'. The hills he roamed came to be very well-known as the Bvumba - along with Nyanga and Chimanimani, one of the most beautiful areas in the Eastern Highlands. This man was Lionel Cripps, who lived on his farm, Cloudlands, until his death in the 1950's.

David Martin also tells us that when the Pioneer Column first came to the country, every member of the column was given at least 4 500 acres of the best land. The first white child to be born in the country was gifted by Rhodes with a farm of 3 000 acres. Handouts of land ranged from relatively 'small' farms like these to others of 29 000, 80 000 or even in one case 800 000 acres! As the land was measured

32 See http://www.sardc.net/Editorial/Newsfeature/07410907.htm David Martin was a British 'writer and photographer, and later in life, a publisher. He was a rigorous researcher and investigative writer'. He observed and wrote over many years on the liberation struggles of southern Africa - Mozambique, Zimbabwe and South Africa in particular. Together with his wife, Phyllis Johnston, he founded the Zimbabwe Publishing House and SARDC (Southern African Resource Documentation Centre).

straight from a map and took no account of hills and valleys, the chunks handed out were even bigger than the official measurements suggest. Much of this land remained in the hands of the original families for over a hundred years and more. When the land was carved up by the white settlers, no account whatsoever was taken of the fact that there were people already living on it.

If one is looking for 'land grabs', this was a land grab – and the process of land-grabbing did not stop there. Right up into the 1970's land never stopped being grabbed from its indigenous inhabitants. It would not be too much of an exaggeration to say that whenever and wherever a white man saw a piece of land he desired, he more or less took it – with the state and the judiciary's connivance, of course. Before 1914 the British South Africa Company was selling the land to the settlers at knockdown prices. When both settlers and indigenous Zimbabweans challenged the company's ownership of the land, the Privy Council in Britain vested all land in the Crown and then ruled that whoever owns the land not yet sold to the settlers, 'the natives certainly do not'! This decision legalised the forceful and indiscriminate land grabs that went on and on from that date right up to Independence in 1980. Whole clans, communities, villages and families were uprooted and transported by force in lorries to alternative sites. Where they resisted, they were shot, beaten and imprisoned. There are no statistics as to how many were killed in the process. Dispossession and forced removal did not even end there. If after they had been dumped somewhere and it was later decided that the land they had been resettled on was good for white settlement, it too could be grabbed – and a number of indigenous communities were forcefully removed from their land over and over again, normally to ever more arid and barren soils and drought-prone areas.

That the original inhabitants of the land were often cast into wilderness that was hardly fit for human habitation, is beyond dispute. Colonial administrators themselves testified to the fact. "Practically useless, owing to the lack of water and rocky nature of the soil," said a white Native Commissioner about the area where the Nambya people were dumped – after almost 3 500 000 acres of their best land had been grabbed without any compensation whatsoever, land which included the Hwange coal deposits, one of the largest coal deposits in the world and from which the country has derived its coal for over 120 years and which, it is said, will last for another 1 000 years. The Nambya people today live in relative poverty in their waterless, rocky reserves, proudly preserving their culture but finding it difficult to eke out a livelihood.

Cripps referred to the little streams he encountered as 'burns', a Scottish word for 'streams'. In addition to the 'burns', Cripps noted the great hills and mountains, forests and waterfalls –and ever since their discovery, whites have never ceased to note the resemblance of the Eastern Highlands to the Scottish Highlands. Many is the settler farm or house in that area that was given a Scottish name. I am not sure how aware they were that the resemblance to the Scottish Highlands did not consist in scenery alone. One of the qualities that so delights the modern visitor to the Scottish Highlands is their empty, desolate grandeur - thus fulfilling the ancient Scottish prophecy that 'the time was nigh when a people might ride for fifty miles among the hills and valleys and no find a reekin' hoose nor hear a crawin' cock'.[33] The Highlands would have presented quite a different picture in the

---

33 Old Scottish prophecy, which was seen to have come true after the catastrophe at Culloden in 1746 and the slaughter of the Jacobite clans. The Corries, the popular Scottish folk group, mention it in one of their songs. A similar prophecy is accredited to the Scottish seer, Alexander Peden, who was born a hundred years earlier. But it is difficult to see the connection between Peden's prophecy, which expressed his woe at the bloody extirpation of the Covenanters in the Lowlands and the suppression of the clans and clearances of the Highlands. Whatever the case, the prophecy presaged powerfully the dismal emptiness of the Highlands today.

years before the Battle of Culloden and the infamous Highland Clearances. The valleys and hillsides would have been dotted with small villages or *clachans* and crofters' cottages, with here and there the homestead of the clan chief. The high areas would have been filled in summer with Highland cattle and other livestock and similarly dotted with the *sheilings*, the small cabins in which those tending the animals stayed. The clansmen would have been wearing the kilt, wielding the claymore and dancing to the *pibroch*. Now their ruins simply add to the 'picturesque' nature of the Highlands. And their inhabitants? Scattered all over the world, many shipped out of Scotland and sold as virtual slaves. In the Barbados, it is said, a shipload of Highlanders was once sold for ten tons of sugar![34]

Similarly, as Cripps noted, when he and the others arrived in Nyanga and the Bvumba, there were well-populated villages and homesteads along with the other structures already mentioned all over the area. The people who inhabited them, like the Scottish Highlanders, were no doubt either cleared or allowed to remain on the white properties or plantations - which their former land became - as virtual serfs. There are no doubt similar prophecies and oral remembrances among the Manyika of that traumatic time but a lot remains to be done in the field of Zimbabwean oral culture.

Zimbabwe is not that big a country. Those who see African tourism as being all about scenic beauty, wild animals, tribal dancing and native crafts, would inevitably cite: *Musi-wa-Tunya* (The Smoke that Thunders), known internationally as the Victoria

---

34 Cited in, among other sources, *The Many-headed Hydra*, by P.Linebaugh and M.Rediker (Beacon Press), a book which suggests a new take on anti-capitalist protest, resistance and, in the concept of the hydrarchy, social alternatives on the Atlantic rim.

Falls; the Kariba Dam; Great Zimbabwe and Lake Mutirikwi; the Hwange National Park; Mana Pools; the so-called Matopos; and the Eastern Highlands[35] as Zimbabwe's major tourist assets.

But if one were to update this rather old-fashioned approach to tourism, Zimbabwe would be seen to have a wealth of other attractions to offer. Its first resource is its people – the people themselves, their culture, their lifestyles, their dance and music. Its second is their history. Zimbabwe is full of places where fascinating historical events and happenings took place, many of them not only neglected but also unresearched and undocumented – let alone developed for tourism. And all over the country there are shrines, sacred mountains, mysterious pools (*madziva*) known to be places inhabited by *njuzu* – water spirits - battlegrounds, political monuments and landmarks. There are ancient stone settlements and their remains. There are ancient mines, both gold and iron. It took someone like the English historian, Basil Davidson[36], to teach us that in the eastern interior of central and southern Africa iron and gold were mined. The iron and gold, along with ivory and slaves, were the basis for the establishment of Iron Age states that participated in the great Indian Ocean trade of the centuries before the arrival of the Portuguese. Davidson tells us that African iron was greatly sought after and that the best swords in the world were manufactured from it in India. Proof of the way in which

Zimbabwe and other parts of the region were integrated into a world

35 Victoria Falls and Kariba Dam are on the Zambezi River, the Hwange (Wankie) Game Reserve is located some kilometers south of Victoria Falls, Great Zimbabwe and Lake Mutirikwi are a few kilometres outside the town of Masvingo, which is halfway between Harare and Beit Bridge, Mana Pools is a game viewing conservancy on the lower reaches of the Zambezi, the so-called Matopos (Matobo) is a region of bald hills and boulders south of the western city of Bulawayo and the eastern highlands are on the border with Mozambique in the east and include the Nyanga Rhodes National Park, the Bvumba and further south the hills and mountains of Chimanimani.

36 See above: Basil Davidson, *Black Mother*

that embraced Ethiopia, Arabia, Persia, India, Indonesia and China is not only the presence of peoples in modern Zimbabwe who derive from the Arabian peninsula but also of Shona-speaking people in Madagascar!

No place in Zimbabwe, even Great Zimbabwe, is more mysterious than the stone remains in what was until recently known as the Rhodes Nyanga National Park. There are hilltop stone structures. There is extensive stone terracing over a wide area. There is a stone homestead that surrounds what must have been an animal enclosure. Such a ground plan is a common feature of homesteads in most of Southern and East Africa but in the case of the Nyanga stone homesteads there is a difference. The animal enclosure is not on ground level but instead takes the form of a large stone-walled pit. The park thus contains all the signs of having once been a relatively well-populated area. Now, there is not a living soul except those who look after the National Park and visitors. How did this happen? Was it empty when Cecil John Rhodes grabbed it or did he just get rid of all the people?

The white Rhodesians inhabited a Zimbabwe full of enigmas. In addition to propagating myths about Great Zimbabwe or creating parks like the Rhodes Nyanga National Park in which to holiday, many white Rhodesians were also gripped by a general amnesia as to who used to live on the land on which they had established their lovely farms and built their lovely homes and what might have happened to them. Not so the people from whom the land had been taken, to whom the shrines were holy and whose ancestors had built the stone and other structures. They never forgot and they never ceased resenting it. Now, after a century of powerlessness, the indigenous people of Zimbabwe had at last the power to take it back – and take it back they did.

The history of the world is based on violent dispossession – and sometimes equally violent recovery. Who has the right to own or possess anything when it comes down to it? What can we say is ours which has not in some way been stolen from others? It is not a question of right and neither would it appear to be a matter of law. Every society or dominant social class makes laws to justify and protect its own property. The land that was grabbed from the Shona and Ndebele peoples in Zimbabwe was legalised – and the descendants of those who grabbed it claimed they held legal title to the land. As a result, they called the post-2000 Land Reform 'illegal', a 'land grab' and 'farm invasions'.

Grabbing - grabbing land, grabbing property, grabbing possessions – is not about right or law. It is at bottom simply about might. Historically, the strong grab from the weak, justify that possession by promulgating rights and laws to legalise their possession, and then enforce them by their power – their might. If this were not so, why is it that today it is the vanquished and the weak that appear before tribunals that try international crimes, like the International Court of Justice at the Hague. The United States does not even acknowledge the Court! When will the US, Britain, France, the Portuguese, the Belgians - to name but few of the main historical perpetrators of international crimes, be brought to book, be made to stand trial for their crimes? Only when they are defeated, when their might is no longer powerful enough to enforce exemption. Or when people are brave and persistent enough, like the Kenyans who were mutilated and brutalised by the British during the so-called Mau-Mau uprising and have finally forced their old overlords to accept that they have a case to answer.

One may wonder how self-professedly 'civilised' and Christian nations such as Britain, France, Holland, Spain and Portugal could have, full-bloodedly and without any qualms, prosecuted one of the greatest crimes of all time, the Slave Trade. They found justifications, even Christian ones. And then colonialism – it too had its moral and religious justification – after all, the Christian Church and its missionaries were in the forefront.

There is no justification in the world for what the slavers and colonialists did. Their actions were pure expressions of self-interest and might.

And so in Zimbabwe, Rhodesian state propaganda also manufactured justifications for the dispossession of the indigenous inhabitants. They taught their people that when the whites in the Pioneer Column crossed the Limpopo, they found vast tracts of land that were uninhabited and a people that had achieved nothing with whatever they had.

What to make then of what were called the 'Zimbabwe Ruins'? To concede the truth, namely that Great Zimbabwe was built by the Shona people whose descendants had inhabited the land they had seized, would have been to contradict that fact. So official Rhodesian government explanations propagated various far-fetched myths – that, for instance, among other things the stone structures were King Solomon's Palace or built by the Phoenicians or the Arabs.

However, the truth was that the land they were referring to *was* inhabited and its inhabitants derived their living from the land. The bottom line was that the settlers had the power to take it. Thus the white occupation of Zimbabwe was nothing but a farm invasion and a land grab on a massive scale – a grab that continued for over 90 years. It was a violent invasion, a ruthless land grab and countless people not only lost all they had, their land, their homes and their livelihood but uncounted numbers lost their lives and uncounted others were maimed and hurt, including women who were raped. There was no valid justification for this either in right or in law. It all boiled down to the fact that they had the power to take the land – and maintain possession of it – for 110 years. That's all. Then, in 1997, they lost the power – and with it quite a lot of land.

The third decade of Zimbabwe's Independence is the Decade of the Land. At the bottom, everything that happened in this fateful decade came down to the land. The First *Chimurenga* saw the people of Zimbabwe struggle to hold onto their land and then lose it to the white settlers. The Second *Chimurenga* saw them fight to get it back. The land in the sense of *nyika* was won at Independence. But the struggle for the land in the sense of *ivhu* had yet to begin. When, in the third decade of Zimbabwean Independence, it did, it was called the Third *Chimurenga*.

In that great hymn of the liberation war, the comrades sang these lines:

Nyika yedu yeZimbabwe	(Our land of Zimbabwe is where we
ndimo matakazvarirwa	were born
Vanamai nanababa ndimo mavanobva	Our mothers and fathers come from there
Tinoda Zimbabwe ne upfumi hwayo hwose	We want our land back with all its wealth
Simuka Zimbabwe!	Zimbabwe, arise!)

For twenty years after Independence the land in which the comrades had been born and from which their fathers and mothers came, along with all its wealth, remained largely in the hands of those who had taken it from them and against whom they had fought for decades. It was certainly about time they rose and took it back. How and why this happened and what then happened when it happened – this is the story of Zimbabwe's Third Decade of Independence.

The whites no longer had the power – at least, in the short term - to hold on to what they had grabbed. Black Zimbabweans had acquired the power to take it. But the key question - and it is to be wondered how many have given much thought to it - was - and still is: did they – do they - have the power to keep it?

CHAPTER EIGHTEEN:

MYTH AND THE LAND

'The breadbasket of Africa'

Since that fatal moment in the history of Zimbabwe and indeed of Africa, when the die was cast, there have been countless papers, books, television programmes and newspaper articles on the Land Reform in Zimbabwe, which in all this material was more generally referred to as 'the land invasions in Zimbabwe'. The vast body of this material has propagated various assertions about the Land Reform, almost all of them with very little basis in fact and not supported by empirical evidence and research. They were propagated and repeated until they came to be accepted as truths. Now at last published research findings are disputing much of it.

Shortly after the road from Harare to Masvingo was nicely tarred, the expression '*Masvingo necarpet*' became current. It literally meant '(travelling) to Masvingo on a carpet'. And it was from Masvingo that, in 2010, right at the end of the third decade, a breath of fresh air came and stirred up the new winds of change with regard to the Land Reform in Zimbabwe. What lent the breeze from Masvingo its freshness, was the crispness of fact, data, research and testimony that the book by Ian Scoones and his team of Zimbabwean field workers brought to the discussion of the topic. This is not to say that previous researchers, like my former comrade and colleague, Sam Moyo, had not published similar findings based on equally fastidious and professional research data – they have and the Scoones team quotes their work profusely. However, these were only Zimbabweans and any Zimbabweans who opposed the official 'international' line, were branded ZANU-PF and then no-one would listen to them. Of course, the converse was true. Zimbabweans who supported and pandered to the 'international line', *they* were accorded international recognition, awards and other emoluments. The payer pays the piper, to adapt the saying, who plays the tune called.

Zimbabwe's Land Reform: Myths and Realities is really a sort of geography book. It is not particularly concerned with the politics, sociology or history of the situation, either local or global. What it is concerned with is the problem of agriculture in countries like Zimbabwe and a lot of it deals with various theories or models relating to the organisation of agricultural production. It highlights a number of very interesting and significant agricultural features with regard to the Zimbabwean phenomenon and the discovery of these features is based on field work and research into actual experiences and phenomena on the ground in one province of Zimbabwe, namely Masvingo. These discoveries and the debate that swirls around agricultural production and its various models, are readily accessible in the book and there is no need to go into them here.

What *is* relevant here is the way in which Scoones and his team note 'the lack of empirical data' to substantiate much of what has been propagated about land reform in Zimbabwe by the media and others. The result, they say, is 'the generation of a series of oft-repeated 'myths' – simple ways of explaining the world, which may have only a tenuous basis in fact – which have gained the status of 'truth'.' They list five such 'myths' – a list that is strictly limited to the researchers' geographical focus - namely: that the Land Reform in Zimbabwe has been a total failure; that its only beneficiaries are Mugabe and his political cronies; that there has been no investment in the new settlements; that agriculture in the country is in ruins and food insecurity pervasive; and, finally, that the rural economy has collapsed. They then proceed to demonstrate from their research that these 'myths' are largely far from the truth. Obviously, the findings of this study cannot uncritically be extrapolated to make a case for the Land Reform in Zimbabwe nationally. For a start, many of the Masvingo case studies relate to land that was once given over to large-scale cattle ranching. Studies from the better-watered farming areas to the west, north and east of Harare, for instance, where massive farming of crops such as tobacco, maize and cotton used to take place, or from the Eastern Highlands where fruit, coffee and tea farming as well as forestry were to be found, might reveal a somewhat different picture.

One therefore cannot generalise from the Masvingo findings. On the other hand, neither can one confidently pronounce on what happened in Zimbabwe's Land Reform until and at such time as similar studies reveal the true situation in other regions of the country nor can one do so without taking into account the findings from Masvingo.

To these myths I myself have already added - and would like to add other - 'myths' of my own. Myths I have already mentioned are: that ZANU PF should not have waited so long to take the land; that the whole thing was engineered from above; and that the land reform in Zimbabwe was discredited by its disorganisation and chaos. The other 'myths' I would like to add are as follows: that black farmers cannot farm and by corollary only whites can; that when the whites were farming Zimbabwe was 'the breadbasket of Africa'; and that the process of taking back the land was based on terrible violence, destruction and killing.

Lastly, there is an overall 'myth', lie, deception or misconception – whatever one wants to call it - namely that the situation in Zimbabwe was simple and straightforward and can be blamed totally on the evil of Robert Mugabe and his party, ZANU-PF. Mugabe and 'his cronies' were the baddies and the poor white farmers, these 'heroic pioneers who opened up and civilised wild Africa', were the goodies. It is only thanks to this wilful or thoughtless distortion of the truth that the media stereotypes – and the 'myths' noted above – can possibly have been sustained and perpetuated as they have been.

Zimbabwe's Land Reform: Myths and Realities shows incontrovertibly that in one prescribed subject area, namely the geography of land and agriculture, and in one province of Zimbabwe the situation in Zimbabwe cannot and never could be understood or explained by recourse to simplistic, stereotypical and/or polarised judgements. The book goes on to show that this complexity is the feature that characterises what happened on the land in Zimbabwe in the third decade of its independence and that the five assertions it lists, which have been universally propagated in a cavalier fashion by the international media, the South African press and uninformed or misinformed people all over the world as facts, are in fact 'myths'.

A myth, I take it, is not the same as a lie, a deception, a fabrication or a mistaken belief. Myth is closely related to truth whereas lies and deceptions are less so. A well-known encyclopaedia explains a myth as: 'a symbolic narrative, usually of unknown origin and at least partly traditional, that ostensibly relates actual events and that is especially associated with religious belief'. Every myth enfolds a core of reality, subjective or objective. In fact, a myth is another way of expressing a truth. The actions and the characters it describes may never have actually existed but their meaning or significance is usually compellingly real. The reality a myth expresses may be a social practice or tendency or it may simply be a yearning or a desire, perhaps a way of compensating for what did not happen or never can happen but what human beings dream and long for to happen. A very beautiful example of a myth is the myth of Cadmus's founding of the city of Thebes, which was described at the beginning of the book. In purporting to tell of the founding of a city, it gives its inhabitants a moral lesson on war, peace and harmony.

There must have been a lot of people who wished for or needed what Scoones and his team called 'myths', to be true. Generally, the truth they wished for or needed to be true was important to them because of the particular interests they had in the question of the land in Zimbabwe. If we go back to the early days after independence, when Rhodesia had been lost and many people were confronted by the new Zimbabwe and they witnessed the old world that was so good for them, slipping away into the past, they comforted themselves and each other by finding fault in everything new they saw around them. In a way, they were myth-building – the myth of Plato's Golden Age, the myth of an idyllic Rhodesia where everything was better than what they found fault with on a daily basis in the new society that was taking shape. For many the nostalgia never faded.

In those who left to make new lives in South Africa, Britain, the United States, Australia and elsewhere, nostalgia was curdled by bitterness. They comforted themselves by refusing to call the new country Zimbabwe and expecting everyone in their circle to swallow their myths about the backward blacks, what a great country Rhodesia had been and how Robert Mugabe destroyed it.

Many of those who stayed behind clung to the same myths and shared much of the same nostalgia. Yet, despite their grumblings, they continued to live in Zimbabwe, which even they, many of them, refused to call so. For another twenty years after the collapse of their Rhodesia, they lived a life of ease and pleasure, which, if they had paused to reflect, was in many ways so much better than the days of UDI. Gone were the sanctions, gone was the old black and white TV, gone were the restrictions on international travel and participation in sporting events. With Independence they had lost their Rhodesia but in Zimbabwe they remained with their privileges and material possessions intact and a lot of advantages they had never had before.

Then they lost their land. Just as they had needed the myths to sustain themselves when Rhodesia went, now they needed new but related myths to deal with the disaster of losing their land. They had a vested interest in the myths being true and a vested interest in getting others to accept them as true. They still had hopes that things would change and they would get 'their' land back and so the myths they clung to became propaganda, an important weapon in their campaign to get 'their' land back. In this, they had many advantages and many allies and they were resourceful in capitalising on them. First of all, they began to dominate the published literature on Zimbabwe and take possession of the internet. Their myths even to this day are almost all there is to be seen in this terrain. Secondly, their vested interests coincided with those of the most powerful forces on earth.

There is one thing that is a red rag to the bulls of capitalism – and that is the violation of the sanctity of private property. Don't talk to me about any other sanctity. The most Christian, the most fundamentalist religious right-wing capitalist, can find a way to live with sacrilege – if it is profitable. But the sacrilege of violating the right - or the principle of the right - of private property, they will never accept or live with. The violation of private property wherever it happens, they never forget. Between 1959 and 1962 some of them and others of their class lost their property in Cuba. The land was re-distributed to the people and the sugar mills nationalised – over fifty years ago. They have never forgotten Cuba and they never will forget it until that land and those mills are returned to the owners or the descendants of the owners who held them in the epoch of Batista. Cuba can do what it likes but *el bloqueo* is here to stay – until that day.

Similarly, Zimbabwe can do what it likes but the sanctions are here to stay – until, as the US quite candidly put it, the land tenure situation returns to the situation that prevailed in the late 1990s. The fact that in pilloring both Cuba and Zimbabwe their propaganda stresses human rights, the rule of law, freedom of expression and various other 'rights' they care not a fig for and which the armed fist of their power, NATO, violates all the time all over the world with impunity, should not obfuscate the issue. The bottom line in the hysteria of the Western media and the establishment concerning Zimbabwe is the land and its wealth – the rest is mere camouflage or, put another way perhaps, opium for the people (see Chapter 24).

So this is where the Rhodies, international capitalism and the MDC came together. They shared a fundamental vested interest in the myths that I have listed above being true – and they possessed the most powerful media and propaganda machine the world has ever seen, to see to it that - with no scruples, with no reverence whatsoever for the facts and with absolutely no concern for the professional ethics of journalism - the myths became fact, became truth, became history - for people all over the world.

Simply by way of illustration as to how unsubstantiated assertions establish themselves as myths to the point that they are universally parroted without question or any scrutiny whatsoever, let's take the contention that Rhodesia was once the 'breadbasket of Africa'. The use of this phrase is routine and pervasive all over the world yet it is so absurd that it is extraordinary that it can have remained unchallenged and that it has continued to be bandied about the way it has all these years. One would have thought that it was obvious that even if its braggadocio were to be significantly downsized and the statement changed to, say, 'Rhodesia was the breadbasket of southern (or even central) Africa', one would still have serious difficulties trying to sustain it. Being the breadbasket of a geographical region – in this case a continent! - implies that the countries in that region depended on that basket for their bread or that it produced more bread than any other country in the region. Is there any proof that any countries in Africa at all, outside of those in the immediate vicinity, ever benefitted from Rhodesian 'bread' or food? Do we have any statistics to show that no other African country could rival little Rhodesia in the production of food, including that breadbasket of the Roman Empire, North Africa and Egypt? If there is any truth to the claim at all, it would surely have to apply to the period of the Federation and it is possible that Southern Rhodesia did help feed Nyasaland and Northern Rhodesia, just as the latter's minerals contributed to the wealth of Southern Rhodesia. It certainly did not feed South Africa or the other members of the Southern African Customs Union – Bechuanaland, Basotholand, South-West Africa and Swaziland. As to be expected with wild assertions, there is no attempt to define the phrase in terms of chronology – when precisely is it claimed that Rhodesia was the breadbasket of Africa? It wasn't long after the collapse of the Federation before the Unilateral Declaration of Independence and the imposition of international sanctions. Even if Rhodesia had ever fed Africa or been the greatest producer of food on the continent, after the imposition of sanctions this would have been impossible. In any case, the imposition of sanctions led to a serious contraction in Rhodesia's export ability. During this period, tobacco exports formed up to 50% of total agricultural output. Yes, Rhodesia in good years had a surplus of maize and possibly wheat but unless you classify tobacco as food, it never really generated anything serious enough to deserve the phrase 'breadbasket'.

In the years after Independence there were a number of droughts and in any case the trajectory of white commercial farming in the period was away from food crops, dairy and beef towards the more lucrative cash crops such as flowers and game. Black farmers had already overtaken white farmers in the growth of many food crops and were beginning to make significant inroads into the tobacco and horticultural sectors. This is not to detract from the achievements of the white commercial farmer. Anyone who lived in Zimbabwe as long as I did, could not fail to appreciate the superlative quality of Tanganda tea, Bvumba coffee, Mazowe orange juice and some very good Mukuyu wines.

However, the breadbasket assertion, along with all those other wild and absurd claims that derived from the narrow illusions of an isolated community, should either be proved or dumped into the dustbin of history. However, it has been taken up by the media, writers and ordinary people all over the world and, quite unquestioned, waved incessantly as a universally accepted stick with which to beat the Land Reform in Zimbabwe.[37]

My point – and basically Scoones and his team's point - is that a lot of the stuff that the media and a whole lot of other people are

37 Ironically, even members of the ZANU-PF government seem to have swallowed it, as Ministers, when discussing agricultural development, even now talk of restoring Zimbabwe's status as the breadbasket of Africa.

saying about the Land Reform in Zimbabwe is simply not true. In order to make this point it is not necessary – and it would be tiresome – so take each myth one by one and illustrate its falsity. A few of them should suffice. So, how about taking 'Land Reform in Zimbabwe was a total failure' for a start?

CHAPTER NINETEEN:

THE LAND REFORM REVISITED

Failures, cronies and no investment

Myth 1: Land Reform in Zimbabwe was a total failure

Opponents of the Land Reform in Zimbabwe paint a bleak picture. They quote statistics which show how production figures across the board plummeted. They describe how vast areas of once productive farmland became desolate wasteland, uncultivated, vandalised and reverting to bush. They love the telling and damning aphorism - and they use it a lot - “From breadbasket to basket case.”

In terms of the Land Reform’s impact on production, it is true that the initial picture was alarming – but really, what did people expect? Farming is a business that takes years, even in the best of circumstances, to achieve successful and profitable production. How much more so in the Zimbabwe of the years after 2000! However since the stabilisation of inflation and the slow return to what normality can be achieved under sanctions, there have been encouraging signs that the many new farmers will soon equal the best production levels achieved by those few white commercial farmers who monopolised the land in days of yore – there is even reason to believe that they have the potential to dwarf them – and more importantly do so in a *completely different – and much more democratic - way.*

The point is that logically land reform in Zimbabwe was inevitable – for two reasons. Firstly, there was the historic injustice of the colonial land grab and the glaring inequality in land ownership and access to wealth that characterised the new Zimbabwe. Zimbabwe and all its wealth belong to its people – goes the song. Every people has the right to confront its own destiny – and this includes the right to fail.

Secondly, the capacity for growth and development of a colonial economy is by definition limited – something South Africa has not yet come to terms with. In pure economic terms, it stood to reason that opening up the agricultural sector to the majority and bringing under cultivation vast tracts of land which the tiny white minority had no hope of utilising, had the potential to expand production on a massive scale.

Given this, it seems to me extraordinary that it never occurred to the white commercial farmers – until too late - that the situation could not and would not continue as it was forever. Perhaps secure in the entitlement their understanding of history and what they felt their title deeds afforded them, they did not see the need to think – or feel. I would have thought that the fundamental injustice of the situation would have made them a little uncomfortable. I would have thought that the danger of the situation would have been a little obvious to them. They must have been perfectly aware that the main goal of the liberation struggle was winning back the land. Why did they not, starting at Independence, begin to make the accommodation that might have secured their future? They were after all rather fortunate that independence had come through negotiation and not as a result of total defeat. In the latter case, they might have lost their land a lot earlier. Why did they not begin a dialogue with government with a view to bringing in black farmers and partners and through sharing their land and training, assist in bringing about a transition which would not only have righted the historic injustices but also ensured continuity and expansion of production as well as their own futures? But many of them were quite myopic, not to say, intransigent and often contemptuous and insulting. Many were the stories of farmers who told their workers on their farms that 'this is not Zimbabwe, there is no Mugabe here'. Many, too, were the instances of degrading punishments, atrocious living conditions and horrific farm schools – something which I witnessed for myself on the commercial farms in the Darwendale area. Some maintained their fatal racist attitudes to the end. Even with their farms already occupied by base camps led by veterans of the liberation struggle, they refused to share their land in defiant and contemptuous terms. Scoone's and his team quote one farmer's wife who reportedly told those on her land to their faces that she did not want 'to live with kaffirs'. When local civil servants suggested to the owner of a farm that was being occupied, that he sell beef to the community, he retorted by saying that he did not sell beef to ZANU-PF!

That a more far-seeing approach would very likely have brought about a completely different outcome in Zimbabwe is illustrated by the fact that some farmers, who worked well with their workers, whose attitudes were not discriminatory and abusive and who worked closely with their black neighbours, the people in the communal areas nearby, the officials in the party and the administration, and who shared their land and expertise, did mostly survive *Jambanja* and even the later, far more unpredictable period when the political heavyweights weighed in with their own land grab - and many retained possession of a farm or a sizeable part of their former farm.

The farmers whose ancestors transformed Rhodesia, so we are told, into 'the breadbasket of Africa', developed their farms in quite different circumstances from those the new farmers of the Land Reform experienced. Wherever agriculture has been successfully developed from scratch, notably in colonial societies like North America, Australia, South Africa and Rhodesia, the farmers benefitted from massive and sustained assistance from the state. They hardly had to pay anything for the land in the first place. Farm allotments were generous in size. They received long-term, interest-free or very low interest loans and sustained support in the form of inputs and subsidies. They were able to count on the state to pass legislation that provided them with the requisite cheap labour. It was not some miraculous or inborn talent for farming that created what the Rhodesians call their 'breadbasket'. It was years and years of very favourable conditions and support.

The situation which faced the new black farmers when they went onto the land in Zimbabwe, was quite different. First of all, the amounts of land and people involved and consequently the dislocations were massive. The failure or otherwise of a massive agrarian revolution of the type that took place in Zimbabwe, could only be fairly and realistically assessed after at least a decade – and even that would be too short a time. Yet commentators highlighted the immediate and inevitable downturn in productivity as a way of proving its failure. This was surely unreasonable.

Most of the land taken over and most of the new farmers moved onto land in areas which came to be pegged for the A1 villagised or self-contained small plots. In these areas the land the new farmers moved onto was largely land which previous farmers had not farmed either as they were using it for cattle-rearing or simply because they had never had the capacity to make full use of it. On this land, the new farmers had to start from scratch. Thus it was obviously going to take some time before these A1 farms began to produce significantly. Also the figures quoted to illustrate the collapse of agriculture would relate to production that was registered in the formal or previous market. Yet a very high percentage of these farmers declared an increased livelihood from even their very early efforts – and their production would not have got into official records. Very importantly, the success of the Land Reform cannot be measured in national production figures alone but should also take into account the livelihood impact on those now involved in production. This is what Scoones and his team refer to as 'accumulation from below'.

Where the new farmers were taking over land that had previously been developed – mostly the A2 commercial model farms – they faced many problems. In some cases their tenure was either challenged or even reversed. In many cases the equipment and infrastructure required for continued production - dairy equipment, pumps, irrigation pipes and dams - were destroyed and vandalised or simply carted away by the previous owners and so they too had to start from scratch. In the case of sugar, for instance, the mill owners would not pay them for their crop as they refused to recognise their legality. When this happened in Cuba, the mills were nationalised. It is interesting that this did not take place in Zimbabwe and much of the sugar-growing industry in the south-east of the country was left relatively intact and in fact amplified by the entry of many new farmers.

All the new occupants, both A1 and A2, required capital and support at a time when the state could do little to assist. The banks had neither the capacity nor, in most cases, the will to assist them. Remember that some of the major banks in Zimbabwe are British or South African – Standard Chartered, Barclays, Stanbic or Standard. In any case, bank requirements for agricultural borrowing required title deeds and in the situation that prevailed at the time, most of the new farmers could not satisfy that requirement. The United Nations, the IMF, the World Bank and the traditional donors did not, for obvious reasons, come on board. As a result, not only did the new farmers have to face a total unavailability of capital but they had to operate at a time of sanctions.

Chapter 22 talks of how Zimbabweans used to say that there were two sanctions people suffered from – one the external sanctions imposed by the West, Japan and others, the other the internal sanctions in the form of rampant corruption. The combined effect of these two forms of sanctions meant that supplies of seed, fertiliser, water, electricity and diesel were at best erratic, at worst non-existent. As we shall see, even when efforts were made by the state to provide them, ruthless abuse, opportunism and profiteering by those with access to power sabotaged their effectiveness.

I am not qualified to contest the 'myth' that the Land Reform is a total failure with research and statistics. I leave that to people like Scoones and his team. Suffice it to say that it is far too early to pronounce on its success or failure and that no simple answer is possible at this time. On the contrary, it is already clear that the simplified 'truth', widely propagated, that it was a failure is premature and an irresponsible distortion of the complexity and variety on the ground. There would already seem to be copious evidence to suggest that far from being a failure, the Land Reform in Zimbabwe has registered significant and interesting successes and has provided thousands of people with a new opportunity to make something of their lives. Commenting on the success rate in Masvingo Province, Scoones and his team had this to say: "In the eyes of those who have moved onto the new land, and contrary to the views often propagated, the land reform has been far from an unmitigated disaster." Their research in Masvingo reveals that the Land Reform is interestingly diverse and full of important potential for the future and that many of those on the land see it as an effective means of improving their livelihood.

In fact, in terms of the global debate on appropriate methods of developing a successful agricultural base in countries such as Zimbabwe, the Land Reform in Zimbabwe has put land reform back on the agenda and suggested new ideas. Scoones and company note that the new A2 farms – the larger formerly white commercial farms – are not replicas of what had existed before and neither are the new A1 – smaller farms – simply an extension of patterns in the communal areas. They note that those farming the new farms are younger, more educated, with a wider range of skills than their forebears. Though the state has not had the resources to impact meaningfully on their operations, there has been a process of developing wealth from below. The jury is definitely still out on Zimbabwe's Land Reform and the premature judgements and apocalyptic visions and prophecies of disaster do not do it - nor the people of Zimbabwe - justice.

Myth 2: The Land Reform in Zimbabwe only benefitted Mugabe and his political cronies

'Crony' originally meant 'close friend' or 'companion' – virtually synonymous with 'chum'. Now it has attracted a negative connotation, implying a companion in activities that are not quite wholesome. When people said that it is Mugabe and his cronies who got the land, I think we can take it that they meant he and his political cronies got the land. Let us assume it refers to members of the politburo of the party and other powerful figures in the provinces, to Ministers and Deputy Ministers, Permanent Secretaries and other top Civil Servants, higher-ups in the armed forces etc – and their families. Well, if it does, it refers to quite a lot of people. And to some extent these were the kind of people who were given the A2 commercial type farms - or just muscled in and grabbed them for themselves.

But the taking of the land came in two main waves. The first one seems to have been initiated by chiefs, liberation war veterans, local people and in some cases even the workers on the farms. The war veterans participated in two ways – either as organised by the Zimbabwe National Liberation War Veterans Association (ZNLWVA) or as freelance agitators. To a large extent such people went onto farms that were subsequently pegged out as A1 small-scale farms. The second wave came in the period of indiscriminate grabbing when Mugabe's 'cronies' - if you like – weighed in in a big way and grabbed multiple farms – in their own, their wives and their relatives' names. They often took away farms or land that had previously been occupied by other ordinary black Zimbabweans, including war veterans, who naturally resisted fiercely. The greed of the cronies was not confined to the rural areas. There are cases I know of personally where urban plots and houses were grabbed.

If this latter wave had been all that happened, one would have to agree that the statement that the land went to Mugabe and his cronies, was, though not the truth, somewhat closer to the truth. But it was not all that happened. In the Masvingo study, 1,169 people got themselves the larger A2 farms and 32,500 the smaller A1 farms. If one counts the families of the farmer – male or female, as possibly for the first time rural women were able to hold land in their own right - this amounted to some 200 000 people in all. These figures exclude the 8,500 families occupying informal settlements. Here we are talking of only one of nine provinces in Zimbabwe.

On the A1 farms nearly half of the beneficiaries were ordinary rural *povo*. Other beneficiaries included urban *povo*, civil servants, some but not many members of the security forces, a few businessmen and some farm workers. The majority of the beneficiaries on the A2 farms were not Mugabe's cronies. They were ordinary people from the towns, followed by civil servants. Global figures for the

Masvingo study show that in the informal settlements 92% were povo, rural and urban, in the villagised A1 they were 69%, in the self-contained A1 58% and on the A2 farms they were 58%. An interesting figure is that for the war veterans. Despite the key role they played in spearheading the re-possession of the land, they constituted only 8.8% of the total beneficiaries.

Figures of this kind are not to my knowledge available for the rest of the country. But the figures from Masvingo alone, taken by themselves, cast serious doubt on the assertion that the Land Reform mainly benefitted Mugabe and his cronies. The figures can be complemented by my own and many other people's first-hand knowledge of the many ordinary and apolitical beneficiaries of the Land Reform that in no way could be counted among 'Mugabe and his cronies'. Incidentally, beneficiaries also included members - and some prominent - of the main opposition parties – and even one or two whites!

Myth 3: there has been no investment in the new settlements

By this assertion is meant that when the new farmers got onto the farms that had been built up over many generations through investment in infrastructure, equipment, irrigation, stock etc. by the previous white owners, they either simply utilised what they found there or let the place run to rack and ruin, owing to the fact that they had no capital and could not, like the previous farmers, invest in the farm.

It has already been noted that one of the difficulties faced by the new farmer in Zimbabwe during the third decade of independence was the lack of capital – and the reasons for this have been given. Investment capital was not available for them from the state, the banks or other investors, including the United Nations agencies such as FAO or UNDP, the World Bank and the IMF as it had been for the previous farmers or as it had been for farmers in other countries where they were starting from scratch. But this did not mean there was no investment. Sources were limited. The problems of the economy, which affected the majority of Zimbabweans, meant that private resources were limited – but astonishingly investment there was.

As Scoones and his team write: "Overall, we argue, the scale of investment carried out by people themselves, and without significant support from government or aid agencies, is substantial, and provides firm foundations for the future." They cite investment in clearing the land, in livestock, housing, tree planting, soil conservation and water development. This raises the question: from where then did the resources for investment come?

Masvingo was a province over much of which cattle-ranching held sway. Yet the new farmers were interested in cultivating the land. Thus a great deal of land clearance was required. However, it is by no means certain that this made the Masvingo example totally idiosyncratic. In other provinces, the same might also have been to a greater or lesser extent the case, owing to the fact that on many farms, even those that were commercially cultivated, vast tracts had not been brought under cultivation or utilised at all before.

In some few cases, the land was cleared mechanically but in most it was done by hand. The research estimates that probably an average of 11 hectares of land were cleared on each farm – those farms where no clearing took place being for the purposes of statistics included. Taking the cost of hiring labour to clear and de-stump a hectare, this comes to an average investment of about US$350 per household.

Also because a lot of the land had been given over to cattle-ranching, the new settlers had few existing farmhouses to occupy – unlike some other regions in the country. So to a large extent they were forced to build their own houses. What they built depended on a number of factors, including security of tenure. For instance, had they received an offer letter? Was the habitation for themselves or for their workers? Did they live on the property or did they have their main residence somewhere else? Owing to uncertainty as well as in some cases local usage, many homes were built in the traditional way – what from colonial times has been called 'pole and dagga' or 'wattle and daub', referring to the use of mud and timber in the construction of the walls and thatch in the construction of the roof ('*udaka*' means 'mud' in Nguni languages, hence the Shona borrowing '*madaga*'.) However, where there was security of tenure and on the A2 farms, a very high percentage of houses or buildings had brick walls and asbestos roofing. The Masvingo report's estimate of average investment on building per homestead – arrived at in the same way as that for land development – was US$630. The incidence of brick and asbestos structures is significantly higher in the new settlements than in the neighbouring communal lands.

In terms of cattle, basically herds on the A2 farms declined – reflecting the high incidence of cattle-rustling and disease. However there was a major increase in cattle numbers in the A1 over the period. In almost all instances farmers' herds increased, sometimes owing to investment in stock but mostly through natural causes and also because of the improved grazing. The proportion of cattle to people in the new settlements became much higher than in the nearby communal areas. Average accumulated value in relation to cattle for households in the study was calculated at US$620.

Equipment is another area where investment took place and the percentage of households that had ox-drawn ploughs registered increases across the board with almost all of the most successful households – A1 villagised and self-contained, A2 and Informal – owning them, with the percentage for the least successful households improving. Added to this, in some case studies, specifically on the sugarcane farms, almost all have acquired tractors. It is true that there were numerous state-sponsored loan schemes and tractor donations but no farmers in the study benefitted from them and instead bought their own equipment. Ploughs, cultivators and scotch carts (donkey carts) were also bought. Because of the decline in public transport nationally, transport became a serious problem for the new farmers and there was a dramatic rise in the number of bicycle and even car and truck purchases.

And so the story continued – with relation to toilets, gardens, wells and boreholes and impressively many examples of community development – schools, churches, markets and other structures. The study sums up its figures with the following food for thought: "While state investment in the new resettlements has been very low, and that of donors and aid agencies effectively zero, settlers themselves have been investing on an impressive scale." The study estimates that if the whole province were taken into account, the investment could come to over US$90 million. "To put this into perspective, the total overseas development aid to the whole of Zimbabwe averaged US$289.6 million over the period 1999 – 2008." It goes on: "The myth that there is no investment on the new resettlements can thus be safely dismissed."

Myth 4: black farmers cannot farm and by corollary only whites can

The media doesn't actually put it like this. Only the most rabid Rhodesian racists would - but the belief is there, mostly unspoken, sometimes implied but there. Attitudes to the Land Reform tap into the deepest veins of racial prejudice in all sorts of way – as does, I believe, the intensity of the vilification Mugabe has endured. The unspoken or spoken belief is that blacks can't do what whites can. Leave farming in Zimbabwe to the whites. They're the experts. It goes back to Fanon and his black surgeon in France or to Haiti when the first black government in modern history emerged. Ronald Suresh Roberts embedded it in the title of his book on Thabo Mbeki, *Fit to Govern.* In my opinion, it underlies the crescendo of white and even much black criticism of the ANC government in South Africa.

I remember being struck with humility in 1999/2000 listening to Zimbabweans from all walks of life participating in the consultative process on the constitution and talking knowledgably about things relating to constitutions which I, despite my ten years of university education, a doctorate and exposure to many different countries, societies and languages, knew very little about. I was always struck too by the knowledge and expressiveness of participants in Mai Chisamba's television discussion programmes. Speaking in Shona, men and women of no special social status or education held lively debates on all sorts of topics. They were articulate and confident. There were numerous experts who participated in various talk shows, say on agriculture or the economy, and demonstrated impressive ability and know-how. I was struck too by the way in which Zimbabweans organised elections, contrary to the image projected by the 'international' media, and the way in which they organised other large-scale national events such as the All-Africa Games in 1995. I was struck by the ability of Zimbabweans to master finance, banking, internet communications technology, theories of corporate management, accounting, marketing, media and so many other sophisticated 'modern' technologies and technical and scientific functions from which they had been excluded for decades

In the arts education organisation in which I worked, young men and women, coming straight from the ghetto, the so-called High-Density suburbs, with a relatively low standard of education at pretty abysmal schools, would pick up digital editing or theatre lighting and master systems which boggled my mind. Well, either this meant that I was very stupid, which may well be the case, or they were very bright. I prefer, obviously, to believe that they were very bright.

It is not about race. Successful black farming cannot rise from the dead or pop up like a genie from a bottle. It is about training, experience and opportunity.

In terms of training, Zimbabwe invested considerable resources in education, including agricultural education. Tertiary institutions that train farmers, graduate in the region of 400 a year. Many of the A2 farms went to people with farming qualifications. So there are also quite a few educated farmers out there. There is also a long tradition of black farming in the region and in Zimbabwe.

In South Africa, black South Africans, as Colin Bundy recounted in his *The Rise and Fall of the South African Peasantry*, showed themselves quite capable of adapting to the demands of the urban vegetable market in the early days of white settlement in Natal - until the rug was pulled from under their feet by the colonial administration. In pre-independence Zimbabwe under white government, black commercial farming was suppressed by legislation or made impossible by land grabs.

The situation in Zimbabwe is different from, say, that of South Africa. Though black Zimbabweans were removed from their land and dumped in marginal or totally unsuitable areas, most, even when they lived and worked in town, were still rooted in the rural areas. The degree of urbanisation was far lower in Zimbabwe than it was in South Africa. Almost everyone went '*kumusha*' (to the rural home) regularly and often spent their leave there during the sowing or harvest season working in the fields. Black agriculture therefore has a long tradition in Zimbabwe. The produce of their labour was not allowed to compete with white agriculture but it provided significant inputs into the food consumption of black families not only in the rural areas but also in the towns.

After independence, when such restrictions were lifted, black farmers in the rural areas (or communal lands, as they had been called) were able to produce food for the urban markets and expand their production. Some were able to buy plots and farms in what were previously reserved for the whites. In the period before the Land Reform when agricultural production was still largely divided into black communal and white commercial production, by 1985 the communal farmers, despite having inferior land, were producing more maize and by 1990 more cotton than the commercial sector. The same was true for millet, sorghum and sunflowers. There was a general trend, as mentioned before, for white farmers to move into more profitable production, leaving black farmers in the communal sector to produce more and more of the food.

Then the Land Reform gave many of them the opportunity of a lifetime, one could say, of generations – for over generations they were never offered such an opportunity.

I mention all this not to prove that all black farmers will be success stories overnight. I mention it simply to show that there is a long tradition of farming by black farmers in Zimbabwe for the new farmers to draw on and that many of the new farmers are not totally inept and inexperienced but on the contrary experienced and qualified.

Rome was not built in a day. White agriculture in Zimbabwe was not built in a day. And there is no reason to expect that black agriculture should be so. The point is that so many ordinary people, who had very little in their lives, have been given hope – and the opportunity. Some have the training but now all are getting the experience – an opportunity they did not have before.

By way of example, this is the testimony of a new farmer on a reclaimed farm. He and his family were in the second success band, described as 'Getting on but with potential'. It is just one of many testimonies, almost all telling the same moving – and ultimately inspiring - tale:

> *I was born in Gutu in 1979. I am married and have one child. In Gutu I had very little land to farm. It was not a good life for a young family. We had to rely on others. In 2000, I decided to join the invasion groups. Before I had no cattle but now I own five head, all purchased through farming. I have also managed to buy a plough. Now I help my family back in Gutu during drought years with food, and I send cash for my young brothers to pay for school fees. All of this is from our hard work. I have cleared four hectares of land and I employ workers on the farm, who stay with us. My wife has a vegetable garden and sells tomatoes and onions locally. She also has a small business selling second-hand clothes. The new land has transformed our lives.*
>
> *(from "Zimbabwe's Land Reform- Myths and Realities")*

Myth 5: the process was based on terrible violence, destruction and killing

Really one's patience wears thin on this one. The people of Zimbabwe took their land back from the whites whose antecedents had, through a century-long process of the utmost savagery, dispossessed them, then suppressed them and treated them like third and fourth class citizens in the land of their ancestors, and in one decade they brought about a profoundly revolutionary restitution that radically restructured society and transformed property ownership and production with an extraordinarily limited amount of violence and killing. The whites were at their mercy yet no white woman, girl or child was raped or killed and very few white men suffered injury or were killed. Compare what happened during the Land Reform with the following. This is one of the many distressing tales of what happened to those who lived in the fertile environs of the then white city of Salisbury, who seemed to have been particularly vulnerable, in earlier times:

> *The most painful account came from hundreds of Seke villagers who were ejected from the commercial farms in Ruwa, about 20 kms east of Harare...investigations established that during forcible removals their wives and daughters were 'seized', raped and used to induce the males to accept work on the farms.*

As one of the villagers put it:

> *It was a painful experience, one I would not want to repeat. If what our sons and daughters are doing (going onto the farms) is anarchy, then what do you call what was done to us? It was worse than anarchy.*

The most extraordinary and revolutionary social and economic upheaval took place in Zimbabwe, the kind of change that at other times and in other countries has led to massive bloodshed, dislocation and catastrophic warfare. Everyone knows the stories of what happened in France when the *povo* rose up against their oppressors - the mock trials, the tumbrils and Madame Guillotine. In the United States, the uprising of the colonists led to a full-scale war with England, pitched battles on land and at sea and considerable death and destruction. In Russia, the Czar and his family copped it and a Civil War ensued, which surely produced some of the most amazing examples of suffering, human endurance and heroism in history. Need we mention the Chinese Revolution and the Civil War between the Red Army and the Nationalists under Chiang Kai Chek?

Or, closer to home, the genocide of the Herero at the hands of the Germans as they rose up against the colonial yoke, the rising of the long-oppressed Hutu against their historical overlords, the Tutsi, in Rwanda, that most criminal of conflicts in Mozambique when Frelimo set about creating the New Society and the Renamo bandits were let loose upon the land or in Zimbabwe itself when ZIPRA went back to the bush after ZANU-PF's victory at the polls after independence. *There* was violence, *there* was death and destruction.

What must have been the images of horror, the fears and the dreaded expectations in the white imagination when they first began to entertain the possibility that the 'Communist' Mugabe and the 'terrorists' in the bush might one day seize and rule their beloved Rhodesia? Violence, death, destruction – and worse. What about rape, that great white spectre of black revenge? And if anyone had said to the white farmers and their families in independent Zimbabwe that soon a time will come when the people in the communal lands, the wretched of the Zimbabwean earth, and their old nightmare the 'terrorists', the liberation war veterans, will come onto their farms and take them back? The mind boggles.

That historic moment came - when after more than a century of dispossession, oppression and hatred, the povo of Zimbabwe and their soldiers, the liberation war veterans, went on to the white man's land. Compare what actually happened with white imaginings and fears. If a single white woman was raped during the Land Reform, I personally never heard of it. If there was destruction it was the destruction of plant and equipment by the white owners before they fled. As for white or other deaths, there were relatively very few.

How was the land taken?

Scoones and his team included in each of their case studies a detailed record of exactly how each farm was taken. The very first thing they note was that no single case was like any other – each farm was taken in a different way. They list what happened: in some cases there was a struggle but rarely involving violence, sometimes the former owner stayed on or nearby and relations with the settlers were 'at least cordial', in others the farmer and his family fled. One case of violence was when the farmer hired and armed people from elsewhere to come and drive the settlers off. There were other cases where farm workers were loyal to their employer, who armed them to take on the settlers and there was fighting, in which people *were* killed, black people. However these cases were few and far between. Quite often the occupation was characterised by *dialogue* – of different kinds – between the leadership of the settlers, often a liberation war veteran, and the farmer. What happened after that sometimes depended on the attitude of the farmer. As already mentioned, one or two farmers did not hide their refusal to share their land, vacate or otherwise co-operate with the settlers and couched it in what were in the circumstances highly provocative and openly racist terms.

As noted before, Masvingo Province differs in a numbers of respects from other provinces. The fact that a lot of it was given over to cattle ranching meant that white settlement was not as dense.

Many of the farm owners did not actually live on the property. In other provinces, more of the white farmers had their homes and communities on the farms. Thus their relations with those who came onto the farms to take them, might have been quite different and would probably have resulted in more incidences of violence. However, I doubt whether the pattern documented in Masvingo Province was dramatically different in the other provinces.

So to sum up, in my opinion, instead of making noise about all the violence, I would have thought that people would have expressed their astonishment that such a momentous process happened with the loss of so few lives and such little destruction. On the issue of violence perpetrated by the political parties at election times, especially round about the presidential re-run in 2008 and at others, much is still to be said – that will come later (Chapter 23). On the way in which sections of the local Zimbabwean media and almost all the foreign media worked hard at creating the impression that Zimbabwe's Third *Chimurenga* was soaked in blood, that too will be dealt with later (Chapter 25).

Controversial as some might find it, I would characterise the Land Reform upheavals as by comparison extraordinarily and quite miraculously gentle and even – dare I say it – polite. There was little that was gentle or polite about the way in which the ZANU-PF fat cats threatened, cajoled and bullied their way into other people's businesses, homes and properties. But the story on the ground, involving the liberation war veterans, the rural and urban *povo* and other ordinary people going onto the white farms, was in most cases quite different. Where there was violence, it seemed to have been largely unleashed by the farmers themselves - and the very few white deaths that were recorded during the land reclamations, seem to have mostly resulted from violent and often armed conflict orchestrated or organised by the white farmers themselves.

There was a time, during the *Jambanja* period, when the spirit of *Jambanja* came to town. The leader of the liberation war veterans, Joseph Chinotimba, played a leading part in settling workers' grievances with their white bosses at companies and factories in Harare. As a white, living in a large house in one of the low-density suburbs, it began to dawn on me that if the farms can be taken in the countryside, there was no reason why people living in the overcrowded high-density suburbs of Harare, who also would have liked a better place to live, shouldn't just move into the suburbs and start squatting in people's gardens, moving into their houses, chucking their white owners out – me included. I don't think there really was much to stop them at that time. They didn't. They could have looted too. They could have gone on all sorts of rampages – and if it was vengeance they wanted, there were lots of helpless white women to rape and old men like me to hack to pieces. Nothing of the sort ever happened.

My final comment, concerning the Land Reform and all the 'myths' it generated, is that even if all the 'myths' were true, it was better that it happened in the way it did than that it did not happen at all. The land and all its wealth (*'nyika ne upfumi hwayo hwose'*) belongs to its people. Kwame Nkrumah put it in a nutshell: "It is far better to be free to govern, *or misgovern yourself*, than to be governed by anybody else" (my italics). Every people has the right to try - and the right to fail. The land is in the hands of the Zimbabweans – it is up to them to see what they are going to do with it.

No-one can describe the historic impact of the Land Reform for thousands and thousands of ordinary Zimbabweans better than they can themselves. Scoones and his team, after having met so many of them, seen the proof of their struggles and heard their stories, have a bash at summing that up when they write:

Despite the hardships and challenges, the commitment to a future in the new resettlements was tangible and inspiring, particularly among the A1 farmers interviewed. A2 farmers were somewhat different...(but) some...have seriously invested in their new farms, and despite all odds, have made a go of it, with great plans for the future.

CHAPTER TWENTY:

THE MOVEMENT FOR DEMOCRATIC CHANGE

From Comrade Tsvangirai to 'Mr Tsvangison'

As ZANU-PF's failings and the contradiction between its rhetoric and policies and its actual behaviour became more marked in the first two decades of its rule, the need for an opposition that proposed a democratic alternative more closely aligned to what the ordinary people of Zimbabwe had sacrificed so much for, became more and more glaring.

The problem with ZANU-PF was – as it was in other countries in which a nationalist liberation movement had come to power through revolutionary struggle – that it had appropriated the Left. Though it was not a Left entity, it adopted a Left rhetoric, and claimed to occupy the space and to be taking care of the Left agenda. It is true that its programme did include a number of elements normally associated with the socialist agenda, for example, land to the people, subsidised basic commodities and services, education not a privilege but a right and so on. Other policies such as indigenisation and black empowerment implied a position which African Marxists commonly refer to as the National Democratic Revolution, and which they would therefore support as an intervening stage in the struggle to build a socialist society. However, ZANU-PF was not moving towards socialism and it was not implementing a National Democratic Revolution. Instead the process of indigenous embourgoisement was seen as an end in itself.

This was accentuated by the actual behaviour of the leadership as opposed to the policy goals of the party.

Not only was ZANU-PF's appropriation of the Left agenda an obfuscation, it offered little to the working class. Its commitment to indigenisation did not include a transformation of the relations of production or a role for the workers. Instead it amounted to capacitating the black petit-bourgeoisie and assisting them to take over the existing role of the whites in business, banking, finance and service. Apart from that, it was to the rural rather than urban masses that ZANU-PF turned. Right from the beginning ZANU-PF placed the emphasis on redressing the inequalities between town and country as inherited from the colonial past in favour of the rural areas. After all, the vast majority of Zimbabweans lived in the countryside. This had been their base during the liberation struggle and it would continue to be their electoral base after Independence. ZANU-PF never placed much emphasis on the particular needs and demands of the urban masses and the workers in particular.

Obviously, the relations of production in the colonial state had been repressive and exploitative but it was five years after Independence before the government enacted its first labour legislation aimed at bringing the labour laws of the country into line with international conventions. This legislation however applied to employees in the Private Sector alone and, with the introduction of ESAP, some of these provisions were reversed.

Though ZANU-PF won the Independence elections and became the government of Zimbabwe with what appeared to be overwhelming support, the appearance was misleading. If the whole thing had been a game of Bridge and the four suits had stood for traditional rulers and rural masses (Spades); urban masses and workers (Hearts); urban black petit-bourgeoisie (Diamonds); and white owners and employers (Clubs), ZANU-PF would probably have had honours in Spades – in other words, all the royals - the Ace in Hearts, the Ace and King in Diamonds and a singleton in Clubs. Its feet of clay lay in its potential weakness in the urban areas and with workers, potential loss of support among the urban petit-bourgeoisie, potential if not inevitable opposition from the whites and, because of its designs on the land and its commitment to indigenisation, possible alienation of the international capitalist establishment. At that stage, ZANU-PF needed a partner who would come in with the other honours in Hearts and Diamonds so that when the confrontation came with the whites – assuming it was unavoidable given the determination to take back the land – their hands together would have been strong enough to ensure game. ZANU-PF did not set about finding that partner. On the contrary, it was not long before it fell out with the newly constituted Zimbabwe Council of Trade Unions (ZCTU).

The ZCTU's forerunner, the African Trade Union Congress (ATUC), was founded by Josiah Maluleke and he had some prescient things to say about the importance of his congress and its relation to the liberation movement and the future government of an independent Zimbabwe, for example:

> *We as a trade union are fully prepared to throw our weight behind the nationalist party's fight - after all, we all want to get rid of the present minority government, but we want to do so as workers, with our own organisation. For after independence the party will be the government and will be as much concerned as any government to increase production to develop the country. This may happen at the expense of the workers' wages and general standard of living. Then we want our own organisation to defend our position and our rights; if we, then, are merely an arm of the party we as workers will be defenceless.*

Salutary advice for African labour! In country after country in Africa, after labour had supported the nationalist movement in the struggle for political independence, a confrontation developed between the interests of the unions and the government, resulting in many cases in the suppression of the unions and their replacement by a compliant surrogate. This is partly what eventually happened in Zimbabwe. The ZCTU was never suppressed but after it had established the MDC and began to pose a serious threat, ZANU-PF created its own Zimbabwe Federation of Trade Unions (ZFTU) – a phenomenon repeated in a number of African countries eg. Obote's Uganda. It remains to be seen how the relationship between the ANC government and COSATU will work out in South Africa.

The Movement for Democratic Change (MDC) was founded in 1999. In an article on the MDC website, the author refers to the decision taken in February, 1999, at a 'working people's convention' to set up a political party, as 'timely'. By now, having worked our way through the chronology of Zimbabwean Independence, we can hopefully appreciate why. The establishment of a new opposition party at that time was the logical outcome of the events of the previous 19 years, the combined effect of all we have been describing – Lancaster House, corruption, debt, drought, ESAP, Clare Short, the move on the land and Western opposition. It was a year in which I wondered whether ZANU-PF was looking at the cards. If it had, it would have realised that it was facing an opposition with a very strong hand. Though not totally stacked against ZANU-PF, the cards looked ominous – especially when compared with the hand they had held at Independence. Arraigned against them were the whites – business, industry, farmers, in short the bulk of the bosses –the urban masses, many professionals, intellectuals and student leaders, 'civil society' (read NGOs) – a new force, as it had hardly existed at Independence - the trade unions and the Western World. Matebeleland could easily – and actually did – defect *en masse* from PF-ZAPU, which since the Unity Accord had been a junior partner in ZANU-PF. All that was required was a credible organisation to galvanise and unite these forces in opposition to ZANU-PF. On the party's side – and only if they acted to retain their support – were the armed forces, the liberation war veterans, the traditional chiefs and the rural masses outside Matebeleland.

The MDC's roots were in the trade union movement. It called its founding convention a convention of the 'working people'. Its leadership was almost totally made up of ZCTU officials. This was a case of a labour movement, as organised in the trade unions, deciding to enter politics. But it was clear from the start that the ZCTU was not going to set up a political party, a party that would fight for the rights and interests of the workers. It was adopting a different, perhaps more ambitious agenda. Basically it was setting itself up – as its name implied – as a movement, not a party.

Characteristically a movement is a political alliance of interest groups who come together *for a time* to bring about change. Movements may consist of disparate interest groups who, though they may have quite opposite intentions or objectives in some spheres, share one overriding common objective. The United Democratic Front (UDF) in South Africa was a good example. Its participants had many different ideologies and intentions but all were united in their determination to end *apartheid*. In the case of the MDC, their common objective was to get rid of the ZANU-PF government and its President, Robert Mugabe.

It is obvious that ZANU-PF had opened up its flanks to attack from a very wide social and ideological spectrum, from the extreme Left to the extreme Right. For instance, earlier in this chapter we discussed how ZANU-PF had appropriated the Left terrain. It had disguised the vacuum there by its rhetoric and some of its policy objectives. However, as its real agenda became clearer, the gap on the Left of the party widened. As a result, there was even a Trotskyite International Socialist who joined the MDC – and became a member of parliament in the same party side by side with right-wing white farmers and businessmen.

As we have seen, ZANU-PF's position in the towns and in relation to the trade unions was precarious. The urban population was the easiest target for non-ZANU-PF influences. It had access to opposition newspapers and later on to anti-ZANU-PF radio and television broadcasts. In the trade union movement (ZCTU) they had another organisation other than ZANU-PF to give their allegiance to and when that organisation began to pursue an independent line, especially when that line began to run counter to that of ZANU-PF, the party was in danger of losing them. Also because the war had not touched the towns in the way it had the country, the support that many gave them at Independence was ephemeral. What the people in town were concerned about was ZANU-PF delivering the goods – and when it didn't and with the introduction of ESAP in fact seemed to have brought untold suffering instead, they easily became disgruntled. It was they too who suffered most from the alienating effect of King Pressure and all the indignities outlined above.

We noted the possibility of ZANU-PF losing large sections of the urban petit-bourgeoisie. We also noted that winning the support of these social forces was essential in order to deal with the inevitable confrontation with the whites and more ominously the West. ZANU-PF had not won their support and thus they found themselves going into a crucial strategic phase, that of the Third

Chimurenga, confronted by a new party or movement that would combine all their foes in a campaign to bring them down.

The trade unions were able to found a movement which embraced the enemies of ZANU-PF across the spectrum. In addition to their domestic support i.e. in Zimbabwe, there was Britain, Europe, North America and the White Commonwealth. A number of whites and blacks in Zimbabwe, who had opposed the liberation struggle, were able to fly their flags again as born-again champions of democracy and human rights. At the head of this coalition of anti-ZANU-PF forces was Morgan Tsvangirai.

When I was working at the University of Zimbabwe in the 1980's, making and performing political theatre with Zambuko/Izibuko and organising showings of alternative cinema and political 'culturals', Morgan Tsvangirai was the newly elected Secretary-General of the Zimbabwe Congress of Trade Unions (ZCTU). He was a comrade in the general alliance within society of left-wing or 'progressive' forces – all, at that stage, accommodated in the progressive alliance that had been ushered in by the triumph of the revolutionary struggle led by the Patriotic Front. Some who worked with him in the ZCTU, were also working with us at the University. Our political theatre group, Zambuko/Izibuko, performed specially devised political theatre pieces, referred to as *ngonjera*, on occasions such as May Day, commemorated as Workers Day in Zimbabwe, often in partnership with the ZCTU at mass rallies at Rufaro Stadium in Harare or at special workers' lunchtime performances at the University. The working class was a part of the progressive alliance and there was as yet no contradiction between it and ZANU-PF.

I left the university in the mid-1990's. In all the years since, I met Tsvangirai only once. I have three abiding memories of him in the years after the founding of the MDC and they seemed to sum him and the MDC up for me rather aptly.

The first was watching Tsvangirai on television addressing a rally - in the 'high-density' suburb of Highfield, I think - and promising that, if Mugabe did not want to go peacefully, the people would make him go by force. It was sensational. The response to this from a lot of people, especially in the high-density suburbs, was ecstatic. Tsvangirai was shattering the silence of fear - fear openly to oppose and speak out against the President and the ruling party - that had hitherto prevailed. He was just about the first person to stand up and challenge the President publicly. In those days, one thought twice about speaking out against the President or the ruling party. But even more significantly, he was not only speaking out against them but also warning them that he would oppose them with force. I wondered whether he really knew what he was taking on and what he was starting.

In a way, Mugabe and Tsvangirai were birds of a feather – or, shall we say, bulls in the same kraal. If Mugabe's obstinate refusal to be budged on an issue he felt was important, no matter the consequences and no matter how powerful and prestigious the opponent, was one of his defining characteristics, now here was someone in the political arena who displayed a similar characteristic. It takes just one dog to stand up and defy a long standing top dog for others to follow. For those who had previously lacked the courage, Tsangirayi, in a manner of speaking, broke the ice - like the child who spoke out what everyone else was thinking but feared to say openly, namely that the Emperor was walking through the town with no clothes on. Tsvangirai said it, openly declaring Mugabe to be a dictator and threatening his removal by force. His example was electric. After many years of deference to Mugabe, who had hitherto seemed to be above criticism, when someone now stood up and confronted him openly - in public, with no apparent fear at all and nothing happened to him - it made the impossible seem possible. It proved that opposition was possible and could perhaps just turn out to be the beginning of what might, many people hoped, be the end of Mugabe and ZANU-PF's political hegemony.

However, as we see from the example cited above, from the very beginning much of the MDC's rhetoric was violent. This was inevitable given the support of the urban youth and lumpen elements and the influx into the organisation of veterans of radical student politics, in particular the annual demos at the University of Zimbabwe. I was particularly well-placed to know the latter and observe their activities. As someone who was involved in politically-charged cultural work and also one of the very few members of the university staff who was regularly on campus after hours, I had my fair share of demos, tear gas, and police and student confrontations. I remember taking part in a performance in the New Lecture Theatre (NLT) 400 on campus the night before one of the annual demos. It was a Zambuko/Izibuko play about Mozambique, which was being performed on the anniversary of the assassination by the apartheid regime of the charismatic leader of Mozambique's Frelimo, Samora Machel. The students were psyching themselves for the battle of the morrow and were already part possessed by the 'rage' – like the old beserkers of Viking days. We had hardly started our performance before the students stormed the stage and took it over, dancing, singing and wielding our props, which included flags and wooden replicas of AK 47s. Avant-garde theatre fans might have considered this to be exciting audience involvement but when the students' participation continued in the form of irreverent ribaldry at the expense of the solemnity of the occasion, the leader of our theatre group, himself a liberation war veteran, had to interrupt the performance to address them so as to try and steer their anarchic indiscipline in a more constructive direction.

And this was the feature of student disturbances at the time, an almost total lack of any coherent direction or ideological consistency. As previously mentioned, on one occasion they demonstrated because the new curtains in the residences did not match the bedspreads! The veterans of student mayhem that entered the MDC no doubt contributed to the movement's tendency to indulge in violent, irresponsible and sometimes criminal statements and behaviour, including beating each other up and assaulting the leadership.

I am no supporter of political violence and I always thought ZANU-PF's use of it was counterproductive and tactically disastrous, something Mugabe himself has often stated. However, before throwing a stone at ZANU-PF, we need honestly to acknowledge the inherent proclivity for violence in the MDC too – violence among themselves as much as violence directed against their enemies. One of the dragon's teeth of Zimbabwe's history – as of South Africa's – was the tendency to settle disputes through violence. It was endemic in the society. Supporters of rival foorball teams like Dynamos and Highlanders regularly clashed. When, for example, a political opposition incites a stay-way and talks of marching on State House for 'the last push', i.e. to overthrow the government, which is what the MDC did on one occasion, I think they had it coming to them. One should not idealise the MDC on the question of violence. The MDC was no Ghandiist passive resistance movement. It was the first opposition entity that was prepared to match ZANU-PF blow for blow. Their only constraint was that they did not have the solid network of party branches, particularly in the rural areas, with which effectively to do so. However, in the urban areas, with the youth and lumpen on their side, they did their fair share of burning buses, killing policemen, fire-bombing police stations and other forms of mayhem. They also displayed a tendency to settle their own internal disputes violently.

My next memory of Tsvangirai was again on television. It came out on the evening news. There was a news clip of Tsvangirai - the trade unionist, the leader of the workers, he who had been part of the left-wing alliance of progressive forces in the years after Independence - lounging nonchalantly, not to say arrogantly and seemingly perfectly at home, at a table *al fresco* on a white commercial farm - as white farmers, in their traditional dress of khaki shirts, shorts and veldskoens, queued up to contribute their cheques to the MDC coffers!

I think this clip of Tsvangirayi on the commercial farm has to go down in history as one of the most sensational scoops in the history of politics in Africa. It must have damned him in the eyes of thousands. It is just a pity that the Western media had more sense than to take the image up and show it to the world. But then Tsvangirai is a politician whose blunders have become, like those of the late Vice-President Muzenda, rather like van der Merwe jokes. The clip had all the ingredients of disaster – fraternising with the traditional and historical enemy, whose land at last was returning to the people; a black man at home in a white environment long associated with racism and discrimination; a black man being paid to do the white man's work: and, fatally, an exposure of the real agenda of the MDC – to oppose and reverse the land reforms.

The element of white support for the MDC was quite different from the non-racial comradeship in the African National Congress, for instance. Working with the likes of Bram Fischer and Joe Slovo to bring about democratic change in South Africa was a different kettle of fish to rubbing shoulders with white commercial farmers and various other 'new democrats', discredited by their role in upholding or never opposing the racist rule of the Smith regime. When this was allied to the support of Britain, the colonial oppressor, white South Africa and the whole international white capitalist establishment, the MDC may have lined up some very big guns but for Zimbabwe, southern Africa and Africa itself, the PR was terrible. The name, Tsvangison, given to him by ZANU-PF and its media, thus attempted to capitalise on the Uncle Tom-doing-the-whiteman's-work image Tsvangirai had allowed himself to attract.

My third and last memory of Tsvangirai was a chance encounter with him in the reception area of the Netherlands Embassy in Harare. When visitors got to the gate at the Embassy, their particulars were taken and they were asked what their business was. The guard would then phone the relevant person in the embassy and, if all was well, the visitor would be admitted. Visitors would then march up the driveway and into the Embassy building. There they would sit – in the reception area - and wait until the person they wanted to see was ready to receive them. The embassy official would come down and fetch the visitor from reception and take him or her into the Embassy's inner sanctum.

And this is what happened to me. After completing formalities at the gate, I arrived in the embassy reception area and what was my surprise to see my old comrade, Morgan Tsvangirai! But he was no longer my old comrade, the Secretary-General of the ZCTU, an ally in the progressive struggle for socialism and a better deal for the working class. He was now the much feted leader of the MDC, the darling of the West and white South Africa, hobnobber with the white commercial farmers, the Great Black Hope. But what was he doing sitting here in reception, just like me? As someone who had to grovel at various embassies, begging for funding for our arts education organisation, I was used to being treated in this way. I was used to sitting in numerous reception rooms waiting for the important though actually quite ordinary person who controlled the purse strings, to find the time to see me. Surely, I thought, if someone like Tsvangirai, the leader of the MDC, the darling of the West etc visited an embassy, he would be driven straight into the compound and whisked up the stairs to see the Ambassador. But here he was, sitting in reception, leafing through magazines and waiting patiently to be called. The Embassy knew that, if they had their way, the man in reception was the possible future president of Zimbabwe – and they treated him like they treated people like me! It seemed to be a situation that spoke volumes.

Obviously the reason was that they knew that he and I were no different really. He too was a supplicant. He too was waiting until the important but quite ordinary person who controlled the purse strings, could find time to see him. And I wondered whether he too was feeling what I was feeling. Was he bridling inside at the indignity but forcing himself to suppress his feelings because the MDC needed the money? Was he aware of his client status with these people and what their attitude to him was – someone from a small but for various reasons rather important little country, whom they were supporting in order for him to sort things out to their advantage?

I also thought of the address to the parliament of the Netherlands he had made a few months earlier and his call for sanctions – and how this had impacted on our little organisation, something to talk about later (Chapter 21). It was MDC policy openly to call on its allies to impose sanctions on Zimbabwe, their own country and their own people. They even urged South Africa to impose a blockade at one stage – what was it? Fuel? Electricity? Something they were sure would 'bring Zimbabwe to its knees'. And when their allies did impose sanctions, they made it clear that they would only lift them on the MDC's advisement. This was because they were sure that the MDC would only call for the lifting of sanctions when the land had been returned to its pre-1997 occupants. After all, that was their main reason for assisting them.

I personally think Tsvangirai and his comrades in the ZCTU failed Zimbabwe. They failed the working people of Zimbabwe and they failed the peasant masses. Entering the political terrain as a trade union organisation was not the problem. The problem was how they did it. As far as I am concerned, they were hijacked. In fact, from what I could see, they actually courted hijacking. What was really required in the situation was a party not a movement. That party should have been built on the patriotic and democratic leadership of the revolutionary working class. It should not have made a polarised and undiscriminating antagonism to ZANU-PF its core objective. Instead it should have embraced the ideals and objectives of the liberation struggle and endorsed ZANU-PF's progressive agenda to the extent that it was based in these ideals and objectives. On the other hand, it should not have hesitated to condemn ZANU-PF's lapse into corruption and betrayal of the struggle. It should have supported the taking of the land but rallied support around its abuse. It should have supported indigenisation but pressed for effective and equable processes. It should have supported the new constitution of 2000, which would have given them an advantage. It should not have discredited itself by allowing its agenda to be contaminated by white revanchism or its credentials to be discredited by an unprincipled alliance with the untransformed whites, the former colonial powers and the international capitalist establishment. It should not have tried to win power by calling for sanctions against its own people. Instead it should have relied on its own people to bring it to power. It should have endorsed ZANU-PF's progressive foreign policy but avoided its destructive and unstatesmanlike expression and implementation. It should have campaigned for free and fair elections, for freedom of expression, human rights, non-violence and democracy on this just and fair basis. It should have worked to unite all Zimbabweans in the struggle for national reconstruction, welcoming those of other races into the party who genuinely supported transformation.

I believe if they had, the ZCTU could have created a genuine alternative to ZANU-PF, which would have attracted the support of the vast majority of Zimbabweans, including the liberation war veterans and genuine cadres in the armed forces. This is more like the role one would expect the representatives of the working class to have played. In short, I would have welcomed a Comrade Tsvangirai as president but not a Mr Tsvangison.

CHAPTER TWENTY-ONE:

SANCTIONS

A letter from the British Ambassador

From the Ambassador

British Embassy
Harare

3 Norfolk Road
Mt Pleasant
(P.O. Box 4490)
Harare

Tel: +263 4 338800-338817
Fax: +263 4 338828
Email: mark.canning@fco.gov.uk

9 March 2010

Dr Robert McLaren
13 Mountbatten Drive
Marlborough
Harare

Dear Dr McLaren,

The Director of the British Council has copied me your recent letter to the Director of the National Arts Council about the cultural Indaba. In that letter you make the patently absurd assertion that the British Government is in some way responsible for the economic damage which Zimbabwe has suffered in the recent past. Please allow me to respond.

The restrictive measures which the EU enforces on Zimbabwe comprise the following elements:– a ban on military sales; a travel ban on some 197 individuals and an investment ban on around 35 companies (which are owned, predominantly, by two individuals and which have never benefitted the national good).

The EU has gone to great lengths to ensure that these measures do not affect the economic health of the country. Indeed the UK will, this year, be spending around $100 million in a variety of areas including health, education, water and sanitation. We were also a strong supporter of the recent decision to restore IMF voting rights to Zimbabwe and indeed to the programme which allocated special drawing rights totalling around $512 million to this country. These are hardly the actions of a country which is bent on damaging the economy.

The reasons for the damage inflicted on Zimbabwe are patently clear – years of mismanagement, violence and corruption on the part of the former Government which the UK, and its partners, is now working hard to redress.

Mark Canning

I was never a great one for ambassadors or cabinet ministers or any of that ilk. Robert Burns said it all for me a long time ago. "A man's a man for a' that/The rank is but the guinea's stamp/The man's the gowd for a' that". Ambassadors and Cabinet Ministers tend to put on airs and want to be treated above the rest of us. I was never good at that.

So when one day an Embassy car pulled up outside my house in Marlborough and a uniformed driver brought in a letter, it was quite an occasion. The letter came from the British Ambassador to Zimbabwe, who had the same family name as another who, a few centuries back, was Foreign Secretary and Prime Minister for a bit. I suppose being an ambassador or a minister in countries like Britain must run in the family.

In order to appreciate the story of the letter from the Ambassador, something needs to be said about the new British Embassy in Harare. Before the 'troubles', the British had an office suite in town in a high rise building. But with the souring of relations and increased unrest, they decided to move. As it happens, the European Union felt the same and so right next to each other they built new offices out on Norfolk Road, which runs from what was once called the Golden Stairs Road to Pendennis Road on the edge of the rather upmarket suburb of Mount Pleasant, opposite our not so upmarket suburb of Marlborough. Did the street and suburb names make the Embassy staff feel at home or were they just mocking reminders of what once was - for the new house that John Bull built in Harare did not suggest he felt at home at all.

I have never seen any photos of Abu Ghraib prison in Iraq from the outside but I have seen a few from the inside – photos that are so shocking that one wonders how the United States can lift its head up in public and say a word about torture and abuse in Zimbabwe

– or anywhere else for that matter. Well, Abu Ghraib was the first thing I thought of when I saw the new British Embassy for the first time. It is built like a fortress or a concentration camp, with high fences and razor wire, guard turrets and grim brick walls. This is not a photographic description – I may have the details wrong. I am just trying to share with you the impression it had on me the first day I saw it.

I only actually tried to go there once. I started out with misgivings because what I wanted to talk about with them was organising something to commemorate the 250th anniversary of the aforesaid Robert Burns' birth. Well, Burns isn't Wordsworth or Shakespeare - so I was not quite sure how interested they would be in a commemorative concert for the national poet of Scotland. I needn't have bothered. What I had planned was to talk to someone at reception and explain my plan so that they could direct me to the appropriate person. I never got past the gate. I was grilled through a small window by an extremely bellicose guard, who hadn't the slightest capacity to assess what I wanted. Once he somehow tumbled to the fact that it was something to do with culture, he abruptly cast me off, telling me to go to the British Council. I drove out in a fury, knocking over an orange bollard as I reversed. At that the guards started forward in my direction and for a moment I thought they were going to arrest me. I wondered whether the new British Embassy in Harare didn't have dungeons.

Now here was this letter from the Ambassador. The background to it was that the British Council had put up some money to hold a national Artists' Indaba. Artists' Indabas are hosted by the National Arts Council of Zimbabwe from time to time to give artists an opportunity to come together and grouse about their problems and recommend ways of alleviating them. Every Indaba is exactly the same as all the others for the simple reason that nothing ever gets done about the problems from one Indaba to the next. On this occasion the British had put up some money and I was invited by the National Arts Council of Zimbabwe and the Zimbabwe Culture Fund to attend and make a presentation. I wrote *them* a letter telling *them* that as the problems the artists would be talking about were largely a result of sanctions and as Britain was the initiator and main instigator of the sanctions, it was a bit of a cheek that the British Council should put up money for the artists to come and discuss their problems. The British Council must have got hold of a copy and forwarded it to the Embassy – hence the letter from the Ambassador.

Those countries that have imposed sanctions and the so-called 'International' media, with the South African media predictably following suit, have been insisting for years that there are no sanctions against Zimbabwe. All there are are travel restrictions imposed on individuals with connections to the government. And this is what His Excellency was telling me in his letter.

Like the issue of the land, that of sanctions is a bitterly contested terrain. Those who are alleged to have imposed them, deny they have done so. Those upon whom they have been imposed, assert they have.

It is difficult to comprehend how those who continue to maintain that there are no sanctions can live with their consciences. Any Zimbabwean, from the highest to the lowest, could tell them all about sanctions because all of us suffered from them every day of our lives – and we still do. The sanctions imposed on Zimbabwe by Britain, the European Union, the United States, Japan and the white Commonwealth, are well documented. However one or two general statements relating to sanctions need to be made before going any further.

First, unless they have some basis in international law, sanctions are illegal. Unless they have been endorsed by the United Nations or some such body with legal jurisdiction in relation to the countries involved, sanctions are illegal and simply a form of international bullying. In the case of Zimbabwe, the sanctions have not been endorsed by the United Nations - and the other bodies with some claim to jurisdiction, the African Union and SADC, have both called for them to be lifted. Thus, the sanctions against Zimbabwe are illegal.

Second, sanctions are like a weapon of mass destruction. Whereas they may affect those they are targeted against, they in fact negatively affect countless others, including the lives of men, women and children who in no way deserve to have their already existing tribulations and disadvantages exacerbated.

Third, there are other measures that complement the effect of sanctions *per se*, including negative media coverage, cutting of sporting and cultural ties and travel restrictions, which can to all intents and purposes be labelled sanctions, along with the more conventional economic penalties relating to trade, investment, loans and grants, banking and foreign currency.

Fourth, the imposition of sanctions is incompatible with a democratic solution. Sanctions are an unfair and violent intervention in the democratic process aimed at supporting one side against the other. Therefore, where sanctions have been imposed, the demand for free and fair elections, the rule of law, the end of violence, freedom of the press and the electronic media, human rights etc is simply hypocritical.

Lastly, sanctions began to be imposed in Zimbabwe as soon as the proposal to take back the land began to be implemented. Whatever the bluster, the reality is that sanctions against Zimbabwe were directed against the Land Reform and are a concerted illegal effort to bring about regime change in order to reverse the reforms.

Let me start off by illustrating the nature of the sanctions and their impact on people in Zimbabwe by referring to my own personal experience in the arts education organisation I worked in. This organisation worked with children and young people in Zimbabwe in an effort to make their lives a little happier and a little better than they might otherwise have been.

The organisation began as a purely voluntary service on the part of its founders and it had no offices, no full-time staff and no funding. Children paid fees and from the fees the arts educators were paid a modest sum. The organisation began to buy equipment with the money. Parents chipped in with costumes and other things. And so the organisation grew, other centres were established in schools, money came for Bursary Centres in disadvantaged high-density suburbs and also for spreading its work to places outside Harare. Infants as well as high school children were now attending and a programme was running for children at Emerald Hill School for the Deaf. It was time to go full-time and get some kind of office and staff.

The Cultural Attaché from the Netherlands Embassy attended an event and saw for herself what the organisation was up to. The upshot was two years of funding from the Government of the Netherlands to establish an office and a full-time staff.

At the end of that initial two-year period, in order for what the organisation had achieved to be sustainable, it was reasonable to expect that the Netherlands Government would continue its support for at least another term. The funding was not continued. The leader of the new political party, the Movement for Democratic Change, my old colleague, Morgan Tsvangirai, had gone to the Netherlands, addressed the Dutch Parliament and called for sanctions. Netherlands Government policy with the relation to Zimbabwe changed. The new policy withdrew funding to Zimbabwe except for that aimed at regime change or humanitarian assistance. That was just the beginning. Rapidly the traditional funders of the arts and culture and work with children withdrew. Some, like the Danish, left Zimbabwe. Others like the Netherlands restricted their support to regime change, HIV/AIDS and humanitarian relief. This was coupled with difficulties in accessing money from Europe and elsewhere as banks were refusing to send money to Zimbabwe. Thank goodness the Swedes in the form of SIDA (Swedish International Development Agency) and after them the Norwegians (NORAD) refused to abandon the arts sector – and us.

Another instance of how sanctions affected our organisation related to ASSITEJ (Association Internationale du Théâtre de l'Enfance et la Jeunesse). We had pioneered its introduction into Zimbabwe and were instrumental in establishing the Zimbabwe Association of Theatre for Children and Young People (ZATCYP), which became the Zimbabwe chapter of ASSITEJ. ZATCYP then proceeded, with the support of SIDA, to spread ASSITEJ to other countries in the region – until the new Secretary-General of ASSITEJ, who was a Swede, neatly side-stepped Zimbabwe and continued what we had begun, with other African countries which were considered acceptable, namely Zambia and Uganda – the Swedish Government obviously preferring that regionally its money not go to Zimbabwe. After that, ZATCYP was allowed to decline – almost to the point of extinction.

Again, a few years later our arts organisation was involved in a project developed by music teachers in Norway. Again the funding was from government – the Norwegian in this case. The idea was to bring young musicians from three southern African countries, namely Mozambique, South Africa and Zimbabwe, and from Norway together in a music camp. Zimbabwe was included in the first place owing to ties established some time back by the famous international advocate of Zimbabwean music, Dumi Maraire. The camps were planned to rotate from one partner country to the other. Norway was soon ruled out owing to the prohibitive cost of airfares involved. When it came to Zimbabwe's turn, it was quietly skipped and the camp began to 'rotate' between Mozambique and South Africa. It never came to Zimbabwe.

Again, in an effort to make our website more effective and easier for those who wished to support the organisation through payments or donations, we tried to link it to Pay Pal. Internet purchases could not be made on banks in Zimbabwe and an account was opened in Canada. Pay Pal would also not accept payments to a Zimbabwean organisation. So with help from sympathisers in Canada this was circumvented. Now payments could be made. However in order for the payment to enter the Pay Pal account, it had to be validated. This is where we had to come in. We managed to access the site and tried to validate a payment. A message flashed up on the screen along the lines of: "You seem to be trying to access this page from a sanctioned country." So much for no sanctions!

The most recent incidence of how sanctions have impacted on us related to the proposal to hold an African conference on the theatre of a European playwright. Our professional youth theatre company and the organisation itself had already established Zimbabwe's reputation with relation to work on plays or based on plays by this playwright and we felt that Zimbabwe would be an obvious place to host the conference. Instead it was hosted in Zambia – which had no track record whatsoever with regard to this playwright. It later emerged that the European funders had refused to allow it to take place in Zimbabwe. They would pay for Zimbabwe's participation but not for a conference in Zimbabwe.

Now, if this happened to us, one can imagine how many more – and far worse - instances there must have been of how sanctions impacted negatively on people's lives. How many musicians who, attempting to ply their trade, were blocked from entering the UK and European countries in order to tour or participate in a concert or festival? How many ordinary Zimbabweans were blocked from attending family births, graduations or marriages? I personally witnessed one, beautiful, dignified old lady from the countryside at the US Consulate in Harare, who wished to attend a family event in the US and had been there and returned numerous times before. She was told rudely by a boorish young official that he was sure she would never come back and she could not have a visa!

Collect the stories, just collect the stories. *There* is a tale of anguish that would emerge – and we are not talking here of the top brass, the party fat cats, the government officials. It is the ordinary people of Zimbabwe, the struggling middle classes and the *povo*, rural and urban, who can tell the stories of what they have endured or succumbed to – as a result of sanctions.

'*Quem deus vult perdere, dementat prius*' (whom god would eliminate, he first makes mad). Obviously in those days the powers on high had their own strategy as to how to deal with troublesome mortals. Nothing has changed – except the means. Right now, NATO is the power on high. Thanks to modern technology, the strategy they employ to deal with troublesome mortals is somewhat more sophisticated than it was in the days of Zeus or Jupiter. Now, the power on high does not quite make its victim mad. Instead, it digs its grave by means of a co-ordinated campaign, involving, among other things, the media and sanctions, a campaign designed to destroy the offender's economy in the first instance, though a lot else is destroyed in the process.

Mugabe was the offender. In the eyes of the West, Mugabe was a thorn in their flesh. Zimbabwe, as we have seen, is a rich country and rich in important resources. It is not just that it is richly endowed with minerals eg. gold, asbestos, chrome, coal, platinum, nickel, copper and recently diamonds, not to mention coal-bed methane gas that is yet to be exploited -- but many of the minerals it has in abundance are of strategic technological and military importance. There is chrome (manufacture of stainless steel, protective plating), nickel (stainless steel, armour plating, batteries, magnets) platinum (explosives, autocatalysts, petroleum catalysts, spark plugs, strategic electrical and electronic uses), phosphates (fertilisers), tantalum and niobium (key uses in tele-communication electronics) and rare earth metals (military electronic devices and communications industries).

But Mugabe just wouldn't play ball and let them get at it. He also had an uncomfortable way of getting standing ovations in international fora for stating the truth about NATO and its many violations. When he finally crossed the Red Line and sanctioned state-supported confiscation by the indigenous inhabitants of white settler property, he had to go. So the campaign machinery was wheeled into action.

The first phase of the campaign is typically for the media to get domestic and international public opinion on their side and then mount a negative publicity onslaught (see Chapter 25). The media had fired their first salvoes the moment Zimbabwe began making noises about taking the land. By the time they had really got going,

Zimbabwe had lost its tourism industry. Tourist figures rose during the 1990s to 1.4 million annually but by the end of the 1990s and during the early 2000s, the industry suffered a 75% decline with only 20% occupancy in the hospitality industry. Naturally, this not only led to loss of income but also the loss of many jobs, the collapse of many companies – and all the attendant suffering this meant for the families of those who lost their jobs.

I once spent the night in the rather large but very unusual and splendid Lodge at the Ancient City, which overlooks the valley that rises on the far side to the majestic and compelling remains of Great Zimbabwe. The Lodge has the most extraordinary main hotel area. The bars, dining room and other public spaces are housed in a massive and towering structure of timber and thatch that straddles the countryside almost in its natural form - here a large boulder, there a staircase of stone and I am sure there is even a tree inside, a large one! The chalets are no less prepossessing, built in and of rock, also with thick poles and thatch. I don't know how many visitors the hotel can accommodate – but on that particular night I was the only one.

At the same time, the new Harare Airport International Terminal opened to a dismal scene as major Western airlines had stopped flying to Harare. Sport followed as the English cricket team refused to come to Zimbabwe, citing, initially, 'the situation in the country'. After that Zimbabwe was chucked out of the Commonwealth – and so it went on.

All this was *before* the formal imposition of conventional sanctions! The major achievement of the media campaign was to bamboozle the public internationally as to what was really going on. Thanks to the West's media, their own citizens and those of other countries all over the world were conditioned to believe almost anything their governments and the other big stakeholders had to tell them about Zimbabwe. The first objectives had been achieved.

It was then that Britain, the European Union and the United States got out their heavy artillery - the Zimbabwe Democracy and Economic Recovery Act (2001) and EU Council Regulation (EC) 314/2004 CFSP (2002). And when they did, the public that by now was ready to believe anything on the question of Zimbabwe, believed them when they said that they were not imposing sanctions – simply targeted travel restrictions. So to this day, the Europeans, the North Americans, the Australians, the New Zealanders, the South Africans and many others all over the world deny that there are any sanctions and the problems in the country are nothing to do with sanctions but are all Mugabe's fault.

What does this quaintly named legislation, the Zimbabwe Democracy and Economic Recovery Act, entail? The following passage from an article by Balfour Ankomah in *The New African* (March, 2005) says it rather well:

> *The bill (Zimbabwe Democracy and Economic Recovery Act) had been pushed through the US Congress by Senator Jesse Helms and his friends led by Senator Bill Frist. The cynicism in this bill is exposed when one looks at Helm's history regarding African liberation. For all his life, Helms had fought against black majority rule in Zimbabwe. Yet, the same man — when the land issue blew up in Zimbabwe, a land issue that had taken land from white farmers and given to black farmers - now suddenly becomes the front for a bill supposedly aimed at giving black people more democracy in Zimbabwe. The main objectives of the Act are: (1) to provide for a transition to democracy and promote economic recovery in Zimbabwe. (2) block debt relief and other financial*

assistance to Zimbabwe from all international financial institutions until President Bush authorises it.

The Act defines "international financial institutions" as the multilateral development banks and the IMF. By "multilateral development banks", the Act means; "the World Bank, the International Development Association, the International Finance Corporation, the Inter-American Development Bank, the Asian Development Bank, the Inter-American Investment Corporation, the African Development Bank, the African Development Fund, the European Bank for Reconstruction and Development, and the Multilateral Investment Guaranty Agency." In effect, Zimbabwe could not even borrow or benefit from the services of our own African Development Bank and the African Development Fund. And America, Britain and "Africa's best friends" keep telling the (people) that they have not imposed economic sanctions on Zimbabwe!

Additionally, the Act authorises the US executive director of each international financial institution to oppose and vote against; (1) any extension by the respective institution of any loan, credit, or guarantee to the government of Zimbabwe; and (2) any cancellation or reduction of indebtedness owed by the government of Zimbabwe to the US or any international financial institution. Any US official in these institutions who disobeys this law is liable to be prosecuted at home. On top of this, President Bush was authorised to use provisions under the US Foreign Assistance Act of 1961 to "support democratic institutions, the free press and independent media, and the rule of law" in Zimbabwe. In this respect, $26m was immediately made available to him in 2001. The following yearly allocations were also made; in 2002, Bush got $21m to spend on regime change in Zimbabwe, 2003 $18rn, 2004 $12m, 2005 $7m, and 2006 $4m.

> *As a result of this mandate, Studio 7 of the Voice of America has been beaming propaganda every evening for the past two years into Zimbabwe. Please don't ask me which "independent" media outlets or NGOs inside and outside Zimbabwe are benefiting from the Bush largesse.*
>
> *When the bill was passed on 4 December 2001, Cynthia Mckinney, that great daughter of Africa, and Congresswoman for Atlanta, stood up in Congress and said; "Mr Speaker...when we get right down to it, this legislation [the Zimbabwe Democracy Act] is nothing more than a formal declaration of US complicity in a programme to maintain white-skin privilege. We can call it an 'incentives bill', but that does not change its essential sanctions nature. It is racist and against the interests of the masses of Zimbabweans..."*

There is no way that anyone can pretend that the US Zimbabwe Democracy and Economic Recovery Act is legislation that confines itself to military support and travel restrictions against 'targeted' individuals. The financial and commercial reach of the document is a blanket held over the head of the targeted economy, Zimbabwe. With these sanctions in place the European Union's later scrap of dishonesty and hypocrisy is almost superfluous as sanctions applied by the US, even when unilateral, are binding on the entire western establishment. Look at the trouble the European banks got into for going against unilateral US sanctions against Iran – they have forked out billions in fines! For something the EU never legislated on, something that was unilaterally imposed by the US! When the US imposes unilateral sanctions, the rest are compelled to fall into line, whether they like it or not.

The Europeans have been around a lot longer than their cousins in the United States and consequently they don't often call a spade a spade. Their relationship in this regard to the US is aptly suggested in a piece of dialogue in Oscar Wilde's play, *Lady Windermere's* Fan:

> Cecily (read US): This is no time for wearing the shallow mask of manners. When I see a spade I call it a spade.
>
> Gwendolen (read Europe): I am glad to say that I have never seen a spade. It is obvious that our social spheres have been widely different.

The European Council Regulation (EC) 314/2004 CFSP) is a much more subtle instrument than the Zimbabwe Democracy and Economic Recovery Act. The EU regulation does admit that the measures against Zimbabwe involve 'sanctions' eg. 'the Member States shall lay down the rules on *sanctions* applicable to infringements of this Regulation and shall take all measures necessary to ensure that they are implemented. The *sanctions* provided for must be effective, proportionate and dissuasive'. However, the wording of the document enables them to say that the legislation is only about restrictions which include 'inter alia, a ban on technical assistance, financing and financial assistance related to military activities, a ban on the export of equipment which might be used for internal repression, and the freezing of funds, financial assets and economic resources of members of the Government of Zimbabwe and of any natural or legal persons, entities or bodies associated with them.'

But then again, as I have said, they really didn't have to do much more – or admit to much more - because the US bill did it for them. The EU has therefore been able to continue 'squeaky clean' by claiming that they are not imposing sanctions, only targeted travel restrictions. They omit informing the world that they are bound by the US conditions and implement - and even exceed - them faithfully.

While Europe and the United States openly and publicly organised sanctions against Zimbabwe's new-found wealth in diamonds, they continued doggedly to reiterate that the sanctions they imposed were simply targeted against certain individuals.

But the cat always finds its way out of the bag and, in 2012, it was reported that the head of the EU Delegation to Zimbabwe, Ambassador Aldo Dell'Ariccia, in the process of promising an improvement in the EU's relations with Zimbabwe, stated that 'the EU used to extend more than US$130 million humanitarian aid to Zimbabwe'. This aid had been withdrawn on the imposition of sanctions. Jack Straw, when British Foreign Secretary, in response to a question in the House of Commons as to what his government was doing about Zimbabwe, replied that 'extensive sanctions' had been applied.

So, all this hooey about British and EU sanctions being restricted to the travel of targeted individuals and military activities was just a smoke-screen. European undeclared sanctions went a long way beyond this. These two examples are but two of the many that illustrate that what they say to each other when they are by themselves, is quite different from what they say when they are hoodwinking the world.

The official 'sanctions' legislation the EU and the US tabled, as stifling as it is, doesn't come anywhere near revealing the full weight and might of what the West has inflicted on Zimbabwe. In actual practice Western sanctions against Zimbabwe go far beyond the scope of the legislation and the letter of their own laws. They are pervasive across the whole spectrum of international relations, development and even humanitarian aid. Zimbabwe has often been excluded from regional and global funding in numerous sectors, including AIDS and other diseases, drought and flood relief (Cyclone Helene!)[38], tourism and agriculture. If to this is added their impact on the activities and opportunities of companies, institutions and individuals and families in business, sport, culture and private life, it must surely be apparent that the combined effect of international sanctions on Zimbabwe cannot be underestimated and is a far cry from what the Western Media – or the British Ambassador - pretend to be the case.

A Zimbabwean Senator, A. Georgias, decided to take the European Union's imposition of sanctions to court.[39] He described the sanctions as an 'arrogance of power' and went on to say: "we have seen what the collapse of national morale can do with the economic hardships we are experiencing and the alienation of our people into the Diaspora. This why I am even advocating class action by parliament, that we may protect what is our national core, our endowments, our people – young, educated and dynamic population." A Quixotic gesture? Quite likely. If Justice was a girl, Wealth and Power would get her any day.

But this is not the end of the sanctions story. Neo-colonialism refers to a situation where a country, usually a former colony, though

38 In February 2000 what were billed as the worst floods in 30 years struck Mozambique, South Africa and Zimbabwe. The situation in Mozambique was the most critical but the northern regions of South Africa and southern Zimbabwe also suffered. Bridges were washed away, roads buckled, peoples' houses destroyed along with schools and other infrastructure. A massive relief effort was mounted to assist the victims in Mozambique. South Africa was able to take care of itself but Zimbabwe, that needed assistance, was virtually ignored. Damage wreaked by the cyclone has still not been repaired in some cases to this day.

39 Currently (April, 2014) the case is being heard in the General Court (ECG) of the European Court of Justice in Brussels

it has 'flag independence', is economically – and therefore politically – controlled by the neo-colonial power. In other countries in the region, excluding South Africa, the national budgets are to varying degrees subsidised by foreign donors. In Mozambique, for instance, in 2003 direct budget support from foreign countries was in the region of 30% - and this excludes other channels for development-linked aid. In Zambia, direct budget support, again excluding development aid, was in the region of 7% of public expenditure. In 1999 Tanzania recorded external income receipts of 11.3% of Gross National Income. Automatically, this means that these countries are in effect to a greater or a lesser extent neo-colonies. With the imposition of sanctions on Zimbabwe all balance of payments or budgetary support was withdrawn. Thus, as far as I can make out, in effect Zimbabwe has survived, since the imposition of sanctions, on its own resources – with the exception of occasional budget support from South Africa. Is this a blessing in disguise? Does the harsh medicine of sanctions suggest a cure for Zimbabwe? Given its resources, could Zimbabwe not join South Africa as an independent country, independent and self-sufficient without falling again into the 'dependency syndrome'? I believe the answer is 'yes' if...

It is a big 'if' because Zimbabwe's efforts to mitigate the effects of the external sanctions on its economy and its very life have been disastrously undermined by another form of sanctions – what people came to call the 'internal sanctions' – corruption, the subject of the next chapter.

CHAPTER TWENTY-TWO:

CORRUPTION

Between a rock and a hard place

In traditional culture, the grain is pounded between the *duri* and the *mutswi* – the mortar and the pestle. Two women usually pound together, in rhythm with each other, each holding a *mutswi*. As the one goes up, the other comes down, pounding the grain in the *duri*. The grain being pounded could be said to be between the *duri* and the *mutswi*. Another way of expressing it is the English expression, 'between a rock and a hard place'. And that is where the ordinary people of Zimbabwe found themselves, 'between a rock and a hard place', between the *duri* and the *mutswi*, being ground to dust between Western sanctions - and local corruption.

If international sanctions against Zimbabwe were the rock, corruption within Zimbabwe was the hard place. Whichever way you put it, for the people of Zimbabwe there was no escape. Reeling from the effects of sanctions, their strength and stamina on which they relied to resist them was scandalously and treacherously sapped by the looting and corruption of those they relied on to lead and protect them. While the people suffered, the fat cats grew fatter and fatter.

There was a housing co-operative in Harare, one of a number in the country. This particular co-operative involved some of the poorest people around. Every month they paid to the co-operative some few Zimbabwe dollars from their very meagre income, cherishing the hope that one day a house would be theirs. The co-operative was a great idea and it had been pioneered by a rather high-flying liberation war veteran. Whereas the members of the co-operative lived in shacks, this 'comrade' lived in one of the most affluent suburbs in Harare, drove the usual spectacular motor car the Harare new rich drive around in, sported glamorous and fashionable clothes and hairstyles and went abroad from time to time. The contrast could not have been starker.

This might have been perfectly OK if she had been an upper-class philanthropist of independent means who, while living the high life was, in the spirit of capitalist charity, genuinely assisting these representatives of the 'the wretched of the earth' to get houses. Or even if she had been a 'comrade' who had taken her opportunities, made a packet but not forgotten where she came from. Unfortunately, she was neither. Like many of the Zimbabwean new rich, she relied on political power and '*madhiri*' (deals) to pay for her extravagant lifestyle. And, like many others, her greed knew no bounds and it seemed she had lost her conscience *mumasango* - in the bush - fighting for independence.

Houses were indeed being built with the funds that had been paid in by the hopeful members of the co-operative and were accumulating in the co-operative's account and from time to time the building contractor would come to the office with invoices or receipts for work done or materials to buy or be paid. This was the loophole of opportunity which the 'comrade' exploited. She would arrange with the building contractor to present bloated or fictitious claims, which were duly paid from the co-operative's account, and equally duly handed over to her by the contractor after payment. As she needed a lot more money for her lifestyle than the members of the co-op did, the sums she siphoned off from their housing fund were considerable and frequent.

This example – a true story, by the way, not a rumour or a 'myth' – burnt itself into my brain as an image of the great betrayal. Here was someone who had sacrificed her youth in the bush to make Zimbabwe free and, ostensibly, make a better life for the ordinary, suffering people, who were *her* people, *her* family and *her* ancestors - the *povo*.

I think this probably explains the way in which many in ZANU-PF, in particular the leadership, behaved after Independence – and from what I can see, many in the ANC in South Africa, where the wealth and consumption was far more conspicuous than it had been in Rhodesia.

This phenomenon however had disastrous and possibly fatal consequences for Zimbabwe. Zimbabwe is potentially a rich country. If the people were united and the leadership honest and committed, the West's sanctions might not have been nearly as effective. This is why in the hard years of the third decade, the ordinary people called corruption, the 'internal sanctions'. They knew that what the external sanctions didn't destroy, the internal sanctions finished off. Worse, they undermined the ability of the country to resist the sanctions and get by on her own resources.

In their day the Rhodesians also felt the sting of sanctions. But in Rhodesia, the whites were united and the leadership, while not honest, was at least committed to the survival of their Rhodesia. Perhaps when you've got it and you are a minority and you are in danger of losing it, it is easier to be honest and committed about defending it. Sadly, the leadership of independent Zimbabwe neither managed to unite its people nor lead its country with the honesty and commitment it so sorely needed. Many in ZANU-PF, like the lotus-eaters in Homer's *Oddyssey*, quite forgot where they came. They forgot, as if they had never really cared, what they had, ostensibly, fought for and gave themselves over to self-enrichment and greed. As the years progressed and they monopolised power and opportunity, their greed and lack of conscience seemed to attain obsessive proportions. All other considerations - love of one's country, dedication to one's people, the ideals of the struggle, *hunhu* - all gave way to a mania of selfish acquisition and accumulation to the point of shameless looting.

Take this. This is a list of the assets of a Minister of Local Government, Urban and Rural Development, which appeared in a report in a local daily on the proceedings of a case in which the minister's wife was suing her husband for matrimonial assets as agreed in 'a signed post- nuptial agreement stating that 50% of all properties acquired – whether held personally or in proxy – during the subsistence of their marriage' will be shared:

> *List of assets*
> *Vehicles:*
> *4 Toyota Land Cruisers*
> *3 Mercedes-Benzes*
> *1 Mahindra*
> *2 Nissan Wolfs*
> *1 Toyota Vigo,*
> *1 Mazda BT-50*
> *1 Bus*
> *1 Nissan Hardbody*
> *1 Toyota Hilux*
>
> *Properties:*
> *2 Glen View houses*
> *2 flats in Queensdale,*
> *A property in Katanga Township,*
> *Stand Number 1037 Mount Pleasant Heights*

4 Norton business stands
3 Chinhoyi business stands,
4 Banket business stands
1 commercial stand in Epworth,
2 residential stands in Chirundu
4 commercial stands in Kariba
1 stand in Ruwa
1 stand in Chinhoyi
2 stands in Mutare
2 stands in Binga
4 stands in Victoria Falls
1 stand in Zvimba Rural
Chitungwiza (two residential and two commercial stands)
Beitbridge (four stands)
20 stands in Crowhill, Borrowdale
10 stands in Glen Lorne
2 flats at Eastview Gardens (B319 and B320)
1 flat at San Sebastian in the Avenues, Harare
Number 79 West Road, Avondale
Greendale house
Number 36 Cleveland Road, Milton Park
Number 135 Port Road, Norton
2 Bulawayo houses
Number 18 Cuba Rd, Mount Pleasant
Number 45 Basset Crescent, Alexandra Park
2 Chegutu houses
1 Glen Lorne house (Harare)
2 houses (Victoria Falls)
Stand along Simon Mazorodze Road
Norton (one stand)
Avondale (two stands)
365 Beverly House (one stand)

> *Bulawayo (three stands)*
> *Mica Point Kariba (one stand)*
>
> *Farming equipment:*
> *New Allan Grange Farm including three tractors, two new combine harvesters, two boom sprayers and two engines*
> *Darton Farm, shared chicken runs, pigsties, a shop, grinding mill, house, mills, tractors, lorries, six trucks, five of which are non-runners, four trailers (three non-runners) and one truck*
>
> *Companies and businesses:*
> *Shares in the family's 10 companies including Dickest, Hamdinger, Landberry and Track in Security Company*
>
> *Other interests:*
> *Mvurwi Mine*
> *Hunting safari lodges in Chiredzi, Hwange, Magunje and Chirundu*
> *properties in South Africa*

Before joining government, this minister was a university lecturer. By the time of this law suit, he had acquired 21 motor vehicles (cars, pick-ups, a bus and trucks), 15 houses (mostly in upmarket suburbs), 78 stands (commercial and residential), 2 commercial farms with equipment, 10 businesses, safari lodges and a mine! This excluded unspecified properties in South Africa.

One would have thought that these revelations would have provoked an outcry, an enquiry, a sacking, a resignation or something. No, life went on as usual. For who was going to throw the first stone? I was told that the minister's assets were chickenfeed in comparison with others! Far from disgraced, the honourable minister was probably being clapped on the back by other aspirants to fat cat status who had not yet made it and saw the minister as a role model! Incidentally, this was the same minister who called me 'Bongo Man' on that occasion out in the commercial farms when he was addressing farm workers and playing the race card.

During the time of the so-called 'melt down' I had a business friend. Let's call her Nyarai. She really saved our organisation's life on a number of occasions. Nyarai was a 'Cross-Border' – but of some class. She had an account in South Africa and for her business purposes she needed to be constantly moving cash – from South Africa to Zimbabwe, from Zimbabwe dollars to rands, from US dollars to rands or Zimbabwe dollars to US. Now it so happened that our organisation, like every other organisation in Zimbabwe at the time, had to do a lot of the same thing, in order to beat inflation or evade the snags of sanctions. Nyarai was running a for-profit business. Ours was a not-for-profit Trust. We were opposite sides of the coin and so her needs and ours dovetailed exactly. Many is the time Nyarai would come to the office with a box full of Zimbabwe dollars in the boot of her car and save our lives.

Now it so happened that one day I found Nyarai not her usual buoyant, busy self. That things were not going so well for her was confirmed by the fact that for once she could not help me. "Sorry, I can't help," she said. "I've no liquidity at all." So I said to her: "Nyarai, you're not your usual self. What's up?" "It's hard," she said. "*Zvakaoma*." Then she told me the story.

One of the things that Nyarai used to do was accumulate US dollars and then get orders from companies in Zimbabwe. She would then go out of the country, purchase whatever the company wanted and make a profit. Now that Air Zimbabwe had introduced their new direct flight to Beijing, Nyarai, like women from all over Africa, had taken a ticket on the gravy plane to China. On this particular occasion, she had got a very good order from a certain company to supply IT equipment. She had gone to Beijing as usual, bought the stuff – sinking a lot of foreign exchange into the deal – and loaded it on Air Zimbabwe. She was now waiting in the departure lounge for her flight to return to Harare with all the equipment. She knew she was going to do very well out of this transaction.

Unbeknown to Nyarai, the First Lady, Grace Mugabe, had also been to Beijing on a commercial shopping spree. Grace was the top 'Cross-Border' in the land. But there were significant differences in the conditions of trade between Grace's and those of Nyarai. Nyarai had to buy her foreign exchange on the black market. Grace got it from the bank at a basement bargain rate – more of that later. Nyarai had to get her goods onto the return flight to Harare in the usual way. Grace didn't have to bother about any of the usual ways. She was the First Lady. So, as I started saying, unbeknown to Nyarai, Grace Mugabe had come to the flight in Beijing late with a whole load of goods and in order to accommodate the President's wife's goods, Nyarai's and other good down-to-earth Cross-Borders' dearly-earned purchases were offloaded and left behind in storage. Nyarai arrived back in Harare with no cash and no goods and the company who had contracted her furious. When I found her, she had been waiting for three weeks for her stuff. It was not easy to get your goods onto Air Zimbabwe flights from Beijing – if you were not the President's wife, that is. Nyarai lost her contract with the company – and she was not able to help us...till next time when, being a Zimbabwean, the ever dynamic Nyarai had bounced back and was doing business again.

It starts at the top! That is what the angry artists were saying at a meeting held to discuss the National Healing[40] process in the early days of the Inclusive Government some years later. We had been addressed by one of the Vice-Presidents and by a minister of the cloth, whom the artists knew very well and what he was. They were incensed. Put briefly, what they were saying was that the wounds that needed healing had been perpetrated by the people at the top and if any National Healing was going to happen, it had better start with them. Until they came clean, confessed their crimes and mistakes and asked the people for forgiveness, all this National Healing business was a farce. The artists were saying 'healing starts at the top'. This must surely be true of any nation in other respects too. It is certainly true of corruption. In Zimbabwe, corruption started at the top – and spread down until by the year 2010 it was a poison that had corroded the entire fabric of Zimbabwean society - and who now knows how Zimbabwe can be restored to health again?

There was another even uglier side to the corruption. The members of the housing co-op were ripped off and Nyarai was done down without any danger to life and limb. There were other stories, however, of people who experienced something more dangerous. I knew someone well who had been a top manager in an important company. Let's call him Maredza. There were some misunderstandings and he was forced to leave the company. After

40 An aspect of the Global Political Agreement signed by the political parties, was the need for National Healing. The Inclusive Government then set up the Organ for National Healing, Reconciliation and Integration to respond to this need. Its mandate included coming up with a 'mechanism for national healing, cohesion and unity and laying the foundation for a society characterised by mutual respect, tolerance, and development and where individuals enjoy the freedoms as enshrined in the Constitution' – it was seen as a process closely linked to the need for a new constitution and involved developing a National Framework for Peace.

some time, he disappeared and it was only after a couple of years that I met up with him again. He had a sad story to tell. The reason that we had not seen him around was that he had managed to buy a hotel in one of the small towns between Harare and Bulawayo. It was pretty run down when he got it but with his managerial skills, he turned it round and soon it was undergoing something of a renaissance. Business was much better as well – and all seemed to be rosy, until one day a man came to see him.

The man was perfectly friendly and in the course of the chat, he asked Maredza how much he was prepared to sell the hotel for. Maredza laughed and told him he wouldn't think of it. That seemed to be that. But the same man came back again a few weeks later and told him that he had been sent by the local party heavyweight. This heavyweight had noticed that the hotel was doing quite well and he was expressing his interest in taking it over. Naturally, my friend, Maredza, thought that this meant the man was interested in buying it. Again he indicated that the hotel was not for sale. He had a couple more visits after that, each one more insistent than the last, until one day the party man came himself. He challenged Maredza by asking him whether he was aware that it was he who had said that he wanted to take over the hotel. Maredza said yes, he was aware but, as he had explained on a number of occasions, he did not want to sell. The party heavyweight grew incensed and pulled out a gun. Pointing the gun at Maredza, he warned him to vacate and never come back again if he wanted to stay alive.

Maredza abandoned his hotel. No money was paid - until he took the matter to court and received a token sum in compensation. But that was the end of his hotel. This was corruption and *Jambanja* at the same time. Senator Georgias was suing Britain for what he called 'arrogance of power'. His cause was just – but what about all those in the party he belonged to, who were equally guilty of 'arrogance of power' and used it to grab whatever they wanted, not from need but out of pure selfishness and greed?

In the desperate days when there was no fuel at the pump and one was forced to buy it in England at a reasonable price or pay exorbitantly for a *chigubhu* of dubious stuff *mumarayini* (in the 'hood'), we had a young man in our organisation who was ever ready to offer us diesel or even petrol at black market prices. When asked how he happened to have such an ever-flowing supply of the precious liquid, he innocently explained that his uncle had a farm. Now this might have explained little for those who never went through those years in Zimbabwe. But for us it was as clear as day. We refused to buy it.

What he was saying was that as a new farmer, his uncle had access to very cheap diesel. This diesel was made available to farmers along with tractors, fertilisers, seeds and other inputs either for free, like the tractors, or at far below black market prices. It was part of government's efforts to assist the new farmers to get their operations off the ground. This assistance from government was precisely what was needed and what, as we had noted earlier, had been received by new farmers in many other countries, including Rhodesia. If you remember, Scoones and team noted that most of the new sugarcane farmers covered in their survey had acquired tractors but that, although farmers were being given tractors by the state, they had not been able to access any of these tractors and all their tractors they had purchased themselves.

There was a connection between the facts that this young man's uncle had abundant diesel and the new sugar cane farmers never got any of the tractors. One could say that there was a connection also with the fact that the honourable Minister of Local Government, Urban and Rural Development, whose assets we had a look at a few pages back, had a number of tractors standing around on his farms. In a situation of rampant inflation and extreme shortages, it made a lot more sense for a farmer to take his cheap inputs and sell them on the black market rather than toil away all year for dubious returns in a currency that lost its value from one day to the next. The profit to be made from accessing and then re-selling the cheap inputs was so great that anyone who was anyone or had any connections or any party or government clout, would get their hands on the stuff long before it reached the needy farmer and sell it openly on the black market. Thus Government's policy was good, its efforts laudable. But two factors negated Government's efforts - one, the macroeconomic environment (external sanctions), two, the 'arrogance' of power and corruption (internal sanctions). The two fed on each other.

If this was true for agricultural inputs, it was criminally far truer for foreign exchange. There was a time when Zimbabweans took their foreign currency to the bank and a time when they could request foreign currency from the bank. With the rise of the black market, foreign currency disappeared from the banks. People kept it at home and traded it on the streets or through private deals. The Reserve Bank Governor, Gideon Gono, whose resourcefulness is by now legendary, as unfortunately is his own participation in the orgy of corruption, came up with the innovative idea of a foreign currency auction. This brought the value of the Zimbabwe dollar relatively closer to that of the US dollar. Dramatically the rate of inflation fell until it had dropped below 100% per annum and was still falling. Then came the elections in 2005 and various other political expenditures and the Zimbabwe dollar began to go out of sight again. However, the auction having been abandoned, the official rate against the US dollar was kept static at a totally unrealistically low figure. Despite the fact that zeros were being regularly lopped off the Zimbabwe dollar, which was attaining astronomical figures, the official foreign exchange rate continued unchanged. Of course, no-one took any foreign currency to the bank. Instead, if they had the good fortune to lay their hands on any, they made a killing on the black market. And of course, no-one could access foreign currency from the bank at the official rate – except the chosen few. And there was the rub. The rest of us, the innocents, looked on in amazement. Why was government not seeing the obvious? Why did they not raise the official exchange rate, which would get forex back into the system and make it available for business and for servicing the needs of society? For people like me, it all seemed to be a mystery until one day I asked someone who had been President of one of the big financial bodies representing industry and big business. He shook his head at my naiveté and gently explained to me that those with power were accessing foreign exchange at that rate – and that was very nice for them – so why change it? They accessed it and sold it on the black market or used it for other extremely profitable deals. Others used it to indulge in luxurious consumption and amass motor vehicles and houses. Some, the minority, like the President's wife, at least used it for 'Cross Border' trading.

While those at the top were doing all this and fuel, fertiliser, foreign exchange, tractors – you name it – were being corruptly accessed for profit, inflation had eroded the earnings of the rest of us. Unless one was paid in foreign currency, one's salary became meaningless. In effect, vast sections of society stopped earning. This included the civil service, the teachers, the police, customs officials etc etc. The situation did not improve with dollarization as the state did not have sufficient dollars to pay its employees a living wage. In the absence of a salary, many just stayed at home – their salaries hardly covered their fares to work and back. Not only did they stay at home but they could no longer go on paying for electricity and water. For some years people simply got them for free – which partly accounted for the power cuts and water shortages.

Because teachers and nurses could not afford the transport to get them to work, they too stayed at home. This meant that the entire national education system collapsed for two school terms as a result and hospital services deteriorated dramatically. Others used the opportunities for corruption their jobs afforded them, to pay themselves. And that is why, from that time, Zimbabwe by and large ceased to have a *bone fide* police force. The police virtually gave up combating crime and spent their days doing their best to bully commuter omnibuses and innocent citizens into paying them bribes. For once the Zimbabwe Republic Police were conspicuous. They were out in the streets all over Harare issuing unreceipted spot fines and every little police station between Harare and Beit Bridge would on a daily basis erect its road block on the national road. Not only Zimbabwean motorists were cajoled or tricked into paying. They began to invent new crimes for foreign motorists, which must have negatively affected tourist numbers, bad as they already were. Telephone technicians would not attend to your phone unless you bribed them. Then they would do it for free – in other words you would not have to pay the telephone parastatal, you paid them instead – thus undermining the viability of the parastatal. The much maligned ZESA, the electricity authority, of all service providers, was a partial and sometimes heroic exception.

An experience of mine illustrates the ambiguity of that time, the crazy conflict between survival, greed and duty. One night I was woken up at about three in the morning by an almighty crash. Someone had thrown a kind of siege weapon, an enormous rock placed in one of my large flower pots and bound about with a swathe cut from my lounge curtains, through the large bedroom window, two and a half metres from my head,. Before I even had time to wake up, a gang of six men came tumbling in through the broken window. This is not the time to tell the exciting and rather idiosyncratic story of my burglary. I simply want to make a point – and the point is this. Detectives from ZRP Southerton did a wonderful job. The gang had made their getaway with all their loot in one of the cars they found in the garage, hence the involvement of Southerton, which is the vehicle section. They caught the burglars. I met them after their capture. A detective and I were able to interrogate them at Homicide Harare – they were an armed gang – and ask them where all my property was with the result that most of my possessions were found. In fact, the detectives tracked me down using my own Samsung cellphone, which had been in the gang's possession when they were arrested. A detective came to my house with the cellphone in his hand. The Southerton police had retrieved my laptop and made Homicide sign for it when they handed it over. I had personally gone into Police Headquarters to identify my property.

I never saw any of my property again. Having done a wonderful job catching the robbers, the police at Harare Headquarters managed to 'lose' my property. When, accompanied by detectives from Southerton, I went to claim it, the officer in charge at Homicide was not able to find any record of it in his books and suggested that it had gone to Lost and Found. Found and Lost, I think, more like!

HONDO (WAR)

PART FIVE
THE BATTLE FOR ZIMBABWE

When ZANU-PF announced its intention to move on the land and the first incursions onto the farms began to take place at the end of the Second Decade, it was basically a declaration of war. Indeed it came to be called the Third Chimurenga, *the war to complete the Second* Chimurenga, *which had brought political independence. This was now a war for the control, in fact, ownership of national resources, principally the land but also the economy and natural resources in general, including its minerals. It was also a war for national sovereignty, in other words, a rejection of imperialist or neo-colonial control. As these objectives were opposed, in the first instance by the MDC and their supporters, it should be viewed as a Civil War too. Therefore, to judge what happened subsequently as if it all took place in peace time, is not, in my opinion, an honest, valid or helpful approach. I believe that what happened must be viewed as taking place in a war situation, in which local forces were aided and abetted by the most powerful foreign nations on earth.*

To fight this war both sides employed whatever available weapons they could get away with. ZANU-PF, despite the MDC's hold on the urban areas, had the advantage within the country as it was the government and was supported by the uniformed forces and a majority – albeit diminishing - of the peasantry outside Matebeleland. The MDC had the advantage internationally as they were supported by the West. The latter used the usual big guns at their disposal. Their most effective weapon was withdrawal of all financial support and the imposition of economic and political sanctions. Their ownership of the world media was another extremely powerful weapon and they used it to advantage, particularly by pretending that a war situation did not exist, by claiming the moral high ground and lambasting the Zimbabwean government on the issues of democracy, human rights and the rule of law.

ZANU-PF, fighting for the objectives of the Liberation Struggle at the same time as fighting for its life, used its control of the state, the armed forces, the traditional structures, television, radio and whatever newspapers it had – and, interestingly, as in the Second Chimurenga - *culture to fight back. One other very important ally was SADC and it was its support which was crucial in sparing them the full force of the West's venom, in particular an armed assault.*

Being a desperate struggle, there were no holds barred.

CHAPTER TWENTY-THREE:

THE 2008 ELECTIONS

Snatching defeat from the jaws of victory

The trumpets sound, the banners fly,
The shining spears are ranked ready.
The sounds of war are heard afar
The battle closes deep and bloody.

Robert Burns, "The Silver Tassie"

I will never forget the lull before the storm in the week days leading up to the elections of 2008. It must have been a little like this, I thought, in Britain and France when Hitler's Panzer divisions went into Poland and people wondered what would happen and what should happen, knowing that, one way or the other, the storm was about to break.

The day before the elections were to take place I had a few people round to dinner. I enjoy my dinners and one way I make sure I do, is to ban politics. Of course, during those years, politics was the bane of social intercourse. You either talked about the hardships or the politics. Neither makes for a convivial discussion round the dining room table with interesting people, good food and plenty wine.

But this particular dinner party had to be different. One, it was the day before what we all knew might be the first phase in the Battle for Zimbabwe, the harmonised elections of 2008. Two, coincidentally present that night were four rather prominent intellectuals; one well known for his anti-government theatre productions;

another a film-maker and polemicist, equally well-known for his staunch support of ZANU-PF; the third a university academic and poet, who had written beautiful poems inspired by the liberation struggle; and the fourth the enlightened and intellectual director of a cultural funding institution.

No politics, I announced at the beginning of our soirée. I might have been King Knut commanding the mighty ocean not to roll. It just started coming in, creeping in, dodging and darting until finally it was there – and it went on into the early hours. A wonderful political discussion of diametrically opposed views, of passion but no rancour. O, I thought, if only Zimbabwe had been able to talk this way all these years, we wouldn't be in quite the position we were in that evening.

And then I remember, later that night, thinking about what the morrow would bring. In our children's arts education organisation, for very obvious reasons, political or religious canvassing was banned. I would never have given the Zimbabweans working in the organisation any political advice, just as I would not give them the benefit or otherwise of my religious opinions. I think they all knew that I had been a ZANU-PF supporter and a liberation activist. But we never talked about it. However, on that night, on the eve of the most momentous elections in the history of Zimbabwe, I imagined myself saying to them: "*Veduwe, ndirikuziva kuti hapana anoda ZANU. Asi ukavotera MDC mangwana uchamukira urimuRhodesia kuswera mangwana!*" (My people, I know none of you wants ZANU-PF but if you vote for the MDC tomorrow, you will wake up the next day in Rhodesia.)

The forces that had lined up for the battle reminded me – as a South African - of the Battle of Gqokli or Qokli Hill, when the man who was to become Emperor Shaka the Great drew up his meagre but highly trained forces on the top of a conical hill a little way south of the site of a much later but even more fateful battle at Ulundi. Spread out before him in great numbers were the forces of his great adversary, King Zwide of the Ndwandwe confederation:

> *The mountains roared with the great anthem of the Ndwandwes.*
> *They stamped the ground, pointing their spears to the sun.*
> *The river trembled, jolting the trees on the overhanging mountains...*
> *The big army of Zwide, like the young of the locust in spring,*
> *Spread over the body of the Qokli hill.*
>
> - *Emperor Shaka, the Great*,
> an epic poem by Mazisi Kunene

As a South African of Scots descent, it reminded me too of that great battle of the Bannockburn. There the enemy forces consisted of the flower of English chivalry, hundreds of heavily armoured earls, bishops and knights mounted on enormous destriers, the tanks of medieval warfare. Behind them and key to success were our fellow Celts, the Welsh bowmen, selling out to 'the auld enemy', who was as much their enemy as he was ours. And behind *them* 40 000 foot soldiers, in a procession of English military might that stretched back miles and miles into the Lothians. Opposing them were a scattering of Scottish light cavalry and the wild and kilted Highlanders with their dirks and claymores, my ancestors, mustering all of a few thousand. No heavy cavalry to speak of and no archers.

So the forces lined up in Zimbabwe on that fateful day. On the MDC's side was the West and white South Africa with their sanctions, their media, including the so-called 'independent' media in Zimbabwe, and their financial support for NGOs and activities targeted at 'regime change'. They had seized the 'moral high ground', from which they were able to shower down the equivalent internationally of the Welsh arrows – calls for democracy, human rights and the rule of law. Also on the MDC's side were the trade unions, the urban masses, what whites remained, much of the black middle class and intelligentsia, the vast majority of the population of so-called Matebeleland and increasing numbers of the rural masses in other parts of the country too. In short, a very impressive line-up.

On ZANU-PF's side were the government and its resources, including the uniformed forces, the government-owned media (print and electronic), well-entrenched and organised party structures, the majority of chiefs and people in the rural areas outside Matebeleland, the liberation war veterans – and SADC.

Thus, inside Zimbabwe, MDC and ZANU-PF were rather equally matched. Internationally, the MDC had the overwhelming advantage except for the crucial exception of the other governments in the Southern African region, many of them like ZANU-PF tracing their origins in liberation struggles. For years now the white press in South Africa had been baying for Zimbabwean blood and Mugabe's head but the ANC government had resolutely refused to budge. There is also little doubt – and Blair admitted it recently – that the West would have relished the opportunity to use military force to get their way in Zimbabwe – if SADC had not held firm and opposed it.

I have drawn up this inventory of the forces arrayed on each side so that the battle and the way in which the adversaries fought, can be seen in context. Too many Zimbabweans and others tended to see the conflict in purely parochial terms, as if it was taking place in a hermetically sealed country and the only adversaries were those inside it. Yet, in order to understand the reality of the situation and why the combatants fought in the ways they did, it is vital to see the conflict in its global context.

Earlier, I spoke of a storm that was about to break. This may have given the wrong impression. Perhaps for those who knew the fatal potential of the upcoming elections, it might have been an accurate description. But generally in the country at large the atmosphere during the run-up to the elections was not that which precedes a storm. In fact, the situation was extremely calm. Both sides had called for a peaceful process and there was a sense that with the MDC and ZANU-PF having already opposed each other in a number of elections, a more mature approach to campaigning and voting had begun to develop.

For instance, I was in Warren Park in the weeks before the election, at the place that was called Mereki. Warren Park, as its name implies, was not the traditional urban 'township' or 'high-density suburb', associated with the colonial days, such as Mbare, Mabvuku, Mufakose, Kambuzuma, Dzivaresekwa and Highfield. It was a sort of medium-density suburb but in many respects the social milieu was similar to a high-density suburb. Mereki was an example of this. In the centre of Warren Park there is what is called a 'rank', in other words, a bus and taxi terminus. As is typical of a 'rank', there were also lots of vendors of various descriptions and many liquor outlets with popular music blaring, like the Dendera Kings, Alex Macheso and Orchestra Mberikwazvo, Leonard Zhakata and the Zimbabwe Stars. These particular vendors were a common source of commodities at times when commodities could not be bought in the shops – sugar, mielie-meal, bread, cooking oil etc. But what was distinctive about Mereki was its '*gochi gochi*'[41]. On the pave-

41 From '*kugocha*', meaning 'to roast'. '*Chisanyama*', literally 'burn meat', meaning braai or barbeque.

ments outside the liquor outlets a thriving chain of *chisanyama* braais had been set up – and people came from all over Harare to enjoy the meat, the liquor, the music – and no doubt other things on the side.

Well, I happened to be there and I was chatting to some *gochi gochi* customers and I noticed that one or two of them were openly wearing MDC T-shirts. Many is the man or woman in the rural areas who has been made to pay dearly for the privilege of wearing such a T-shirt. O, so in town, where the MDC rules, maybe the roles are reversed, I thought. I wondered what would happen to someone who pitched up at Mereki in a ZANU-PF T-shirt. So I asked the guys. They shrugged and said it wasn't a big deal these days. One of them actually pointed to a woman who was indeed wearing one.

And this remained very much the spirit of the campaigning and also of the voting, when people went to the polls peacefully, in an orderly fashion, and the results were, after a delay, announced slowly but methodically.

But what was the outcome? A bombshell. The results of this well-organised, extraordinarily peaceful and, dare I say, mature voting process, was a victory for the two MDCs. The MDC had split into two factions, one, the smaller one, led by Arthur Mutambara, ex-UZ student activist, the other, led by Tsvangirai. MDC (Tsvangirai) had won 100 seats, ZANU-PF 99 and MDC (Mutambara) 10, all in so-called Matebeleland. The ruling party, the party that had been instrumental in bringing Independence to Zimbabwe and had ruled the country for 28 years, was the ruling party no more!

What is more, in the presidential election, which was held concurrently with the Parliamentary elections, the leader of the MDC,

Morgan Tsvangirai (47.87%), polled more votes than the incumbent, Robert Gabriel Mugabe (43.24%). For the first time, Mugabe had lost an election. But Tsvangirai was not yet home and dry. According to the constitution, if no candidate in the presidential election wins 50% or more of the votes counted, there must be a second round of voting to decide between the two candidates who polled the most votes in the first round – a common enough provision and a provision which prevails in many countries.

And that is when the storm broke – that is when the First Battle for Zimbabwe was joined in earnest.

To say that the 'election' that followed, was discredited by violence and social upheaval is to miss the point. It was not an election any more. It was a battle. When PF-ZAPU lost to ZANU-PF in the Independence election in 1980, they made for their weapons caches – and both parties were committed to the national sovereignty of Zimbabwe. Both had fought against Smith. Neither was going to hand the country back to the whites if they won. But they fought each other. How much more would this be the case in a situation where there was little reason for ZANU-PF (which now included PF-ZAPU) to believe that the MDC was committed to defending the national sovereignty of Zimbabwe and every reason to fear that they would hand the country – and the land - back to the whites and foreign interests.

ZANU-PF had fought the 2008 elections on the twin issues of the land and national sovereignty. 'Zimbabwe will never be a colony again' was one of its slogans. It was clear that, for ZANU-PF, the victory of the MDC was a victory for Imperialism and Neocolonialism, for the white commercial farmers and the white bosses, a victory that would lead to the loss of the land, in both senses *nyika* and *ivhu*, for which Zimbabwe had fought three *Chimurengas*.

The military was led by men who had played prominent parts in the liberation war. Members of the top brass had already made it clear – in so many words – that they would not accept an MDC government. They made it clear that they would defend the gains of the liberation struggle if the results of an election endangered them.

For the MDC, victory meant payback time. Tsvangirai and his party had accepted the financial and diplomatic support of the West and the whites. If or when they won, the MDC would be expected to give them what they wanted. The Imperialists wanted unfettered access to Zimbabwe's resources and its realignment with the West. They and the whites demanded the repeal of legislation empowering the state to designate and confiscate land and the restoration of land ownership rights as they existed before 1997 – in other words, to give back the land. Already, so the stories that did the rounds after the first round of elections had it, whites were streaming back into Zimbabwe from South Africa. Many of them were visiting the farms they had previously owned and crowing that now the MDC had beaten ZANU-PF, they would soon take them back again. People spoke of mysterious light aircraft circling over their farms etc. etc.

A victory for either side might have been disastrous for the country. If Tsvangirai had won the presidential run-off and the MDC had come to control not only parliament but also the presidency, the resultant situation would have been extremely serious. I do not believe that after a century of struggle Zimbabweans would have handed over their Zimbabwe to a coalition of what they would consider to be sell-outs or reactionaries and their Imperialist masters. Having got Zimbabwe back, along with its land and increasingly its wealth, it is very unlikely that they would have accepted the result meekly. As I have made clear, we are not talking about democratic elections. We are talking about war – the war for Zimbabwe. The President of Zimbabwe is also the Commander-in-Chief of the armed forces. It is unlikely that the armed forces would have accepted Tsvangirai as their chief. It is unlikely that the military would have recognised an MDC government. The liberation war veterans would have joined forces with them and, like their ZAPU predecessors, made for the arms caches. The only difference this time was that they would not have had to dig them up. The arms were with the military. The new farmers and the chiefs who stood to lose their land, would also have readied themselves for resistance. I do not think surrender was an option.

If ZANU-PF had won or had either fraudulently manipulated the outcome or refused to take an MDC victory lying down, not only would there have been a dramatic increase in Western condemnation but it would have been extremely difficult for SADC to continue to protect Zimbabwe from their retribution. It is difficult to know what SADC would have done in such circumstances, namely a situation in which the government of a member state refuses to accept the results of an election and step down. It is possible that it might have been obliged to intervene. A precedent for this had been established in 1998 when a SADC force, consisting of South African and Botswana detachments, intervened in Lesotho following disputed elections. An intervention by SADC forces would have provoked a military conflict in Zimbabwe. And if SADC had declined to go in, it is likely that nothing would have stopped NATO this time. The West had for some time been itching to intervene directly in the Zimbabwean conflict, including military intervention. With SADC holding the line, they were not willing to alienate the whole region. But with SADC too condemning a ZANU-PF fraud or hijack, there would have been nothing to restrain them. In the event of a military intervention, there is no doubt that the West would have enlisted the involvement of other compliant countries in the region, possibly Botswana, Rwanda and Uganda. The Zimbabwean armed forces, loyal to the revolutionary party and the goals of the liberation struggle, would have resisted. The liberation war veterans and the new farmers would not have been left out. Zimbabwe and possibly the whole region would have been engulfed in a conflagration that would almost certainly have had disastrous consequences. The smouldering ruins of Afghanistan, Iraq, Libya and Syria bear testimony to what might have happened.

As it happened, it didn't come to that. The lead-up to the re-run of the presidential election was, as I have said, not an election campaign. It was a battle in a war, the First Battle for Zimbabwe.

It pitted Zimbabweans against Zimbabweans. They beat each other up, they called each other names, the police and the army brutalised Zimbabweans, on one side, while Zimbabweans co-operated with their foreign allies to trash their Zimbabwe in the world media and intensify sanctions against their own Zimbabwean people, on the other side.

ZANU-PF used everything in the book, every weapon it had, to see to it that Tsvangirai was not elected, including compulsion, violence and intimidation. The MDC responded in like manner and with its own weapons. Sometimes it was impossible to say who was doing what to whom. Youth in Mbare were mugging other youths and forcing them to *toyi-toyi* and attend all night *pungwes* at which they sang ZANU-PF songs. ZANU-PF youths in Mbare! First we had heard of them. Mbare had long been an MDC stronghold. Also the tactic was so fatally counter-productive that it is almost impossible to believe that it was orchestrated by ZANU-PF. Was it an MDC ploy? Like bombing opposition newspaper offices, knowing that the international media would immediately blame ZANU-PF? Yet in the countryside just such tactics were being used by them. Stories and rumours, accusations and counter-accusations, fear and confusion, were the signs of the time.

The battle raged – and then, when victory seemed to be there for the taking, Tsvangirai, the 'hero of the people's struggle for democracy', fled the field! He handed Mugabe the victory on a platter. He withdrew from the election.

Over the years, Tsvangirai showed great courage - in his rhetoric. There he has been fearless, outspoken – even reckless. Not so, it would appear, when it came to action. Is he really a sort of *miles gloriosus* - the boastful soldier of Classical and Renaissance comedy, all bombast and no action? Whether it be true or not, it is what the people say – as we saw earlier, every myth has a kernel of truth - they said that on one of the numerous occasions when he had run away from Zimbabwe, claiming that it was too dangerous for him to stay, he was urged by the Botswana President to return. Tsvangirai consented on the condition that he be given an armoured car! Was it true? How could one know what to believe? As it is, half way through the Battle for Zimbabwe, Tsvangirai fled, running off to that very same embassy where I had found him, a supplicant, those many years before– the Royal Embassy of the Netherlands. He told the Dutch and the rest of the world that he feared for his life. And indeed his life was in such danger that he left his sanctuary in the Netherlands Embassy on at least one occasion to drive off across Harare to his home to talk to his best friends, the Western, South African and local 'independent' media. The press conference over, the situation was again be adjudged to be life-threatening - whereupon he scuttled back to his refuge in the Dutch Embassy.

And this was the Tsvangirai who had publicly proclaimed that if Mugabe did not want to go peacefully, he would 'remove him violently'. This was the Tsvangirai who had called for 'the last push' to overthrow the government. I suppose it is always easier to call on others to do it than take the risk yourself. Yet back in the days, he was with us when we lamented but praised the courage and sacrifice of Salvador Allende of Chile, who stood his ground to the end, and when we commemorated the heroism of the children of Soweto, who braved the might of the apartheid state.

Tsvangirai's party was cast in his image. It was one of the perennial weaknesses of the MDC that instead of organising on the ground and concentrating their energy on fighting to overthrow ZANU-PF inside the country, they tended to rely on their external allies to do it for them. When Tsvangirai withdrew from the re-run of the presidential election in 2008, he and his supporters might have believed that they had registered a famous victory by demonstrating to the 'international' media how violent and undemocratic ZANU-PF was. It certainly gave them lots to write about in their newspapers and show on television. By running away and refusing to fight, he might have won the media war out there in the outside world but he forfeited victory in Zimbabwe. The 'election' went ahead and Mugabe, being the only candidate, won it and thus, according to the constitution of Zimbabwe, became the *de facto* President of Zimbabwe. After you have died in a road accident, it's no good protesting 'but it was my right of way!' 'All's fair in love and war', they say. Though the MDC maintained its slender majority in parliament, it lost the presidency when it might have been there for the taking - and in so doing left the state and its armed forces in the familiar hands of their long-time Commander-in-Chief, Robert Mugabe, thus paving the way for the Global Political Agreement (GPA) and the Inclusive Government.

Which, when one considers the alternatives, was probably the best possible result for Zimbabwe in the long run.

CHAPTER TWENTY-FOUR:

THE MORAL HIGH GROUND

The arrows of the Welsh

If you remember, I referred to the arrows of the Welsh as a metaphor for the West's fusillade of accusations directed against ZANU-PF and Zimbabwe from 'the moral high ground' concerning democracy, human rights, 'rule of law' violations and violence. Bowmen or archers were really quite an important factor in medieval English battles – you might remember Agincourt, Crecy and Poitiers where the archers wiped out the flower of French chivalry. It was the same against the Scots. The Scots never really had archers and it was Robert the Bruce's neutralisation of the archers at Bannockburn that opened up the possibility of victory. So, basically, the Welsh archers were a pretty devastating asset in a battle. There was one compelling reason to believe that the Welsh were on the MDC's side. The MDC Secretary-General until the split in 2005 and, at the time of the election in 2008, Secretary General of the Mutambara faction of the MDC, was Welshman Ncube!

The whole question of Mugabe and ZANU-PF's violations of democracy, human rights and the rule of law is, like the Land and Sanctions, another key contested terrain. ZANU-PF was not able to do much about it as it was a terrain fought almost entirely in the media where the opposition held almost all the aces (see Chapter 25). Nevertheless, it is important to explore to what extent the West and the MDC's allegations were justified or whether ZANU-PF had some kind of case which, owing to its media disadvantage, was not done justice.

Though modern battles are fought with a wide variety of weapons on many different fronts, taking possession of the moral high ground is essential. It is a front in itself. In their conflict with Zimbabwe, the West moved pretty smartly to seize and occupy it. They had the power to do it – but did they have title?

Castigation of Zimbabwe was usually pretty sweeping and the allegations were rarely spelt out in any detail. Often they went no further than a general condemnation of Zimbabwe's 'democracy', 'human rights' or 'rule of law' record. All sorts of people criticised Zimbabwe and in their criticism these were the catchphrases they characteristically resorted to. Mostly they just repeated them as if everyone knew they were facts and therefore really why go into the details? However, if one unpacked what the West meant by being 'democratic', it really boiled down to something like: "Well, you know, being like...I mean...like us really." Until Africa is a mirror image of them and plays the game the way they like it, Africa's democracy, her human rights and her rule of law will never be quite up to scratch.

Which is a bit much, when you come to think of it. Europe barged into Africa, shipped a whole load of people over to the New World and sold them as slaves, divided the place up amongst themselves with straight lines and rivers on a map, called the space in the middle a country – their colony, of course – ransacked it for almost a hundred years and then one day turned round and said: "OK, this is your country. Now you run it." So what happened? The erstwhile colonised woke up one morning to hear that *their colony* is now *your country*. The colonizers had specifically made sure that the colonised never got any practice in running a country, any country, especially the one they said was theirs, and then after that they said: "Now you run the country – and run it our way!" If in two year's time the government and the country is not running it their way as well – or as badly (depending on your viewpoint) – as say Her Majesty's Government, the grousing starts: "Where's the democracy? No human rights! What happened to the rule of law? It was better when we ran the show!"

Why I think that the West has been very unreasonable is explained by a rapid glance at history. Take England, the major critic - when could England first claim to be a country? Was England a country before 1066 - when the Saxons ran the show? Or did she have to wait for William the Conqueror to call it Angleterre. I don't know. But let's say England has been a country for roughly 1,000 years. How long did it take them to have a parliament that all English men could vote for? 918 years! How long before an English woman could vote? 928 years! How long did it take them to have free and fair and above all peaceful elections? The hustings of the early 19th century were renowned for their brawling as competing candidates hired local thugs to break up each others' meetings! I don't know when they managed to sort that out. Maybe when they introduced the Football Association and everybody got a chance to fight each other over football instead of politics.

This aside, who, really, among the so-called 'Western democracies' was qualified to cast the first stone against Zimbabwe when it came to democracy and human rights? For Britain with its colonial record of a century of injustice and crimes against humanity to lecture Zimbabwe or any other African country on democracy and human rights was a pill too bitter to swallow – and Mugabe was not the man to swallow it. As Mugabe snorted: "Democracy! Who's talking? Where was democracy in Zimbabwe before we sacrificed our lives for it?"

And then, why Zimbabwe? How many totally undemocratic and notorious abusers of human rights has the West been cosy with? For how long did the US cuddle up with the murderer of Lumumba, Mobutu Sese Seko? Or the murderer of Allende, Pinochet? Now with their 'War on Terror', they have made no bones of the fact that as far as they're concerned, the very basics of international law and human rights do not apply to them at all. For a country that kidnaps and assassinates all over the world with impunity, that tortures and incarcerates people at Guantanamo, including a 15 year old child, with no recourse to due process of law – openly, brazenly and ruthlessly – for a country such as this to pass a law against Zimbabwe called the Zimbabwe Democracy and Economic Recovery Act – well, what can one say?

And then, in the wake of this so-called 'War on Terror', what inroads have been made in the democracy, human rights and 'rule of law' of their own countries, the so-called 'Great Democracies' of the West, inroads into the rights and liberties of their own citizens and those of other countries, including their allies?[42]

No, they have no claim to any 'moral high ground' when it comes to Zimbabwe. If their claim to occupy the 'moral high ground' is untenable, so is it hypocritical. It is hypocritical because if they were genuine about democracy, human rights and the 'rule of law', they would have found themselves so busy denouncing states that infringe them all over the place that they wouldn't really have had the time to bother about Zimbabwe – or even consider it a priority case when its record is compared with those other countries they would be busy with. But they are not busy with them. They are silent about them. Instead, they are very busy and very vocal about Zimbabwe. Why?

42 Many authors have detailed this process, including, most tellingly, Asim Qureshi in *Rules of the Game*, not to mention the cyber espionage exposed by Edward Snowden.

Whatever anyone's opinion as to their freeness and fairness, Zimbabwe has had regular elections since Independence – 1980, 1985, 1990, 1995, 2000, 2005, 2008, 2013. Guinea, the second country in sub-Saharan Africa to become independent, had its first democratic election four years ago in 2010! Uganda, like the MDC, a Western protégé, did not have multiparty elections between 1980 and 2006, during which time it was a one-party state! So all those years while Zimbabwe was having its much maligned elections, Uganda really wasn't having any at all! Ghana, the first sub-Saharan country to achieve Independence, in 1957, did not have any elections between 1972 and 1992. Kenya, another state that the West has generally got on rather well with, never had multiparty elections between 1963 and 1992, during which time it too was a one-party state.

A similar survey of Zimbabwe's legislative framework, the functioning of its judicial system, its record on gender and the freedom of its press would also reveal that, despite its failures and abuses, there were lots and lots of countries in Africa and elsewhere whose records could not bear comparison. Again, it begs the question: 'Why Zimbabwe?' On Zimbabwe, they could not say and write enough. To Zimbabwe, they could not devote enough time and energy. For Zimbabwe, they could not find enough column space in their newspapers or airtime on their television stations. And this from newspapers, television stations and governments which spend most of their time acting like they've never heard the African continent exists! Why then all the interest in Zimbabwe?

They demanded free and fair elections - like Florida, we may ask? They said they wanted freedom of opinion, speech, assembly and the media and human rights - like Guantanamo? They said they wanted the 'rule of law' in Zimbabwe. They pretended that they really wanted all these things for the good of the poor people of

Zimbabwe for whom they had such a soft spot that they slapped sanctions on them. Since when have the sufferings of ordinary people in Africa bothered them? Why now? Why all of a sudden Zimbabwe?

No, the human rights the West and white South Africa were really concerned about, were the human rights and the 'rule of law' that relate to the sanctity of private property – to those of the white farmers who lost their land - and, by corollary, to theirs! They do not bother all the other transgressors who daily violate democratic norms, abuse human rights and disregard the rule of law, because whatever the other lot is doing, they are not threatening the West's fundamental economic interests and the rights and laws that protect them.

What about the MDC then?

MDC stands for Movement for Democratic Change. Presumably, by calling their movement this, the founders meant two things. One was that whatever democracy existed in Zimbabwe was flawed and the MDC thought they could improve on it. The other was that they were going to go all out to change the government i.e. regime change, by *democratic* means i.e. 'democratic change'. One wonders whether removing the Head of State by force or a last push on State House is now considered 'democratic means' – or calling for the imposition of sanctions, for that matter.

The MDC's allegations relating to democracy, human rights and the rule of law would have been a lot more credible if they had not teamed up with the white commercial farmers, the white bosses and the West. If the MDC had been a genuine democratic party, rooted in Zimbabwe, it would not have spent *all* its time criticising ZANU-PF and only ZANU-PF. It might have found a little time too to say something about the democratic record of the commercial farmers, the white bosses and the West and the unjust anomaly that 4,500 white farmers owned 80% of the land!

The MDC's behaviour has consistently been characterised by political opportunism and lack of principled conviction. This was prefigured at a very early stage when its leadership were still trade unionists. In any trade-unionist's book, teaming up with the bosses, as the ZCTU did in the days of the 'stayaways', is surely as bad as scabbing? Labour in bed with the bosses! Then later, a Zimbabwean party calling itself the Movement for Democratic Change, in bed with the white commercial farmers and the former colonial power and calling on the latter to impose sanctions on their own people!

Lest anyone accuse me of sweeping abuse and violations in Zimbabwe under the carpet, let me say that demonstrating that the West's and the MDC's preoccupation with Zimbabwe's democratic, human rights and 'rule of law' record was hypocritical, dishonest and self-serving in no way implies my acceptance of abuses and violations, whether they be in Zimbabwe or elsewhere. I do however urge those who would judge Zimbabwe and Africa in general to clean up their own house first and secondly to see such things in the context of Africa's and their own history. Yes, though it is true that ZANU-PF (this includes PF-ZAPU) brought democracy to Zimbabwe, they very soon began to undermine their achievement through the arrogance of power and the betrayal of the ideals they fought for. As we have seen, corruption is not just about money and the dishonest accumulation of wealth. It is about accountability. It is about transparency. It is about not being above the law. At a parliamentary investigation of abuses in Masvingo a couple of years ago, witnesses stated that they feared to name the perpetrators as they were 'high-ups' and to name them was too dangerous. Corruption corrupts democracy, it undermines human rights and it makes a mockery of the law. There were indeed serious problems with democracy in Zimbabwe and they needed to be challenged, exposed and opposed. But the MDC, through its political opportunism and its inappropriate alliances and tactics, forfeited the mandate to do so.

So, in my opinion, the West was able to take possession of the moral high ground not because they had any right to it but simply because they had the power to seize it.

On the question of free and fair elections, the problem of sanctions has already been raised. Imposing sanctions in order to bring about a preferred result and then calling for free and fair elections, is a contradiction in terms. There can be no free and fair elections in Zimbabwe before the lifting of sanctions. Sanctions prejudice the democratic process in favour of one side and if the other side proceeds to counter their unfair influence in the best way it can, including the rigging of votes or violence, who has any right to complain? This does not make rigging votes or violence right. It should be condemned – along with illegal sanctions.

The 'rule of law'? Somewhere in Dickens someone calls the law 'an ass'. Hear, hear! History is full of the scepticism of intelligent minds concerning the so-called sanctity of the law. But as for the phrase the 'rule of law', I don't remember really hearing much if anything about it for years. Then suddenly everyone was saying it. I mean everyone – all the time! I asked myself, where does this phrase come from? Is it an old phrase that for some reason, 'its hour come round at last/slouches towards Bethlehem to be (re) born'? Or is it a new coinage?

Apparently the first known use of the phrase goes back to the 18th century. Dr Johnson has it in his Dictionary. The guy people quote a lot these days is A.V. Dicey, a Nineteenth Century legal theorist. Basically it means what it says. As the skinheads of old would have said it: "The law rules, OK." It means the law rules but it also means that a society's legal system should not be subject to interference from the powers-that-be in government or from parliament itself. It means that everyone should be protected by the law and the law should know no favour or respect no rank or status. Here's how the European Union Commission for Democracy through Law put it: "The rule of law in its proper sense is an inherent part of any democratic society and the notion of the rule of law requires everyone to be treated by all decision-makers with dignity, equality and rationality and in accordance with the law, and to have the opportunity to challenge decisions before independent and impartial courts for their unlawfulness, where they are accorded fair procedures. The rule of law thus addresses the exercise of power and the relationship between the individual and the state."

Which is all very well, as it goes. But what people seem to be conveniently leaving out is the question as to what is the law. The problem is not with the rule bit. It is not the *rule* of law that is controversial, in my opinion. It is the *law* itself. Who would not accept the jurisdiction of law if the law was a law for all, if all were really equal before the law, rich and poor, weak and powerful? Who would have a problem with the rule of law if the law was accessible to all and safeguarded the interests and rights of all? That character in Dickens did not say that the *rule* of law is asinine. It is the *law* he said which is an ass.

Two ideas characterise scepticism about the law. One is that it is a great respecter of persons, expressed in sayings that can be paraphrased as 'the law is a spider web and the little insects get caught in it while the large ones break their way through', in other words, that for the law to be just, all should be equal before it. The other is that a law can be unjust and an unjust law is not a law, a concept dramatised in Sophocles' play *Antigone*, also taken up and powerfully adapted to the *apartheid* situation in *The Island*, by Athol Fugard, John Kani and Winston Ntshona. But when is a law unjust and how can this be determined? There is the rub.

The rule of law in the West has its antecedents in ancient Athens. As with everything Greek, the law, like democracy, in Ancient Athens, has been greatly deferred to. Yet though it might have worked wonders for all the free *men* who were the citizens of Athens, it might not have worked so many wonders for those who were not, namely the women and slaves.

Roman Law is acknowledged to be probably the most influential tradition in the development of the law in the West. Yet again no-one would deny that its fundamental function was to protect the rights and interests of the patricians or rich and powerful land-owning families as well as Rome's interests vis-á–vis the subject peoples and provinces of its empire. And so, from one society to the next, the law went on, always reflecting and protecting the interests of those in power and keeping them and their property safe from those for whom the law was not such a good deal – what, one author notes, was quite often referred to as 'the many-headed Hydra' [43] - the people.

The Law did not come down to Mankind from Jehovah via Moses on the Mount. That was the Ten Commandments. The Law is not an absolute. Law has no transcending validity. It is fallible. It is human, a man-made set of rules drawn up by those in power - to

43 *The Many-headed Hydra*, by P.Linebaugh and M.Rediker

protect their interests and those they rule on behalf of. The law is just another aspect, along with religion and ideology, of the intellectual expression of the economic relations and interests that a society is founded on.

Not only does the law express, protect and facilitate the interests of the dominant social group, it also favours it in its practice. It is always much easier for members of the dominant group to access the law, either to use it to their advantage or to evade culpability. As a result, when a society changes, all the more when it is revolutionised, the new rulers and those *they* rule on behalf of, change the laws - and often the judges. Just as it is the dominant social group that makes the laws, so it is they who appoint the judges to administer them.

That is why, with regard to Zimbabwe, where a lot of things were changing, the 'rule of law' became like the sound of a cracked record. Every Tom, Dick and Harry spouted the hackneyed phrase in solemn, unthinking and holier-than-thou tones as if it were a quotation from the Bible or inscribed by God on stone tablets. It was as if all anyone had to do was say 'rule of law' for everyone to stop thinking, nod solemnly and somnolently agree: "O, yes, the rule of law. *(Nod, nod.)* Zimbabwe. What a disgrace!" To them, the law was the law and it must be respected. Their concept of the law was fossilised, static. It did not seem to have occurred to them that the law may and, sometimes must, change. The laws of Zimbabwe relating to property suited the rule-of-law parrots fine – and that is why they insisted on their being respected.

The first charge relating to Zimbabwe's violation of 'the Rule of Law' was a perceived interference by the Executive (Government) in the Judiciary (the Law). The substance of this charge really consists in the feeling that ZANU-PF used its majority in parliament to make new laws and then appoint judges who could be counted on to interpret and apply these new laws in the spirit in which they were intended.

With the coming of Independence in Zimbabwe there was no way in which the government could fulfil its mandate within the racist and discriminatory legal framework inherited from Smith's Rhodesia. As a result, in the years after Independence many new laws were passed democratically. They were democratic laws. New judges were appointed to interpret these laws. When the ZANU-PF government was busy doing that, no-one said anything much about the 'rule of law' and interference by the Executive in the Judiciary. The 'rule of law' only became a problem when ZANU-PF found itself confronting a completely new and revolutionary social development, a development which the existing legal framework, as amended after Independence, could not accommodate, namely the Land Reform. It was when Zimbabwe began to pass new laws with which to enable that development to go ahead that the 'rule of law' became a problem. ZANU-PF believed that the restoration of the land to its original historical owners was just and its justice should be expressed and enabled through law.

It was this, the making of new laws, the nature of the new laws and 'the rule of law' that related to those new laws, to which the critics objected – laws which gave legality to the Land Reform. It was a disagreement over law. One side believed that correcting an historical injustice as it related to the land in Zimbabwe was just and therefore laws that expressed and enabled it were just. The other side believed, for its own reasons, that the rights of property must be upheld in law - history and circumstances notwithstanding.

Another thing that was criticised was the creation of new judges. If judges were absolutely impartial and could interpret laws absolutely objectively, there would be no reason to replace them. But there is a great deal of room for manoeuvre when it comes to interpreting laws. If there wasn't, panels of judges would always be unanimous in their judgements and different political parties, when they get into power, would not have to appoint their own judges.

In Zimbabwe, the new laws needed new judges. A judge brought up and embedded in the old dispensation cannot always be relied on to interpret the new laws in the spirit in which they were intended. Put simply, a judge in Zimbabwe, who was used to Rhodesian or pre-Land Reform legislation and did not share the aspiration of the people of Zimbabwe to take back their land, could easily interpret the new laws so as to obstruct them. What were needed, therefore, were new judges and these were appointed. The ZANU-PF government passed legislation that enabled the Land Reform and appointed judges who would interpret the new laws in the spirit in which they were intended - the outcries of jurists who were products of the past or members of law societies that upheld different interests notwithstanding.

There is nothing very new in this – and nothing reprehensible about appointing judges who will understand and identify with the ruling party's interests and objectives. In Britain, High Court judges are selected through a process in which what is called 'the secret soundings system' is decisive. This piece of detective work is done by the Lord High Chancellor's department. For those of us who do not know who this august being, the Lord High Chancellor, might be, he or she (has there ever been a she?) is the second most senior member of government, a member of the cabinet, appointed by the Queen on the advisement of the Prime Minister and in charge of the Law, basically – a kind of highfaluting Minister of Justice. In other words, the selection of High Court judges in Britain is subject to review by a party political functionary.

As is usual with European processes generally as opposed to those in the United States, the political nature of the appointment of judges in Britain is less blatant than in the United States. In the US there is no pretence. The appointment of judges is political. They are openly appointed by the President in consultation with the Senate. A Democrat President is not going to appoint the same judges as a GOP[44] President.

The situation in Zimbabwe, under the constitution at the time of the Land Reform, seeing as how the 2000 draft constitution had been rejected, was not in essence very different from that of the United States. Judges were appointed by the President. The main difference was that the body the President consulted, the Judicial Services Commission, unlike the US Senate, was also appointed by the President. This did not in any way augment the extent to which the judges' appointment was political as the Senate in the United States is voted in along party lines.

So, it is difficult to understand what the hue and cry about the appointment of judges in Zimbabwe was all about.

The other charge against Zimbabwe relating to 'the Rule of Law' is that Zimbabwe denied to its citizens the opportunity to 'challenge decisions for their unlawfulness before independent and impartial courts, where they are accorded fair procedures'.

There are two aspects to this question. One involves the operations of the law-enforcing agencies. The other is the recourse to law in the courts. On the latter, I do not believe Zimbabwe has a case to answer. When a case involving government and the party came to judgement, government and the party were frequently roundly beaten. Just ask Beatrice Mthethwa, a Zimbabwean lawyer, who

44 Nickname for the Republicans and standing for 'Grand Old Party'

has defended and prosecuted a whole lot of cases for the opposition with great aplomb and appropriate militancy. If she is honest, she will tell you that she has won a great deal – and also tell you that despite her outspoken denunciations of the government, she remained free to practise throughout the period in question.

After the disputed elections in 2005, the MDC took the results of almost every disputed constituency to court. ZANU-PF followed suit. The judges clearly did their best to interpret the constitution without fear or favour. Both parties won some and lost some. Tsvangirai and two other MDC officials were acquitted on numerous counts in Zimbabwean law courts, including the count of High Treason.

On the question of the law-enforcement agencies, there was no doubt that Zimbabwe did have a case to answer. The law-enforcement agencies were intrinsically biased in favour of the ruling party. Many was the complainant who reported to the police only to be told that so-and-so is a big chef or 'they are those of the ruling party and nothing can be done for you'. Not only were they biased but their methods of interrogation and intimidation indubitably included violence as a matter of routine, which at times, in fact often, were tantamount to torture. This was bad and there was no excuse for Zimbabwe on this.

But neither is there any excuse for exactly the same behaviour, if not worse, that takes place routinely in the new South Africa. As I write a South African television programme featured a number of cases in which investigating officers forced individuals to confess to crimes they have never committed through torture. This torture involved placing black plastic bags over their victims' heads, drawing them tight so that they could not breathe, applying electric shocks to their bodies and beating them up with fists, boots and other brutal objects. Victims have been left blind, impotent and permanently crippled. All efforts to seek redress and have the perpetrators punished come to nought and the officers are seen moving around, untouched, doing more of the same no doubt in the course of performing their daily duties.

Such brutal behaviour by police is not confined to Zimbabwe and South Africa. Research would reveal that to Africa's shame it is almost a standard pattern all over the continent where not only the police but the army have a sad tendency to inflict violence on their citizens. There is no point speculating as to where this behaviour comes from – though it is easy to suggest theories. The point is that what took place in Zimbabwe was scandalous but that it was not a problem that is peculiar to Zimbabwe. In many different countries in Africa it seems endemic in the culture. Our domestic disciplinary procedures take various forms of corporal punishment for granted. Parents smack or beat their children. Husbands beat wives. Supporters of one football team beat those of the opposing football team and are beaten in turn. There is a readiness to solve disputes or react to slights or impose one's will through violence. We do not value each other enough to shrink from hurting or even killing.

It was a characteristic of pre-colonial justice and warfare. It was a characteristic of the colonial nightmare. It seems to go right back to a world when no-one thought anything of thousands and thousands of people dying in the Attic mines in Greece or building pyramids in Ancient Egypt or digging canals at Suez from the Pharaohs to Ferdinand de Lesseps, or working on colonial plantations or railroads – 120 000 Africans perished building the Congo-Océan railway for the French – or in hell-ships on the Middle Passage from Africa to the Americas, dying like flies on a Friday night in apartheid Soweto, bus passengers mowed down on the side of the road by Renamo, or men, women and children burnt or hacked to death in Rwanda, Mozambique, the Eastern Congo, Northern Nigeria and Liberia, slaughtered in refugee camps by the Rhodesians or dumped into drums of acid and thrown down disused mineshafts, or the Fifth Brigade doing more or less the same in Matebeleland, or Steve Biko, beaten and naked, thrown into the back of a truck and driven to his death – on and on it goes, what human beings do to other human beings, what Africans have done to Africans and what was done to them.

In Zimbabwe, a parent has a child who takes to drinking beer or maybe taking drugs. He steals everything he can lay his hands on to get money. He is violent. He swears. He commits criminal acts. The time comes when a parent must decide that prayer, that love, that talking to him, is not working. What the boy is doing are crimes. He must learn that a crime is a crime – whether he commits it against his own parent or another. Surely the answer is to report to the police? Maybe the parent does. They ask whether he or she wants to press charges. No, just deal with him. They have him overnight in a cell. They rough him up, they beat him. They are doing it for the parents, trying to teach the boy a lesson. He comes out and he has learnt no lesson. If anything he is worse. The parents cannot go on like this – can they send him to prison? There have been cases when this has been done and the child has emerged after some time and burnt his parents' house down in bitterness and revenge. Everyone knows the police are violent, the criminals in jail are violent. The police extract confessions through torture. How can one send anyone into that system, especially your own son? Suffer anything rather than let the police get hold of him.

So, yes, on this issue, if anyone wants to use the 'Rule of Law' and violence as a stick to beat Zimbabwe with, they can. But against whom in this world can you not use that stick? Look at what the US soldiers did in Abu Ghraib or in Guantanamo or the British in southern Iraq. Yes, beat Zimbabwe if you wish but then you must beat mankind. You will beat because you too are human and beating is all you know.

Sanctions are a big stick. A very big stick with which to beat boys who are naughty. So is a negative media campaign. When it comes to ZANU-PF's use of violence to hold onto power, I have this to say. In comparison with the instruments with which ZANU-PF was being beaten, the sticks ZANU-PF had at their disposal, were mere straws. As ugly and unacceptable as it is to hit someone on the head with a stick or cut them with a machete or hang them upside down or apply to their bodies electric shocks, as awful and painful as it is to be the victim, they are nothing in comparison with international sanctions and negative media campaigns – and nothing but the desperate tactics of the weak. In the face of helicopter gunships, rockets, tanks, heavy machine guns, what can the weak do when they have had enough of stones? Make their own bodies the missiles they do not have but with which the enemy daily blows them up, missiles they can guide and guide out of rage, out of desperation and the hopeless admission of their weakness.

The point is that when the powerful abuse their power, their immense power, to get their own way, those that try to resist, to defend their own interests, will lash out with whatever is left to them. Some in ZANU-PF, in the armed forces, were confronted with the end of their corrupt practices, their abuse of power, their opportunities for enrichment and fought in whatever way they could to hold on to them. Others saw the country they had fought for, the land they had at last recovered, in danger of being lost and they too fought in whatever way they could to hold on to it. It's not about blame. It's about interests and the application of force to protect them. The powerful brought massive force to bear. The weak found strength where they could find it to oppose force with force. While I will not defend the actions of ZANU-PF over the years and in particular during the Battle for Zimbabwe, I will not join those who whitewash their opponents.

Just as it was with sanctions and corruption so it has been for the *povo* down the years. The little elephant in Zimbabwe trampled the grass. When a herd of much bigger elephants came along and the little elephant battled to survive, the big elephants and the little elephant together trampled the grass. There is an old African proverb – which I have just invented – which goes: "It is better for the grass to be trampled by a small elephant than by a small elephant *and* a herd of big elephants."

CHAPTER TWENTY-FIVE:

THE MEDIA

Zimpapers and ZBC vs the Rest

On 2nd February, 1990, the African National Congress, the Pan Africanist Congess and the South African Communist Party were unbanned. I had not set foot in my mother country since 1976. In Britain, Addis Ababa and finally in Harare, my wife and I had been part of the large population of South African exiles, coming from across the spectrum of South African opposition politics. It was not long before the exiles in Zimbabwe began to go home and soon we found ourselves almost alone in Harare. That was when I made my first visit to my native land in twenty-five years.

And, after that first visit, as the years of my life in Harare rolled by, I visited again and again. When the tensions rose and the situation in Zimbabwe became more and more a focus of world attention, an unsettling schizophrenia developed in me. Zimbabwe, the place I lived in, and the place I read about in my motherland and elsewhere seemed to be two different places entirely – until it got to the point when my youngest daughter, who by that time was living and working in South Africa, made sure that when I came visiting, I did not lay my hands on a South African newspaper until at least a few days had gone by because she knew reading what it said about Zimbabwe would spoil my holiday. The South African press (along with the world media in general) had entered its manic phase of wilful derangement and disinformation with regard to Zimbabwe.

What made me so angry was first of all the abandonment of all journalistic ethics as they relate to objectivity and balance. Then there was the inaccuracy, the distortion and the lies. What they were writing was not what was happening in Zimbabwe and what *was* happening was of vital relevance to South Africa. How was South Africa going to learn the lessons of Zimbabwe without some appreciation of what was really going on? I knew that what I was reading was no longer journalism. It was simply an expression of the white man's terror, the racial nightmare coming true – and just over the border. Between the lines of what they were writing was the nervous question: what will happen to us if it all spills over and South Africa is engulfed by the demons we imagine to be on the rampage in Zimbabwe? Or is this going to happen to us someday?

When I was a little boy in South Africa, there were all those stories about what happened in the Congo after Independence, nuns being raped and so on. And then there was Mau Mau where, we were told, old and faithful servants slit their master and madam's throats in their own homes. There were the horrific images of '*die swart gevaar*' (the Black Peril), propagated by the National Party of South Africa. Now all of that was suddenly looming up over the border, like a *djinn* let out of the bottle – in Rhodesia, of all places! Salisbury and all that? Horror! South African white society was already full of Rhodesians who had either never given Zimbabwe a chance and fled on Mugabe's taking power or decided to 'gap it' later - disgruntled and scathing in their criticism of bungling 'Afs' messing up their beloved Rhodesia. Many of them were working in the media in South Africa. They were joined by the black Rhodies - and, quite frankly, pure and simple mercenaries. The *Mail and Guardian* came to be 'owned' by a black Zimbabwean.

The South African press had its own special interest in the Zimbabwean situation but its coverage was not substantially different from that of the Western Media in general. The function of the so-called 'international' media is to take up the moral justifications the politicians churn out, mostly clichés whose main function is to mask and obscure the bottom line, and then get their viewers to buy them.[45] They do this in a number of ways. They pretend to debate and interview on the issues but do so within the parameters of the legitimated 'take'. Newspaper journalists no longer seem to search for the truth. Instead their job is to come up with 'the story' the newspaper and the powers-that-be require. And I am not only talking about the gutter press. Even the most 'reputable' newspapers propagate judgements as if they were facts and by repeating them over and over again get most people to believe they are. Media 'tags' with which to label individuals, governments or even ideas, are a favourite ploy. Once tagged, they are never mentioned without adding, whether relevant or not, their emotive and 'don't you forget now' tabs, like 'dictator', 'Stalinist', 'Trotskyite' or 'Marxist', 'extremist', 'blood diamonds', 'the ship of death' etc. Robert Mugabe's 'dictator' tag, discussed earlier, is an obvious example.

This sense of schizophrenia with regard to the reporting on Zimbabwe was not mine alone. Almost everyone I have met, having read what was being daily propagated in the newspapers and on television all over the world, and actually coming to Zimbabwe, said the same thing – two different countries, two different worlds. For instance, the media depicted a country that was dangerous, where whites were being attacked by blacks, where everything was falling into rack and ruin. I myself as a white person living in Zimbabwe had constantly to reassure people that I was OK and if anyone was in danger it was not whites like me. They had got their public to believe that there was a race war going on and blacks were killing whites. Yet this was very far from the case. Black people had a lot more to fear from inter-party violence than whites

45 Herman, Edward, and Chomsky, Noam, *Manufacturing Consent*

had at the hands of blacks. Travel almost anywhere in the country was peaceful and safe. The tourist sites were completely peaceful. The hotels enticing, ready, waiting – and empty.

Harare has been dubbed, by *The Economist* among others, *the* worst or the fourth worst city in the world![46] Just imagine what must be the impressions of those who actually do come to Harare and spend some time there for themselves! Nothing would drive home the message more that there is a whole lot of very dishonest bamboozling going on out there.

"We were shocked to discover on our own how wonderful Zimbabwe and its people are... and it became clear to us that the British Press is lying to the public for their own reasons," said the leader of a group of British tour operators, who had initially been very worried about being subjected to abuse in the streets by black Zimbabweans. This is but one of many such statements.

I remember speaking to one of my publishers in Johannesburg over the phone from Harare. I happened to say to her that she should not worry about me as what she was reading or seeing in South Africa was a far cry from reality. Then, very naively I thought for a publisher, she said: "Images don't lie." There used to be a saying: "The camera never lies." I wonder when the last time anyone used that expression was - for nowadays it is more like 'the camera almost always lies'. Just the other day a South African journalist was sacked for airbrushing out the dead bodies in a picture showing a minibus that had been blown up in Kabul. He wasn't sacked because he changed the picture. He was sacked because he did it without prior editorial approval!

---

46 See 'Is Harare really the worst city on Earth?' by Andre Vitchek (www.trinicenter.com)

For years now the world's media has been full of photographs– from Syria, Bosnia, Egypt, wherever – claiming to be depicting 'the people', 'the rebels', 'liberated' Iraqis celebrating - all purporting to be genuine photos of events in the news. Genuine photos exist, taken sometimes at great risk by extremely courageous photographers. But that so many others are put up jobs is painfully obvious. Anyone with an elementary grasp of the fundamentals of photography - or theatre for that matter – can tell a posed or directed image from a real one. Ask Meyerhold![47]

One day, a friend sent me a distraught email from Zambia with a photograph attached, asking me if this is what is really happening in Zimbabwe. Allow me to describe to you what the photograph she sent to me looked like. In the middle of the picture was an elderly white man, wearing a Kentucky Fried Chicken T-shirt. I spell KFC out because, believe it or not, despite being, significantly for the impact of the photo, a great white favourite in South Africa, it is not a brand known to everyone in every country all over the world. KFC does not exist in Zimbabwe. Now, if it had been Chicken Inn or Nando's, Zimbabweans would know what I'm talking about. Standing on either side of the elderly white man – in order not to mask the KFC lettering on the T-shirt, mind – were two black men. Each had a fist, menacingly poised but not tensed, in a pose that suggested that they were in the process of punching the elderly white man's tummy. And, *mirabile dictu*, behind the three, like an amateur crowd scene at the Reps Theatre in Harare, was a rather friendly looking, 'seething mob' of 'blacks', all in a neat semi-circle, watching - or rather half watching – the proceedings. I say half watching because they all had half an eye on the camera. And there they all posed, waiting for the cameraman

47 Vsevolod Meyerhold (1874-1940) is a famous and innovative Russian theatre director who was critical of Stanislavskian efforts to reproduce real life on stage.

to say: "Watch out for the Dickey Bird." All it lacked as a theatrical scene was getting the crowd to say: "Rhubarb, rhubarb."

My friend who had sent me the photo, is probably the most awarded actress in Zambia. The whole thing was so contrived, so amateurish, that it was difficult to believe anyone, especially her, could be taken in by it. But there is no limit to what human beings will believe if they are already believers.

Another example was a news clip broadcast by a well-known British television station – I don't think for a moment they had actually filmed it themselves. While I do not respect the particular television station's ethics, I do give them credit for being able to make a decent film. The clip was intended to show how awful things were on the farms where war vet thugs and local rabble were invading and causing wild and wilful destruction wherever they went. It showed some of the aforesaid rabble attacking some farm outbuildings. The extraordinary thing was that there was a man hitting the wall of a rather solid structure with a *bemba*. Now a *bemba* is a slim piece of metal, about the length of a shooting-stick, which is curved at the bottom and sharpened. It is used for slashing grass or weeds. Well, it was hardly the poor man's fault that the 'directors' of the video clip did not have anything more appropriate to give him as a prop. He certainly earned his money by enthusiastically belabouring the rather bored-looking wall with the *bemba* – and then, after each lusty blow, looking, as most beginner actors will do, at the director to see how he was getting on. What 'farm-invaders' would be trying to destroy farm buildings for is anyone's guess!

It was not only video footage that was concocted. Photo-stories were also faked – unfortunately with devastating effect. A relative of a very close friend of mine was taken to a house in Mt Pleasant, a suburb of Harare, made up to look like he had been in the wars, photographed, given some money and then published in the local opposition press as a graphic example of ZANU-PF thuggery. The photo and the story were taken up uncritically by the international media too.

You may think I exaggerate. I do not. Opponents of the government were providing all sorts of articles, photographs and video clips to the Western media – and the media lapped them up. The media knew they had got everyone so horrified by what was happening in Zimbabwe that no-one would smell a rat even if it was dead and a week old. The viewers did not question - because by then it was what people expected from the Zimbabwe the media had created for them. The enemies of the Land Reform and those out to make a quick buck cashed in on the demand big time.

Alright – you still think what I am describing could not possibly happen in the West? BBC, CNN, Sky, the *Guardian*, the *New York Times*? *They* would never do such things? Ok, then what about a Zimbabwean scribbler called Basildon Peta, who very soon got onto the gravy train. He wrote for the most prestigious and respectable newspapers of the British and South African establishment. He could make a police road block in Zimbabwe read like the Seventh Circle of Dante's Inferno or a politician's car crash an assassination attempt worthy of Hollywood. One day he produced an article headlined something like 'A night in Mugabe's prison'. I wondered about that. I knew the old man had a gym but a prison! Well, of course, Mugabe was the demon people loved to hate and so every enormity that one could think of in Zimbabwe was directly traceable to him. Certainly makes for chilling headlines. Anyway, in graphic detail, our mercenary Zimbabwean scribbler described his night of horror. The only problem was that a few days later it turned out that the whole thing never happened. Peta had made it all up! He meant to enter it for a short story competition – he just made a silly mistake and put it in the newspaper instead.

There must surely be something that happens to a journalist when he or she does such a thing – and gets caught out. I mean, for plagiarism at a university a student gets chucked out. What happens to a journalist who makes up the news? Isn't there a Commission for Journalistic Ethics or something that strips him of his licence or bans him for life – like they do lawyers and judges? That poor guy who airbrushed dead bodies out of a photo, got the sack. What happened to Peta? Well, the answer is...er... nothing really. He was in the dog box for a little while but soon he was back and his articles can be read regularly to this day in the same prestigious British and South African newspapers. The point is he hadn't really done anything wrong as such. He had just gone a little overboard on this one, that's all. He was in demand precisely for his ability to make up stories, to spin the kind of fictitious nightmares the editors wanted out of the rather less sensational but very much more interesting reality of what was actually going on in Zimbabwe.

My point is that media coverage of the situation in Zimbabwe was orchestrated to support the West's agenda and had very little to do with providing the public with balanced and objective information or an in-depth understanding of the real issues raised by the events the news reports. Although the media served its masters well, it served the world and, in particular, the people of South Africa badly. In its anxiety to provide the prescribed story, the media abandoned most of the ethics that laymen like me expect should govern the noble profession of journalism. Sources were not checked. Apocryphal and often fictitious material was projected as fact. Few bothered to get both sides or other sides of the story. There was little historical or contextual analysis. Unsubstantiated clichés were peddled as if they were unarguable facts. File tapes depicting past events were passed for original news footage.

However, one question always came to mind – and when people questioned me about what was really happening in Zimbabwe, I often raised it and asked them to ask themselves: "Why is it that Zimbabwe, a small African state, dominated the media in your countries when generally, in your media and in your countries, what happens in Africa is seldom worth a mention?"

And really this is what happened. The media coverage of Zimbabwe was nothing short of sensational. I remember one sunny Sunday morning in Hartford, Connecticut, opening the front door to collect the *New York Times* from the doorstep, and, after being engulfed in a cloud of jasmine coming from a line of bushes that ran down the driveway past the kitchen, I was more than a little surprised to see a photograph and an article on Zimbabwe on the cover. It was continued on the inner pages along with two more articles on other Zimbabwean topics. I said to myself, three articles, one on the cover and a cover photo! On Zimbabwe! In the NEW YORK TIMES!!! Why? What was it that touched the Western nerve in this way? Or put another way, what nerve did it touch? Although I have in this book offered some of my own explanations as to why the West was so obsessed with Zimbabwe, I can't ultimately explain it. When I thought of what has been going on in the Eastern Congo for decades or the horrors, monstrous happenings and atrocities that poor Mozambique had to go through at the hands of Rhodesia and later apartheid South Africa's proxy bandits, Renamo – I asked myself: "What kind of coverage do they or did *they* get? What did all these papers and all these television stations that are so besotted with Zimbabwe, do about them?" Very little, I'm afraid. Why? So the question remains – why Zimbabwe? In the answer to this question lies the rebuttal. Yes, Zimbabwe did lots wrong. Mugabe made his mistakes. But whatever happened, it was not the way the media made it out to be.

Meanwhile what was the Zimbabwean government doing – what could it do – to counteract the West's monopoly and abuse of the media?

There was virtually nothing the government of Zimbabwe could do about the external media. The cards were stacked against them right from the start. Imagine, virtually all the television stations anybody watches – including Al-Jazeera, that started off so promisingly, and the South African Broadcasting Corporation – all against them. They had hostile foreign-funded radio stations beaming propaganda against them into Zimbabwe from neighbouring countries. Then there were the newspapers. Inside Zimbabwe was the so-called 'independent' press. In fact, all 'independent' meant really was that it was independent of the Zimbabwean government. These included over the years *The Financial Gazette*, *The Daily Gazette*, *The Daily News*, *The Independent*, *The Standard*, *News Day*, the South African *Sunday Times* and, financed and printed in Britain, *The Zimbabwean* - all of these free to publish virtually whatever they liked and all rabidly anti-ZANU-PF and pro-MDC and the West.

Then there were all the newspapers of Europe, North America, South Africa, Australia and New Zealand – all against ZANU-PF. Finally, where did all the newspapers I have mentioned as well as all the other newspapers in the world I have not mentioned, get their stories and their slant from? Reuters, Agence France-Presse, Associated Press – all originating in and owned by companies based in countries mentioned above. I never saw a story from the Chinese news agency, Xinhua, or from RIA-Novosti or ITAR-Tass (Russia) in either the local 'independent' media, a South African newspaper or any of the 'mainstream' western papers. And then the internet – we all know who owns and dominates that.

So, for years, while this enormous, gigantic apparatus maintained, with one voice, its unrelenting anti-ZANU-PF barrage, what did ZANU-PF have to put into the field? Zimbabwe Broadcasting Corporation (ZBC) – one television channel, a couple of radio stations - and Zimpapers, which included in its stable *The Herald*, *The Chronicle*, *Kwaedza*, *The Sunday Mail* and *The Sunday News*. Full stop! That is why I called this chapter 'Zimpapers and ZBC vs the Rest'!

Quite understandably, the situation being what it was, ZANU-PF was not going to let anyone else get a look-in. People complained that ZANU-PF would not allow them to open up other television channels. They wanted ZANU-PF to deregulate the media! How out of touch can you get! ZANU-PF was not born yesterday. They knew there were plenty people out there who would be only too happy to put up the money for some more television channels – and they knew very well who and why. People also complained that ZBC and government newspapers were simply the voice of ZANU-PF! Well, all I can say to that is two things: "And the so-called 'independent' newspapers, whose voice are they?" and then, really, "What did they expect?"

ZANU-PF never had much media savvy and though it did possess some newspapers, television and radio stations, it didn't really have much of a clue as to how to use them to their advantage. They had also long since neglected the 'songs that won the liberation war'. The cultural struggle had been an important element of the Second *Chimurenga*. Now in the thick of the Third, they either did not think of or were powerless to revive it. In the next chapter we look at someone who helped them out in the nick of time.

CHAPTER TWENTY-SIX:

CULTURE

The professor's jingles

I believe I heard or read once that in the newspaper business there is a saying which goes: "Never interfere with the crossword!"

Well, every day, virtually without fail, *The Zimbabwe Herald* ran a double crossword – the Easy and the Cryptic. Until very recently, the Saturday crossword was larger and quite a bit more difficult. It was in fact a significant component of my survival apparatus during the dark years of Zimbabwe's Third Decade – along with literature, the guitar, the piano, a cigar from time to time and - when my ancestors sent me – a bottle of Scots single malt whisky.

Apart from the crossword, the Saturday edition of *The Herald* had little in it for the likes of me. It was a good illustration of ZANU-PF's attitude to culture. *The Herald* had abandoned all pretence at covering anything one would call the arts or culture. Its entertainment supplement was full of gossip, articles on marriage and infidelity, Zimbabwean pop 'stars', and pages on celebs, Big Brother and overseas idols – more or less what also happened to the Tonight section in the South African newspaper *The Star*. There was a bumper section on sport, including copious coverage of the English Premiership. And there was Hagar the Horrible and Andy Capp. So when there was something wrong with the crossword - like, for instance, when the type was so faded as to be illegible or a dark ink smudge obscured it or when some wise guy decided to set it on a dark green background or when the clues didn't match the puzzle – I was not happy.

But what do we make of a cryptic crossword, 30 years after Independence, in a newspaper that is notorious for being a government and ZANU-PF mouthpiece, a newspaper that in its political manifestation goes on and on about sovereignty, indigenisation, colonialism and imperialism? What do we make of such a newspaper still carrying Andy Capp, filling two enormous pages on the English Premiership and decorating its entertainment section with the romps and frivolities of US American singers and film stars? What do we make of that?

For many, many years after Independence, many in the culture sector hoped for a cultural revolution which would turn around theatre, arts and culture from its colonial onto a popular, community-based, even socialist course. We fretted at the lack of interest in and therefore coverage of the work we were doing in *The Herald* while it was at the same time running a weekly column by an antediluvian 'critic' ('pander' would have been a better word), inherited from the previous regime, who confined his sycophantic theatre spectrum to what went on at the virtually segregated white Reps Theatre in Harare! This was the theatre the mythology of which included the assertion that theatre came to Zimbabwe with a performance by the Pioneer Column of a play by Shakespeare on the banks of the Tuli (Thuli) River![48]

The ongoing historical dialectic of continuity and change produced many strange and apparently anomalous phenomena in Zimbabwe. For instance, the parliamentary regalia of the English parliament, itself archaic but at least based in English tradition,

48 The origins of theatre in Africa are a contentious issue in African theatre historiography as many European scholars, Ruth Finnegan, for example, have claimed that the continent did not have a theatre tradition before the coming of the Europeans. This has been contested and scholars have pointed to the massive evidence that would seem to prove that Africa, like any other Europe and Asia, had its own indigenous theatre traditions.

later adopted by Rhodesian parliamentarians, is still the regalia of the parliament of the independent African republic of Zimbabwe today. Was the theatre column in *The Herald* another example of this?

No, I think there was a little more to it than change and continuity. What I think was at the bottom of it was the fact that culture and the arts, when weighed in the balance with politics and economics, were found wanting. ZANU-PF saw politics and economics as serious business and consequently its newspaper, *The Herald*, took them seriously. Arts and culture were not. I am sure *The Herald* had an editorial policy on politics and economics, which was based on what its owners, the ZANU-PF government, perceived to be in their interests. I do not believe they felt it necessary to have a policy on the arts and culture. I think that probably the only thing that concerned them was that its entertainment coverage be innocuous, popular and sell the paper.

This is something that was not peculiar to ZANU-PF. Our liberation movements knew the power of the arts in times of struggle but the moment they seized power, they forgot all about it. We have already mentioned Alex Pongweni's publication, *The Songs that Won the Liberation War.* After winning the war, though the songs still served their limited purpose and were routinely sung at rallies, ZANU-PF seemed to be quite blind to the vast opportunities that confronted them. Those songs sung by their cadres in the camps, in the bush, and with the people at *pungwes* in the village, had helped to power them to victory in the armed struggle. How could they not have seen how much more the arts as a whole could do for them - and, if properly used, for Zimbabwe - in the changed circumstances of independence when, as the government, they controlled a national apparatus with which to foster and project them? They didn't. That is why there was no cultural revolution.

A cultural revolution is something that accompanies and gives expression in cultural terms to the political and economic changes that a revolution brings about or aspires to bring about. They say 'every revolution has its poets'. This saying refers to the symbiotic relationship that exists between the revolution and the arts. The former shapes the latter and the latter not only gives expression to the former but assists it in its task of transforming society. It is a mistake to reduce the role of the arts in transformation to assisting in the material development of the new society, as many of us do in a desperate effort to get our governments to take the arts seriously. The arts, including literature, play the crucial role of preparing the *people* to play its part in the shaping of the new society and of ensuring that the new society and its people are in sync. Any amount of factories, bridges, freeways, hospitals, schools, irrigation schemes and housing will not do that. They will provide the material and physical shell of the society. It is language, literature, philosophy, theatre, dance, music, the visual arts, architecture, film and the media that transform the people's soul and create a national character which makes the material transformation worthwhile.

There has been debate as to what precisely is meant by a cultural revolution. In China, the idea was that a cultural revolution should sweep away all relics and exponents of the cultures of the reactionary and oppressive past. In Russia the exponents of the *proletkult* (short for 'proletarian culture' in Russian) had similar views. They advocated sweeping away feudal and bourgeois art and replacing it with the completely new art of the classes the revolution had brought to the fore, namely, the proletariat and progressive peasants. They said you can't put new wine into old bottles, new wine needs new bottles. Wisely, Lenin opposed this view. He pointed out that human civilization has evolved over millennia. The society the revolution was trying to shape was simply its highest form but it grew out of all those past years of human endeavour. As in the process of any biological culture, like making yoghurt, for instance, it is the old that gives rise to the new. Lenin counselled that the cultural revolution should re-interpret the old where it was oppressive, preserve and value the best of it and go on to build and develop the new from the old.

So, in Zimbabwe, committed artists had hoped that the new government would actively promote the transformation of the arts, literature and media by moving to re-structure the institutions inherited from the colonial regime as well as to encourage popular participation in literary and artistic production. They had hoped it would ensure that the arts were re-oriented in form and content so that they could play their part in the transformation of society and the development of Zimbabwe. Though there were indeed some sporadic initiatives of this kind in the early years after Independence, they soon petered out.

As far as I could see, there seem to have been a number of reasons for this. First and foremost was the attitude described above – that basically the arts are of low priority and now that the *chimurenga* had been fought and won, there were other more important things to attend to. When it came to national budgeting and the government's negotiation of development assistance with donors, culture was either totally excluded or given perfunctory attention. To a large extent, the ZANU-PF leadership seemed to be happy to demobilise struggle in general and as far as they were concerned the serious arts were a weapon of struggle reserved for *chimurenga* time. So, the theatre and the songs that had served them so well, went into mothballs - to come out twice a year on Independence and Heroes Days.

However, there was something else. Knowing the role the arts can play in political struggle, many in government were probably nervous as to how much trouble they might cause in the new Zimbabwe. It didn't take me long to learn this. If you remember, at the theatre for development workshop I came down from Ethiopia to attend in 1983, a government functionary noted that theatre for development could be compared with fire. You can cook with it but it can also burn the house down. It is inevitable that this fear of theatre for development would extend to literature and the arts in general. Writers and artists have always had a reputation for being troublesome. It is one thing to have them on your side when you are fighting an oppressive government, another when you are the government and you now have them on your back. Of course, government knew that Zimbabwe had to have something, there had to be arts of some kind – and, strategically, as far as they were concerned, the sillier they were, the better. And, seriously, what could be sillier than the Broadway musicals and British farces the Reps Theatre in Harare served up or the fascination with Big Brother and the so-called 'celebs' that take up space in the weekend newspapers!

Another reason for ZANU-PF's lack of interest in anything resembling a cultural revolution was that most of its leadership and government functionaries were schooled in the British education system. In other former colonies, generally non-Anglophone, there arose ideologues, who had the perspicacity to note the role played by the arts and literature in their own subjection and therefore the importance of culture in the struggle for freedom. Amilcar Cabral of Guinea-Bissau, Agostinho Neto of Angola and Stephen Bantu Biko of South Africa were noteworthy examples. There does not seem to have been any such consciousness in the Zimbabwean revolution. The top brass both in the party and in government were either quite philistine in that they did not enjoy literature and the arts at all – a feature of British colonies in the region - or their preferences were for those nurtured by their education in Rhodesia and their membership of the new Christian educated elite - as a result of which traditional, popular and African art forms were of no interest to them whatsoever. As mentioned before, a measure of the lack of understanding of the role of arts and culture in social transformation was the fact that for the vast majority of Zimbabweans the word 'culture' meant – exclusively - traditional rituals and customs, the equivalent of '*tsika*' in Shona or '*amasiko*' in Ndebele.

People of the generation of Robert Mugabe and Professor Walter Kamba, the first black Vice-Chancellor of the University of Zimbabwe, were very uninterested in the arts - with the exception of those traditionally associated with the educated elite. From my experience, in the whole time I have been in Zimbabwe, Robert Mugabe never attended a cultural event that was not an adjunct to a political one. While I was in charge of the development of the arts and culture at the University, the only form of art that Professor Kamba supported and obviously enjoyed, was choral music - *makwaya*. He did attend the first play we presented in the Beit Hall in 1985 but he did so only because, on my appointment in August 2004, he had summoned me and peremptorily 'ordered' me to produce a substantial theatre production by the end of 1984 – which I did. He never again attended a cultural event at the university to which he was invited that was not choral music.

In the absence of the hoped-for cultural revolution, initiated and supported by government, the people, as so often happened in Zimbabwe's history, got stuck in themselves. Without government support and despite being undermined by government at times, the people gave birth to and developed the rich arts and culture of contemporary Zimbabwe. Although there were serious casualties during the tough years of the late 2000s, the artists and their arts continued to astonish. The story of the growth and development of the arts and literature of Zimbabwe is an inspiring and a humbling one and remains to be done justice.[49]

By failing to reform the arts sector or support it, government did not know that it was digging its own grave. Its negligence led to a situation where television and radio, to take the most conspicuous examples, were dominated by foreign, particularly US American, content, both in the form of soaps and films as well as music and music videos. As a result, the local arts production industries, such as film, video and music, remained underdeveloped – and this left them almost exclusively in the hands of white Zimbabweans. Though indigenous music flourished on the popular circuit and to some extent in the export market, it was not featured prominently in the government-owned media. Indigenous theatre, dance and music struggled to survive on the fringe and the visual arts, despite Zimbabwe's extraordinary achievement in sculpture and its recognition internationally, were completely peripheralised. When it came to literature, the ZANU-PF government presided over the virtual extinction of indigenous readership. Whereas the pre-Independence Rhodesia Literature Bureau had at least encouraged the production of literature – albeit of a strictly controlled and censored content - the Zimbabwean government did nothing at all really except to levy exorbitant customs duties on the import of books. Cultural achievements such as the Zimbabwe Book Fair and the Harare International Festival of the Arts depended exclusively on the donations and support of foreign donors.

So, those who had expected that a cultural revolution would accompany the political one, came to realise it wouldn't. They

49 Comparatively little has been written on this. Joyce Jenje-Makwenda is a conspicuous exception. She has laboured long and at great sacrifice to research and make known the story of the popular music of Zimbabwe, in particular the role of women (see *Township Music* – film and book).

contemplated the arts and culture landscape in the succeeding years with dismay - until, to their astonishment, the Godot[50] they had been waiting for and who all these years had never come, unexpectedly, suddenly, pitched up – over twenty years after his cue. He was certainly not the Godot they had expected. In fact, he was probably an imposter, a false Godot. But imposter or no, the results of his appearance on the Zimbabwean stage were sensational. Late is not always better than never – and in this case, it remains a moot point as to how much it was and how much it wasn't.

Two things seem to have prompted this Godot to make his entrance at last. The first was the fact that it was *chimurenga* time again. The second was that there were a number of new kids on the block in ZANU-PF – and he was one of them.

In the period after ZANU-PF began, willy-nilly, to return to the revolutionary agenda of twenty years before – when the reclamation of the land was coming off the back-burner, land seizures were slowly accelerating and the Constitutional Consultation process and the elections in 2000 were looming - fresh life and vigour seemed to possess the party. Certainly, its leader, Robert Mugabe, who had shown distinct signs of either hibernation or senility – or both – began to jump about like the proverbial spring chicken. A number of relatively young talents rose to prominence at that time and became members of the cabinet. These included Patrick Chinamasa (53) in Justice, Joseph Made (44) in Agriculture and Francis Nhema (approximately 41) in Tourism – this at a time when the party was led by Robert Mugabe (76), Simon Muzenda (78), Joseph Msika (77) and John Nkomo (66). Joshua Nkomo had only just died at the age of 82. In comparison with the veteran nationalists of Mugabe's generation, these new kids on the block

50 In Samuel Beckett's famous play, *Waiting for Godot*, two clowns are depicted waiting over two acts for someone called Godot. Godot never comes.

seemed veritable Young Turks as in their various portfolios they pursued energetic goals, were eloquent in defence of their policies and committed to their programmes. Well, the Third Decade of Zimbabwe's Independence was *chimurenga* time and ZANU-PF's back was to the wall.

I first sensed that one of the new kids on the block was special around about the year 2000. For years the party and the government had taken a hammering from the so-called 'independent' and international media without seeming to be capable of standing up for itself. I am talking here of standing up for itself in the arena of public polemics and debate. People who saw things more or less along the same lines as I did, noted the hypocrisy, the flaws, the reactionary tendencies of much anti-government criticism. But there didn't seem to be anyone who could forcefully and cogently point them out, who was able to answer back and give as much as he got in the cut and thrust of public political debate. All the university intellectuals seemed to be on the other side. ZANU-PF desperately needed all the help it could get – not only did it not seem to have the capacity to compete in the polemical arena but it seemed to have no clue as to how the arts, culture and the media could assist them.

At that opportune time, it so happened that it acquired the services of a university intellectual who had a nicer appreciation of the power of the arts and, by corollary, the media than the rest of them put together. He was also able to fill an important gap. He was an ideologue, a polemicist. At last, ZANU-PF had someone who was able to refute the criticism, ridicule the inconsistencies and expose the foreign agenda - in short, carry the battle to the enemy. The column and the style he created with his pseudonymic persona, 'Nathaniel Manheru', on a Saturday morning in *The Herald* with its talismanic signing off flourish '*Icho*!', was a first in Zimbabwean satirical political journalism and initiated many acerbic but amusing exchanges between the muckrakers of the so-called 'Independent' newspapers and himself and his successors, because after his departure, others maintained the tradition.

This man was Professor Jonathan Moyo, who was 43 at that time.

Moyo was a revelation. Only someone who knows nothing about the arts and culture and their importance in fighting battles and transforming society, will downplay the extraordinary impact he had on the development of Zimbabwe and the revolutionary impact of his role in helping to carry ZANU-PF through the stormy seas of the Land Reform and its aftermath. Perhaps one way of describing him would be to call him a sort of Gideon Gono[51] in the ideological and cultural domain!

All these years, the spirit of the liberation struggle and its culture had been left to rust in a backroom. Now that the revolution and its goals were being revived, now that another *chimurenga* had begun, the spirit of the struggle had to be re-invoked. It was Moyo who did it – but he did a lot more. Moyo knew that culture is not outside the mainstream of social development. He knew that culture too is an arena of struggle. He knew that the battle needed to be fought there too.

---

51 Gideon Gono (b. 1959) was Governor of the Reserve Bank of Zimbabwe (RBZ) throughout the crisis. He steered the ship in a most innovative, iconoclastic and sometimes clearly illegal way. It would appear that he himself participated in the pervasive looting and speculation that characterised Zimbabwean finance before the introduction of the dual currency. However I believe it would be difficult to deny that without his fiscal gerrymandering and highly unorthodox methods the Zimbabwe meltdown might well have taken place. For this reason he was not popular with those who were eagerly awaiting exactly such an event.

All along ZANU-PF had permitted its enemies to wage the cultural war unopposed. Moyo knew that globalisation, Hollywood, US television soaps, celebs and music videos and their idioms, dress, slang and symbols like Coca Cola – all these things played the same part in the struggle for the minds of Africans as the Christianity brought by the missionaries in the time of colonialism. He also knew that the deregulated, hedonistic, anarchic but essentially meaningless freedom they inculcated, was a Trojan Horse that gave Zimbabwe's enemies the entry they needed into the minds, behaviour and ultimately allegiance of the nation and thus the free hand they required to interfere and control not only the nation's culture, its thinking and its allegiances but also its economy and resources.

Jonathan Moyo, as Minister of Information, introduced important legislation to regulate the print and electronic media - the Broadcasting Services Act, the Zimbabwe Broadcasting Corporation (Commercialisation) Act, the Access to Information and Protection of Privacy Act and the Public Order and Security Act. This legislation provoked an outcry among ZANU-PF's internal and external detractors, who claimed that he was attacking freedom of speech. I saw little evidence that the legislation in question did more than block the use of the Zimbabwean print and electronic media by ZANU-PF's Western adversaries to further their campaign to unseat the government and roll back the gains of the Land Reform. I believe, too, that Dr Tafataona Mahoso, the head of the Division of Media and Mass Communication at Harare Polytechnic, in a series of articles in the press, made a convincing and learned case to prove that such legislation was not peculiar to Zimbabwe and that the so-called Western democracies had long ago put in place similar measures to protect themselves from strategic interference and destabilisation by foreign powers.

The point was, as we saw in the previous chapter, the media had a crucial role to play in the Third *Chimurenga* and for the media in Zimbabwe to be the deadly weapon the MDC and their foreign allies wanted them to be, they needed to be liberalised and deregulated. I believe that is the primary reason for why they kicked up such a fuss. Zimbabwe was at war and I can assure you that the legal restraints the British, United States and other governments have imposed on their media during wartime, including that one on 'Terror', made Moyo's measures seem like child's play.

Apart from introducing the legislation cited above, Moyo took the following practical steps relating to television, radio and the performing arts: he directed both television and radio to programme and broadcast 75% local content; he commissioned the first Zimbabwean 'soaps', one from Harare (*Studio 263*), the other from Bulawayo (*Amakorokoza*); he commissioned the so-called 'jingles', short video advertisements featuring a catchy song, dance, a dramatisation and text supporting government programmes, in particular, the Land Reform; he lifted import duty on the importation of equipment related to music and video production; he began a tradition of national cultural galas and what came to be called 'Splushes' (Splashes), free shows, featuring top musicians and performers and commemorating patriotic occasions such as Independence Day, Heroes Day and Umdala Wethu or 'Father of the Nation' (Joshua Nkomo); he sponsored the national football team and exploited the media and performing arts to the full to whip up patriotic support for it; he wrote songs that supported ZANU-PF's Africanist ideology; and he sponsored music groups, music videos, plays and dance groups. As an Ndebele-speaker himself, he was able to spread the artistic spectrum so as to include Bulawayo in the mix. In the process he transformed not only the arts but the national ethos itself.

Moyo's innovations happened to coincide with the extraordinary explosion in the techniques and equipment of digital sound and video editing that has transformed film, video and sound recording all over the world. Suddenly film, video, music video and music became much more affordable as well as much easier to make. The youth of Zimbabwe took to it like kapenta to Kariba. In no time there were little studios all over the place producing local stuff, new directors, new production houses, new singers and new music groups. So-called 'Urban Groove' music now jostled for popularity with Sungura, Chimurenga, Rhumba and Gospel – and each of these four also expanded and multiplied in response to television and radio's need to fill their quota of 75% local content. Some of it was pretty wonky at first but rapidly improved. I remember listening to the gospel diva, Fungisai Zvakavapano, when she first started. She was literally singing out of tune – but that did not stop ZBC from airing her songs and videos. Then later I attended an Independence Cultural Gala and she was on the programme. I groaned inwardly. I needn't have – having been given that exposure while she was still cutting her teeth, she had gone on to perfect her art and was now a professional – almost arrogant - in the mastery of her art.

Churches made their videos. Schools – all sorts of community groups - came up with work ranging from the abysmal to the promising to the very interesting. Few had ever seen or heard the male choirs of the Vapostori (Apostolic Faith Mission) before but now they wowed the nation with their gospel lyrics and harsh harmonies. There were music videos of groups, backdropped by the ever popular scenic sites of Harare – the bald rocks and hills of Domboshawa, the dam wall at Lake Chivero, the park at Cleveland Dam, Harare Gardens in the CBD. Now we began to hear *mbira*, marimba, traditional and revolutionary songs, watched traditional and other local dances, like *kongonya* and *jiti*, saw 'street theatre', school theatre – and were fascinated by Mai Chisamba and her Shona-language topical discussion show and programmes such as '*Toringepi?*', which featured the different peoples and clans of rural Zimbabwe, their history and their cultures. Whatever the motive for making all this possible, this really was a cultural revolution – and the Zimbabwean arts have never been the same since. Whatever one's view of Moyo and whatever one may think of his motives, in real terms he transformed the media and cultural industries.

Then there was the overt political propaganda. Note, 'propaganda' literally means 'that which is to be propagated, like 'agenda'- 'that which is to be actioned' - or addenda - 'that which is to be added'. Propaganda's pejorative connotation is not derived from the fact that it refers to 'propagating' *per se*. It is derived from the way it is used or abused – or, to be frank, sometimes whether someone likes what is being propagated or not. People who did not like what Moyo was propagating, likened him to Goebbels, the Nazi propagandist. Clearly his techniques were similar – but was his content?

The jingles, some of them featuring the songs and dances of the Liberation Struggle, others new compositions, promoted the land redistribution campaign and exhorted Zimbabweans to farm. A title such as '*Rambai makashinga*' (meaning, literally 'Keep on giving it your all and never fear') was typical of the political jingles which were featured by the national broadcaster incessantly - all day, every day. One would have thought they were going to drive the entire nation mad. Not a bit of it. There they were - being sung by children, even tiny tots, in every township – and many a suburb - of the land. The song composed to rally every Zimbabwean behind the national football team, 'Go, Warriors, Go', and Zimbabwe Television's programme song, 'Sisonke' – 'we are together (or one)', caught on like wildfire. They had a very powerful effect. They made everyone, except anti-ZANU-PF die-hards, feel that the whole country was together, that they were Zimbabweans and that they were proud to be so.

The famous Ghanaian novelist, Ayi Kwei Armah once wrote: "There is something so terrible in watching a black man trying at all points to be the dark ghost of a European." It was in the time of Moyo that the Zimbabwe nation laid that ghost. People began to relax and relish their Zimbabweanness. Gone was the colonial hangover - being embarrassed about who you are. The things that made Zimbabweans what they are, different from other nations, special – even the funny little things that used to make people embarrassed, the idiosyncracies, the failures, the blunders, the ignorance – all the human things that summed up being a Zimbabwean, seemed now to be accepted in the spirit of 'this is what we are. We may laugh at ourselves, we may recognise that others have things better than we do but they are not Zimbabweans and we are – and we are proud of it.'

Take the new radio station that replaced Radio One. It was meant to be a Sport Channel and as a result it was called 'Spot FM' – someone wrote 'sport' the way it was said in Zimbabwe. No-one changed it and to this day it is still 'Spot FM'. Take the Heroes' Splushes. Same thing – that's how you say 'splash' in Zimbabwe – like people's once English names, now spelt as they are pronounced. They are not wrong. They just cease to be English names – they are Zimbabwean and no-one raises an eyebrow.

We have already had occasion to mention the wonderful email that did the rounds a few years back, entitled 'You are a Zimbabwean if...' It collected many of these funny little things that make Zimbabweans Zimbabwean. It made one laugh, it made one cry, it touched the heart – because it was one's own - us, our us-ness. So even now when Zimbabwe comes up with a new cost-cutting airline and it is called 'Fresh Air', it goes viral on the Zimbabwe network. 'Only Zimbabwe could call an airline 'Fresh Air'", people say, laughing at the ridiculous name but tickled pink. Yes, that's Zimbabwe. Haven't you noticed? People do. South Africans in South Africa do. They notice this thing about Zimbabweans, especially the younger generation – happy with what they are, proud of their country with all its peculiarities, free in a real sense from all that colonial doubt. Their own people in their own country.

We in our children's art education organisation were visited a number of times by children and young people from South Africa and Namibia – where everything is said to be so much better, lots of money, swanky malls and so on. By the time they had spent a week or so in Zimbabwe, they didn't want to go back. Excuse me if I put it in these terms but I can't think of any other way of saying it. South Africa may be the 'Rainbow Nation' it is touted to be but ultimately it is a country made in the image of Europe. Zimbabwe used to be like that. No more. Zimbabwe is an African country and Africans feel nice in it.

The realisation as to what had happened really hit me hard one evening, sitting at home watching the Miss Zimbabwe contest on television. There was a band playing. They struck up one of the jingles, one of the political jingles defending the Land Reform. The audience was young, very stylish, pleasure-loving and not, not by any stretch of the imagination your ZANU-PF supporters. But when they heard that jingle, as one the whole audience rose to its feet and danced and sang like there was no tomorrow! That is when I saw how the whole thing, this whole thing that was going on, had changed the national ethos.

This was not the cultural revolution I and others like me had had in mind and the government-funded cultural galas and 'Splushes' were a far cry from what we tried to do in the early 80s. The cultural revolution we had in mind was never intended to be 'propaganda' in the crude sense and the political performances never mercenary. We artists in those early years were committed to building the New Society and we did our performances not for money but for commitment and belief. We tried in our performances to inform and educate, to depict and explain the revolutionary objectives of the struggle and encourage the audiences to support them. The performers at Moyo's state galas were, with very few exceptions, Comrade Chinx[52] being one of them, professionals who were performing for the money and mostly they went ahead and performed at the galas the very same material they did in the bars, clubs and hotels where they earned their living all over the country.

I suppose it wasn't the professor's fault that bringing out all the old *chimurenga* songs and dances from mothballs after so many years, especially when ZANU-PF had betrayed them in deed and in spirit all these years, smacked of cynical opportunism and manipulation. Perhaps if he had been a ZANU-PF cadre in the 1980s and not the bitter opponent he was, and if he had been in government, he might have done it all at the right time and in the right way. As it was, Jonathan Moyo did it all the same. He did it as the main ZANU-PF propagandist in his role as Minister of Information. It was done consciously to win national support for the Land Reform and ZANU-PF's programme of indigenisation and national sovereignty. He used it as a weapon in the Battle for Zimbabwe. He turned out to be an excellent captain of culture for the party. It is a pity for ZANU-PF that the 'Young Turks', including Moyo, were

52 Comrade Chinx ((Dickson Chingaira), a lead singer in the camps during the *chimurenga*, developed a successful musical career after independence and is still performing today.

squashed by the septuagenarians of the struggle after the so-called 'Tsholotsho Declaration', and Moyo was thrown out of the party.[53]

Every year, the National Arts Council of Zimbabwe holds its NAMA Awards (National Arts Merit Awards) Ceremony. It is said that when it came to the award for the person who had done most for the arts in the year, Moyo was the unanimous choice. However, having by that time been sacked from his post and having stood against the party as an independent – and won, what's more – there was no way the professor, jingles and all, could be given the accolade the selection panel clearly believed he deserved.

Professor Jonathan Moyo was a greatly reviled personality in some quarters. Artists aligned with the MDC couldn't stand his guts. He mobilised those artists who were prepared to support ZANU-PF, its ideology and in particular its policies of land redistribution, indigenisation and black advancement to produce work that helped to propagate the cause. Those who would not support ZANU-PF and did not appreciate its policies, were outraged. However, one way or the other, the Professor's jingles, along with all the other measures he took to promote indigenous Zimbabwean arts, thoroughly transformed the media and culture industries in Zimbabwe and transformed the nation – I believe, on balance, for the good.

53 The 'Tsholotsho Declaration' emerged from a meeting held in Tsholotsho, Moyo's constituency, in 2005, which, it was alleged, was convened to challenge the Old Guard of the party and to promote Emmerson Mnangagwa for Vice-President as opposed to Joyce Mujuru, Mugabe's preferred candidate. Moyo lost his post in Information as a result and Chinamasa came close to losing his in Justice. Moyo later re-joined the party, becoming Minister of Information again after ZANU-PF's landslide election victory in 2013.

CHAPTER TWENTY-SEVEN:

THE GREAT ESCAPE

Another fateful year

1980, 1987, 1990, 2000, 2008 and now 2013 were probably the most fateful years in the history of the independent nation of Zimbabwe: Independence, followed by the Unity Accord; the introduction of ESAP; the constitutional referendum and the Land Reform; the Great Escape; and the landslide ZANU-PF electoral victory. These were deciding events. They shaped irreversibly what was to follow, what is now and even what is to come.

Why I call the events of 2008 'the great escape' is that it was in this year that things were so bad that it was difficult to imagine how Zimbabwe could go on – except to get catastrophically worse. Everything was short, the Zimbabwe dollar was disappearing into the stratosphere and government had virtually ceased to govern. Electricity and water were erratic or unavailable. The state school system had collapsed. The health system had collapsed and cholera was on the rampage. The formal banking system was in chaos.

Hyperinflation was like a tsunami. It destroyed everything in its path but it carried those who could find a way to ride it to unimagined lengths and undreamt of heights. Such people became extraordinarily rich over night. The Black Market of course reigned not only supreme but virtually alone. 'Burning money', get-rich-quick rackets involving Zimbabwe dollars, '*madiri*' – deals - and the Black Market were the order of the day. Those who could manipulate the system bought luxury cars in large numbers and began to erect palatial dwellings all over the northern suburbs. Those who could, were buying food in South Africa and fuel in London

It really looked as if the great 'melt-down' the South African and western media had been predicting for years, was in its throes. This would surely mean the end of Mugabe and the ZANU-PF government. All the efforts of the regime changers (or the democratic changers – whatever your perspective), with their sanctions, international media onslaught and NGOs seemed certain to be about to pay off. The Third *Chimurenga* would end in defeat and the white farmers would get back their land.

Not a bit of it. Zimbabwe once again astonished the world – and probably herself – and did a Houdini act. She did not go down. Instead she survived and began a famous come-back. Three events were responsible for this in my opinion. The first was the solution to the crisis of hyperinflation – the introduction of the Dual Currency in January. The second was the elections in March and June, which wrested power from the one side but did not quite give it to the other – thus averting what would almost certainly have been either foreign intervention or civil war. The third was the Global Political Agreement in September, which brought the contesting parties together in the Inclusive Government.

When the decision was taken to abandon the Zimbabwe dollar and permit transactions in US dollars and the South African Rand, the transformation was dramatic. The result was somewhat similar to the first flush of ESAP – things to buy but not enough money to buy them with. Almost overnight the shortages disappeared. The shops and supermarkets filled up. Fuel queues disappeared and goods became available. However, many companies, organisations and individuals who had quadrillions of Zimbabwe dollars stashed away in the bank, anyone, in short, with a healthy Zimbabwe dollar bank balance or a pension and who had not found a way to convert it to a foreign currency in time, was wiped out. As for those with multiple fancy motor vehicles in their yards and flamboyant mansions in the building, they came down to earth with a crash. Harare was glutted with expensive cars for sale at ordinary prices and the shells of unfinished mansions litter the northern suburbs as monuments to a bubble that burst.

Money was very short. It was not that there were no dollars and rands in the country. Though Zimbabwe did not have the reserves to import foreign currency, there was no shortage in real terms as the Black Market was awash with it. But this store of dollars was in the hands of the dealers, the speculators, the racketeers. For the ordinary people, the situation was desperate. Whereas the problem previously had been the proliferation of the almost worthless 'Zimdollars', now there was almost no money at all. At this point, I should imagine that if it hadn't been for the diaspora many people would have been very hard put to survive. Many people did not have even this to fall back on.

Now that everything had to be paid in foreign currency and there was pretty little foreign currency available, salaries suddenly became very low. For a long time after the abandonment of the Zimbabwe dollar, high-ranking civil servants, university professors and school teachers were not getting much more that $100 a month. The police and the armed forces were being paid a pittance. The same went for the workers. Those who survived by selling and could access goods through foreign exchange, found it hard to sell anything. The bottom of course fell out of the Black Market. Those who had previously been able to access foreign currency and change it into Zimbabwe dollars at Black Market rates and so make a killing, found their advantage had suddenly evaporated. People selling goods or services still thought of the US dollar as the dollar they knew – the Zimbabwe dollar – and so they charged ludicrously high prices. A plumber thought nothing of doing a few hours work unblocking a drain and demanding US$250 for the service. This confusion and the total lack of a way to evaluate services led to rentals, fees and rates skyrocketing. Supermarkets, used to frequently raising prices, continued to - and still do - frequently raise prices – with no more justification than that the public still pays them and they make more profit. Thus not only were the precious dollars hard to get hold of but they went very quickly when you got them. Those organisations which were supported by foreign donors, felt the pinch in another way. Whereas previously the budgets they submitted were considered modest by foreign standards but in Zimbabwe went a long way, now they seemed exorbitant. As a result the donors cut them down ruthlessly, which obviously affected the organisations and their operations.

Inflation vanished. The situation became stable. But it stabilised at a very low level of subsistence and it stabilised to the point of stagnation. Not as bad as 'stagflation', which is stagnation coupled with high inflation and unemployment, what characterised the period between 2008 and 2010 was a depressed stability at a low level with negligible inflation, a money supply so restricted that economic growth of any kind was extremely difficult, high prices and wages that were way below the poverty datum line.

When that gang burst into my house through the bedroom window, I could see they were desperate. They were hungry and they needed money. They couldn't wait to lay their hands on the remains of my cottage pie – once I had assured them that it was more than edible - on my profuse supply of sweet little bananas from my little plantation at the back and on the loaf of bread that was still warm in the bread machine. Of course, having demolished the loaf, they took the bread machine.

Thousands of people in those years were in the same boat as these young men. There was hardly anything they could do to get hold of US dollars and yet without them they would have nothing to eat. That is why so many of them skipped Zimbabwe's borders and continued their desperate search for money and food in other countries.

However, despite the privation and desperation, few would have wanted a return to the days of rampant inflation. It was as if Zimbabwe had stabilised on the ground floor and could now slowly drag itself up the stairs to the first floor, the second floor – slowly recovering, slowly recuperating and slowly developing a capacity to get to the top. In those early days – even now - it had to be the stairs as the lifts didn't work – they were either broken down or there was no electricity.

Zimbabwe needed this breathing space - a time to let the dust settle and build anew. For this to happen, economic stability had to be backed by political stability. 'Politics is the concentrated expression of economics', Lenin tells us. This was made possible by two decisive events. The electoral stalemate and the formation of the Inclusive Government provided a moratorium on political conflict for five years.

First, the 2008 elections. Let us go back to the situation that existed in the wake of the 'Harmonised Elections' of 2008. By the way, given what happened, on the face of it 'harmony' must have appeared to be the very last word that would have leapt to mind to describe those elections. As it happens, they were called 'harmonised' because the local government, parliamentary, senate and presidential elections were all held together at the same time. After the results had been announced and the presidential elections entered the second round, all hell, as we have seen, broke loose. I called the hell that broke loose after the 2008 elections, the First Battle for Zimbabwe, a battle between those who had launched the Third *Chimurenga* and those who seemed determined to roll it back. As you will recall, just as a victory for the MDC and their Western allies had appeared inevitable, Tsvangirai withdrew from the race and a stalemate resulted. Mugabe of ZANU-PF continued to be President and, while ZANU-PF had a majority in the Senate, MDC controlled Parliament.

In my opinion, the actual result of the Harmonised Elections in 2008 was probably the very best any Zimbabwean or any African could have hoped for. It was a stalemate and so the warring parties had to declare a truce, a truce which resulted in the so-called Inclusive Government. ZANU-PF and the two MDCs, bitter enemies, 'puppets', 'thugs' and 'sell-outs', formed a government and were forced to govern Zimbabwe together – as Zimbabweans!

The instrument which made this possible was the Global Political Agreement (GPA). The southern African regional grouping, SADC, has achieved a fairly high degree of regional unity and co-ordination. Globally, when a crisis has occurred in a member state, SADC has been quick to come to a consensus and move decisively to deal with the crisis. The situation in Zimbabwe had been an item of concern for the regional grouping for some years and Thabo Mbeki, both as President of South Africa and after, had been tasked by the Commission to broker an agreement between the warring parties. Supporters of the MDC, both in Zimbabwe and in particular in South Africa, have hurled all sorts of abuse at Mbeki for his handling of this task. They would - because supporters of the MDC are also supporters of 'regime change' and Mbeki (and SADC) did not support the concept of 'regime change' i.e. external forces interfering in a sovereign state to bring about the change of government they desire. SADC never supported this principle. It deplored it in Iraq and Libya and would not consider it in Zimbabwe for the obvious reason that SADC is a grouping of sovereign nations and 'regime change' in Zimbabwe today could be 'regime change' in any one of its members tomorrow. Besides the governments of a number of its members were once liberation movements and so they have a nice appreciation of what lies at the root of white South African and Western hostility towards Zimbabwe.

Mbeki negotiated what came to be called the Global Political Agreement (GPA), which all three parties, ZANU-PF, MDC (Tsvangirai) and MDC (Mutambara), signed. The GPA is an extraordinary document, a true southern African document, an African document. It brought together the two sides in the Zimbabwe conflict in their capacity as Zimbabweans and thus laid the basis for a historical agreement between Zimbabweans, an agreement which did not kowtow to the agenda of the foreign allies of the MDC.

The GPA starts with a detailed Preamble, preliminary comments which together make up the context and rationale of the agreement. The Preamble cites recent 'challenges' and 'threats' facing the nation, the need to 'uphold, defend and sustain Zimbabwe's sovereignty', 'the sacrifices made by thousands of Zimbabwe's gallant sons and daughters in the fight against colonialism and racial discrimination', and 'the polarisation, divisions, conflict and intolerance' existing in the country. Thus, the three fundamental issues of the time – the liberation struggle and Zimbabwe's national sovereignty, the economic crisis and the divided nation – were recognised at the outset. The three parties then commit themselves to putting their people and their country first and respecting the constitution and all national laws, the rule of law, observance of Zimbabwe's national institutions, symbols and national events. They accept and acknowledge 'the values of justice, fairness, openness, tolerance, equality, non-discrimination and respect of all persons without regard to race, class, gender, ethnicity, language, religion, political opinion, place of origin or birth (as) the bedrock of (their) democracy and good governance' and express their determination to 'build a society free of violence, fear, intimidation, hatred, patronage, corruption and founded on justice, fairness, openness, transparency, dignity and equality'. Thus the major concerns of both ZANU-PF and the two MDCs were fully acknowledged.

The Preamble stresses 'loyalty to Zimbabwe, patriotism and commitment to Zimbabwe's national purpose, core values, interests and aspirations' as well as the 'centrality and importance of African institutions in dealing with African problems' – thus setting out the common Zimbabweanness and Africanness of the protagonists.

There was nothing in this agreement that ZANU-PF or the MDC could object to. It contained all their most cherished ideals. It was obvious that Zimbabweans who could agree to the above, would have a genuine basis for working together. As long as the issues of national sovereignty, the goals of the liberation struggle and the irreversibility of the Land Reform were guaranteed, ZANU-PF had no objection to accepting the MDC's emphasis on democracy, human rights, rule of law and other civic virtues. After all, as Mugabe often reminded people, it was they who brought democracy to Zimbabwe in the first place.

All this was then spelt out in a series of articles. These included articles on the restoration of stability and economic growth, the need for a democratic process to come up with a new constitution, the fostering of equality, national healing, cohesion and unity, free political activity, rule of law and respect for the constitution and other laws, the freedom of assembly and association and the framework for a new government in which government posts were distributed among the three parties.

Extremely significant were the articles on sanctions, the land, external interference and regime change. The agreement on these burning issues was quite historic. On sanctions the GPA endorsed 'the SADC resolution on sanctions concerning Zimbabwe', namely, that 'all forms of measures and sanctions against Zimbabwe be lifted in order to facilitate a sustainable solution to the challenges that are currently facing Zimbabwe' and committed the signatories to 'working together in re-engaging the international community with a view to bringing to an end the country's international isolation'! Wow! The MDC agreed to that!

On the issue of the land, the GPA accepted 'the irreversibility of the said land acquisitions and redistribution'! What did those white farmers who signed all those cheques and presented them to Tsvangirai in the television footage described above, have to say about that, I wonder, not to mention Jesse Helms, Blair, Gordon Brown and the rest! On external interference and regime change, the GPA was a star: "Parties reaffirm the principle of the United Nations Charter on non-interference in the internal affairs of member countries" and agree "that no outsiders have a right to call or campaign for regime change in Zimbabwe".

It is significant that despite the signing of the GPA by the main parties, the US, Britain and the EU did not lift sanctions, they did not recognise the irreversibility of the land requisitions and redistribution and neither have they shown any signs at all of respecting the UN principle of non-interference or giving up their 'right' to bring about regime change in Zimbabwe or any other country where they don't like the government.

The three warring parties signed the GPA and with that set about setting up the Inclusive Government.

From the start, the situation was a difficult one. The parties had already experienced a decade of bitter conflict. The MDC too was outraged at having been robbed of what they considered to have been a victory at the polls by ZANU-PF violence and intimidation. They went into the GPA sulking. ZANU-PF on the other hand was smarting and as a result feeling pretty sore about the MDC. It had got the shock of its life and it was determined to make sure that next time there would be no mistake. All the parties realised that the arrangement was simply a truce and went into the agreement with their own agendas. MDC-T believed that they would be able to exploit their participation in government to further their plans to unseat Mugabe and ZANU-PF. ZANU-PF wisely decided to learn its lessons and rectify its mistakes in time for the next election when it came. Thus, the Inclusive Government was the very unlikely marriage of unwilling and diametrically opposed parties - certainly not the ideal climate for an experiment in national unity.

Robert Mugabe remained President and Tsvangirai became Prime Minister. The Deputy Presidents were from ZANU-PF and the deputy Prime Ministers from the two MDC factions. The cabinet was enormous - with a host of duplicate ministries formed in order to give the three parties a share of the cake. There were squabbles over the respective powers of the President and the Prime Minister. There were numerous MDC walk-outs and boycotts. MDC ministers blocked funding or otherwise obstructed support for sectors or projects they deemed to be either supporters of ZANU-PF or in line with ZANU-PF policy, for instance the armed forces, the new farmers, agriculture in general and even industry. Along with sanctions, their policies and actions had always been designed to turn Zimbabwe into a failed state so as to bring about regime change. ZANU-PF did its best to undermine the ministries headed by the MDC.

Nevertheless, although it did not seem to be a great prescription for efficient and productive government, the Inclusive Government did bring peace on the ground for the majority of the people, a lessening in pressure from outside and a slowly improving economic situation. On balance it was a relief from crisis but at first not an auspicious experiment in an alternative form of democracy. However, the Inclusive Government was to surprise us.

THE FOURTH DECADE

PART SIX

'THE NEXT FORK'

THE HOE MAKER: It's impossible. Look, here are my orders. It says, go and get Peter Gwindi because he was not what he was intended to be. Put him in the fire and melt him down. So come quietly, mudhara, *and don't cause trouble.*

PETER: Never. You must be mad. What if you're making a mistake.

THE HOE MAKER: Here it is in black and white.

PETER: Just give me some time and let me prove to you that all my life I have been myself.

THE HOE MAKER: Prove it? How?

PETER: All I ask is that you lend me myself. It won't take long.

THE HOE MAKER: OK – but remember we meet at the next fork in the path.

In the Zimbabwean professional youth theatre company, New Horizon's, adaptation of Henrik Ibsen's Peer Gynt, *which they called* A Journey to Yourself, *Peter Gwindi comes back home to Zimbabwe after a full and not very exemplary life in faraway places. On the home stretch he meets the Hoe-Maker (equivalent of Ibsen's Button-Moulder), who accuses him of never having been himself. At each meeting Peter asks for more time in order to prove he has. At the end of each meeting, the Hoe-Maker warns him that he will meet him at the next fork in the road – at the next crossroads.*

As Zimbabwe begins its fourth decade, like Peter Gwindi, she is still searching for herself. Until she finds herself, she can never be true to it. In the first three years of the decade, she experienced a period of relative calm and slow recovery. Politically this was made possible by the coming together of ZANU-PF and the two MDC formations in the Inclusive Government. But in 2013 general elections were held and ZANU-PF swept back into power with a landslide. The results were bitterly contested by Tsvangirai, the leader of the MDC-T, and his Western backers.

Now Zimbabwe seems to be standing at another crossroads. If ZANU-PF decides to ride its success at the polls and considers it a mandate to go it alone, it sets out on what may prove to be a rocky road, namely to intensify its indigenous ownership campaign and to revive sectors of the society that fell into decay during the hard times of the third decade in the teeth of opposition from the West and with a nation divided. Such a national programme is unlikely to succeed in the circumstances. After all, despite ZANU-PF's victory, one third of Zimbabweans and the two major cities oppose it.

It therefore has a choice – go forward in unity (a possibility suggested by the potential of the Inclusive Government) or, echoing Abraham Lincoln's famous words, remain 'a house divided in itself'.

CHAPTER TWENTY-EIGHT:

THE INCLUSIVE GOVERNMENT

"Unequally yoked"

> *"Be ye not unequally yoked together with unbelievers: for what fellowship hath righteousness with unrighteousness? and what communion hath light with darkness?*
>
> *- 2 Corinthians: 6:14*

On Christmas Day, 1914, German soldiers initiated a day of friendship across the trenches with their British enemies. The 'Tommies' and the 'Huns' met in No-man's-land, shook hands, sang carols, drank beer, played football and told each other how sick they were of the war. In some sections of the trenches this lasted into the New Year. The officers disapproved and further 'fraternisation' with the enemy was strictly forbidden. It did not happen again in the Christmases that followed and millions died on the Western Front. In July 2012, an article describing a rather similar event, in its way, certainly an extraordinary event, appeared in one of the pro-ZANU-PF local dailies, *The Herald*.

The event is question was reported to have taken place the previous day. Out there in the rural areas of so-called Matebeleland it must have been dry and a bit chilly because of course July is the middle of winter for Zimbabwe and although, during the day, the sun can be quite warm, often there are leaden skies and a slightly chilly wind but no rain.

At first sight, the 15 000 people who attended the event, might not have noticed anything unusual. They had gathered officially to commission the Landa J. Nkomo High School and launch an e-Learning Centre in the rural district of Tsholotsho in so-called Matebeleland. Of course, for such an event, government representatives would have had to be there and they were – in force. On this important occasion, no less than the President of Zimbabwe himself, the Honourable Robert Gabriel Mugabe, was attending. With him was a heavyweight team of government representatives, one of the two Deputy Presidents of Zimbabwe, the Deputy Prime Minister, the Minister of Education, Sports, Arts and Culture and the Minister of Information Communication Technology.

What made the event extraordinary was not the presence of the President and other government dignitaries because that was what was expected. What made it extraordinary was who the government dignitaries were and what they said.

I attended the funeral of the late Vice-President of Zimbabwe, Cde Simon Muzenda, at Heroes' Acre in Harare in 2003. I liked Muzenda because I thought he was a sincere and down-to-earth man and he enjoyed dancing his traditional dance, *mbakumba*, with the people whenever the opportunity presented itself. At that stage ZANU-PF made much capital over the way in which whites and the MDC did not attend national events, like Independence Day, Heroes' Day or State Funerals. If I am not mistaken, the leader of the MDC, Morgan Tsvangirai, did attend Cde Muzenda's funeral with other MDC officials. The others attending were overwhelmingly ZANU-PF and I couldn't help feeling that it was in very poor taste that the President attacked the MDC and ridiculed Tsvangirai in front of all the mourners, as I seem to recall he did in his speech. When he sets out to make a fool of someone, Mugabe does exactly that. It is something he is very good at and his jibes are very amusing and popular with his audience. But on this occasion I felt it was not right – for how could ZANU-PF complain that whites and the MDC did not attend national events when the events were treated as if they were ZANU-PF party rallies and anyone who attended who was not a member of the party, could be and often was subjected to humiliation? I believe this was an aspect of Mugabe's lack of statesmanship as well as his tendency to be divisive that I noted earlier.

It is against this backdrop that the event in Tsholotsho which I have been describing, should be seen – a backdrop that made the event all the more extraordinary. For, in addition to the President, the government representatives attending were Vice-President John Landa Nkomo (ZANU-PF, ex PF-ZAPU), after whom the school had been named, Deputy Prime Minister, Thokozani Khupe (MDC-Tsvangirai), Minister of Education, Sports, Arts and Culture, David Coltart (MDC Mutambara, later Ncube) and Minister of Information Communication Technology, Nelson Chamisa (MDC-Tsvangirai).

Well, if you knew what these particular individuals had had to say about each other in the past, the names they have called each other, the accusations they have levelled against each other, just the fact that they were sitting peacefully together on the podium representing the Government of Zimbabwe was miraculous enough. But listen to what they were saying.

The newspaper reporter opened his report of this august occasion by saying: "President Mugabe yesterday charmed Deputy Prime Minister, Thokozani Khupe, when he described her as a beautiful and meticulous lady." The President, according to the report, then went on to remark that 'the directors of ceremonies had mistakenly omitted Deputy Prime Minister Khupe in their introductions'.

The President was reported to have 'drawn amusement from the gathering by going on to say: "I don't how she could be omitted because she is always in my mind. A beautiful lady . . . a meticulous lady. How can anyone forget a person of that charm, a very charming lady?" This from President Mugabe for a leader of the MDC! Was this just a flash in the pan? Not a bit of it. The meeting continued in this vein.

President Mugabe commended Coltart and Chamisa 'for their hard work through their ministries in ensuring that Zimbabwe was abreast with the rest of the world in adopting modern learning approaches'. He also noted that Coltart, 'though being a white man, had shown a lot of commitment towards working with ordinary Zimbabweans'. "We all have the right to freedom of choice and it is that choice that made Mr Coltart to choose to be among us. When the Inclusive Government was formed I thought it was going to be a challenge for him to be among so many black people. Well, we may have differences of political outlook but what matters is that we are all Zimbabweans." Excuse me!

Then 'turning to Minister Chamisa, the President said the minister was a young leader who was endowed with great wisdom'. "I encourage him to go forward. We call him the youngest among us and we wonder why he has the wisdom of the elders," he said.

The Mutual Admiration Society continued its affable effusions with Coltart showering praises on President Mugabe, 'describing him as a visionary leader whose passion for education has led the country to embrace the global technological revolution of E-learning...through his guidance, we have been able to acquire software programmes for E-learning at primary schools... the President is an unwavering pillar of strength for the country's education system'. Coltart also paid tribute to Vice-President, John

Nkomo, and Chamisa ended his remarks by praising President Mugabe and Vice-President Nkomo, saying they were 'exceptional leaders'. The MDC youth firebrand and student leader, who was kicked out of Harare Polytech, Nelson Chamisa, never known for his temperate language or behaviour and very well known for his virulent anti-ZANU-PF utterances! Mugabe an 'exceptional leader'! Chamisa!

People attending the meeting could have been forgiven for asking themselves what is the world – and Zimbabwe – coming to? Leaders of the bitterly opposed political factions, ZANU-PF, MDC-Tsvangirayi and MDC-Ncube, showering praises on each other like this! What had happened to the divisive Mugabe, the man who could always make the audience laugh at his witty put-downs of those he considered his enemies? What about that notorious description of the urbanites of Mbare, Harare, who no longer supported him – '*vanhu vasinamutupo*' (people with no totem)? Had he finally learned statesmanship? He certainly seemed to have learned at last that whatever their differences, Zimbabweans were all Zimbabweans together. How had such a miracle, a totally unforeseen situation like this, come about?

The Inclusive Government lasted from the signing of the GPA in 2008 to July 2013. The above-described amity and acceptance between the partners in the Inclusive Government is something which developed, after a rocky beginning, gradually over the five years of working together in government.

In a sense, by stressing the common Zimbabweanness and Africanness of the three parties, the GPA created the potential for driving a wedge between the MDC and their right-wing white and Western supporters. The dichotomy between what the MDC as patriotic Zimbabweans agreed to in the GPA and what their funders and backers really wanted them to do came to characterise the behaviour of the MDC and, in particular, that of Tsvangirai during the years of the Inclusive Government. One moment, Tsvangirai found himself being a Zimbabwean when talking to Zimbabweans and the next the supplicant of the West when his powerful allies called him to heel. *The Herald* had a field day. In a secret communication with one of his Western backers, made public by Wikileaks, Tsvangirai called on the representative of a foreign power to continue sanctions for regime change and disregard what he was saying in public! And so, one minute, Tsvangirai was corroborating what close to 100% of the Zimbabwean population would agree with by telling them that there would be no rights for homosexuals in the new constitution, the next he was recanting and pledging himself and his party to ensure there were. One day, he was telling people that sanctions were bad for Zimbabwe and he personally was appealing for them to be lifted, the next he would be saying that sanctions will not be lifted because ZANU-PF is not respecting the GPA. One month, he was saying there was no way the land would be given back, the next he was saying that the whole question of the land needed to be revisited. When in very recent times he seemed to forget which woman he had promised to get married to, Tsvangirai's tendency to dance to other people's tunes ended up providing entertainment for the whole nation!

This aside, the GPA and the Inclusive government was an extraordinary exercise in which, I believe, lay the seeds of true democracy – and, in particular, true African democracy, one in which people whose ideas and beliefs appeared to differ, can, even when they have a tradition of enmity, come together as Zimbabweans and Africans and *find a way* to work together in the interests of their country. We who observed the process, saw how the fighting, the snubbing, the discomfort of sharing such a bed with such a political partner, which was the situation in the initial stages, gradually gave way to grudging and surprised expressions of appreciation for each other. Members of the three different parties began to speak on national issues with one voice – as in the interparty parliamentary committees which knew no party whip or party line but tried to thrash out issues in the interests of their Zimbabwe as Zimbabweans together. I couldn't help feeling that there, in the awkwardness and challenges of the Inclusive Government, something miraculous was taking place and that perhaps there lay the answer to Zimbabwe's – and possibly many other African countries' - future. When eventually the grudging and surprised expressions of appreciation became 'a very charming lady', 'a meticulous lady', 'visionary leader', 'exceptional leaders', 'unwavering pillar of strength', a young man with 'the wisdom of the elders' – one could only hold one's mouth in astonishment and say: "Viva! Long live!"

By agreeing to the GPA and then being forced to work together, practically, in the business of government, Zimbabweans who had spent the last ten years in bitter opposition, calling each other names, were forced to recognize in each other their shared nationhood. It is this process, in my opinion, which ultimately led to the Mutual Admiration Society the reporter described in his article on the launch of the regional ITC centre in Tsholotsho.

The extraordinary thing is that very few people have remarked on this process and seen in the miracle a better way, perhaps, to govern Zimbabwe – and even to achieve the goals of national sovereignty, self-sufficiency and indigenous ownership. The reason for this is, I believe, the entrenched polarisation in the country, the interference of the Western powers, who do not have a Zimbabwean or African agenda but rather their own peculiar interests at heart, and the fact that the war for Zimbabwe has not yet been fought to its conclusion. Instead of seeing the potential of their inclusivity as a way to wean the MDC away from its backers and persuade them to work together in the spirit of the GPA – in this way possibly paving the way for a situation in which the whole country would back the government in its plans for the consolidation of the revolutionary gains and the continued transformation of the economy – ZANU-PF clung to the old script. According to the old script, ZANU-PF is the revolutionary party and those Zimbabweans who are not a part of it, are the counter-revolutionary '*vapanduki*' (traitors) who have opposed them ever since the liberation struggle. According to this script, the only way to achieve its goals is for ZANU-PF to win another election and be free to implement its programmes unfettered and unconstrained by other Zimbabweans who have a long history of collaborating with the white man. They did not believe in the possibility of winning the backing of all Zimbabweans but preferred to put their faith in going it alone in a divided nation.

But surely, someone must have noticed what had happened. The President certainly seemed to be aware that it was something extraordinary and often in public he referred to how amazing it was that he and his party were working with people who had long been their enemies. He repeatedly put this down to their common Zimbabeanness, saying that though they might not see eye to eye exactly, they were able to work together because they were Zimbabweans.

So when I heard the President, despite the progress that had been made - despite this miracle - clamouring for elections, I wondered – as I often have with Mugabe – how he reconciled his appreciation of his MDC colleagues and their shared Zimbabweanness with an election in which they would become opponents again and the MDC would be thrown back into the arms of the West. Obviously the key factor for ZANU-PF was that while Unity was possible with another revolutionary party or leader – as in the Patriotic Front and the Unity Accord with PF-ZAPU - Tsvangirai and the

MDC had gone beyond the pale by calling for sanctions and embracing a counter-revolutionary agenda. It is a pity. Was he not aware of how he himself had progressed from divisiveness to inclusiveness and was now gradually being recognized as a leader - in fact, even a father - of his people? Did he not see the way in which Zimbabweans who were not from ZANU-PF, were now working together – even whites, as he noted in his remarks at Tsholotsho – with ZANU-PF as Zimbabweans. Zimbabwe was at last being seen as bigger than the party. He himself had said 'but what matters is that we are all Zimbabweans'! Why call for party elections and dig it all up again – ZANU-PF versus MDC? A competitive election? We fight over competitive football matches – what is going to happen when Mugabe gets the election he is calling for? And what will happen when one side 'wins'?

And then I come to a question I have often asked myself: "Why do countries in Africa and other places try to replicate a parliamentary system of government developed over centuries in a small island off Europe that later became their colonial master. Can we really not do better?"

CHAPTER TWENTY-NINE:

THE 2013 ELECTIONS

The greening of Zimbabwe

On 31st July, 2013, I woke up oppressed by a sense first of all of the significance of the day and then by feelings of dread and foreboding. Zimbabwe was going to the polls. Just the day before, I had spoken to my son-in-law in Cairo. We discussed the situation in Egypt and the overthrow by the military of the democratically-elected Muslim Brotherhood government there. I remembered his comment. "Never have a people fought so hard for democracy and then thrown it away so easily" is what he had said. I feared that the people of Zimbabwe might this day do just that. In their case it would not be democracy as such they would be throwing away but the gains of a revolutionary struggle that goes back 130 years to the First *Chimurenga*. ZANU-PF, for all that one can justly say in criticism of them, did in the end deliver on many of the most sacred goals of the liberation struggle. If they lose the election, say goodbye to all that, I thought.

A verse that has already been quoted more than once in this book, taken from one of the great songs of the struggle, came to mind:

> *Nyika yedu yeZimbabwe ndimo matakazvarirwa*
> *Vanamai nanababa ndimo mavanobva*
> *Tinoda Zimbabwe neupfumi wayo wose*
> *Simuka Zimbabwe!*

Which translated means: "Our land of Zimbabwe is where we were born, is where our mothers and fathers come from. We want/love Zimbabwe and all the wealth in it. Zimbabwe, arise!"

The land came back and - with the indigenisation legislation and implementation - ownership and control of the economy and the resources of Zimbabwe, particularly its land and minerals, have passed or are passing into the hands of Zimbabweans in a process unparalleled in Africa.

I think it would be true to say that - to echo another song of the liberation war - "*Zimbabwe yauya*" (Zimbabwe has come back). If Zimbabweans vote the MDC into power, they might as well sing: "*Zimbabwe yaenda*" (Zimbabwe has gone). But why would this be such a crushing blow to me? I asked myself. After all, I am not Zimbabwean.

The answer that came to me is that there was a moment in my life when I began to dedicate myself both in my life and in my thought to the struggle for a better world for all. I grieve and feel deeply for the poor, the deprived, the downtrodden and the wretched of the earth and I note with disgust and rage the rich and powerful, who with their selfishness and greed, their hypocrisy and distortions, perpetuate a system which not only prolongs their looting and accumulation but casts the rest who are not too poor to participate, into a wasteland of degraded values, mindless consumption and slavish imitation. And, ever since that moment, apart from fleeting but ephemeral victories, I have seen the tide of human existence flow remorselessly against me and against all those who feel what I feel and see what I see.

So, if the struggle, the blood, the sacrifice and the sufferings of the people of Zimbabwe had come to naught on that day and all their gains were lost – if *they* had once again triumphed and once again *we* had got a whipping, I did not need to have a Zimbabwean heart for it to be broken. To me it would have felt like the last straw and after this – well, at the risk of being melodramatic but as an expression of how I really felt – to quote the Bible (not something I do a lot) – I could only ask: "O, Death, where is Thy sting?" (King James Version, 1, Corinthians, 55)

Yes, the elections Mugabe was calling for during the time of the Inclusive Government were upon us. In the interim I had tried to go back and live in my native land, South Africa, failed in the attempt after only a year and a half and came back to Zimbabwe to live and die. Now my heart was in my mouth as to what the day would bring.

When I left Zimbabwe to go back to South Africa, the Inclusive Government was in place, the subject of the previous chapter. Don't get me wrong. When in that chapter I wrote that 'something miraculous was taking place and that perhaps there lay the answer to Zimbabwe's future', I was neither ignorant of the severe shortcomings of the Inclusive Government nor suggesting that such a government was the answer to Zimbabwe's problems. The parties that were 'unequally yoked' together were the products of a competitive party political system. The two MDC formations owed their allegiance to foreign powers. It was a miracle the three of them could work together at all. Nevertheless something miraculous did happen and I was only suggesting that in this miracle lay the seeds of a completely different way for Zimbabweans to govern themselves, different from that which they had adopted from their colonial masters - a genuine, indigenous democratic alternative. Now, as was inevitable, instead of nurturing the seeds of this miracle, the erstwhile partners were again at each other's throats and the elections were going to decide who would triumph.

The day came and went. My most fundamental dread and forebodings were swept away by a most spectacular victory. The President, Robert Mugabe, at the age of 89, and his party, ZANU-PF, swept to victory in a landslide - with Mugabe winning 61.09% of the vote and the party 160 seats. The MDC formations had been thoroughly trounced - with Tsvangirai coming in with a paltry 33.94% and his party with 49 seats. If the constituencies on the map of Zimbabwe won by the MDC were coloured red and those won by ZANU-PF green, Zimbabwe had indeed been considerably 'greened'.

Yet, what about the fears expressed in the questions with which I ended Chapter 29: "...what is going to happen when Mugabe gets the election he is calling for? And what will happen when one side 'wins'?" Mugabe got his election and we now know what happened. One side won – comprehensively. But do we know what will happen next? In such an election and at such a time, are there – can there be – any real winners?

True, much to my and thousands of Africans and Zimbabweans' relief, the gains of the freedom struggle seem for the moment to have been secured – but at what cost? History has shown that revolutions that cannot resolve the fundamental contradiction of revolutionary change, namely that it is based on conflict and division, are never secure and often end up being reversed.

In the last year of the Inclusive Government, Mugabe and ZANU-PF had been pushing for elections. Tsvangirai and the MDC did their best to stall them. During this period, a number of important studies and newspaper articles had appeared in the West, which suggested that the Land Reform project in Zimbabwe was by no means a failure. Also in a windfall for the embattled nation, a treasure trove of diamonds had been discovered in Marange. As the time for the election approached, pollsters and columnists began to suggest that support for ZANU-PF had increased exponentially while support for the MDC had correspondingly declined. It was widely predicted that ZANU-PF would win the election comfortably. A position began to emerge outside Zimbabwe that it would be wise for western governments to abandon their efforts to bring about regime change in favour of constructive engagement with whichever government resulted from the elections.

In the short space of time available to them, the MDC formations had little chance of improving their fortunes. For reasons we shall discuss, during the Inclusive Government the balance of support in the country had indeed shifted away from them. They and their western sponsors faced two possible scenarios – either to accept a ZANU-PF victory as the likely outcome of the elections and, in the spirit of the position referred to above, prepare the ground for constructive engagement or to disrupt and sabotage the elections so as to render a ZANU-PF victory null and void.

Offered a wiser alternative, died-in-the wool Imperialists as they are, the MDC-T's Western coalition characteristically opted to repeat all their old mistakes. They opted to try and render the elections null and void. For this tactic to succeed it was crucial that not only Europe and North America accept that the elections were not free and fair but that SADC itself did so as well – and they obviously believed that they could engineer that conclusion. The twin-pronged approach they seem to have adopted, involved, one, trying to delay the elections as long as possible while pushing for various measures aimed at re-grading the playing field in their favour and, two, beginning a campaign to discredit the elections even before they happened so that when they did happen and when ZANU-PF won, they would be able to convince the world and pressurise the AU and SADC into accepting that they were fraudulent or at least not free and fair - and get them annulled. Failing this, they calculated that the MDC-T's urban supporters, believing that ZANU-PF had stolen the election, would come out into the streets as the opponents of Morsi did in Cairo and in this way block ZANU-PF's path to power.

In order for this strategy to succeed, their best bet was to return to the GPA and push for provisions in the GPA that had not been implemented, claiming that, until these were, a free and fair election could not be held. The two provisions they particularly focussed on related to reform of the media and of the security apparatus. Deregulation and liberalisation of the airwaves in Zimbabwe would have given them the kind of advantage ZANU-PF would have been hard put to beat (see pp.364-5). They also knew that the higher ranks of the security apparatus – both the uniformed forces and the secret service – were thoroughly loyal to ZANU-PF, the bulk of them having been involved in the liberation struggle. Even if the MDC were to win the election, they could face opposition from them. If they attempted to reverse the revolutionary gains, this opposition could easily take the form of armed intervention.

ZANU-PF was perfectly aware of all this and they retorted by pointing out that the GPA also called for the lifting of sanctions and the closure of hostile pirate radio stations broadcasting into Zimbabwe from neighbouring countries. They rejected the reforms the West was pushing for and basically turned round and said that if the MDC wanted to bring about the desired changes, they should win the election and do so. ZANU-PF was not going to dig its own grave for their sake.

However, the MDCs and their allies' tactic was for a while relatively successful as even SADC endorsed their complaints and called on Zimbabwe to approach the courts, which had ruled that the election should be held by 31st July, for a two week postponement. When the courts threw this request out and the President announced that they would indeed go ahead on the 31st, the MDC/

Western alliance then attempted to put the kibosh on them by flooding the courts with litigation. All this did nothing to delay the elections but it did have the useful consequence of making it very difficult for the tri-partite Zimbabwe Electoral Commission (ZEC) to get everything ready for the elections in time, resulting in chaos during the Special Elections.[54] It also meant that the completion of the voter's roll and the provision of copies to the participating parties were delayed. These two hitches were of course gratefully utilised by those who wished to discredit the elections.

It is important to stress that the organisation of the elections was not in the hands of one party. It was the Inclusive Government and structures put in place by the Inclusive Government that organised them. JOMIC (Joint Monitoring and Implementation Commission), which had the largest team of monitors and from which ZANU-PF had actually withdrawn, claiming that it was being abused in favour of the MDC and their allies, was funded very liberally by the West. Its 30 000 monitors, with at least three observers to each polling station, were made up of Zimbabweans drawn from the three partners in the inclusive government. Besides, the elections were taking place in accordance with the new constitution that had been democratically formulated in consultation with the people and endorsed by all three partners in the Inclusive Government and their principals, including Tsvangirai himself.

When it came to polling day itself and the people trooped out in their millions to cast their votes, peace reigned - just as it had in the first round of elections in 2008. I must say that the 2013 elections

54 The Special Elections were a new feature in the Zimbabwe electoral process, designed to permit members of the uniformed forces, secret service and election officers a special day to vote at least 16 days before actual polling day. This was combined with postal voting for embassy staff.

were yet another humbling experience for me. I have had a number of such experiences in Zimbabwe as I marvel at Zimbabweans organising and staging massive and complicated processes with extraordinary facility. I have never met Justice Rita Makarau, the Chairperson of the Zimbabwe Electoral Commission (ZEC), but I do know her deputy, Joyce Kazembe. We were together at the University of Zimbabwe. Those who so often castigate Africans for negative gender balances, were so busy slamming the elections that they somehow managed not to notice that this extraordinary event, which had been subjected to almost unbearable scrutiny and pressure ever since it was mooted, was organised essentially by two women. I watched the footage and saw the two of them sitting together, sisters who had been through fire and come out triumphant. My heart went out to them.

All the party leaders had stressed over and over again the need for peacefulness and people of all different persuasions stood in line without duress, intimidation or being subjected to party slogans. This contrasted dramatically with elections in some other African countries, including Nigeria, as Orji Uzor Kalu, a member of the African Union Observer Mission, noted in an article she wrote about the Zimbabwe elections. What was extraordinary was the way in which candidates from the different parties fraternised, as they did on that doomed Christmas Day on the Western Front. Even after the results were announced, many congratulated each other and the losing candidate in Gokwe (MDC-T) explained that he and his victorious opponent from ZANU-PF were not enemies. "We come from the same town," he explained. "We just happen to belong to different parties."

In the last days before the election even Tsvangirai seemed to be confident of the elections, knowing the equal part his party had played in its planning and organisation, and early on the day of the elections itself he was filmed proudly casting his ballot and beaming at the camera. However, only a few hours later he was in front of the cameras again. It was quite a different Tsvangirai and a quite different message. Now he was angrily denouncing the elections as a farce, a joke, a fraud - before the elections were even over. They were rigged, he said. Western ambassadors, British and Australian in particular, added their hear-hears. It was not very long before their allegations were on all the news channels in the world. Watching Tsvangirai cast his vote in the morning in front of the television cameras, for all the world like the future president in an election he seemed to have no problem with - and then seeing him fulminating a few hours later and dismissing this same election as a farce, was a sad sight indeed.

The Western countries that had imposed sanctions, had not been permitted to send observers and, with the partial exception of the European Union, they as a bloc denounced the elections, citing various irregularities which they claimed invalidated the results. They called for an 'independent inquiry' or even a re-run. In particular, they cited the fact that the voters' roll had not been made available in electronic copy, that a high percentage of voters had been turned away, particularly they claimed in MDC strongholds, and that there was an abnormally high percentage of assisted voting – where an individual for one reason or another had to be assisted by an electoral official to cast his or her vote. Of course they also selectively cited the 'reforms' which, they alleged, were required for a 'free and fair' election. They would – but they made no mention of sanctions and pirate radio stations.

On the other hand, those who had observed the elections had a quite different story to tell. Despite pressure on them to come out with a condemnation of the elections, both the African Union and SADC observer missions gave the elections a thumbs-up and pronounced them a free and fair reflection of the people's will. Other SADC observer missions, COMESA (Common Market for Eastern and Southern Africa) and SADC, African, Caribbean and Latin American countries did likewise.

The MDC-T refused to accept the results and filed an appeal with the Electoral Court. But all their legal and media efforts to discredit the elections and invalidate the results came to naught. The British, the United States, Australia, Canada and other nations within the Western orbit refused to accept them and vowed to maintain sanctions. Other nations outside their orbit hailed their success – including Russia, China and India. The United Nations Secretary-General, Ban Ki-moon, hailed the peaceful nature of the elections. This left the European Union, which managed to impale itself on the horns of a dilemma. Very fairly and quite commendably, the EU had announced that it would be guided by SADC. SADC endorsed the elections yet here were some of their members - Britain, Germany and others - vociferously refusing to accept them. What to do? Nothing, of course. By the time of writing, the EU had not yet come out with a definitive statement – and what did it matter? The results were now a *fait accompli*. Robert Mugabe was duly sworn in as President and ZANU-PF formed a new government.

In retrospect, the Zimbabwe elections of 2013 beg four questions. The first three are: how come the MDC did so badly? Who contested the validity of the elections and why? Why does the West (in the main) find it so difficult to credit Africa with any integrity or pay any attention to its opinions and decisions?

So, first question, why did the MDC lose in a landslide? This was the party that came within a whisker of upsetting the applecart in 2008. If Tsvangirai had not chickened out of the re-run of the presidential elections, he might have won – and that would have been the end of Mugabe, ZANU-PF and the revolutionary gains, many of which had already been chalked up by that time.

First of all, the Movement for Democratic Change (MDC), has never really been a party (see Chapter 20). It was an anti-ZANU-PF front, fronting for all those in Zimbabwe who wanted to see the end of Robert Mugabe and ZANU-PF and for all the others in the world, mostly the West, who wanted the Land Reform to be reversed and the country opened up to their unfettered 'investment' As such it won support not on the basis of its policies nor its campaigning nor its party organisation. It won support actually without doing very much at all – *mahara* really (for free), as people would say in Zimbabwe.

The bottom line was that the narrow squeak in 2008 had woken ZANU-PF up whereas it had lulled the MDC into complacency. In the years leading up to the 2013 elections, MDC-T had done very little to canvas and organise for support. Its woeful lack of organisation at the branch level was demonstrated in its chaotic and bitterly contested primaries, which were sparsely attended and often marred by those who did attend totally rejecting the candidates the leader of the party, Tsvangirai, was trying to introduce to them. Many unsuccessful candidates refused to accept the primary process on the grounds that the leadership was manipulating it, refused to support the candidates put forward and in many cases campaigned against the party as independents.

Secondly, instead of organising for the election, Tsvangirai spent all his time opposing it, visiting other countries to win their support, pushing SADC and the courts to postpone it and adopting a strategy of sabotaging the process by bringing a series of litigations on numerous issues to the court.

This is related to the third reason why the MDC lost. Tsvangirai and the MDC have never fought the battle for Zimbabwe in Zimbabwe. They have always put their faith in their powerful sponsors' ability to hand it to them on a platter through the international media, sanctions and diplomatic warfare.

Other reasons relate to Tsvangirai's leadership. His private life was the subject of much national entertainment for quite some time. But his main problem was and is that Tsvangirai is at heart, I believe, a patriotic trade unionist. But he fell into bed with partners – and I am not referring to his wives and mistresses – who had a quite different agenda, with the result that he was always yo-yoing between his heart and what his masters told him. One day he would reassure Zimbabweans that gay rights are not acceptable in Zimbabwe, the next he would be telling the world that it must be a key provision in the new constitution. After opposing the election so bitterly for such a long time, he pulled off a *volte farce* (if I may coin the phrase) that was sensational even for him. He suddenly claimed that it had been the MDC all along that had been clamouring for an election and it was ZANU-PF that was stalling. In addition, in his campaigning, he had little to say that was not negative and went around insulting all sorts of important constituencies. It was common knowledge that the MDC would be compelled to return the farms to their original white owners but he went further by disparaging the new farmers, belittling their farming skills and saying they would be better off coming back to town and working in the factories. No wonder they mobilised *en masse* in support of ZANU-PF, ferrying people who would otherwise not have been able to get to a polling station in their newly acquired pick-ups and tractors. He insulted China, the ANC and the current Secretary-General of the African Union, Nkosazana Zuma-Dhlamini. He spoke disparagingly about the liberation war vets and belittled the peasants by telling them that they go around without any underwear because of the ZANU-PF they vote for. Taken all in all, Tsvangirai's contribution to his own downfall was fairly plain to see.

But far more substantial than even all this was the fact that while the MDC continued to depend on its anti-ZANU-PF rhetoric and its support from abroad and did very little to consolidate or increase its support base, it failed to notice that ZANU-PF's policies had improved the lives and given hope to hundreds of thousands of ordinary people all over the country – the kind of people I mentioned at the beginning of the chapter, those who are or always have had a raw deal. People coming from many different parts of the country speak of the quiet but effective work that was being done by ZANU-PF, bringing tangible benefits to the people. The Land Reform was a major source of benefits. There was the substantial income from tobacco. In Nyanga new farmers who specialised in growing potatoes commercially, prospered and now sported expensive new 4 x 4s. In the Lowveld others were growing sugar-cane. All over the place, the new farmers were slowly developing their allotments and growing their income. But this was not all. The community share ownership trusts, resulting from the indigenisation of local companies, were bringing communities unparalleled investment in schools, dams, electrification, boreholes, clinics as well as shares in mining operations. Many observers noted the support for ZANU-PF this time round on the part of the youth. The reason for this was obvious. Over the last few years thousands of youth projects had been established and financed all over the country.

Above all, ZANU-PF had done solid groundwork at the branch level, was no longer divided as it had been in 2008 and had worked hard to get its voters registered. In the end 93% of Zimbabweans entitled to vote were registered, one of the highest percentages in Africa.

Then, really, it was not as if ZANU-PF's victory was a total surprise. Only Tsvangirai seemed to have been unaware – unless of course when he expressed his incredulity at the fact that he had been trounced, he was playing a part. Opinion poll after opinion poll, including those of US institutions, and prominent Western media corporations such as *The Guardian*, the *New York Times*, CNN and Reuters had all predicted it. Many pro-MDC organisations outside Zimbabwe were already predicting a ZANU-PF victory and even the MDC's own survey had shown that support for their party had sagged dramatically while that for ZANU-PF had surged.

Having accepted that ZANU-PF was likely to win, the pro-MDC camp decided that its best strategy was to denounce the election results and press for them to be declared null and void. This tactic they seemed to have decided would be accompanied by efforts to engineer an Egyptian or Turkish situation. According to this scenario, ZANU-PF would be overthrown by MDC supporters in the two main cities, Harare and Bulawayo, both MDC strongholds, taking to the streets. Unfortunately, their hopes in this regard were destined to be disappointed as the anticipated popular demonstrations failed dismally to materialise.

The second question - who contested the validity of the elections and why - relates to the credibility of the election. There were thousands of observers and numerous observer teams and they were able to observe the process over weeks - some of them, including SADC and the African Union - all over the country. SADC monitored the election process starting on 15th July. They had 600 observers observing all 210 constituencies. To the best of my knowledge, there was no observer team that observed the election in Zimbabwe that refused to endorse the elections. All commended the peacefulness and overwhelming numbers in which Zimbabweans voted. They commended the punctuality of the opening of voting stations as well as the adequacy of materials required in the voting process. Opposing candidates of the two main parties congratulated each other after the results were announced. Voting was observed, counting was observed, the posting of results was observed, the announcement of results was observed – observed not only by observer missions but by representatives of the contesting parties themselves. Not only did the observer teams endorse the elections but some were clearly astonished by what they saw. The African Union, SADC observer mission, SADC electoral commissions team, SADC lawyers team, COMESA (Common Market for Eastern and Southern Africa), the Chinese and Caribbean observer teams, Namibia, South Africa, Kenya and countless other countries - all endorsed the results of the elections and congratulated the people of Zimbabwe. Left at that, the elections would have been a deserved feather in the cap both of Africa and Zimbabwe.

But no, the proponents of regime change went all out to muddy the waters. As expected the foremost dissenter was the leader and the leadership of MDC-T - not the rank and file or even many of its influential supporters. MDC Ncube accepted the results. MDC-T's Matebeleland North chapter upheld the results and put their loss down to the imposition of candidates by the leadership. Even Professor Brian Raftopolous, an inveterate ZANU-PF basher and political adviser to the MDC, pronounced that there was no evidence of vote-rigging. In a report released by the Solidarity Peace Trust, Raftopolous put ZANU-PF's election victory down to hard work, listening to the people, not imposing popular local candidates and desisting from violence. He also noted the massive registration campaign it had mounted, which added over a million new voters to the roll.

Adding fuel to the fire the MDC leadership was battling gamely to stoke were the Australian Ambassador and the British Ambassador - in the forefront - and their Governments, the US Embassy and its Government, the German government, to a lesser degree the European Union. In chorus, all of these cried foul. It is extraordinary that the only countries to cry foul were the countries which did not have teams on the ground to observe the elections! They were joined by some Zimbabwean NGOs who benefit from their support –the Zimbabwe Election Support Network, being the prime example.

Why did they not have teams observing? They were banned. Why? Because these are the countries that have over ten years contributed to making the lives of Zimbabweans a misery by unleashing a relentlessly negative media campaign and comprehensive sanctions on the country (see Chapter 21). To reiterate, economic sanctions are an illegal method powerful countries use to impose their will on weaker ones. There is no such thing as a free and fair election in a country on which sanctions have been imposed because sanctions are a naked and brutal attempt to influence the outcome. They support a biased agenda and, in the case of Zimbabwe, aim to effect the reversal of the Land Reform and bring about regime change.

The reasons that these countries imposed sanctions on Zimbabwe are the same as those that prompt them now to oppose ZANU-PF's stunning victory.

When it comes to the spurious objections to the process they have raised, there are arguments and explanations on both sides but, whichever way, none of them is serious enough to have made any significant impact on the vote. Taking them, briefly, one by one:

the voters roll – the main objection was that the contesting parties were not given electronic copies. Hard copies were available but the MDC-T refused to accept their voters roll in that format and only eventually collected their hard copy late on polling day. Zimbabwe is by no means the only country in Africa that is not able to provide electronic copies of their voters' roll.

Next, the percentage of voters turned away from polling stations: it is important to note that the figures do not necessarily refer to those who were disqualified to vote. They also included significant numbers of people who went to vote at the wrong polling station and were then referred to the right one. This meant that many of those initially turned away, did indeed vote. Those others who were denied the right to vote included many who could not produce IDs. Even then, including all those turned away for whatever reason from a polling station, the percentage of registered voters in the Zimbabwe elections who were turned away, came to 4.8%. In Botswana, the percentage was 23%, with Zambia and Namibia doing a lot better with 2% and 1.3% respectively. This figure was not representative of previous elections in Zimbabwe and it is likely that it was caused by the rushed nature of the elections.

Finally, the high numbers of assisted voters: what characterised the 2013 elections was the very high percentage of registered voters – 93% of those eligible. This meant that ZANU-PF's efforts to get the people registered must have not only included very many new voters but in addition large numbers of voters from the rural areas. Then there was the complicated nature of the Harmonised Elections. Each voter was voting for the President, for the House of Assembly, for the Senate and for the local authority. Given the number of first time and rural voters and the complication of the voting process, surely it was only natural that many voters would need assistance. Assistance was not provided by just anyone. The secrecy of the ballot was preserved and voters were assisted by election officials drawn from all three parties that made up the Inclusive Government.

The third and last question is about the West's general failure to trust Africa. One of the most depressing developments in recent history is the general lapse of sections of the media from informing and educating into state or establishment propaganda (see Chapter 25).[55] Many have warned of the danger of this, not only to the people who consume it but to the states and establishments that mean to benefit from it. The folly of the socialist government of the German Democratic Republic in not allowing the people to know the truth about the West became disastrously apparent with the fall of the Berlin Wall. The US media's hype about Saddam Hussein's regime in Iraq led to their soldiers being astonished that they were not welcomed as liberating heroes when they entered Baghdad. My old colleague, Julie Frederikse's book, *None but Ourselves*, demonstrated the catastrophic delusions of Ian Smith's media that continued, even when he himself knew it was a lie, to assure the white Rhodesians that they were winning the war and Robert Mugabe was a ruthless terrorist. They were left stunned when suddenly they found they had not only lost the war but faced the prospect of Mugabe as their Head of State. And what about the Western reporter who was astonished to see the people of Zimbabwe going imperturbably about their business after the results of the recent elections were announced? "Aren't you upset?" she asked the people in the street incredulously. And the saddest of all, Tsvangirai, so out of touch with reality that he told his Western media that after the announcement of the results there was a state of national mourning in Zimbabwe!

A number of countries in Europe and the United States have a lot to answer for when it comes to Africa. They profited from the slave

55 See Chomsky, Noam, *Manufacturing Consent*

trade and colonialism and then after political independence they continue to impose neo-colonial or imperialist relations. There was a lot of propaganda in those days justifying slavery and later colonialism. In the same way, the media has worked assiduously to justify the West's post-independence role in Africa. This it has done through the images of Africa it serves up to its populations. It is no secret that for decades the situation with regard to media rapportage in the West has been that very little good is reported out of Africa. Yes, Africa emerging from two centuries of bondage and exploitation, has had more than its fair share of nightmares but these have never been able to eradicate the good. While the former is grist to the mill in the Western media, the latter hardly gets a show-in.

As a result, good people in the West, kind people, people who would know human greatness and goodness when they saw it, are confused in a situation like the one we witnessed in the days following the elections. Once again there was a horror story out of Africa, a crisis, African villains, corrupt processes – 'on the knife edge', 'about to tumble into civil war'. This is what their media was telling them - yet again - about an African election – and in particular about Zimbabwe, the horror stories of which country never seem to end. As one European friend of mine said to me when I tried to tell him that on the ground here in Zimbabwe it was all quite different to what his media were telling him: "I am confused. Who can I believe? Is there any institution in Zimbabwe we can trust?"

I looked at the footage and pictures of the people, dressed in their warm layers, ordinary people, not rich, not stylish, standing in line, laughing, chatting, waiting patiently to cast their vote - the salt of the earth. They have been through a lot – we all have in Zimbabwe over the last thirteen years. The two amazingly dedicated and courageous women who organised this whole thing, even Mugabe himself laughing, moving among children, having a joke with the opposition – all this they never see. The goodness of Africa, the plain, down-to-earth courage, endurance, ingenuity, talent, ability, expertise – but above all the pity and human sympathy – it is all here, in Africa. But none of it is reported. No wonder good people in Europe don't know who to trust in Africa.

And who can blame them when their ambassadors and statesmen sweep the informed and honest assessments of observer teams of sincere, conscientious people from the African Union, from SADC and African countries contemptuously aside – as if they either didn't exist or – nudge, nudge, wink, wink – *we* (we Westerners) know how corrupt all these African governments and officials are, don't we? That is when I became infuriated – to see the British Ambassador in Harare telling British television that the election was a sham when she had not observed it and she knew that those who did observe it, had declared otherwise. But, you see, they were Africans.

And so we had a very clear situation in the post-election period, clear for all Africans who wanted to see - to see...and to think about it. On one side, Africa unanimously endorses an African election in Africa, on the other, Australia, Britain, Germany and the United States 'know better' and reject it. Where is this taking us?

Unlike in the 2008 elections, in 2013 one of the two sides won decisively – and so, the fourth question is, what now?

CHAPTER THIRTY:

THE END OF INCLUSIVITY

"Tsvangirai can go hang"

Two principles have characterised the political life of Zimbabwe, going right back to the First Chimurenga, namely Unity and Division, and generally Unity has been a lot better for the country than Division.

When the European settlers first came to Zimbabwe, relations between Mthwakazi and the Shona-speaking peoples either took the form of vassalage or constant raiding and pillage. When Mthwakazi tried to resist the invaders alone in what was called the First Matebele War, it was not very successful. However when both Shona and Ndebele took up arms in a united uprising to drive the Europeans out, they posed a much greater threat and it took a number of years – and the Maxim gun - before the uprising was finally suppressed. From antagonistic, subservient and divided relations, the indigenous peoples found a common cause in their opposition to dispossession and brutal subjugation at the hand of the Europeans. They were also united in their worship at the shrine of Mwari or Mwali at eMthonjeni (Matopos)[56].

Then in the era of nationalist politics the unity of the Zimbabwe African People's Union (ZAPU) gave way to the divisions and discord of the period ushered in by secession and the formation of the Zimbabwe African National Union (ZANU), an unfortunate division that soon came to be characterised by ethnic difference - with Ndebeles tending to remain with ZAPU and Shonas joining

56 See Ranger, *Voices from the Rocks*

ZANU. The two organisations fought the war of liberation for the most part divided but came together in the Patriotic Front and their unity enabled them to negotiate majority rule.

At Independence Zimbabwean society was already a dangerously divided one.[57] But at a time when unity was desperately needed, ZANU-PF made what was in my opinion a disastrous mistake by deciding to fight the elections in 1980 not as the Patriotic Front but as ZANU-PF. This ensured that the liberation forces would not embark on the transformation and building of the new state of Zimbabwe as a united force – a development which was inevitably going to reinforce the dangerous divisions of Zimbabwean history in the colonial period.[58] The consequence was the ZIPRA rebellion, the terrorism of Super-ZAPU and the new government's excessive reaction, namely the Gukurahundi campaign in Matebeleland. It was a consequence which set up one of the most corrosive elements of Zimbabwe's post-independence politics - the estrangement of the people of Matebeleland from the national destiny.

With the signing of the Unity Accord, once again division was replaced by unity. As praiseworthy as this accomplishment undoubtedly was, it was not enough to bring about unity at all levels of society. It brought the leadership of the two parties together but left other elements in the party as well as the population of Matebeleland, especially those that had borne the brunt of the 5th Brigade killings, sullen and unreconciled. However unity, even though only partial, was a distinctly more acceptable outcome than unfettered civil war.

The unity of ZANU-PF and PF-ZAPU in the form of the new ZANU-PF carried the country through the second decade. But

57 *See Chapter 1*

58 *See Chapter 8*

as problems multiplied and social divisions increased the basis for yet another fundamental division emerged in the form of the Movement for Democratic Change (MDC). With the re-taking of the land, the problems and divisions not only intensified but proliferated. The MDC came to serve as a cat's cradle for all the disaffected sections of the population, both of longstanding and recent provenance - but with a new and alarming addition, namely the involvement of powerful forces outside the country. Between 2000 and 2008 the country and the people were, sadly, bitterly divided. Zimbabwe was polarised, the people locked in a desperate struggle - with one side massively assisted by external forces.

The year 2008, rather similar to 1987, saw Zimbabwe hovering on the brink of civil war. Indeed a kind of war was already being waged. ZANU-PF called it the Third *Chimurenga*. Their opponents called it Regime Change. Fortunately, again, for Zimbabwe neither side won. It was a stalemate and Thabo Mbeki was able to get the warring factions to sign the General Political Agreement (GPA) and form the Inclusive Government.[59] For almost five years peace reigned in Zimbabwe and the bitter enemies came to realise, not before experiencing considerable unease and discomfort, that they shared a common Zimbabweanness, that they could work together and, in fact, that they could appreciate each other's gifts and hopefully points of view.

With the coming to an end of the Inclusive Government, Zimbabwe again reached a fork in the road, one prong leading to increased and more effective unity, the other a return to disunity. It was inevitable that the Inclusive Government would give way to elections. In fact, it was stipulated in the GPA that the parties oversee a consultative process to come up with a new constitution and in accordance with the constitution move to a general election.

59 *See Chapters 23, 24 and 28*

Zimbabwe is still far from re-considering the Westminster democratic model of competitive winner-takes-all party parliamentary elections in favour of an alternative system based on national unity rather than division (see Preface to the Future). But surely there was – and still is perhaps – a choice. Surely Zimbabwe can, after its peaceful election process, choose to go down the road of unity rather than blunder off again in the other direction.

During the Inclusive Government the 'international media', as was to be expected, constantly stressed its dysfunctionality. The local so-called 'independent' press overall did the same – again as was to be expected. *The Herald* did not drop its strident factionalism. ZANU-PF fretted. The President may have expressed from time to time his delighted and avuncular surprise that he could actually work with the MDC but in actual fact I believe he and his party saw the Inclusive Government as a straightjacket and couldn't wait to get out of it and rule again.

The result is that little attention was paid by anyone to what I called the 'miracle'. Was ZANU-PF so intransigent not to perceive the immense political advantages that accrued to them on account of their participation in the Inclusive Government? I have already indicated[60] that I believe that in the Inclusive Government, for all its frustrations and inadequacies, lay the seeds of a form of government far more suited to many African countries, Zimbabwe included. The GPA itself was an extraordinarily important document. It represented what could be the common ground for almost all Zimbabweans – as it was for the MDC and ZANU-PF. The fact that the three parties signed it indicates that there is the possibility of a progressive political consensus in Zimbabwe. And then there is the valuable experience of Zimbabweans coming from different political traditions, for example, the liberation struggle,

60 *Chapter 29*

trade unionism, academia and student politics, working together. Very important too is that working in government with ZANU-PF, MDC-T became for a period less tied to the apron strings of its Western sponsors. MDC-T's dependence on the West must have been a defining factor inhibiting their relations with their main partner in government. If the West would stop meddling in Zimbabwean politics, I believe there is every likelihood that Zimbabweans, left to themselves, could iron out their differences and work together.

If we refer to the critique of Mugabe and ZANU-PF in the early chapters of this book, we would see that many of what I consider their shortcomings, were mitigated by the experience of working with other Zimbabweans with whom they could agree on a basic vision – that of the GPA – but at the same time differ. To take one or two examples: there was the unfortunate tendency for the President to calumniate all those that do not support his party – to the extent that in effect for decades he was never a president of Zimbabwe but in effect really only a president of those Zimbabweans who supported his party. He was a ZANU-PF president. Then there was his poor statesmanship and the racial tendency of his politics. During the time of the Inclusive Government, Mugabe began to develop a greater stature. He seemed to be transmogrifying into a sort of elder statesman, the father of the people, more and more a president for all Zimbabweans. His ability to work with the white man, Coltart, and the student rabble-rouser, Chamisa, and not only work with them but give them their due, was a sign of his growth. Above all, the man who had openly and publicly insulted and defied him over many years and almost unseated him in 2008, Morgan Tsvangirai, Mugabe was able to sit down with him and establish a relationship with him akin to tutelage - something Tsvangirai himself acknowledged.

What was happening to Mugabe was also happening to the party. Clearly their near defeat in 2008 was a shock and clearly the positive way in which they responded was one of the main factors that led to their victory in 2013. I have heard from someone whose family home is in Chinamora (Domboshawa) that not only did the ZANU-PF Member of Parliament, Biata Beatrice Nyamupinga, do a great deal for the people in her constituency but, very different from the ZANU-PF of the pre-2008 years, she did not simply address the villagers but sat with them to hear their problems and suggestions and made those the basis of her constituency work. If this was being done by many more in the party, it does indicate a very important change for the better.

Other promising developments – in particular, the work of the inter-party parliamentary committees – have already been touched on in Chapter 29. Added to these is a new spirit in local government where MDC majorities have voted in ZANU-PF mayors and the Mayor of Harare has openly claimed that his council is not a council of ZANU-PF or MDC representatives but simply councillors who are going to work together for the benefit of their city. These are considerable gains and they must to a large extent be put down the experience of the Inclusive Government. It is for this reason that I believe that by stressing the shortcomings we have failed to recognise the potential and in particular the significance for the future of both the GPA and the Inclusive Government.

Let us imagine what might have happened if the spirit of the inclusive Government had gone onto shape events during the election period and after. ZANU-PF and the President win in a landslide. Tsvangirai's foreign backers, having agreed to defer to their decisions, have the maturity and respect to keep quiet until SADC and the AU pronounce on the elections. When these two organisations endorse them, Britain and the rest show a modicum of political maturity and strategic nous. While perhaps expressing their reservations, they accept the results of the election and congratulate the winners, deciding that, as Michael Holman in an article in the London *Financial Times* savvily suggests, it is in their long-term interests to give up their regime change agenda - including sanctions - and re-engage with Zimbabwe.[61] Tsvangirai follows suit. The spirit of the Inclusive Government now sets the tone. Mugabe accepts his erstwhile Prime Minister's congratulations and commiserates with him on his defeat. As the President of all Zimbabweans – not just ZANU-PF supporters - he calls on all Zimbabweans to come together in a spirit of togetherness and reconciliation and help make Zimbabwe great. He forms a government which, while not exactly a government of national unity, brings in some of the losers. Then the whole nation celebrates Heroes Day together. The President and the party, instead of fulminating against those who did not vote for them, do some serious consultation and research as to why one third of the nation did not support them. Where their opponents' ideas or differences can be accommodated in a common Zimbabwean vision, they entertain them and do their best to bring them on board without necessarily insisting they join the party.

In this way what had been achieved during the implementation of the GPA and the Inclusive Government is built upon and the unity and mutual respect of one Zimbabwean for another is carried forward as the country moves into the future

This has not happened. Once Zimbabwe was definitively committed to elections, both parties dumped inclusivity and its benefits like an uncomfortable pair of shoes. It was a case of unity is over,

61 Interestingly Holman doggedly reproduces the myth about sanctions being 'modest travel and banking sanctions on Zimbabwe's elite'

inclusivity over, bring on division and bring on disunity. Yet, as I have tried to show, the history of Zimbabwe has demonstrated that in unity she stands and flourishes, in division she suffers and threatens to fall.

This tendency was intensified predictably as the canvassing and campaigning got off the ground. We were back to all the old allegations and aspersions. The Mutual Admiration Society that a reporter had described in his article on the unveiling of a district IT centre in Tsholotsho (see Chapter 28) was no more. Back at the hustings, gone were all the memories of the Monday morning teatimes when Mugabe used to sit down with his Prime Minister to discuss the affairs of the nation or joint service in the inter-party parliamentary commissions or public appearances together at various official functions where they praised and deferred to each other. Now ZANU-PF found nothing of any value or validity in the two MDCs nor they in it. Mugabe reverted to type. The maturity and wisdom of his years at the helm of the Inclusive Government gave way to serious lapses of judgement during the run-up to the elections – as in his wild and dangerous boast that Zimbabwe could do without SADC and his unacceptable abuse of President Zuma's international adviser, Lindiwe Zulu, his belated apology notwithstanding.[62]

When the results were announced, as we have seen, despite the endorsement of the AU and SADC, Tsvangirai claimed they were rigged, the MDC-T rejected them and their sponsors condemned them and called for an 'independent inquiry'. This in turn infuriated Mugabe, his party and his supporters.

62 Ms Zulu had been a thorn in Mugabe's flesh, presenting a report on the situation in Zimbabwe at the SADC summit in Maputo which ended up calling on Zimbabwe to appeal to the Court for a postponement of the elections, and then going on to issue a statement in South Africa commenting unfavourably on preparations for the elections in Zimbabwe.

The Western tactics, namely to rubbish the elections, try and have them declared null and void and if possible overturn the results through Egyptian or Turkish style popular protests, set the stage again for confrontational politics. In the face of the behaviour of the MDC-T and in particular the Western ambassadors and governments, Robert Mugabe was taken right back to the days of the struggle. Robert Mugabe will not brook abuse or arrogance at the hands of his old colonial and Imperialist masters. It does not help that all the countries that were dishing it out are 'white'. The result was a burst of reckless and triumphalist hysteria. No doubt to the embarrassment of the African Union and SADC it threw the party and its supporters into an Africanist war with Europe – 'Africa versus Europe' screamed the banners at Heroes Acre. Well, what did they expect?

Now in the aftermath, with the elections lost and won, the post-elections situation saw Tsvangirai sulking in one corner, Mugabe rampaging in another and the West busy stirring it up – while Zimbabwe prepared to suffer. As in the bad old days, though the MDC-T withdrew its petition to the Electoral Court and seemed to accept the results of the local authority elections, it boycotted the President's speech at the opening of Parliament. Once again the country is divided. Like a spectre, polarisation once more stalks the land. Zimbabweans who worked together in government as Zimbabweans only a few months ago are now at each other's throats. The President who has won a famous victory, tells those who did not vote for ZANU-PF - in Harare and Bulawayo - that they will be punished for it[63]. Overzealous party cadres and youth take him at his word and a witch hunt begins to track down MDC-T supporters and punish them. People who campaigned and voted peacefully together, now terrorise those who did not

63 This statement was taken back a few days later but it illustrates the mood of the times.

vote for the winning side. The man the President worked together with as his Prime Minister for five years, he tells to 'go hang'.

Like Orsino and the upper-class characters at the festivities which mark the end of Shakespeare's *Twelfth Night*, Robert Mugabe, ZANU-PF and their supporters gather at Heroes Acre twelve days after their victory and bask in the euphoria of their spectacular election triumph. A feature of the Inclusive government had been the fact that national events such as Independence and Heroes Day should be attended by all and not be used for party political ends and this had been a rule by and large respected. Now the leaders of the MDC formations and their supporters again do not attend the Heroes Day commemorations at the Heroes Acre and the President uses the occasion to tell them to 'go hang'.

"I'll be revenged upon the whole pack of you," snarled Malvolio, the Puritan, excluded from Orsino's feast and bitter at his humiliation. Like Malvolio, the shell-shocked Tsvangirai continues to dream of a miraculous reversal, reassuring his supporters at the 'victory celebrations' in Mutare marking the 14th year of the MDC's existence that all is being 'sorted out' and the victory that he obsessively believes is rightly his, will materialise after all. In South Africa, the battered Rhodies like Roy Bennet and Ian Kay, who had just lost his Marondera Central seat - swear vengeance, violent demonstrations and outright revolution in an interview with the London *Sunday Times*.

The victors claim that all this is irrelevant. Zimbabwe has moved on, they say. ZANU-PF is free again to govern alone and to hell with those who disagree or have something different to suggest. After all, they have a two thirds majority in Parliament and can even modify the constitution. The election whitewash has given the President and the party the opportunity to take the country back to the old days when Zimbabwe was virtually a one-party state.

There is great euphoria in ZANU-PF and among its supporters. There is a feeling in the country that now the unwieldy and inhibiting yoke of the Inclusive Government has been exultantly cast aside, there will be dramatic developments. The new MPs profess a zest to get down to business and the cabinet ministers pledge themselves to make things happen. There is an excitement and an air of expectancy.

The MPs are sworn in. ZANU-PF appoints a new cabinet. The President delivers an impressive speech on the aims and challenges of the new ZANU-PF government. Parliament opens and the President again delivers an impressive speech, describing the legislation the party is lining up for the new parliament. Interesting enough, though the MDC-T is not there, their sponsors are – the ambassadors of Britain, the United States and Australia. They all praise the President's speech. What is going on?

ZANU-PF's programme for the future, already powerfully expressed in its election manifesto, was ably and at length spelt out in his own unique way by the President. Robert Mugabe, like me and many other older men, like to tell the younger generation stories about the past – and this is what the President did, trying, for example, to inspire the new generation of MPs to restore the greatness of Zimbabwean industry in the national industrial capital, Bulawayo, by reminiscing about his own experiences as a child and a young man in the City of Kings. The new government believes that during the Inclusive Government many of the things it wanted to do were obstructed by the MDC. It now wishes to redress this situation. It spells out ways in which it is going to free up a lot of idle finance and use it to forge ahead with its programme based on

National Sovereignty, Indigenisation and People's Empowerment. It places emphasis on production – industrial and agricultural, proposing a raft of measures to revive industry and support the already significant progress made by agriculture. The President makes much of the need to revive Bulawayo as the industrial hub of the country and a major centre of employment. He outlines plans and enabling legislation energetically to make improvements in many different sectors, including communications and transport, mining, education, health and the youth.

ZANU-PF has a two-thirds majority. It has ambitious plans for the country. Zimbabwe has moved on, they say. But has it? Is two-thirds enough?

In my opinion, it is not. Zimbabwe needs to break with the negative in its history, namely division and polarisation. Unless the gains of the GPA and Inclusive Government are recognised and the spirit of co-operation among Zimbabweans on the basis of a shared progressive agenda is restored, Zimbabwe will not have moved on. On the contrary, it is in danger of moving back. Those who do not back the winning side or the winning president constitute approximately one third and more of all Zimbabweans. Zimbabwe's major cities are still solidly anti-ZANU-PF. Those who do not like the ruling party or its president are not known for the moderation of their likings and dislikings. Many are passionately, fanatically opposed. Many nurse historical grudges and entertain longstanding bitternesses. Many have never forgotten *Murambatsvina* and *Gukurahundi*. Others despise ZANU-PF for its corruption, the violence it has perpetrated, its bullying, its arrogance, the sufferings of all different kinds that it has inflicted on them and others.

ZANU-PF itself is not ignorant of the importance of unity for Zimbabwe. In its 2013 election manifesto, it states: "it is impossible to achieve anything that uplifts the livelihood of the people without unity and hence ZANU-PF's call for "Unity, Unity and more Unity". Unfortunately, it would appear that the party's view of unity is rather blinkered. It seems that in its view it was the unity achieved through the Unity Accord in 1987 that constitutes the kind of unity that is required – in other words, the unity of the parties that fought for liberation. Yet again, ZANU-PF demonstrates that its vision cannot entertain anything outside of itself. The lesson of the Inclusive Government surely shows the crucial importance of widening the sights so as to include all Zimbabweans.

Again it needs saying that a programme of material transformation, important as it may be, is not enough. In Chapter 26, I wrote:

> *The arts, including literature, play the crucial role of preparing the people to play its part in the shaping of the new society and of ensuring that the new society and its people are in sync. Any amount of factories, bridges, freeways, hospitals, schools, irrigation schemes and housing will not do that. They will provide the material and physical shell of the society. It is language, literature, philosophy, theatre, dance, music, the visual arts, architecture, film and the media that transform the people's soul and create a national character which makes the material transformation worthwhile.*

There is no mention in the manifesto or in the President's two speeches of constructing anything more than the 'material and physical shell' of the nation. There are serious and very fundamental, even threatening issues, Zimbabwe needs to grapple with in relation to its intellectual, social and moral fabric, particularly as they concern the youth and the children. There are also issues that go a lot deeper even than these – issues that relate to the soul and the spirit of the nation. The killings and massacres of the past must be expiated. In all these issues, it is national unity that is the key.

The West's role in Zimbabwe has been a major source of division. It must lift sanctions and stop interfering. The MDC must cut its ties of dependency and transform itself into a truly Zimbabwean party. And the President and ZANU-PF must have the level-headedness and strategic sagacity to realise that they cannot go it alone. A two-thirds majority is a very nice thing to have. But, given the challenges Zimbabwe is facing in an increasingly unstable and perilous world, two thirds of the country is not going to be enough. Someone has to take note of the lesson the history of the country offers its people – united they stand, divided they fall.

A LUTA CONTINUA
PROLOGUE TO THE FUTURE

Tsela tsela dimatlapa	*(The road is rocky*
Kogae kogae gokgakala.	*And we are from home.)*

- *Tswana choral song*

My life's work has largely been in theatre or things associated with it in some way. Though I have been fairly versatile and involved myself in quite a wide variety of theatre forms, I have specialised in two of them in particular – political theatre and making theatre. Theatre is essentially a very social art – and a practical one. You have to work with other people and for other people. And, as a way of approaching the topic of this prologue to the future, I want to tell you what I have found to be the best way to work together as people, in making theatre, especially political theatre.

What makes the process special if it is political theatre? People who practise political theatre do so because through their theatre they want to say something or show something that will have a political impact. They might even hope that it will change people – and sometimes even change the world! There is no point then in trying to make political theatre with people who have very different ideas about what they want to say or show – or how they want to change people. There is no point in trying to make theatre together with people who want a different world. In other words, there has to be a common vision or something powerful that all the people working together share, some common ground.

However, even among people who do have a common vision and share some common ground, because we are people, different people, no two of them really think alike. So what do we do about that?

In the second year of my time in Zimbabwe, some people came together to form a political theatre group called Zambuko/Izibuko (see Chapter 4). The group included myself, university lecturers and students from different faculties, a female school teacher, university workers and some people from the so-called 'high-density suburbs' such as Mbare, Highfield, Dzivaresekwa, Mabvuku and Kambuzuma. Everyone identified with the group's basic commitment. They were all for socialism and against apartheid and any form of discrimination based on race or gender. But the group included former ZANLA fighters, a member of the African National Congress of South Africa, a young woman who later became a famous writer and was very PAC (Pan Africanist Congress), another who belonged to the International Socialists and others who never declared any particular affiliation but subscribed generally to the group's ideals. Some spoke only English. Others spoke Shona and English. One or two spoke Ndebele. All were Zimbabweans, with the exception of the school teacher and me.

Together we made a play called *Katshaa! the Sound of the AK.* The basic idea behind the play was to explain very clearly, almost diagrammatically, what the situation in apartheid South Africa was like, how the struggle there was structured (the 'Four Pillars of the Struggle') and to motivate the audience to take the struggle in South Africa seriously and give it their support in whatever way they could. We were all agreed that this is what we had to do and we were all committed to try and do it. But how? That was not so easy. What *was* the situation in South Africa? How *was* the struggle structured? *What* forces in South Africa should we encourage people to support? The struggle in South Africa involved many different elements: the African National Congress (ANC) and its multiracial approach; the South African Communist Party (SACP) and its Marxist ideology; the Pan Africanist Congress (PAC) and its Africanist, apparently racial, approach: the Black Consciousness Movement (BCM); the Azanian People's Organisation (AZAPO); and the United Democratic Front (UDF). Was the conflict about class or race? What was the role of the workers? What was the role of socialism? What Socialism – Marxist-Leninist, Maoist, Trotskyite? The pro-ZANU-PF members favoured the PAC. Others the ANC. Which songs? So many things to disagree about.

So here was a group, a cross-section of race, class and gender, drawn from Zimbabwean society. They had a common commitment and a shared vision but they were individuals and their different lives and backgrounds meant that they had different ways of approaching the commitment or formulating the vision.

Some things were relatively easy to create together – the coming of the whites to South Africa, racial discrimination, a workers' strike, apartheid legislation. This we did by reading material together, discussing it and then deciding how to act it out. We listened to everyone in the group, we heard them out, we tried out people's ideas – and then together we chose what we wanted to keep. It is a way of working that hundreds of other theatre groups and political theatre groups have followed.[64] Everyone's opinion is respected and given time. No-one dictates. No-one bullies. No-one laughs at anyone else. The common objective is stressed and together we come to a decision – via consensus. There is no voting that leaves the majority triumphant and the minority crestfallen. We go forward together. The focus is on togetherness and the common goal.

The biggest issue we faced was the apparent irreconcilability of the ANC and PAC positions. Some members very strongly supported the one, others the other. We invited a representative from the PAC to come and watch a run and give comments. We invited an ANC cadre from Lusaka to come down and work with us for a period. At last, we had to finalise our script. We sat up all night debating. We decided that come what may we would not go to bed until we had hammered out an agreement. Each side pushed for what they believed in and then in the interests of coming to an agreement, they tried to find ways to accommodate each other. The dawn was streaking the horizon with red and grey as we finally became one and made for our beds – in the various part of Harare where we lived.

And then we rehearsed the play and, when we performed it, we performed it as one, with the power, intensity and passion that comes from presenting a work of the imagination that each one of those performing it has taken part in creating, laboured long and hard to fashion and finally come to embrace as their own.

I can just hear some people saying what's a ridiculous bit of theatre like this got to do with the big world, the important things of life, you know, politics, economics, Zimbabwe, Africa?

---

64 For instance, see the introduction to John McGrath's *The Cheviot, the Stag and the Black, Black Oil*, in which he described how the political theatre group 7:84 created the play.

My answer to that is, first of all, I have never agreed that art is not as serious and as important to the development of society as all those other so-called 'serious' things. I believe that in this simple example of human beings working together for a common objective lies the answer to greater things. And this brings me back to the question I raised earlier on. Allow me to quote it again: "Why do countries in Africa and other places replicate a parliamentary system of government developed over centuries in a small island off Europe that later became their colonial master. Can we really not do better?"

I believe we can – and I know that I am not the only one. I believe that the Patriotic Front and the Inclusive Government bear me out. It was extraordinarily good for Zimbabwe that the bitter enemies, ZANU and ZAPU, came together as the Patriotic Front to negotiate Zimbabwe's way to Independence together. I believe it was equally bad for Zimbabwe that they then broke up to fight the election separately – the consequences testify to that, I think. I think it was miraculously good for Zimbabwe that the bitter enemies, ZANU-PF and the two MDCs, came together in the Inclusive Government. I believe it was equally bad that they split up and fought an election against each other. I hate to say this but I fear the consequences will testify to that.

I do not think that the model of democracy we inherited from the colonial master is a good one or necessarily an appropriate or a fitting one in our circumstances. I think it needs to be interrogated, rigorously and creatively – in the spirit of those wonderful phrases in the GPA: 'loyalty to Zimbabwe, patriotism and commitment to Zimbabwe's national purpose, core values, interests and aspirations' and the 'centrality and importance of African institutions in dealing with African problems'. We need to search for African ways of governing ourselves. Westminster democracy was born out of the particular history of England and the particular temperament of the English. I am sure we can do better for ourselves if we search for democratic frameworks that derive from our African history and the temperament of the peoples of Africa.

Why do I think this? Some of the reasons have been said before, in the pages of this book, in different places where I thought it was relevant. Now it needs to be stated again along with other things that have not been said before.

When colonialism came along and carved up Africa, it did two things. As Basil Davidson again so usefully notes (*The Black Man's Burden* – not a great title but a useful book), up to the coming of colonialism African peoples had pursued their own organic development trajectories. In other words, Africa's societies were still rooted in their own history. Colonialism came along and more or less said: 'Enough of all that parochial rubbish, we are going to decide for you what countries you all live in and your countries will be what *we* want them to be'. And then they set about completely and arbitrarily – from the African point of view – not only re-drawing the map of Africa but also turning the lives of millions of people upside down.

To understand this better, let's create our own example. Imagine that in a certain region in Africa there are five peoples. One is a powerful kingdom – the Central Kingdom. The Central Kingdom is divided into two language groups and occupies the coastal and central parts of the region. Another influential people – the Eastern Kingdom - also occupies coastal and central parts but to the east of the Central Kingdom. A third is a northern people – the North - closely related to others in other regions, who have a long tradition of migrations, invasions and also trade with the coast and across the desert with North Africa. A fourth is a tribute population – Tributaries - occupying parts of the central region under the Central Kingdom. A fifth – Immigrants - are recent immigrants from another region and they are basically all over the place as they are traders. The Central and Eastern Kingdoms are for obvious reasons great rivals and this rivalry sometimes involves war. They were very much involved in the slave trade in the old days and they have a lot of guns as a result – because the slaves were largely traded for guns. The two speak totally different languages but both are what they call 'animist' by religion. In other words, they worship in the traditional way. The North are Muslims and were once part of one of the great empires of ancient Africa. They are ruled by emirs and they have always controlled the trans-desert and east-west trade. They are, as a result, the entrepôt for the coastal traffic as well. The Tributaries are earlier inhabitants that were conquered by the Central Kingdom. They are greatly looked down on and occupy a status similar to that of slaves. The Immigrants are a very enterprising people. Some are Muslim, others traditionalist. They speak the language of the region they come from, further to the east.

Along come two European invaders – say Ruritania and Transylvania. They are rivals. Both the Central and the Eastern Kingdoms try and use them to get the upper hand in their own squabbles and so the Eastern Kingdom assists Ruritania to conquer the Central Kingdom. Later the Central Kingdom is conscripted by Ruritania to fight against the North. Then the invaders, Ruritania and Transylvania, conclude an agreement and lines are drawn on the map to mark off their different colonies. Rivers are obvious boundaries, despite the fact that quite often people straddle rivers, living on both sides of them. So the area becomes two colonies – let's call them Ivory and Gold. The central boundary between Ivory and Gold follows a great river and thus passes through the territory of the Eastern Kingdom, leaving some of its people in Ivory and some in Gold. It also passes through the territory of the Central Kingdom and does the same, with some of its people in Ivory and some in Gold. And so it goes on.[65]

Many years later the people of Ivory and Gold get a bit sick and tired of the rule of Ruritania and Transylvania. Many of them down in the South have become Christians and have received a Western education. They all know that it was their divisions that made it easy for their colonizers to take them over and so they realise that their only hope is to unite and create organisations that campaign for the freedom of Ivory and Gold on a national basis. So, in the two separate countries of Ivory and Gold all the peoples of the Central Kingdom, the Eastern Kingdom, the North, the Tributaries and the Immigrants try and come together. Others don't want to and so they form separate Central, Eastern or North parties.

Then comes independence. Well, I hope by now that it is fairly clear what a seemingly impossible task it is for these two 'countries', Ivory and Gold, to make a go of it – two impossibly divided 'nation states', divided by language, ethnicity, religion, caste (the case of the Tributaries) and, in particular, by history – wars, rivalry, subjugation – and their experiences of colonialism. For instance, the North was always favoured despite the fact that the southerners became Christians but the southerners became more educated and prosperous and so there is a legacy of mutual suspicion, jealousy and resentment between them. The only way in which the two countries can possibly function as countries is for the new governments to try and instil in the people a loyalty and a sense of their new nationhood and so they coin slogans such as 'One Ivory,

65 The history of Ghana is but one example of this kind of scenario. See Kwame Nkrumah's autobiography or any other history of Ghana such as W.E.F Ward's *A History of Ghana*.

One Nation', 'One Gold, One People'. Their only hope is to go flat out for unity, consensus and working together – what in Shona they call '*mushandira-pamwe*'.

However, not satisfied with leaving their African subjects in 'nations', divided but thrown together by their own ambitions and interests and with no experience in self-government and very little education, Ruritania and Transylvania also stipulate what form of government their erstwhile colonies should have – multi-party democracy! Something which no-one in Ivory or Gold ever knew about before Independence because it was something that Ruritania and Transylvania kept for themselves. And so these chronically divided 'nations', where unity and co-operation are the only hope, are forced to adopt a system of government which is the opposite. Why do I say the opposite? Let us look at Western democracy for a moment.

According to the various models of Western democracy, governments are formed through the conflict of political parties, each trying to win an election. These parties express the interests of different social groups – determined sometimes by class, sometimes by ethnicity or even by language (Canada), sometimes by nationality (Spain). To be able to promote these interests, they have to get into government. Note these interests are the interests of that section of the society the party represents, not those of the nation as such. In the process of competing one with the other, each party tries to show that its ideas are good and the ideas of every other party are rubbish. Despite the fact that they are all citizens of the same nation, whose interests should be the common goal, they slang each other, try and mire each other in scandal, sometimes even destroy each other. To do this they need money – which means that really only those parties that are supported by the rich have much of a chance. Then you have newspapers that support the different parties. Some parties don't even have a newspaper to support them, others have lots of them. If a newspaper does not support the party of the government, it will constantly try and show that everything the ruling party does is rubbish. In other words, it will constantly undermine the government – not in the interests of the nation but in those of the party it supports, claiming to do so in the name of freedom of the press or speech or expression or whatever.

Once in parliament itself, the different parties devote their energies to pulling each other down. Despite the fact that people of other parties might have some good ideas, the fact that the ideas come from opposing parties means that again they are rubbish, they must be voted against – and if any members of the party want to vote for what their consciences tell them, they are 'whipped' into line by a person whose job it is to see to it that they always vote for what the party has decided rather than what they think the people who elected them would like.

Now, given the historical experiences of our African countries, Ivory and Gold, and their make-up at Independence, can anyone in their right mind believe that the legacy of the colonial powers, Ruritania and Transylvania, to Ivory and Gold was anything but a recipe for disaster? In my opinion, it is an utter and total miracle that so many African countries, like Ivory and Gold, have been able to make some kind of a go of it.

The legacy of colonialism is division, quite natural when one considers that the guiding principle of colonial power is '*divide et impera*', divide and rule. Africa and its nation states came into being divided. Many former nationalities and peoples were split up between different states. Many who found themselves in the same colony had no historical tradition whatsoever of a common fate, co-operation or unity with each other, instead many had traditions of enmity, rivalry, often even war. As a result, in the liberation struggles of our various states, the stress was almost always on Africanness, in other words Pan Africanism, because the one common factor that overrode all the divisions was that they were all Africans. The stress was on oneness. Then after Independence, the major thrust of almost all newly independent states was the struggle to build a united nation, to create unity, among the many disparate national components inherited from the past, and to get them to see themselves and each other as one and the same nation. Slogans and songs such as '*masibe munye*', '*mwana wevhu*', '*sisonke*', '*o povo Mocambiçano da Rovuma ao Maputo*', '*tiyende pamodzi ndimtima umo*', '*ujamaa*'[66] and many others stressed the need for unity because of the realisation that the tendencies in the country and within Africa towards division were strong and dangerous.

But then, it would seem to me, the present system of party political elections that we are all trying to make work in Africa is inimical and in direct contradiction to the struggle during liberation and after Independence to unite our peoples. On the one hand, governments have pursued nation-building strategies, the goal being to unite the nation. On the other, governments are chosen by a 'democratic' system which promotes division and divides the nation into supporters of different parties. The goal is no longer the common weal i.e. the welfare and development of the nation. Instead, the goal is for one party to beat the other parties and win the election. Those in parliament devote all their energies to defeating the other side, instead of guiding the political destiny of the nation in the spirit of 'loyalty to (the country), patriotism and commitment to (the country's) national purpose, core values,

---

66 '*Masibe munye (let us be one – South Africa)*, '*mwana wevhu*' (child of the soil – Zimbabwe), '*sisonke*' (we are together – Zimbabwe), '*o povo Mocambiçano da Rovuma ao Maputo*' (the people from the Rolvuma River in the North to the Maputo River in the South – Mozambique), '*tiyende pamodzi ndimtima umo*' (let us go forward together - Zambia) , '*ujamaa*' (brotherhood, family - Tanzania)

interests and aspirations' and the 'centrality and importance of African institutions in dealing with African problems'

But why? Why do we go on accepting this legacy? In Africa there is a strong tradition of working together, of consultation, of community support and in particular of discussion and decision by consensus. If we look into that tradition and analyse our need today, our need for nation-building, our need for a common goal and our need for working together to achieve it, I am sure we can come up with something a lot better than the current failed systems that the West seems to think it is 'teaching' us to implement.

I am not alone in thinking this. A number of eminent African leaders of newly independent states have noted that multi-party democracy is not a good idea and have tried to find other models. Almost all the efforts to avoid the competitiveness and divisiveness of multi-party democracy have been experiments with the one-party state. The reasons given for these experiments usually related to the need for national unity and the rapid and single-minded development of the nation without the distractions of interparty squabbles. They also looked to African history, values and culture for alternatives. Kenneth Kaunda of Zambia, for instance, proclaimed one-party rule in 1972 after the elections of that year had resulted in an alarming level of violence. He was appalled by the way in which elections were dividing the nation, whose slogan had always been 'One Zambia, One Nation'.

However, the first of Africa's great leaders who had rejected multi-party democracy was Kwame Nkrumah himself. He also noted that it was divisive and recognised that a newly independent state 'needed the energy and enthusiasm of all the people to move forward'. He once said: "We, in Africa, will evolve forms of government, rather different from the traditional Western pattern, but no less democratic in their protection of the individual and his inalienable rights."

Mwalimu Nyerere of Tanzania also hoped that Tanzania's single-party democracy, along with other measures like the adoption of Swahili as the national language, would fuse Tanzania with all its many different peoples and languages into one nation.[67] Interestingly, Museveni of Uganda is the only one who went beyond one-party rule to a form of democracy based not on a single or multi-party system. Instead he envisaged elections that are not based on party affiliations. An article in *The Economist* (29th June, 2000), reports that Museveni was also one of those who saw the way in which political parties opened up the religious, ethnic and historical divisions in undeveloped or African countries. He believed that:

> *... they (political parties) created the instability that, in turn, led to the tyranny, wars and bloodshed that tore at the country between 1966 and 1986. Under Mr Museveni's system, parties are allowed to exist, but are banned from campaigning, or backing candidates, in elections. The president encourages local communities to run their own affairs and elect their own representatives, but these representatives have to stand as individuals, not as party members.*
>
> *Within that restriction, politics, at least in most of southern Uganda (the north and parts of the west are plagued by rebellions), have been relatively free, open and broad-based. Feeling*

---

67 See 'Language Reform: How Nyerere killed tribalism', in *The Southern Times* (20th April, 2014), in which Elvis Mboya compares the unity of the Tanzanian people with the ethnic divisions bedevilling Kenya and other African countries. He puts this down to Tanzania's language policy and makes no reference to its single-party democracy.

> *themselves reasonably secure, and granted a good deal of economic freedom, Ugandans have been able to reclaim the lost 20 years.*

The Economist could not refrain from patronising Museveni's efforts by describing them as 'his curious no-party system'. Africa's efforts to find its own systems will always have to contend with sneers of this kind – but she should not be deterred.

For me, the need to go beyond multi-party democracy in the search for more appropriate forms of democratic government in Africa – and in Zimbabwe – is further demonstrated by the Inclusive Government miracle. In my opinion, it is not the Zimbabwe parliament that is the model for government in Zimbabwe. It is the inter-party parliamentary committees. It is in these that we have seen Zimbabweans, irrespective of party, meeting, discussing and trying to do the best for their Zimbabwe on the merits of each case. In other words, this suggests a democratic system in which people who have something in common, politicians who are all Zimbabweans and desire the prosperity and well-being of Zimbabwe, work together, discussing, pooling ideas and coming to an agreement as to what is best for their country. When a decision has been made in this way, those having made it, are committed to it and work for it as one, implementing it 'with the power, intensity and passion that comes from the knowledge that each one of them has been a part of creating it, has laboured long and hard to fashion it and finally come to embrace it as their own'. *Katshaa! Katshuu!*[68]

Consensus, national consensus is a far better goal to fight for than parliamentary divisiveness. If in Zimbabwe there had been

68 In the 1980's in South Africa when the comrades were doing the *toyi toyi* dance during protests they used many different slogans, one of which was 'Katshaa! Katshuu!', which was an onomatopoeic rendering of the sound the AK47 assault rifle makes when being loaded.

a consciousness of the need to come up with alternative democratic models with national unity and consensus as the framework, it might have been far better for the Inclusive Government to have transformed itself into a Government of National Unity on the basis of the principles agreed in the GPA. Those principles, the need for national consensus and alternative ways of democratic governance, could guide the nation in coming up with a new constitution – without Western tutelage. This constitution could move away from divisive party politics and possibly introduce an electoral system where candidates do not stand for parties. Instead, those standing for election put to the people in their constituency their principles, ideas, projects or planned action. Let the people then choose on that basis whom they wish to represent them. Each elected member would come to parliament not as a member of a party but as a representative of the people in his or her constituency. It is then up to them to do their best to achieve what the people voted them into parliament to achieve. No whips. No party divisions. Zimbabweans debating and discussing what is best for the country in the light of what the people have delegated them to do.

Without the protection of parties, the fat cats would not be able to continue their corrupt activities and retain their immunity from exposure and prosecution. Zimbabweans could then stand together and achieve the common national goals that were described in the GPA, namely, eliminate corruption, make government more efficient and sensitive to the people's dignity and needs, work for a strong economy, stand together and, in the spirit of self-reliance, minimise the effect of sanctions by making sure that national resources go towards the genuine development of Zimbabwe rather than into people's private pockets.

As it is, none of this has happened – yet. In the absence of an alternative democratic model, I believe Zimbabwe – both ZANU-PF and the MDC – needs to put the unity of the nation and the interests of the people first by coming together, in good faith, building on the gains of the Inclusive Government, eschewing foreign interference and working together for the common good. Zimbabwe has enough in the way of human and material resources to achieve self-reliance. Zimbabwe needs to be resolute and stand up for its national sovereignty. The gains of the Third *Chimurenga* must not be lost but they must be fairly distributed and efficiently employed. In terms of foreign policy, there is an urgent need for statesmanship and strategic policy. While standing firm on the nation's goals, interests and sovereignty, Zimbabwe needs to avoid unnecessary confrontation and defiance. She has a lot to offer her current enemies by way of a carrot. They want to participate in the economy. Zimbabwe should make this possible on a win-win basis and in the process the enemies may soften their stance on sanctions.

By all means, let Zimbabwe have 'standards' but let those standards be Zimbabwe's own. Let them be achievable and applicable to all. May all the people in Zimbabwe accept that they are Zimbabweans and Zimbabweans first. Give to each other the dignity and respect a Zimbabwean deserves. Stop trying to foster divisions, stop agitating for revenge or dreaming of secession. May those who have taken their skills to other countries, be persuaded to return and bring back with them their experience, expertise and new ideas and may they be welcomed and accepted back into the fold when they do. The struggle was fought for democracy – let there be democracy in the image of the people and derived from their history and culture. Let there be laws that are just for all and let there be the rule of those laws. Let there be human rights but rights in the spirit of *hunhu/ubuntu*. Let people at last realise that science is but the other face of the arts and the arts of science and that a society that develops mechanically but neglects its spirit, its soul and its intellect is little more than a shell.

In our arts education organisation, the children often used to sing a song composed by the South African artist and writer, traditional doctor and mythologist, Credo Vusamazulu Mutwa:

Maye, kumnandi ukuba izingane zelanga	(O, it is so sweet to be the children of the sun
Singabantwana bokukhanya nobuhle	We are the children of brightness and beauty.)

The anthem of our arts education organisation was adapted from another song, a well-known Zimbabwean song, and went like this:

Iro gomo reZimbabawe	(The great mountain of Zimbabwe
Rinevana vakanaka.	Has beautiful children.)

I discovered from personal experience that this is true. Zimbabwe does indeed have beautiful children. Of all the wonderful resources Zimbabwe has, the children are her greatest resource. Let us hope that their leaders will hand on to them the Zimbabwe they deserve. And let us hope that they grow up free of the cruelty, violence, jealousy, envy and greed that their elders have demonstrated in great measure and rather continue in the spirit of the great courage, resourcefulness and endurance their elders have shown also in great measure during the trying but historic three decades of the history of their young nation. For Zimbabwe these years have been full of pain but also great and historic achievements.

It is better to have leapt the hurdle and fallen on the other side than not to have leapt at all. One can always get up. *Simuka Zimbabwe!* Zimbabwe, arise!

POSTSCRIPT: MY ROAD TO WRITING THIS BOOK

I was born into the third and fourth generation of families of Scottish emigrants to South Africa, Duncans on my mother's side, McLarens on my father's. My father met my mother when they were working in the Post Office in Newcastle, South Africa. He later became a life assurance salesman. My mother, when she returned to work after the divorce, managed the office of a large gent's outfitters business.

Despite their relative modest social status, they sent me to two of the most privileged schools in the country, Highbury Preparatory School for Boys and Hilton College in Natal, colloquially referred to as the 'Last Outpost of the British Empire'. At the University of Cape Town I went on to win a Rhodes Scholarship, which gained me entry to that most elite of elite institutions in the colonial metropolis, Oxford.

During all this time I was taught to believe in the British Empire. I read with avidity the novels of G.H. Henty, which glorified the exploits of the great empire-builders – Clive of India, Wolfe of Canada, Kitchener of Khartoum. I believed in the BBC as the voice of truth and liberty and in the values of Britain and the West as the acme of the world's evolution to a civilised, democratic and just society. At that stage in my development, the events of history which belied that belief – slavery, colonialism and capitalism – did not in any way impinge on that belief.

At school, every year on the anniversary of V-Day, the day of Remembrance, I was moved to tears by the hymn "O, valiant hearts, who to your glory came". I mourned as I listened to the lone bugler outside the school chapel playing 'The Last Post'. I was reared in the spirit of Delville Wood and the Battle of Britain. I hero-worshipped Douglas Bader and all the other symbols of that heroic struggle against Fascism.

I knew that something was wrong in South Africa. I knew that the Afrikaner Nationalists were another expression of that racism and Fascism which NATO had so gloriously withstood and triumphed over in the years just before my birth. I knew too – I fervently wished – that the same thing would happen in South Africa and that a just and liberal society of non-racism, integration and justice would replace it.

That there was anything more to it than that did not occur to me. But the seeds began to be planted in Oxford itself when I was confronted by the Vietnam War. I took part in the marches on the US Embassy in Grosvenor Square and I saw the mounted police form a ring around it to protect it. I slowly began to have second thoughts about the great ally, the United States. But Britain? Britain was not like that, I thought. It was the time of the King's Road, flower power, bell-bottoms, long hair, pot and free love. This was the permissive society. The students in British universities, in Paris and the States heralded a new dawn. And then I went back to South Africa, complete with long hair, bell-bottoms and flowery shirts, determined to play my part through popular theatre in Soweto to make a change in my own country.

And there the seeds began to burst and give life to a completely new perspective. I came to see that the system in South Africa was not just an aberration, a unique and isolated case of racial Fascism. I came to see the same system in operation in Brazil and in many other parts of the world. I came to read about Black Power in the States and came face to face with Black Consciousness in South Africa. I read Fanon, Freire, Cesaire, Cabral and – Marx and Lenin. My eyes were opened and my mind too as I heard and participated in the heated discussions of Socialists and the revolutionaries of the Pan Africanist Congress of South Africa (PAC) on my frequent visits to England. I read Walter Rodney, Mahmood Mamdani and the new African history of Basil Davidson. And everywhere I went in South Africa – in the white towns and black townships - I saw an extreme version of a world-wide system being ruthlessly applied.

And so the process went on – while reading for a Ph. D. at Leeds and exposed to the alternative theatre of the 1970s in England, I saw the Western media campaign of vilification and misinformation unleashed against the struggles for freedom in Zimbabwe and South Africa where Robert Mugabe was branded a 'terrorist' by much of the British media and the African National Congress a 'terrorist organisation' by the Reagan government. I heard the BBC propagate lies about the MPLA in Angola and Frelimo in Mozambique.

I witnessed the same phenomenon when, after finishing my Ph.D., I took up an appointment in Ethiopia. I had in the meantime become a husband and a father. While in South Africa I met and subsequently married a woman who could claim descent from

Queen Nandi, the mother of Emperor Shaka the Great. As I was descended from a Gaelic clan that were vassals of the Stuarts of Appia, I think I can say I married above my station.

For various reasons it was not possible to return to South Africa. My wife and I were travelling on United Nations refugee documents. I did not want to stay in England but I needed to get a job and continue my interest in ideology, politics and culture. In Ethiopia, a popular revolution had overthrown the semi-feudal imperial government of Haile Selassie. The so-called Derg, under the leadership of Mengistu Haile Mariam, took control of the revolution and set out to revolutionise Ethiopia along Marxist-Leninist lines. This seemed an ideal place for me to go and between 1980 and 1984 I worked at the University of Addis Ababa.

While there I met members of the Embassy of the newly independent Zimbabwe. I might have stayed on in Ethiopia for a much longer period but there was a concern that Ethiopia was far and isolated from our ageing parents in South Africa and I agreed to transfer to the University of Zimbabwe. Transferring to Zimbabwe was also a move that was in keeping with my interest in the development of arts and culture in a post-revolutionary African country.

So, by the time I landed up in Zimbabwe, the illusions I once had about the BBC, Britain and the United States had been dissipated. My eyes had been opened to a new perspective, quite different from what I had been raised in and spent my childhood and youth imbibing, by the naked machinations in the support of self-interest that came to characterise the behaviour of the West. With the collapse of the Soviet Union and the ushering in of a unipolar world, all checks and balances fell away. NATO, led by what seemed to me to be a totally transformed United States, set about enforcing the so-called New World Order – and woe to any silly country that vainly struggled to uphold its sovereignty and the belief that its resources should first of all benefit its own people.

I became a Socialist – and will always remain one. I am not a member of a political party but my ideological allegiance is to the ideas and objectives of Marx, Engels, Lenin, Fidel Castro and many others who have seen in Socialism the answer to the problems of injustice and inequality created by an economic and political system based on greed and profit.

George Fox, the Quaker, came to his faith not by reading the scriptures but through a direct revelation of the truth and only then afterwards found that the scriptures agreed with it. In rather the same way, my Marxism did not come from theory. It came from the practical experience and observation of capitalism at work, particularly in *apartheid* South Africa, which then found its expression in the theories of Marxism, which I subsequently read, and the practice of revolutionaries. That is why when others deserted ship after the collapse of the Soviet Union, I remained on board. I see Socialism as the only hope for Mankind and the planet.

I am also a supporter of the revolutionary struggles in Africa for independence and sovereignty. For this reason, I supported the African National Congress in South Africa, Frelimo in Mozambique, the MPLA in Angola, SWAPO in Namibia and the Patriotic Front in Zimbabwe. For me the slogan of that struggle, 'A luta continua', never meant the struggle continues until majority government. Majority government was never the final aim of the struggle. It was just a stepping stone. In other words, for me the struggle continues even - and probably especially - now.

In 1985 in Zimbabwe, I and others at the University of Zimbabwe founded a theatre group. We called it Zambuko/Izibuko, meaning 'river-crossing - in Shona and Ndebele respectively. By this name we intended to proclaim what this theatre group stood for and what it would propagate. We saw the river-crossing as carrying us over from one bank, which was characterised by colonialism, capitalism, racism and sexual inequality, to the other, characterised by the opposite, namely national sovereignty, socialism, non-racialism and sexual equality. We called the work of our theatre group, political and socialist, and the group itself a Frontline Theatre group – the frontline being the frontline in the fight against apartheid, made up of the independent countries of Mozambique, Zimbabwe, Botswana and Angola –later to be joined by Namibia.

Non-racialism is my dream. By this, I do not mean multi-racialism or a system of fair distribution of power and wealth to defined racial and ethnic groups. I mean the acceptance of each other as human beings based not on race or ethnic group but on our shared humanity. Now after a long life I am bitterly aware that this is a dream that is as yet remote and far-removed from reality.

I was born, brought up and have lived my life in Africa. I speak five or six African languages. My thinking and my allegiance is shaped by this experience. I am an African. I believe that the events that unfolded in Zimbabwe are of great importance for Africa and that they contain many lessons which Africans and African states can learn a great deal from. It is regrettable that 'mainstream' media coverage of Zimbabwe has by and large failed to provide readers and viewers with the information required in order to understand the lessons and therefore learn from them. South Africa is a country which perhaps more than any other faces and will face many of the same hurdles that faced Zimbabwe. As a citizen of South Africa, I have over the years been particularly concerned that it has been kept in such ignorance by its media of the real issues that it is unlikely that it has learnt anything at all from what happened in Zimbabwe.

I think I can say that I have been privileged – if that is the word - to participate in and observe three extraordinary moments in the history of Africa. The first was the bitter days of *verkramte apartheid* (narrow apartheid) in the 1950s and 1960s and then the rise of Black Consciousness and that extraordinary explosion of children's power in the 1970s when the young people and children of Soweto fearlessly took on the *apartheid* state and in the process set in motion a resistance which culminated in 1994 in the negotiated demise of formal and state-imposed segregation and discrimination.

The second was my experience in Ethiopia in the years following the overthrow of the feudal regime of Haile Selassie and the struggle to build a Marxist state in Africa.

The third was what I went through, with millions of Zimbabweans, in the three decades and a bit between 1980 and 2014, which is the subject of this book.

THINGS TO READ AND WATCH

2001 ZIM: A Study on Street Children in Zimbabwe, Evaluation Report (Unicef)
Ankomah, Balfour, "A Place in the Sun", in *The New African* (March, 2005)
Astrow, Andre, *A Revolution Which Lost its Way* (Zed Press)
Biko, Stephen Bantu, *I Write What I Like* (Heinemann)
Blair, Tony, *The Journey* (Hutchison)
Bundy, Colin, *The Rise and Fall of the South African Peasantry* (James Currey)
Cabral, Amilcar, *Return to the Source*, ed. Africa Information Service (Penguin)
Chifunyise, Stephen, *Vicious*, in *Intimate Affairs and Other Plays* (Cybercard Trading PL)
Cleaver, Eldridge, *Soul on Ice* (Turtleback Books)
Dangarembga, Tsitsi, *Neria* (film, 1993)
Davidson, Basil, *Black Mother: the Years of the African Slave Trade* (Penguin)
Davidson, Basil, *The Black Man's Burden* (James Currey)
Fanon, Frantz, *Black Skin, White Masks* (Pluto)
Gibbon, Peter, 'Structural Adjustment and the Working Poor in Zimbabwe' (online pdf)
Hanlon, Joseph, *The Revolution under Fire* (ZED Books)

Hanlon, Joseph, et al, *Zimbabwe Takes Back Its Land* (Kumarian Press)

Halliday, Fred, and Molyneux, Maxine, *The Ethiopian Revolution* (Verso)

Herman, Edward, and Chomsky, Noam, *Manufacturing Consent: The Political Economy of the Media* (Pantheon Books/ film)

Jenje-Makwenda, Joyce, *Township Music* (Joyce Jenje-Makwenda, book/film)

Lenin, Vladimir, 'On Proletarian Culture', in *Lenin on Literature and Art* or *Lenin on Culture and Cultural Revolution* (Progress)

Mahamba, Irene, *Woman in Struggle* (ZIMFEP)

Malcolm X, *The Autobiography of Malcolm X* (Penguin)

Mamdani, Mahmood, *Politics and Class Formation in Uganda* (Monthly Review Press)

Martin, David, 5-part series on the land from a historical perspective in *The Herald* (Harare)

Martin, David, and Johnson, Phyllis, *The Struggle for Zimbabwe* (Zimbabwe Publishing House)

Mlambo, Alois, *The Economic Structural Adjustment Programme: The Zimbabwean Case, 1990-1995* (UZ Publications)

Modisane, Bloke, *Blame me on History* (Simon and Schuster)

Moyo, Sam, 'Three decades of agrarian reform in Zimbabwe' in *Journal of Peasant Studies* (Routledge)

Mugabe, Robert, *Our War of Liberation: Speeches, Articles, Interviews 1976-1979* (1983 - out of print)

Mzala, *Gatsha Buthelezi, Chief with a Double Agenda* (ZED Books)

Nillsson, Anders and Akeson, Gunilla, *Killing a Dream* (video)

Nkrumah, Kwame, *Autobiography* (PANAF Books)

Nyagumbo, Maurice, *With the People* (Graham Publishing)

Pongweni, Alex, *Songs that Won the Liberation War* (College Press)

Qureshi, Asim, *The Rules of the Game* (Hurst and Company)
Ranger, Terence, *Voices from the Rocks: Nature, Culture and History in the Matopos Hills of Zimbabwe* (Baobab, Indiana University Press, James Currey)
Roberts, Ronald Suresh, *Fit to Govern: The Native Intelligence of Thabo Mbeki* (STE Publishers)
Rodney, Walter, *How Europe Underdeveloped Africa* (Black Classic Press)
Sato, Makoto, 'The Organisation and Effectiveness of Co-operatives in Zimbabwe', in *Southern African Studies.* (Leeds University, June 1988)
Saunders, Richard, '"Zimbabwe" Esap's Fables ii', in *SAR* 11, 4 (July 1996)
Scoones, Ian, et al, *Zimbabwe's Land Reform: Myths and Realities* (James Currey)
Shah, Anup, 'Structural Adjustment—a Major Cause of Poverty' (Global Issues, online article)
Smith, Ian, *The Great Betrayal: the Memoirs of Africa's Most Controversial Leader* (Blake Publishing)
Snow, Edgar, *Red Star Over China* (Left Book Club, Victor Gollancz)
Timba, Jameson, 'The impact of structural adjustment on people-centred development: the experience of the collective/worker cooperative movement and collective self finance scheme in Zimbabwe' (The Common Wealth Network for People-Centred Development, online article)
Tongogara, Josiah, *Our Struggle for Liberation* (Mambo Press)
Ward, W.E.F *A History of Ghana* (George Allen and Unwin)
Zhelokhovtsev, A, *The "Cultural Revolution": a Close-Up* (Progress Publishers)

INDEX

B

C

D

H

I

M

N

O

P

Q

S

T

U

V

W

X

Y

Z

Printed in Great Britain
by Amazon